Y0-CHP-594

BLUE BOOK

OF

QUESTIONS & ANSWERS

FOR

SECOND MATE, CHIEF MATE, MASTER

BLUE BOOK

OF

QUESTIONS & ANSWERS

FOR

SECOND MATE,

CHIEF MATE, MASTER

THIRD EDITION

By

W. A. MacEWEN

Master Mariner

CORNELL MARITIME PRESS

CENTREVILLE, MARYLAND

Copyright © 1962, 1966, 1969, by Cornell Maritime Press, Inc.

All rights reserved. No part of this book may be reproduced in any manner
whatsoever without prior written permission except in the case of brief
quotations embodied in critical articles and reviews. For information,
address Cornell Maritime Press, Inc., Centreville, Maryland 21617

ISBN 0-87033-007-1
Library of Congress Catalog Card Number: 62-15957

Manufactured in the United States of America
First edition, 1962; Third edition, 1969
1982 reprint

CONTENTS

(Subjects are numbered in accordance with Table on the following page)

TABLE 10.05–45 (b).—SUBJECTS FOR DECK OFFICERS OF OCEAN OR COASTWISE STEAM OR MOTOR VESSELS

No.	Subjects	Master Ocean	Master Coast-wise	Master Yachts	Master Limited mineral and oil industry	Chief mate Ocean	Chief mate Coast-wise	Second mate Ocean	Second mate Coast-wise	Third mate Ocean	Third mate Coast-wise	Mate—Limited mineral and oil industry
1.	Latitude by Polaris	X	X			X		X		X		
2.	Latitude by meridian altitude method	Any body	Sun or star.			Any body	Sun or star.	Sun or star.	Sun or star.	Sun	Sun	
3.	Fix or running fix	Any body	Sun or star.	Any body		Any body	Sun or star.	Sun or star.	Sun or star.	Sun	Sun	
4.	Star identification (any method)	X	X	X		X	X	X	X	X		
5.	Chart navigation	X	X	X	X	X	X	X	X	X	X	X
6.	Compass deviation	Any body	Sun or star.	Sun	X	Sun or star.	Sun or star.	Sun or star.	Sun	Sun	Sun	X
7.	(Canceled)											
8.	Middle latitude sailing	X	X	X		X	X	X	X	X	X	X
9.	Mercator sailing	X	X	X		X	X	X	X	X		
10.	Great Circle sailing	X	X			X	X	X	X	X		
11.	Piloting	X	X	X	X	X	X	X	X	X	X	X
12.	Aids to navigation	X	X	X	X	X	X	X	X	X	X	X
13.	Speed by revolutions	X				X		X		X		
14.	Fuel conservation	X				X		X				
15.	Instruments and accessories	X	X	X	[1] X	X	X	X	X	X	X	X
16.	Magnetism, deviation and compass compensation	X		X		X		X		X		
17.	Chart construction	X				X		X				
18.	Tides and currents	X	X	X	X	X	X	X	X	X	X	X
19.	Ocean winds, weather and currents	X	X	X	X	X	X	X	X	X	X	X
20.	Nautical astronomy and navigation definitions	X				X		X		X		[3] X
21.	International and inland rules of the road	X	X	X	X	X	X	X	X	X	X	X
22.	Signaling by international code flags, flashing light; lifesaving, storm and special signals	X	X	X	[2] X	X	X	X	X	X	X	[2] X
23.	Stability and ship construction	X	X	X	X	X	X	X	X	X	X	X
24.	Seamanship	X	X	X	X	X	X	X	X	X	X	X
25.	Cargo stowage and handling	X	X		X	X	X	X	X			X
26.	Change in draft due to density	X				X						
27.	Determination of area and volume	X	X	X	X	X	X	X	X	X	X	X
28.	Lifesaving apparatus and firefighting equipment	X	X	X	X	X	X	X	X	X	X	X
29.	Ship sanitation	X	X	X		X	X	X	X	X	X	X
30.	Rules and regulations for inspection of merchant vessels	X	X	X	X	X	X	X	X	X	X	X
31.	Laws governing marine inspection	X	X		X	X	X	X	X	X	X	X
32.	Ship's business	X	X			X	X					
33.	Such further examination of a nonmathematical character as the Officer in Charge, Marine Inspection, may consider necessary to establish the applicant's proficiency.	X	X	X	X	X	X	X	X	X	X	X

[1] Practical use of the magnetic compass. [2] Lifesaving, storm and special signals. [3] Navigation definitions only.

FOREWORD

This compilation answers the specimen questions for Second Mates, Chief Mates and Masters examinations as published in Specimen Examinations for Merchant Marine Deck Officers, CG-101, July 1, 1963.

The questions and answers are not necessarily the ones a candidate may be asked to answer when taking the examination, but they are representative examples covering the subjects on which the actual questions are based.

The candidate will find that examinations today cover a much broader scope and are of a more technical nature than was the case a few years ago. The Rules of the Road have been revised and emphasized and Radar and other electronic navigation aides have assumed an important place in navigation and ship handling.

Before sitting for the examination for an original license, each candidate should study the sample questions and answers in this book and make careful notes of the subjects covered. He should then read everything he can find on these subjects in the many books listed in the bibliography in the back of this book.

W. A. MacEwen

INTRODUCTION TO CG-101, JULY 1, 1963

Specimen Examinations for Merchant Marine Deck Officers

The specimen examinations published herein are for the purpose of acquainting prospective candidates with the type of questions they will be required to answer in order to qualify for licenses. Candidates will not be asked the same number of questions published under the respective grades and titles; nor are the examining officers precluded from using questions not contained in this publication. However, this book provides a fairly comprehensive guide to the nature of the material used.

In order to conserve space, duplication of questions under the different grades has been eliminated as far as practical. In studying for the higher grades of license, similar subject matter shown for the lower grades should be carefully reviewed. Candidates for lower grades should also acquaint themselves with the material given for required subject matter in the higher grades, although they will not be required to show the same degree of knowledge of the more difficult problems.

Candidates must be prepared to demonstrate their proficiency in the use and adjustment of the sextant; plotting of courses, bearings, and lines of position on charts, and the application of the International, Inland, and Pilot Rules of the Road through the use of models. An actual demonstration of the candidates knowledge of signalling is also required. A minimum qualifying speed of six words per minute is required for signalling with flashing light; and a minimum qualifying speed of eight words per minute is necessary for semaphore.

Effective January 1, 1959, every applicant for an original deck officer's license, raise in grade, or increase in scope of license for service on ocean, coastwise, or Great Lakes vessels of 300 gross tons or over shall be required to qualify as a radar observer. Questions of the type that will be given have been included in this publication under the separate heading "Radar Observer."

Subjects have been numbered in accordance with Table 10.05–45(b). "Subjects for Deck Officers of Ocean or Coastwise Steam or Motor Vessels" in the Rules and Regulations for Licensing and Certificating of Merchant Marine Personnel. A copy of the table is included for convenient reference.

A bibliography of texts which may be helpful is included. This cannot be regarded as complete, and failure to list any specific work is not intended to slight its value. Material in the examination has been drawn from other sources as well as the references cited.

Prior to sitting for a license examination, applicant must meet other requirements. A brief summary of these follows.

AGE AND EXPERIENCE

Applicants must be at least 21 years of age, with the exception of third mates, who must be at least 19 years of age. Minimum qualifying experience is required for each grade of license. These requirements are set forth in detail in CG–191, Rules and Regulations for Licensing and Certificating of Merchant Marine Personnel.

CITIZENSHIP

All applicants for an original, renewal, or raise of grade of license must be citizens of the United States, native born, or fully naturalized. This must be established by acceptable documentary evidence. Persons not able to prove American citizenship will not be examined for an original license.

APPLICATIONS

Form CG–866 (License Applications) may be obtained either by written request or personal application to any Officer in Charge, Marine Inspection, U.S. Coast Guard. It must be completed in all respects. All statements of sea service made therein must be supported by documentary evidence, issued by responsible persons, officers, or organizations. When the application has been completed, it must be presented personally by the applicant at a Marine Inspection Office. Each applicant for an original license is required to have a written endorsement from a Master and two other licensed officers of a vessel on which he has served.

PHYSICAL EXAMINATION

Upon acceptance and approval of his application, the candidate will be sent to one of the offices of the U.S. Public Health Service for a physical examination.

For an original license as master, mate, or pilot, the applicant must have either with or without glasses, at least 20/20 vision in one eye and at least 20/40 in the other. The applicant who wears glasses, however, must also be able to pass a test without glasses of at least 20/40 in one eye and at least 20/70 in the other. The color sense will be tested by means of a pseudo-isochromatic plate test, but any applicant who fails this test will be eligible if he can pass the "Williams" lantern test or equivalent.

REEXAMINATION AND REFUSAL OF LICENSES

Any applicant for license or endorsement who has been duly examined and refused may come before the same Officer in Charge, Marine Inspection, for reexamination at any time thereafter that may be fixed by such Officer in Charge, Marine Inspection, but such time shall not be less than 1 month from the date of his last failure. In the case of another failure, he will not be reexamined until after a lapse of at least 6 months from date of last failure.

A candidate who has been duly examined and refused a license by an Officer in Charge, Marine Inspection, shall not be examined by any other Officer in Charge, Marine Inspection, until 1 year has elapsed from the date of the last refusal without the sanction of the Officer in Charge, Marine Inspection, that refused the applicant.

REQUIREMENTS FOR RENEWAL OF LICENSE

Every Officer in Charge, Marine Inspection, shall, before renewing an existing license to a master, mate, or pilot who has served under the authority of his license within the 3 years next preceding the date of application for renewal, or who has been employed in a position closely related to the operation of vessels during the same 3 year period, require that such licensed officer present an affidavit that he has read within the 3 months next preceding the date of application the Rules of the Road applicable to the waters for which he is licensed and demonstrate his knowledge of the application of the Rules of the Road.

Every Officer in Charge, Marine Inspection, shall, before renewing an existing license to a master, mate, or pilot who has not served under the authority of his license within the 3 years next preceding the date of application for renewal, or who has not been employed in a position closely related to the operation of vessels during the same 3 year period, satisfy himself that such licensed officer is thoroughly familiar with the Rules of the Road applicable to the waters for which he is licensed. A written examination may be required for this purpose, or the applicant may be examined orally and a summary of the oral examination placed in the officer's license file.

PART I. SECOND MATE

1. LATITUDE BY POLARIS

Q. On 25 July, 1959 in D. R. Longitude 160°-03' West, Polaris was observed at morning twilight to have a sextant altitude of 49°-02' and a bearing of 002° by gyro-compass. The chronometer read 2h -18m-12s. The chronometer was fast 6 minutes and 4 seconds. The sextant error was 1' off the arc. The height of eye was 25 feet.

Required:
> The latitude at time of sight.
> The gyro-compass error.

A.

Chron.	14h 18m 12s			H_S Polaris	49° 02. 0'	
fast	− 6 4			I. E.	+ 1. 0	
G. M. T. 25d	14 12 08			Dip	− 4. 9	
G. H. A. Aries, 14h =	152° 31. 9'			App. alt.	48 58. 1	
corr. for 12m 08s	+ 3 02. 5			Refr.	− . 8	
	155 34. 4			H_O	48 57. 3	
Long.	160 03. 0 W.			Const.	− 1 00. 0	
t	4 28. 6 E.				47 57. 3	
	360 00			a_0	+ 12. 6*	
L. H. A. Aries =	355 31. 4			a_1	+ . 6*	
Comp. Bearing	002. 0°			a_2	+ . 3*	
Z (N. A., p. 276)	. 8°			Latitude =	48° 10. 8'N.	
Gyro Error =	1. 2° W.			*N. A., p. 276		

2. LATITUDE BY MERIDIAN ALTITUDE METHOD

Q. Alpheratz is observed on the meridian bearing South with an observed altitude of 75°-03'.8. Declination of Alpheratz is 28°-51'.1 North.

Required: The latitude at time of sight.
Show all work.

A.

H_O star Alpheratz	75°	03. 8 S.	
	90	00	
Z. D.	14	56. 2 N.	
Dec.	28	51. 1 N.	
Latitude =	43	47. 3 N.	

3. FIX OR RUNNING FIX

Q. Enroute from Naples, Italy to the Dardanelles, in D. R. Latitude 36°-21' North and Longitude 19°-45' East, four celestial bodies were observed. Given the following information on the celestial bodies, determine the ship's position.

1

Body	Observed Altitude	Greenwich Hour Angle	Declination
VEGA --------	29°-03'.4	260°-38'.7	38°-44'.5 N.
DUBHE -------	56°-48'.0	14°-20'.8	61°-59'.4 N.
SPICA --------	42°-38'.1	338°-57'.9	10°-56'.2 S.
ALPHECCA ---	59°-59'.2	306°-31'.6	26°-51'.7 N.

A. Candidates may use any method of solution.

Vega G. H. A. 260° 38.7'
      Long.   19 45.0 E.
      L. H. A. 280 23.7
              360 00
        t =   79 36.3 E.

t 79° 36.3'	Log hav	9. 61255
L 36 21	" cos	9. 90602
d 38 44.5	" cos	9. 89208
	" hav	9. 41065
	N. hav	.25742
d—L 2° 23.5'	" "	.00044
ZD 61 02	" "	.25786
90 00		

H_c 28 58.0
H_O 29 03.4
          5.4' toward

Z_n = 61.3° From Lat. 36° 21'N. and Long. 19° 45'E. step off 5.4' in the direction 061°, and draw through the point arrived at Position Line in direction of 331° and 151°.

Spica G. H. A. 338° 57.9'
      Long.   19 45.0 E.
      L. H. A. 358 42.9
              360 00
        t =   1 17.1 E.

H_O 42° 38.1'
Bowd. Table 30 + .9
Mer. alt. 42 39.0
          90 00

Z. D.   47 21.0 N.
Dec.   10 56.2 S.
Lat.   36° 24.8' N.

t 1° 17'	Log sin 8.3502
d 10 56	" cos 9.9920
H_O 42 38	" sec 0.1333
Z_n 178° 17'	" sin 8.4755

Through Lat. 36° 24.8'N. and Long. 19° 45'E. draw Position Line in direction of 268°—88°.

Dubhe G. H. A. 14° 20.8'
      Long.   19 45.0 E.
      t   = 34 05.8 W.

t 34° 05.8 L	hav 8.93426
L 36 21	cos 9.90602
d 61 59.4	cos 9.67175
	hav 8.51203
	N hav .03251
d—L 25°38.4'	hav .04924
z. d. 33°13.7'	hav .08175
90 00	

H_c 56 46.3
H_O 56 48.0
        1.7' toward

Alphecca G. H. A. 306° 31.6
         Long.   19 45.0 E.
         L. H. A. 326 16.6
                360 00
          t =   33 43.4 E.

t 33° 43.4' L	hav 8.92498
L 36 21	cos 9.90602
d 26 51.7	cos 9.95041
	hav 8.78141
	N hav .06045
L—d 9° 29.3'	hav .00684
z. d. 30° 04'	hav .06729
90 00	

H_c 59 56
H_O 59 59.2
          3.2' toward

From <u>Davis's Tables</u>:
Az. = N 28.7°W, or Z_n = 331.3°
From D.R. position lay off 331°
dist. 1.7' to meet Position Line
extending 241° and 61°.

From <u>Davis's Tables</u>:
Az. = S 81.3°E, or Z_n = 098.7°
From D.R. position lay off 099°
dist. 3.2' to meet Position Line
extending 009° and 189°.

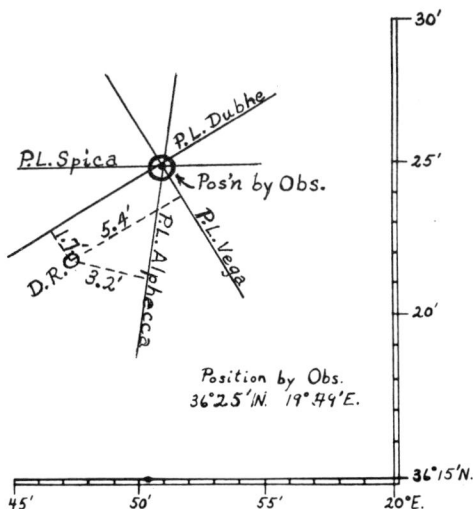

4. STAR IDENTIFICATION

Q. On 18 March, 1959, at Lat. 15° 08'S., Long. 64° 19'E., a p.m. observation is taken at 14h 32m 44s GMT of a star whose corrected altitude is 43° 02.7' and whose azimuth is 338.5° true.
Identify the star. Any method may be used. Show all work.

A.

G.M.T. 18 Mar.	14h 32m 44s	
G.H.A. Aries	25° 23'	
corr., 32m 44s	+8 12	
	33 35	
Long	64 19 E.	
L.H.A. Aries	97 54	
t Star	17 48 W.	
360° - S.H.A. =	80 06 E.	
	360 00	
S.H.A. =	279 54	

Consulting the Star list on page 273, Nautical Almanac, we find nearest star position to that calculated indicates β <u>Tauri</u> or <u>El</u> <u>Nath</u> as star in question.

Az. 338.5° = N 21-1/2°W   L hav 8.5415
H_O = 43°   cos 9.8641
Lat = 15°   cos 9.9849
    hav 8.3905
N hav .0246
Lat + H_O = 58°   hav .2350
90° − Dec = 61°16'   hav .2596
    90 00
Dec =   28 44 N.
Z = 21-1/2°   L sin 9.5641
H_O = 43°   cos 9.8641
Dec = 28° 44'   sec 0.0571
t = 17° 48'   sin 9.4853

Q. Given:

	(1) Alpheratz	(2) Ankaa	(3) Schedar
Date--------	7 Jan., 1959	12 Jan., 1959	17 Jan., 1959
GMT-------	1h 14m 37s	12h 39m 53s	18h 03m 49s
Long.-------	125° 36' West	05° 27' East	02° 58' East

Required: Meridian angle and declination of each star. Indicate whether star is East or West of the meridian in each case.

A.   (1) <u>Alpheratz:</u>   (2) <u>Ankaa</u>   (3) Schedar

	(1) Alpheratz		(2) Ankaa		(3) Schedar	
G.M.T.	7 Jan. 1h	14m 37s	12 Jan. 12h 39m 53s		17 Jan. 18h 03m 49s	
G.H.A. Aries	120°	51.3'		291° 14.1'		161° 46.8
	+3	39.9		+9 59.9		+0 57.4
	124	31.2		301 14.0		162 44.2
Long.W.	125	36.0	Long. E.	5 27.0	Long. E	2 58.0
L.H.A. Aries	1	04.8 E.		306 41.0		165 42.2
S.H.A. Star	358	26.0		353 56.2		350 27.3
L.H.A. Star	357	21.2		660 37.2		516 09.5
	360	00		360 00		360 00
Mer. Angle	2	38.8 E.	L.H.A. =	300 37.2	Mer.Angle=156 09.5	
				360 00		
			Mer. Angle =	59 22.8 E.		
Dec. 28° 52' N.			Dec.	42° 31.9' S.	Dec. 56° 19' N	

Q. The following 3 sextant altitudes of stars were obtained. The height of eye was 22 feet; the sextant index error was 2'.0 on the arc in all observations.

	Observation #1	Observation #2	Observation #3
Star Sext. Alt.------	4°-19'.8	14°-05'.1	48°-56'.2
Bar. Pressure -----	30.6 in.	980 mb	29.6 in.
Temperature ------	92° F.	(−) 20° Celsius (Centigrade)	48° F.

Required: The observed altitudes.

A.

	Observation #1		Observation #2		Observation #3	
H_s	4° 19.8'		14° 05.1'		48° 56.2'	
Dip 22'	− 4.6		− 4.6		− 4.6	
I.E.	− 2.0		− 2.0		− 2.0	
Happ	4 13.2		13 58.5		48 49.6	
N.A.	−11.3		− 3.8		− .8	
front pp.	+ .6		− .5		0	
H_0 =	4 02.5	H_0	13 54.2	H_0	48 48.8	

5. CHART NAVIGATION

Q. How would you assess the accuracy of a nautical chart?
A. By noting the source, or survey basis, from which it is drawn up, as given in the title of such chart. If chart is based upon a very old survey, its accuracy, especially with respect to depths of water indicated, should be accepted with caution. If soundings given are sparsely or unevenly distributed, particularly where irregular depths in rocky areas are shown, extreme care should attend the use of chart.

Q. What type pencils and erasers are best for chart work?
A. Moderately soft pencils, and erasers of the soap-rubber type.

Q. What care should be taken in using pencils and erasers, to keep charts in good condition?
A. Pencil marks should be lightly drawn, consistent with legibility, so that chart's finished surface may not be injured in the erasing process.

Q. How is information concerning magnetic variation shown on Pilot Charts?
A. By isogonic lines, or curves, which pass through all points having the same variation. Given for each degree, 10th and intermediate 5th degrees are indicated by plain lines; all others by dotted lines. An inset chartlet also gives curves of equal annual variation change.

Q. Some foreign charts are published with the depths shown in meters. Convert 10 meters into fathoms.
A. 1 meter = 39.37 inches; 1 fathom = $6 \times 12 = 72$ inches. Thus, 1 meter = $(39.37 \div 72.00)$ fath. = .547 fath. and 10 meters = 5.47 fathoms.

Q. How should charts be stowed?
A. They should be stowed flat, in space provided for full area of charts.

Q. What is the importance of the issue date shown on charts?
A. In that the reliability of a chart may be appraised as to whether or not the latest information may be indicated thereon.

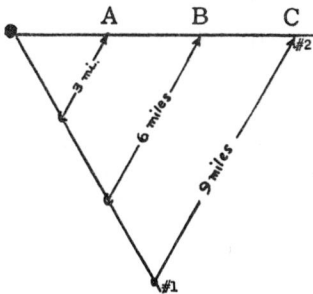

Q. A vessel steams 27 minutes at 20 knots from bearing 1 to bearing 2. Would the position of the vessel at bearing 2 be at point A, B or C, assuming she sailed along one of the tracks plotted?
A. At C.

Q. Where may the issue date be found on a chart?
A. At lower left hand corner of chart. (1st. edition's month and year are given at top margin center).

Q. When Notices to Mariners are received on board a vessel, how long should they be retained before being discarded?
A. Two years.

Q. What is the vertex of a great circle?
A. Point of minimum distance from either pole of the sphere.

Q. What is a chain of soundings?
A. A portion of ship's track, as indicated on the chart in use, along which a number of successively ascertained depths of water are marked, usually also with character of bottom found. It is used to check ship's position by comparison with the charted soundings.

Q. What is composite sailing, and when is it used?
A. When, in connection with great circle sailing, it is decided to limit ship's track to a certain latitude, as on account of probable adverse winds or ice conditions. The great circle passing through departure point and having its vertex at the limiting parallel is followed, thence along the latter, and finally following the great circle passing through destination point and also having its vertex at the limiting parallel of latitude.

Q. How can you determine what charts and publications are to be corrected by the notices listed in the Notices to Mariners?
A. That information is given in the Notices themselves.

Q. What government agency prepares Light Lists for foreign waters?
A. U.S. Navy Hydrographic Office.

Q. What government agency prepares Light Lists for the United States and its possessions?
A. U. S. Coast Guard.

Q. When plotting a fix by means of three cross bearings taken at approximately the same time, what would you assume if the three bearing lines do not intersect in a point or in a very small triangle?

A. That at least one of the bearings is in error.

Q. What branch of the government prepares the American Ephemeris, the Air Almanac and the Nautical Almanac?

A. U. S. Naval Observatory.

Q. Describe briefly the contents of at least two of the three publications mentioned in the preceding question.

A. The American Ephemeris, or astronomical almanac, contains complete ephemerides of the Sun, Moon, and Planets; apparent places for every 10 days of over 200 stars; details of eclipses of Sun and Moon; occultations of stars by the Moon and elements for predicting same; elements for physical observations of Sun, Moon, and planets; and other important data for the astronomer's use.

The Air Almanac, which is intended primarily for aviators' use, in general gives similar information to that contained in the Nautical Almanac. Unlike the latter annual publication, it is issued for every 4 months and giving the epemerides of Sun, Aries, Venus, Mars, Jupiter, and Moon for every 10 minutes of each day, to the nearest 1 minute of arc and 1 second of time. Also for each day is given an ecliptic diagram showing positions relative to the sun, in the zodiacal 16° belt, of 5 planets and the stars Aldebaran, Antares, Spica, and Regulus, together with the moon's parallax in altitude. The above data are tabulated for each day upon a single leaf which may be torn out as it is finished, so that the book opens at current date. Following the daily pages, considerable space is devoted to sky diagrams, astrograph settings, duration of sunlight, moonlight, and twilight diagrams and tables, with other valuable information peculiar to the air navigator's needs.

The Nautical Almanac may be called an abridgment or condensed form of the American Ephemeris. It contains the necessary astronomical data for surface navigation in convenient tabular form. In addition to its handy tables for altitude corrections and finding latitude and azimuth of Polaris, the Almanac gives for each hour of G. M. T. the astronomical places of Sun, Moon, Venus, Mars, Jupiter, Saturn, and First Point of Aries; places of 57 selected stars for every 3rd. day, also those of 173 stars for each month of the year; and daily times of sunrise, sunset, moonrise, moonset, duration of twilight at various latitudes, moon's meridain passage and phase, and equation of time.

Q. Why are the backs of pages in Notices to Mariners left blank?

A. So that any page or portion of a page may be cut out and attached as by an adhesive to the publication or chart affected.

Q. What government agency publishes the Coast Pilot?
A. U.S. Coast and Geodetic Survey·

Q. What government agency publishes the Sailing Directions?
A. U.S. Navy Hydrographic Office.

Q. Describe what is meant by the point of tangency on a gnomonic chart.
A. Point at which a plane, represented by such chart, touches the earth's surface. Conceived as viewed from the earth's center, the area mapped about such point is geometrically projected to the tangent plane·

Q. What information is contained in H. O. No. 205, Radio Navigational Aids?
A. Contains full information on radio beacons, radio direction-finder stations, navigational warnings, distress signals, medical advice procedure, quarantine report stations, time signals, and wartime emergency procedure for U.S. vessels. Also, a complete list of radio stations that perform valuable services for the mariner, with details concerning such services, including regulations of various nations on the subject.

Q. If the co-ordinates on a great circle course are transferred from a gnomonic chart to a Mercator chart and the lines connecting them drawn, what is the appearance of the great circle course on the Mercator chart?
A. A curved line, convexity of which, in either northern or southern hemisphere, lies toward the pole.

Q. How should charts be kept corrected?
A. By hand, from changes given in Notices to Mariners. Date of latest correction should be written or stamped on margin of chart.

Q. What precautions are necessary when charts have laid unused for a lengthy period after the date of issue?
A. Ascertain whether new prints or new editions of the charts have been issued. If so, replace with such later ones; but, in any case, the charts should indicate the latest hydrographic information obtainable, whether by replacement or hand correction from Notices to Mariners.

Q. If a vessel has laid off a great circle track and has departed from the track through bad weather or lack of observations, should she attempt, when her position is determined, to get back on the original track laid down or work out a new course from her determined position?
A. Work out a new great circle course from the determined position.

Q. A vessel on course 000° sights a light vessel dead ahead at a distance of 10 miles. What course should she set to pass the light vessel one mile off her port side?

A. From Traverse Table: Dist. 10', Dep. 1', gives Course 006°.

Q. What information is provided by the Daily Memoranda?

A. Gives a synopsis of late information on navigational aids and dangers to vessels, including reports of ice, positions of derelicts, mine fields, and advance information of the more important material which will be published in Notices to Mariners.

Q. Is the water ever shallower than indicated on a chart? Explain.

A. Yes. If, for example, the chart datum is mean low water, there will be times at which the depth will be less, as well as greater than such charted information. A less depth generally is indicated in the Tide Tables by the minus (—) sign.

Q. In approaching land, what scale chart should be used?

A. The largest scale chart obtainable.

Q. Name the reference planes of soundings used on charts and state how you would determine the reference plane when consulting a chart.

A. On U.S. Coast and Geodetic Survey charts of Atlantic and Gulf coasts of the U.S. and Puerto Rico the tidal datum or "reference plane of soundings" is mean low water; on those of the Pacific U.S. coast and Alaska it is mean lower low water. Most U.S. Hydrographic charts have mean low water, mean lower low water, or mean low water springs. British charts use the plane of mean low water springs, except where the daily inequality is large, in which case the datum Indian spring low water is used. (The last-named is a low datum that is about the level of lower low water at time of Moon's highest declination when it coincides with time of Full or New Moon.)

The reference plane is given in the chart's title.

Q. What precautions would you take when transferring positions from one chart to another?

A. If they differ in scale, care must be taken to use the measurements of both latitude and longitude on the proper chart. Also, to avoid the error of laying off odd minutes of longitude to the right instead of to the left, where West Longitude is concerned, and vice versa.

Q. What information is contained in the Coast Pilots?

A. Coast Pilots cover the coasts of the United States and its possessions, including the Intracoastal Waterway, and contain descriptions of coastlines, harbors, dangers, aids to navigation, winds, currents, and tides; instructions for navigating narrow waters, and for approaching and entering harbors; information on port facilities, signal systems, and pilot services; also, other data which cannot be conveniently shown on charts.

Q. How is the latitude and longitude of a particular point on a Great
Circle chart determined?
A. By use of the latitude and longitude scales in the immediate vi-
cinity of such point.

Q. How would you know of the issuance of new editions of Hydrographic Office charts in order to replace the old corrected charts
aboard ships?
A. From such advice given in Notices to Mariners.

Q. Are parallels of latitude straight lines on a polyconic chart?
Explain your answer.
A. No. The parallels appear as arcs of non-concentric circles having their concavity toward the elevated pole. The distance between
successive parallels is expanded with departure from the central
meridian of the projection. Thus the scale of the chart is correct
along any parallel and close to or along the central meridian only.

Q. Explain the limitations on the use of middle latitude sailing when
crossing the equator.
A. If the distance is 200 miles or less, departure may be considered equal to difference of longitude. For greater distances, the
parts of the course line on each side of the equator should be
considered separately. Generally, Middle Latitude Sailing should
not be used when the latitudes are of opposite names.

Q. In taking a vertical sextant angle, what care is required if the
object observed is situated far inland from the shore?
A. Assuming the basic height is that above sea level, in order to
obtain a correct measurement of the vertical angle, especially at
a comparatively short distance off shore, the observer's eye should
be at the lowest practicable level.

Q. State three methods by which, without obtaining the precise position, the navigator may assure himself visually that he is clear
of any particular danger.
A. (1) By observing whether ship is on the proper side of a danger bearing.   (2) By keeping outside the danger angle between two
known objects on shore. (3) By use of a range as a line of position, as by the lead or direction indicated by two objects in line.

Q. A vessel desires to make good a course of 100° and a speed of
9 knots through a current setting NE, true, with a drift of three
knots.
Required: The course and speed required to accomplish this.

A.

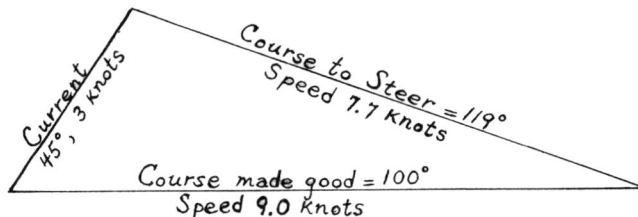

Current 45°, 3 Knots
Course to Steer = 119°
Speed 7.7 Knots
Course made good = 100°
Speed 9.0 Knots

Q. What precautions should be taken when obtaining the position of a ship by means of a bow and beam or four point bearing?

A. That allowance be made for any known current. Especially in a slow moving vessel, such method of fixing ship's position should be considered approximate where knowledge of local current conditions is lacking.

Q. Why should bearings of near objects be used in preference to objects farther away, even though the latter may be more prominent?

A. Because a small error in the bearing of a more distant object affects results by displacing the true line of bearing, in plotting, much more than when an object near ship's track is observed.

Q. What caution should be observed in homing on the bearing of a lightship's radio beacon signal?

A. Bearing observed should be kept a few degrees on the bow, in order to ensure avoidance of collision with the lightship.

Q. Why is a correction necessary in plotting on a Mercator chart bearings obtained through the use of a radio direction finder?

A. The radio bearing indicates the line of shortest distance and therefore is an arc of a great circle which may be drawn on a Mercator chart as a straight line only in the case of a true N. or a S. bearing or, when on the Equator, in the case of an E. or a W. true bearing. With these exceptions, the radio bearing is corrected toward the Equator for plotting on a Mercator chart.

Q. What preparation would you make when planning to enter a strange port?

A. Have at hand the proper chart or charts, Sailing Directions, and Light List. Any information concerning the port in Notices to Mariners should be considered and the master advised accordingly. If a pilot is to be taken, I would see that all is in readiness for his boarding.

Q. A vessel hears a radio distance-finding signal from a light vessel and 10 seconds later hears the sound signal. What is her distance from the light vessel?

A. $10 \div 5.5$, or $10 \times .18$, $= 1.8$ miles.

Q. What measures should be taken to check the accuracy of direction-finder bearings?

A. As opportunity presents itself, simultaneous compass and radio
bearings of a radio-beacon station are observed. Any errors in
direction-finder bearings are then determined by comparison with
the corrected compass bearings.

Q. When taking radio direction-finder bearings off a coast with islands between your ship and the shore transmitter, what care
would you exercise? Why?

A. Caution should be exercised in accepting such bearings as being
correct. What is known as coastal refraction or land effect, due
to difference in the conducting and reflecting properties of the
land and water over which the radio wave travels.

Q. Describe briefly how ocean station vessel's radio beacons may
be located on the chart.

A. Ocean vessel stations are assigned a position within a 10-mile
square. The radio-beacon signal consists of 4 letters, first two
of which comprise the characteristic signal of the station, the
second two indicating its position within the 10-mile square, as
marked out by a grid.

Q. When a vessel equipped with a radio direction finder hears a
distress signal, what measures should be taken?

A. The instrument should be brought into use in order to obtain
the distressed vessel's bearing and thus the course on which to
proceed to her assistance.

Q. What factors must be considered in obtaining radio direction-
finder bearings on a station broadcasting entertainment programs?

A. The station's frequency may differ from that for which vessel's
set is calibrated; transmitting antenna may be far removed from
the known location of the station; if station is synchronized with
others, it may not be possible to tell which station is observed;
and, as most stations of this sort are located some distance inland, land effect or coastal refraction may seriously affect a
bearing observed.

Q. How is a radio direction finder on board ship calibrated for
errors caused by electrical conductors nearby?

A. By observing simultaneously radio and visual bearings of a radio
beacon while ship is placed on different headings, preferably every
20°, round the compass. Antennas, booms, davits, rails, etc.,
should be in their normal positions, as when at sea, during the
calibration procedure.

Q. How are bearing errors caused by nearby electrical conductors
corrected on board ship?

A. By using a calibration table compiled from results of swinging

ship, as indicated in answer to previous question; or, as is commonly done, the direction-indicator may be automatically corrected
by a cam, as it turns in azimuth relative to ship's head.

Q. What is the meaning of the following information taken from the
radio-beacon chart for the stations indicated?
I   San Francisco L.S. 314 (3-6).
II   Farallon 314 (3-6).
III Bonita Pt. 314 (3-6).
A. It means that the three radio beacons named operate as a group
in the order indicated by the numerals I, II, III, on a radio frequency of 314 kilocycles, during the 3rd and 6th 10-minute periods
of each hour in clear weather.

Q. How is night effect usually manifested in radio direction-finder
bearings?
A. It usually manifests itself in wide or changing minimums, thus
giving bearings which are, at best, mere approximations.

Q. Why is night effect unusual when a vessel obtains a bearing from
a position less than 50 miles from the radio beacon?
A. Because the ground wave predominates at such distances. Night
effect is caused by sky waves.

6. COMPASS DEVIATION

Q. Enroute from New York to Cape of Good Hope in D. R. Latitude
31°-26' North and Longitude 55°-17' West, an azimuth of the star
δ (Delta) Cyngi was observed. The following data was obtained at
the time of observation:

Compass Bearing of Star	Greenwich Hour Angle	Declination of Star
329°-00' psc	150°-36'.3	45°-01'.9

Variation for the locality was 18°-30' West.
Required: The true azimuth. The deviation of the standard compass.
Candidates may use any method of solution.
A.

G. H. A.   150° 36. 3'   From Davis' Star Azimuth Tables:
Long. W.   55 17. 0   (Lat. 31°N. ; Dec. 45°N. ; H. A. 6h 20m.)
L. H. A.   95 19. 3   47.8°
     = 6h. 21m. 17. 2s. W.   H. A. corr.   — . 1
Lat. 31° 26'N.   Lat.   "   + .1
Dec. 45° 01. 9'N.   True Az. =   N 47. 8 W.
                                            360. 0
                                 Zn   =   312. 2
                               Comp. Bear'g 329. 0
                               Comp. Error   16. 8 W.
                               Variation   18. 5 W.
                               Deviation   1. 7 E.

Q. At sunrise, March 21, 1964, Lat. 41° 00' S, Long. 175° 00'E, sun's bearing p.s.c. was 114-1/2°; variation 20° E; bearing by gyro 92°; ship's head 50° p.s.c. Find error and deviation of standard compass, gyro error, and true course.

A.

Sunrise, L.M.T. Mar. 21,	6h 11m	Ship's head p.s.c. = 50°
Long. E.	− 11 40	Comp. Error = 24-1/2°E
G.M.T.	Mar. 20, 18h 31m	True Course = 74-1/2°

(Cos Z = sin Dec. × sec Lat)

From N.A., Dec. = 0° 04.3'N.   L. sin = 7.0972
            Lat. = 41° 00' S.   L. sec = 0.1222
            Z_n = 89° 54'   L. cos = 7.2194
          Bear'g = 114-1/2°   Gyro Bear'g = 92°
    S.C. Error = 24-1/2° E. Z_n = 90°
          Var. = 20°   E.   Gyro Error = 2° W.
          Dev. = 4-1/2° E.

9. MERCATOR SAILING

Q. By Mercator sailing, find true Course and Distance from Lat. 41° 00' S, Long. 175° 00' E to Lat. 20° 12' S, Long. 70° 10' W.

A. From Lat. 41° 00' S   Mer. parts 2686.3   Long. 175° 00' E
    To   Lat. 20° 12' S   "   " 1229.9   Long. 70° 10' W
        D.Lat.=20 48   M.D.L. = 1456.4   D.Lg. = 245 10
             =1248' N.   360 00
                                                        114° 50'
                                              D. Long. = 6890' E.

(Tan Co = M.D.L. ÷ D.Long ; Dist. = D.Lat. × sec Co)

D.Long. 6890. . . .Log 3.83822
M.D.L.   1456.4. .Log 3.16328   D.Lat. 1248. . . .Log 3.09621
Co 78° 04'. . . . L.tan 0.67494 . . . . L sec 0.68450
True Course 78°; Distance 6036 miles.   6036. . . .Log 3.78071

Q. By Mercator sailing, find the true course and the distance from Ambrose Channel Lightship (Lat. 40°-27'.1 North and Long. 73°-49'.4 West) to a point in Lat. 32°-22' North and Long. 64°-39'.0 West, off St. David Island Lighthouse, Bermuda. Show all work.

A.

From Lat.	40° 27. 1'N.	Mer. parts 2643	Long. 73° 49. 4'W.

To "	32 22. 0 N.	" " 2042	" 64 39. 0 W.

D. Lat. = 8 05. 1   M. D. L. = 601   D. Long. = 9 10. 4

   = 485. 1'S   = 550. 4'E.

(Tan Co. = M. D. L. ÷ D. Long.   Dist. = D. Lat. × sec Co.)

D. Long.	550. 4'E	Log 2. 74068	
M. D. L.	601	" 2. 77887	
Co.	S 42° 29'E.	L. tan 9. 96181	L. sec 0. 13225
	180 00		
C_n	137 31	D. Lat. 485. 1 Log	2. 68583
		Dist. 657. 8 mi. "	2. 81808

True Course 137-1/2°, distance 658 miles.

11. PILOTING

Q. Running along the coast off a lighthouse listed as 145 feet high. You measure its vertical sextant angle and find it to be 1°-3'. How far off the lighthouse are you?

A. D = . 56h ÷ v, or (. 56 × 145) ÷ 63 = 81. 2 ÷ 63 = 1. 3 miles.

(Or by Bowditch, Table 9, 1. 34 miles).

Q. Steaming South by gyro at 12 knots, a lighthouse was observed bearing 126° by gyro. After a run of 30 minutes the lighthouse bore 100° by gyro. Find distance off at 2nd bearing and abeam.

A. Angle on bow at 1st Bearing = 180 — 126 = 54°

"   "   "   " 2nd   "   = 180 — 100 = 80° Dist. run = 6 miles.

From Bowditch, Table 7, 1. 85 × 6 = 11. 1 miles off at 2nd Bearing.

1. 82 × 6 = 10. 9 "   " when abeam.

Q. A ship is steering 101° p. g. c. , variation 23° East, deviation 3° West, which is 82° p. s. c. A light is sighted bearing 129° true. On what gyro bearing must the light be observed so that the run between bearings would equal the distance off the light when the light bears 191° gyro?

A. Course 82° p. s. c. ; var. 23° E; dev. 3° W, gives 102° true course, and gyro error 1° E. 1st. Bearing = 129° true = 27° on bow. From Table 7, Factor 1. 0; 2nd. Bearing = 148° true = 46° on bow, or 147° gyro.

Note: Problems may be given pertaining to piloting which are under other titles in this book.

12. AIDS TO NAVIGATION

Q. What is the meaning of a red nun marked with a yellow triangle as illustrated?

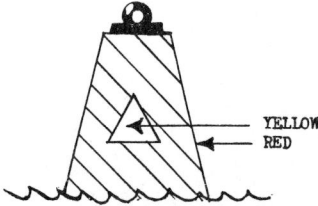

A. A starboard hand buoy in a joint waterway, as where the intracoastal waterway and another fairway coincide.

Q. What is the meaning of the class of a buoy as specified in the U. S. Coast Guard Light List?

A. Class refers to size; largest buoys are 1st class.

Q. When a buoy is in position during a certain period of the year only, how may the dates when the buoy is available be determined?

A. Such information is given in the remarks column in the Light List.

Q. Describe the use of a range (or leading lights) in entering or leaving a harbor. What precautions must be observed in the use of such ranges?

A. By steering toward or away from two lights or daymarks and keeping them in line, or in range, i. e., with the farther one directly above the nearer one, the vessel is kept in a channel or other proper course, as indicated on the chart by a line, usually noting its true direction entering port. As a precaution against running off the range in the event of one of the lights or marks becoming obscured, ship's heading should be checked to coincide with the range, either right ahead or astern as the case may be. Especially where depth of water is limited to a narrow channel, extreme care is necessary when meeting another vessel to avoid departing from the range course any more than is required to pass in safety. Also, in following such leading aids, care should be taken to alter vessel's heading in time, as may be required in turning into another range, rounding a buoy, etc.

Q. What is the significance of the shape of unlighted buoys as used in the lateral system in United States waters?

A. Entering port from seaward, cylindrical-shaped or can buoys are passed on the port hand; conical or nun buoys on the right hand. Either may mark mid-channel, when marked with vertical black and white stripes.

Q. On a clear, dark night, a light is sighted just breaking clear of the horizon. If your height of eye is 50 feet and the charted visibility of the light is 12. 5 miles, what is your distance from the light?

A. Visibility of light is given for 15 ft. above sea level.

Table 8, <u>Bowditch</u>: At 15 ft. horizon is 4.4 miles distant
" 50 "   "   " <u>8.1</u> "   "
Diff.   + 3.7 "
Visibility of light   <u>12.5</u> "
Distance from light   =   <u>16.2</u> miles.

Q. Define exactly what is meant by a group occulting light. (Candidates may submit a sketch such as that contained in the light list to help demonstrate complete comprehension of the term.)
A. A light having groups of eclipses at regular intervals, the duration of light being equal to, or greater than, that of darkness.

Q. Name the different types of buoys sketched.

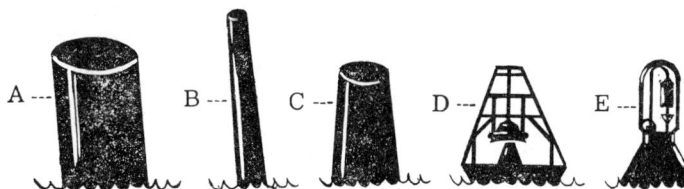

A. (A) Can. (B) Spar. (C) Nun. (D) Bell. (E) Whistle.

Q. Where it is desired to show the need for particular caution, at important turns, etc., what light period is given buoys?
A. The quick-flashing period, or that in which the light shows not less than 60 flashes per minute.

Q. What is indicated by the white buoy with green top as sketched?

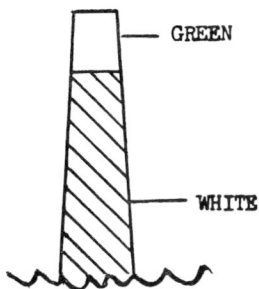

A. Dredging and/or surveying operations.

Q. How would you identify a lighthouse in the daytime?
A. By its description given in the <u>Light List</u>.

Q. Where are station buoys found and what is their function?
A. They are found in close proximity to a major aid to mark the station, as of a lightship, should the regular aid be accidentally shifted from station. They are numbered and colored the same as the regular aid. In the case of lightship station buoys, the letters <u>L</u> <u>S</u> above the initials of the lightship indicate their function.

Q. How far could you see a powerful navigational light, whose height is 100 feet, from the bridge of a vessel where your height of eye would be 80 feet above the water?

A.

From Table 8, <u>Bowditch</u>: Height 100 gives distance to horizon 11. 4 mi.
                        "   80   "   "   "   "   <u>10. 2</u> "
                            Visibility of light   =   <u>21. 6</u> mi.

Q. What word indicates color variations in the characteristics of a light?

A. <u>Alternating</u>.

Q. Define exactly what is meant by an interrupted quick flashing light. (Candidates may submit a sketch such as that contained in the Light List to demonstrate their complete comprehension of the term.)

A. One which flashes at the rate of about 60 times per minute for several seconds, followed by a short period of darkness. Commonly shows quick flashes for about 4 seconds, followed by a dark period of about 4 seconds.

Q. Entering from seaward you sight the black and white vertically striped lighted buoy illustrated.

(a) On which side would you leave this buoy in passing? (b) What number would such a buoy have? (c) What color light would the buoy display? (d) What phase characteristics would the light of this buoy have? (e) How would this buoy be indicated on a chart?

A. (a) On either side. (b) No number. (c) White. (d) Short flash followed by a long one, or "short-long flash," recurring about 8 times every minute. (e) By a diamond-shaped symbol having a line drawn through its longer axis, and a small magenta disc over the dot indicating position of buoy.

Q. How are bearings relating to sectors of visibility of lights stated in <u>Light Lists</u>?

A. They are described as limiting a light's visibility to an arc of the compass between two true bearings of the light (in degrees) as observed from seaward and indicated clockwise.

Q. What are the standard light colors used for lighted aids to navigation?

A. White, red, and green.

Q. What do colored sectors in lights mark?

A. Red sectors cover obstructions, <u>i.e.</u>, dangers lying within the bearing limits indicated, as rocks or a shoal. Green sectors cover the limits of clear navigable approach, as in showing the lead of a channel, or approach to a turning point, in piloting.

Q. How is the power of a light expressed in the Light List?
A. In units of candle power. The International Standard Candle, or candela, is that used as the unit of luminous intensity.

Q. How would you determine if the visibility given for a light is the geographic or luminous range?
A. Since there is no distinction made in the Light List between the geographic and the luminous range of a light, I would find the distance of the sea horizon from the height of the light in question (Table 8, Bowditch) and add 4.4 miles for a height of eye of 15 feet. This gives the geographic range. If the miles-seen column in the Light List gives a lesser value, such would be the luminous range.

Q. Describe the effect of atmospheric refraction on the visibility of navigational aids.
A. Visibility of navigational aids is given for normal atmospheric conditions, with average sea and air temperatures. Abnormal refraction, which occurs with a large difference in sea and air temperatures or an unusually high or low barometric pressure, in the greater number of instances has the effect of increasing the visibility distance given.

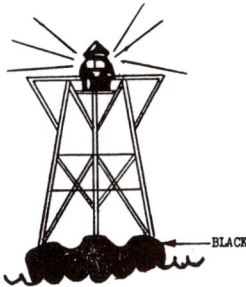

Q. In entering a United States port the black lighted buoy is sighted as shown: (a) On what side should it be left in passing? (b) What type number would it have? (c) What color light would it show? (d) How would this buoy be indicated on a chart? (e) What phase characteristics would this light have?
A. (a) Left. (b) An odd number. (c) White or green. (d) By a black diamond-shaped symbol, with a dot centered in a magenta disc, near one apex. (e) Flashing or occulting, having a frequency of not more than 30 flashes or occultations every minute; if marking an important turn, quick-flashing, or having a frequency of flashes of not less than 60 per minute.

15. INSTRUMENTS AND ACCESSORIES

Q. How would you clean the arc of a sextant?
A. With a piece of soft cotton dipped in ammonia. After wiping clean, with the end of the forefinger apply a mixture of a fine machine oil and powdered graphite, which will preserve the silver against tarnishing and also renew the desirable clear-cut appearance of the division marks.

Q. What is the purpose of the mercury ballistic wicks on the master gyro-compass?
A. To provide ventilation.

Q. Why are corrections for latitude, height and temperature applied to a mercurial barometer?
A. In order to correct its reading to standard sea-level gravity at Lat. 45-1/2°; to sea-level pressure; and to the standard temperature of 32° F.

Q. Describe in detail the procedure of stopping the gyro-compass.
A. Open switches to battery, ship's supply, and all others on the control panel; secure rotor case upright by the locking screw; turn alarm switch to battery to silence buzzer. If compass is to be stopped <u>at sea</u> during heavy weather or when ship is yawing over 10°, proceed as above, except that rotor case should not be secured but compass should be steadied by hand until rotor comes to rest; then lock rotor case upright.

Q. What routine inspection of the gyro-compass should be made each watch at sea? State briefly what you would check.
A. See that proper voltage is supplied; that "hunt" is normal; that master and repeaters are in synchronism; check compass error by observation.

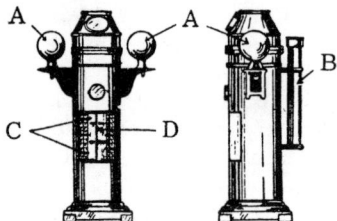

Q. Name the corrector indicated by each letter on the sketch and state the type of magnetism each is designed to correct.
A. (A) <u>Quadrantal correctors</u>. These soft iron spheres are for correcting Coefficient D, or that component of the total deviation which attains a maximum on NE, SW, NW, and SE by compass, and which is caused by transient induced magnetism in horizontal soft iron of ship's structure. (B) <u>Flinders bar</u>, for correcting that part of Coefficient B which is due to induced magnetism in vertical soft iron and which attains maximum value on E or W by compass. (C) <u>Fore-and-aft bar magnets</u> for correcting Coefficient B, or that component of the deviation caused by permanent magin the vessel and which attains a maximum on E or W by compass. (D) <u>Thwartship bar magnets</u> for correcting Coefficient C, or that component of total deviation caused by vessel's permanent magnetism which has maximum value on N or S by compass.

Q. How can the brightness of the reflection from the horizon glass be varied in a sextant?
A. By use of the colored shades for this purpose which are fitted between the index and horizon glasses.

Q. How is the master gyro-compass compensated for permanent errors? Suppose the master gyro heading is 278° and it has been definitely established (by azimuth, bearings, etc.,) that the compass has a 2° easterly permanent error, state how you would compensate the master to read true.

A. Heading 278° by master gyro, with 2° E'ly error indicates ship's head is 280° true. Accordingly, the lubber ring is moved 2° to the right to indicate ship's true heading.

Q. How do you determine the accuracy of a ship's barometer, whether mercurial or aneroid?

A. By comparison with a standard instrument, such as one used by U.S. Weather Bureau for such purpose. If a number of readings — not less than three, with a day between each — show a consistent difference from the standard glass, the instrument may be relied upon as accurate.

Q. Why is mercury used in the barometer in preference to other liquids?

A. Chiefly because its high specific gravity requires a column of about 30 inches only and its sensitive fluidity practically remains unchanged through a range of temperature of from — 38°F. to about 600°F.

Q. Make a rough copy of the sketch shown and on it label the following: E-Layer, F-layer, One Hop F, Two Hop F, One Hop E, Two Hop E, and ground wave.

A.

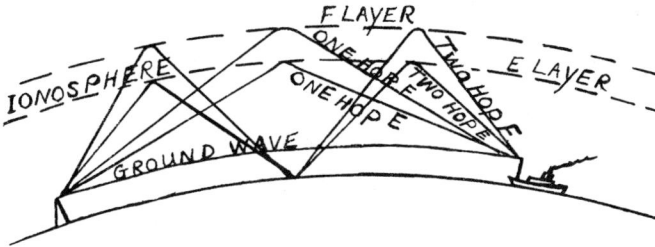

Q. Using the Dutchman's log, determine ship's speed when a floating marker is observed to pass a measured 100 feet of vessel's length in 5 seconds.

A. Ratio of 100 feet to speed S (in knots) times 6076 is equal to that of 5 seconds to number of seconds in 1 hour, or, 100:S × 6076 = 5:3600; wherefore, S = (100 × 3600) ÷ (5 × 6076),
or S = 360,000 ÷ 30,380 = 11.8 knots.

Q. In taking a loran reading: (a) What will be the result of matching a first sky wave with a ground wave, or matching a first sky wave with a second sky wave? (b) What precautions should be taken to insure that the first pulse in a train of pulses is not being over-looked?

A. (a) This will give an erroneous time difference reading. (b) Increase the gain, or power output of the system.

Q. In the loran method of navigation: (a) What is the base line?
(b) What is the base line extension?

A. (a) The line, which is an arc of a great circle, connecting master and slave stations. (b) The base line extended from either master or slave station.

Q. In using a loran chart, the lines on the chart are for ground waves. Where are the corrections to be found when using sky waves?

A. They are found near the intersections of latitude parallels and meridians.

Q. When sky waves are used for computing loran lines of position, are they more accurate close to the station or far away from the station?

A. They are more accurate far away from the station.

Q. What does blinking of a loran signal indicate?

A. It is a warning that master and slave signals are out of synchronization. This lasts usually for a few minutes at most.

Q. How is a chronometer's accuracy checked?

A. By observing whether it maintains a consistent rate. An erratic rate indicates a defective or unreliable instrument.

Q. What is the error of collimation of a sextant?

A. That due to the line of sight through the telescope not being parallel to the plane of the sextant. It gives a greater angle as measured than the true value.

Q. What is a ground wave?

A. The radio wave which travels along the earth's surface.

Q. What is a sky wave?

A. A radio wave which reaches the receiver by way of reflection from the ionosphere.

Q. What is the critical range in loran reception; why is it critical; and what precautions must be taken with regard to the use of signals?

A. The critical range is the distance-limit from the signal transmitters and is, in general, between about 600 to 900 miles by day, and between about 500 and 700 miles by night. It is critical because the ground wave fails at this distance to distinguish itself from a sky wave, or may not appear in the scope at all. In

the critical range use of sky waves only demands considerable
care and skill in their identification and matching.

Q. Explain the construction, principle, and care of the barograph.
A. A barograph essentially is a recording aneroid barometer. From
its partly evacuated chamber the variations in atmospheric pressure are transferred mechanically to a recording chart by a marking pen. The chart, which is laid around a cylinder rotated by
clockwork, thus receives a continuous line to indicate pressure at
any time in its usual record of seven days.
　　With renewal of the recording chart each week the inkwell should
be filled, and the instrument frequently should be checked to insure correct indication of pressure. The barograph should rest
upon a shock-absorbing material, such as sponge rubber.

Q. Upon what 2 natural forces does the directive force of the gyro-
compass depend?
A. Gravitational force and rotation.

Q. State briefly the routine inspection and maintenance care which
should be given the master gyro-compass each month.
A. Inspect general cleanliness and condition of the unit. Clean azimuth motor commutator, collector rings, cosine groove, transmitter. See that all bearings are oiled, including azimuth motor
bearings, transmitter bearings, cosine groove roller, phantom
pots, ballistic link bearing and lower guide bearing. Check level
of oil in rotor bearing reservoirs.

Q. What are the markings of the hand lead line?
A.　2 fathoms from lead, 2 strips leather
　　　3　　"　　　"　　　"　　3　　"　　　"
　　　5　　"　　　"　　　"　　white rag
　　　7　　"　　　"　　　"　　red rag
　　10　　"　　　"　　　"　　piece leather with hole in it
　　13　　"　　　"　　　"　　same as 3 fathoms or a blue rag
　　17　　"　　　"　　　"　　red rag
　　20　　"　　　"　　　"　　cord with two knots in it

Q. What is a hygrometer and what is it used for?
A. An instrument for measuring the moisture in the atmosphere,
or its relative humidity, and thence the dew point.

Q. What is a pitometer log? Describe its principle.
A. A device for measuring a vessel's speed by the dynamic pressure
to which Pitot tube is exposed in passing through the water. The
tube takes the form of a rodmeter which extends about 30 inches
below ship's bottom, and this is surrounded by an outer tube having openings along its sides. By a mechanical arrangement the
difference in static and dynamic pressures is utilized to control
a pump geared to an output of 60 revolutions per minute, which

in turn is transmitted electrically as speed to a master indicator, thence to the several repeaters installed where required.

Q. When a patent log line is hauled in, how do you take the turns out before drying it and stowing it away?
A. Hand in a few fathoms of the line, disconnect it from the register, and pay it overboard from the opposite quarter until rotator is aboard (where log is towed from stern). Then haul in and coil down.

Q. What is a stadimeter?
A. An instrument for determining the distance of an object by measuring the angle subtended by its known height.

Q. What is a hydrometer and what is it used for?
A. An instrument for determining the specific gravity of a liquid.

Q. What is a psychrometer?
A. An instrument consisting of a dry-bulb and a wet-bulb thermometer for determining the relative humidity of the atmosphere, and thence the dew point; a hygrometer.

Q. Where is information concerning loran coverage, charts, and tables available?
A. Tables for plotting Loran position lines are found in the U.S. Navy Hydrographic Office publication H. O. Pub. No. 221. Also, information on such material printed by various agencies is given in H. O. Pub. No. 1-N (Index Catalog of Nautical Charts and Publications).

Q. Which end of a Kelvin sounding tube must be uppermost when taking a sounding?
A. The sealed end.

Q. Describe the glass sounding tube or other depth recording device used with a patent sounding machine, and state how Boyle's Law applies to the principle upon which it operates.
A. The tube is attached to a sinker which is dropped to the sea bottom. Water rises in tube as depth-pressure increases and registers its height either by a discoloration of the tube or by a piston-marker. Since by Boyle's Law "pressure times volume is a constant," if the tube is calibrated to indicate, e. g., 2 inches of imprisoned air at a depth of 50 fathoms, then $2 \times 50 = C = 100$, and at x fathoms the air measurement will be $100 \div x$.

Q. Give a brief description of the principle and operation of the Fathometer.
A. An electrically operated oscillator sends out sounds from ship's bottom of such intensity as will re-echo from the sea floor. The

echo is caught by a sensitive receiver also located on ship's bottom. The difference between times of producing and receiving the sounds then is translated by the indicator into fathoms, usually by a flash of light showing the number on a dial. The installation is put in continuous operation by simply turning a switch.

Q. Explain the use of chemical tubes to record soundings.
A. As in the Kelvin sounding apparatus, the glass tubes are coated on the inside with a salmon-colored chemical (chromate of silver) which, upon entry of sea water in the sounding operation, changes color to the lighter chloride of silver. The height to which water has risen in the tube is thus indicated by the limit of the chemical's change of color.

Q. What effect will an unusually soft bottom have on soundings obtained by Fathometers?
A. Where such bottom covers a harder layer, as of clay or rock, the sound wave may wholly or partly penetrate the soft bottom, with the result that two "bottoms" are indicated. The lesser reading should be accepted as the true sounding.

Q. Explain in detail and in proper order the procedure to be followed in taking soundings with a sounding machine.
A. Have the sounding wire rigged to lead from its proper block or sheave, with sinker and brass container for tube attached (as with Kelvin sounder). Place glass tube in container with open end downwards. Hang sinker free, as over ship's stern or from a sideboom; release brake on machine, and as wire freely runs out, use the feeler to determine sinker's arrival at bottom; apply brake so as to slow up the machine to an easy stop. Then heave in, lift tube from case, keeping open end down. Take sample of bottom from the arming in sinker, if required; read off fathoms on the scale, by measurement of length of unchanged chemical in the tube.

Q. What method is generally employed aboard merchant ships for checking accuracy of a chronometer and determining its rate?
A. By means of radio time signals complete information on which, as used throughout the world, may be found in U. S. Navy Hydrographic Office Publication No. 205, Radio Navigational Aids. Error of a chonometer at a specified date is compared with that observed at a subsequent date, say about 10 days later; then the difference in errors divided by the elapsed time gives the instrument's daily rate.

Q. Why is the morning normally the best time of day for winding timepieces?
A. It is general practice in the Merchant Marine service to wind chronometers at 0800 (8 a.m.). It is held that such duty must first be executed regardless of all other routine, as a safeguard,

not only as beneficial to the instrument itself, but against the responsible officer's attention being occupied at a later hour with unforeseen circumstances, to the probable exclusion of the chronometer.

Q. Where will complete information be found on the times, frequencies of emissions, and characteristics of radio time signals?
A. In the U.S. Navy Hydrographic Office Publication No. 205, Radio Navigational Aids.

Q. On 1 June, a time signal at 1200 GMT shows chronometer "A" 3m-52s fast. On 5 June, a time signal at 1800 GMT shows chronometer "A" 3m-35s fast. An observation is taken on 7 June at 1800 GMT. Assuming a constant chronometer rate, what correction should be applied to chronometer "A"?
A.
Error 3m 52s fast on 1 June at 1200 G. M. T.
Error 3m 35s fast on 5 June at 1800 G. M. T.
          17s loss in 4 days &   6 hours, or 17s loss in 4-1/4 days.
Daily rate = 17 ÷ 4-1/4 = 4 seconds.
From 5 June 1800 to 7 June 1800 = 2 days; 2d x 4s = 8s loss in 2 days

Error 5 June		3m 35s fast
Correction	=	3m 27s fast.

Q. In New York (Zone +5) a time signal was heard, and at 1400 Eastern Standard Time, the chronometer read 18h-35m-38s. What was the chronometer error?
A. Eastern Standard Time 14h 00m 00s

Zone	+	5	
G. M. T.	19	00	00
Chron.	18	35	38
Chron. Error =		24m 22s slow.	

Q. What is the reading of the micrometer sextant illustrated?

A. Sextant reads 41° 30' 20".

18. TIDES AND CURRENTS

Q. Define: (a) Flood tide, (b) Ebb tide. (c) Set of tide. (d) Drift of tide.

A. (a) Periodic vertical rise of sea level at a given place. (b) The periodic fall of sea level at a given place. (c) Direction toward which a tidal current flows. (d) Velocity of a tidal current, usually expressed in nautical miles and tenths per hour.

Q. Where would you find the time of slack water after high or low water in any given port of the United States?

A. In the Tidal Current Tables, issued by the U. S. Coast and Geodetic Survey.

Q. What are subordinate stations, as used in the Tide Tables?

A. Those listed in Table 2 of the Tide Tables, or those for which the predicted times and heights of high and low water are not given for each day, as in the case of the comparatively few reference stations in Table 1. Such tidal information for a subordinate station is found by the application of certain differences to predictions given in Table 1.

Q. What is the purpose of the ratios given in the Tide Tables for computing height of tide and how would you use such ratios?

A. The ratios are given where the constant difference in height would produce unsatisfactory results as applied to the predicted heights at certain reference stations. Height of tide at subordinate station is found by multiplying height at reference station for day in question by the ratio.

Q. Name three planes of references to which soundings and tidal data are referred.

A. Mean low water; mean low water springs; Indian spring low water.

Q. Describe the effect of wind and abnormal barometric conditions on the tides.

A. Onshore winds cause greater heights and offshore winds lesser heights than those predicted for the tides. Local effect, as in a lengthy bay, takes the form of an accelerated flood stream and a weak ebb with onshore and offshore winds, respectively. Abnormally low barometric conditions result in higher tides; high barometric pressure lowers the tide level.

Q. What celestial body is principally responsible for the tides, and what additional celestial body influences the tide?

A. The Moon is principally responsible for, while the Sun has a marked influence on, the tide.

Q. At St. John, New Brunswick, on 7 February, 1959: (a) What is the tabulated time and height of a. m. high water? (b) If the largest scale chart of the locality showed a depth of 10 feet for a given area, what would be the depth at high water at that area?

A. St. John, N. B. , 7 Feb. , 1959: (a) H. W. 1116, or 11. 16 a. m.

$$\begin{array}{ll} \text{Height} & \text{26. 5 feet} \\ \text{Charted depth} & \underline{10. 0} \text{ ''} \\ \text{(b) Depth at H. W.} & \underline{36. 5} \text{ ''} \end{array}$$

Q. At Anchorage, Alaska on 3 May, 1959: (a) What is the tabulated time and height of p. m. low water? (b) If your chart of Anchorage showed a depth of 20 feet for a given area, what would be the depth at low water at this area?

A. Anchorage, Alaska, 3 May, 1959: (a) L. W. 2145, or 9. 45 p. m.

$$\begin{array}{ll} \text{Height} & \text{4. 0 feet} \\ \text{Charted depth} & \underline{20. 0} \text{ ''} \\ \text{(b) Depth at L. W.} & \underline{24. 0} \text{ ''} \end{array}$$

Q. At Deer Island Light, Boston, Mass. Harbor on 28 March 1959: (a) What is the tabulated time and velocity of maximum p. m. ebb current? (b) In what direction does the ebb current flow at this position? (c) What time meridian is used in tabulating the times given for the currents at this port?

A. Deer Island Light, Boston, Mass. , 28 March, 1959: (a) Maximum p. m. ebb current at 1722; velocity 1. 6 knots. (b) 85° true. (c) 75° W.

Q. At San Diego Bay Entrance, California on 13 January, 1959: (a) What is the tabulated time and velocity of maximum a. m. flood current off Ballast Point? (b) In what direction does the flood current flow at this position? (c) What time meridian is used in tabulating ·the times given for the currents at this port?

A. San Diego Bay Entrance, California, 13 January, 1959: (a) Maximum a. m. flood current off Ballast Point at 0845; velocity . 9 knot. (b) 355° true. (c) 120° W.

19. OCEAN WINDS, WEATHER AND CURRENTS

Q. Why is the aneroid barometer preferable for use aboard ship, as compared with the mercurial barometer?

A. Because its readings are not affected by vessel's motion in a seaway, contrary to the case of the mercurial. The latter requires most careful reading in order to arrive at an accurate mean of the mercury column's height which is subject to rapid variations, or "pumping, " due to vessel's pitching or roll.

Q. How is the sea water temperature obtained for a weather observation?

A. Surface temperature being required, a canvas bucket should be used to take the necessary sample, forward of all waste pipes, condenser discharge, etc. Thermometer bulb should be stirred about in the water until the mercury settles at correct reading.

Q. How would you read a thermometer? State the sources of possible error.
A. The eye should be at same height as top of the mercury column, so as to observe its coincidence with the true degree-mark on the scale. Thermometer should be placed in an exposed position, while sheltered from the wind by a louvered cage, as far as practicable from metal bulkheads, in order that a true reading may be obtained.

Q. What does the value 29.75 indicate as the reading of a barometer?
A. That a column of 29.75 inches of mercury in a vacuum is exactly balanced by the pressure of the surrounding atmosphere. This is termed the barometric pressure.

Q. How should a wet and dry bulb hygrometer be placed and what care should be given to this instrument?
A. In a protective cage or cabinet in the open, made to allow free circulation of air around the thermometers. The muslin covering on the "wet-bulb" thermometer should be kept clean and thoroughly moistened at all times; also, the water supply in its cistern should be regularly maintained.

Q. Convert (—) 10° Celsius (Centigrade) into temperature Fahrenheit.
A. F. = 9/5 x C. + 32 = 9/5 x (— 10)+ 32 = —18 + 32 = 14° Fahr.

Q. What is sleet?
A. Frozen raindrops.

Q. Define the term temperature.
A. Temperature is the intensity or degree of heat. It is measured in "degrees" by a thermometer, of which there are several different kinds, that commonly used in America and other English-speaking countries being the Fahrenheit, usually abbreviated F.

Q. On a weather map: (a) An elongated area of high pressure extending from an eminence (or high) is called a .... ?
(b) An elongated area of low pressure extending from a depression (or low) is called a .... ?
A. (a) Wedge. (b) Trough.

Q. What is wave height?
A. Vertical distance from trough to crest of wave.

Q. What wave height should be recorded?

A. The height of wind-driven waves present; or, as given in <u>Bow-ditch</u> (1958), the height corresponding to the force of wind.

Q. How is the visibility determined?
A. By careful estimate by eye, keeping the distance and degree of clearness of the visible horizon in view.

Q. What is a <u>synoptic chart</u>?
A. Also called a weather map; a chart showing the distribution of weather conditions over a region or given area at a certain time.

Q. What is an <u>occluded front</u>?
A. One in which a cold front has overtaken a warm front, which latter is thereby <u>occluded</u> (closed or dispensed with) as the cold air rushes in beneath it.

Q. What is the meaning of the term <u>sky cover</u> and how is the <u>sky cover</u> determined for purposes of weather reports?
A. The percentage of sky surface which is covered by clouds, according to the observer's estimate.

Q. What is meant by the <u>cloud ceiling</u>?
A. The vertical distance between the earth and the base of a cloud that covers more than four tenths of the sky.

Q. How would you determine the <u>cloud ceiling</u>?
A. This usually is done by estimation, having in mind the average heights of the various cloud formations. For low ceilings, however, a reasonably accurate determination may be obtained by means of a "ceiling balloon." The balloon's known rate of ascent times the interval between its release and its disappearance in the clouds gives the required result.

Q. What are the four principal families or types of clouds, and what feature forms the basis of the classification?
A. High, middle, and low clouds; vertical development clouds. The classifying feature is their height above the earth.

Q. Low clouds are defined as those whose mean upper level is 6,500 feet.
   Middle clouds are defined as those whose mean lower level is 6,500 feet and whose mean upper level is 20,000 feet.
   High clouds are defined as those whose mean lower level is 20,000 feet.
   Classify as low, middle, or high the following cloud forms:
   (a) Alto-cumulus. (b) Cirro-stratus. (c) Stratus.
A. (a) Middle. (b) High. (c) Low.

Q. Why are islands or shore lines in the tropics often marked by cumulus type clouds in the daytime, particularly in the afternoon?

A. Because the cumulus is formed by updraft of warm, humid air which occurs over the heated land surface during the day. The volume of rising heated air increases with the hours of sunshine, thus creating maximum cumulus over the land at about 4 p. m.

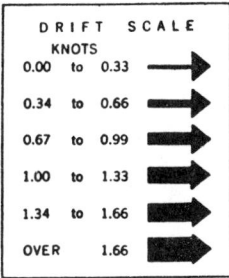

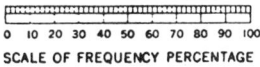

```
DRIFT    SCALE
KNOTS
0.00  to  0.33  ──▶
0.34  to  0.66  ──▶
0.67  to  0.99  ──▶
1.00  to  1.33  ──▶
1.34  to  1.66  ──▶
OVER      1.66  ──▶
```

```
0  10 20 30 40 50 60 70 80 90 100
SCALE OF FREQUENCY PERCENTAGE
```

◀57─◯─▶

Q. Interpret the data provided by the current rose shown from the Atlas of Surface Currents, North Atlantic Ocean. (H. O. Publication 571).

A. Of currents observed, 5% set NE, with average drift .34 to .66 knot; 5% set E, .34 to .66 knot; 9% set SE, less than .33 knot; 5% set S, 1.33 to 1.66 knots; 15% set SW, .34 to .66 knot; 57% set W, .67 to .99 knot; 5% set NW, less than .33 knot. Percentage of observations in which no current was observed, 0.

Q. What is the meaning of the term drift-ice (or pack-ice), used in a wide sense?

A. A large mass of sea ice, consisting of various floes, pressure ridges, and openings here and there, presenting a more or less extensive obstruction to navigation.

Q. Discuss the ice movements in the North Atlantic.

A. Ice of glacier production, or icebergs, which are carried into the North Atlantic shipping lanes latitudes in the vicinity of the Grand Banks, off Newfoundland, by the Labrador Current, have their origin only on the East and West coasts of Greenland, chiefly on the latter. Many bergs from Greenland's East coast find their way with the Greenland Current into Davis Strait, but occasionally are found one to two hundred miles S. E. of Cape Farewell.

Although about 7500 icebergs are formed each year, an average of about 400 only reach Lat. 48°, and of these 35 are carried to Lat. 43° before melting away; but the variation from this average is large. In 1929, bergs numbering 1350 were sighted south of Lat. 48°; 2 only in 1940. This variation, it has been suggested, is due to the degree which the Labrador pack ice obstructs progress of the bergs. A heavy pack forces them well offshore, where warmer water melts them before the shipping lanes are reached; conversely, with lighter pack encountered, the bergs drift closer to shore where colder water prolongs their existence.

Bergs or any type of ice have rarely been sighted South of Lat. 38°, East of Long. 38°, or West of Long. 60°. April, May, and June are the months in which ice may be expected within these limits.

Q. What is fast-ice?

A. Fast ice is the term for the ice foot, or accumulation of ice of varying extent which is fast, or attached, to the shore.

Q. What is the best position for conning a ship in ice?
A. From a position as far above the hull as practicable.

Q. Explain the temperature volume relationship of gases if pressure is held constant. State in words or mathematical notation. (Charles Law).
A. In a gas of constant volume, its pressure increases proportionately with rise in temperature; or, the ratio of pressure to temperature is constant.

Q. How is the correction for an aneroid barometer noted and where should this correction be posted?
A. In the form of an index correction; as $+.05''$ or $-.10''$. It should be posted close to the instrument, preferably on its glass face, as by an adhesive.

Q. How often should the correction for an aneroid be checked?
A. By comparison with a standard barometer, as by such facility provided by the U.S. Weather Bureau, at least every three months.

Q. How is the correction for an aneroid determined?
A. The corrected sea-level reading of the aneroid at a given time is compared with that of the standard instrument, as by telephone. The U.S. Weather Bureau provides such a service at various ports.

Q. What action is taken by the weather bureau when comparison indicates that a barometer is defective?
A. The Bureau will recommend the barometer be replaced by a new or accurate one. If ship is listed as a weather observation vessel, a reliable instrument will be supplied at public expense.

Q. What care must be given an aneroid barometer to assure that it will retain its calibration?
A. It must be mounted permanently, protected from shocks, and in a place free from sudden changes of temperature.

Q. State the precautions necessary to obtain the correct sea level pressure when using an aneroid barometer.
A. The barometer reading must be corrected for height and average temperature between the instrument's location and sea level. On board ship, temperature of the surrounding air is sufficient for this purpose. The total correction is found in Bowditch, Table 11, and is additive.

Q. Describe briefly the relationship between barometric pressures and the corrections that must be applied to altitudes of celestial bodies observed by sextant.

A. When barometric pressure is less than the basic 29.83 inches, or 1010 millibars, correction to altitude is additive; when more than that height, correction is subtractive.

Q. What is vapor pressure?
A. The pressure of a confined saturated vapor; the pressure exerted by a vapor when in contact with the solid or liquid phase of the same substance, under equilibrium conditions, so that neither condensation nor evaporation takes place.

Q. A vessel's true course is 025° and speed 22 knots. The apparent wind direction is from NE. with 16 knots apparent wind velocity. Required: (a) The direction from which the true wind is blowing. (b) The velocity of the true wind.
A. Bowditch, Table 10: Ratio of apparent wind speed to ship's speed = 16 ÷ 22 = .73. Difference between ship's head and wind direction = 20°. Under 20° and abreast of .73 find 141° or relative direction of true wind; and 0.41, or fraction of ship's speed which gives true velocity of wind.
 Therefore (a) Course 25° true + 141° = 166° true, S by E 1/4 E; and (b) Velocity of true wind = 22 × .41 = 9.02, or 9 knots.

Q. To what wind force on the Beaufort Scale do the following conditions correspond?
 WIND SPEED........17 to 21 knots.
 SEA CONDITIONS. ... Moderate waves, taking a more pronounced long form; many white foam crests; there may be some spray.
A. Force 5 on Beaufort scale.

Q. What is a cyclone?
A. An approximately circular portion of the atmosphere, having a center of relatively low barometric pressure around which its winds blow in a counterclockwise direction in the northern hemisphere and in a clockwise direction in the southern hemisphere.

Q. Distinguish between a tropical cyclone and an extra-tropical cyclone.
A. The tropical cyclone differs from the extratropical cyclone in that it usually is of lesser extent but of greater violence in wind velocity. The tropical cyclone originates within the tropics; the extratropical in temperate latitudes.

Q. Describe squall lines and the conditions associated with them.
A. These are the lines along which brief showers and strong shifting winds occur ahead of cold fronts. The squall line may precede a cold front by as many as 200 miles and may be accompanied with much lightning.

Q. How can the barometer show the approach of a cyclone in the tropics?

A. With the accompanying long ominous swell, although weather may be fine and clear, the barometer shows an uneasy "pumping" up and down through a few hundredths of an inch, while averaging normal height or a little higher. About the time cirrus clouds appear, barometer begins a steady fall, its normal daily cycle disappears, and, as bad weather signs with increasing wind and frequency of squalls continue, after a fall of about .20 inch, a cyclone's approach is thus indicated. Thus the barometer, always combined with weather and sea indications, shows the approach of the storm center.

Q. At what latitude (North or South) does a tropical cyclone normally recurve?
A. At about Latitude 30°.

Q. When do tropical cyclones usually move at the slowest speed?
A. In low latitudes shortly after their initial development and also during their period of recurving poleward and eastward.

Q. State two reasons why tropical cyclones are divided into semi-circles, one considered dangerous and the other considered navigable.
A. 1. So that the vessel's position relative to both the cyclone's path and its center may be determined. 2. So that such information will provide the basis for maneuvering ship to avoid, or increase distance from, the storm center.

Q. What is the effect of current upon the waves caused by a storm?
A. A following current increases the length of waves and decreases their height. A current opposing the wind has the opposite effect, and, if strong enough, will cause dangerous breaking waves.

Q. What provides the energy for atmospheric disturbances along frontal zones?
A. Sharp barometric gradients and temperature differences in adjacent air masses.

Q. In winter you are steering W in the North Atlantic; wind SSE, force 7, increasing with rain and general appearance of bad weather prevailing; barometer falling; sea increasing. What change in conditions would you normally expect during next 24 hours?
A. Increase of wind to perhaps force 9, then during lightning in NW quarter, would drop and shift to NW in a heavy squall or squalls with rain or sleet. Then barometer would rise and clear weather again prevail.

Q. What name is applied to tropical cyclones in: (a) The North Atlantic. (b) The western North Pacific. (c) The Philippines. (d) Western Australia.
A. (a) Hurricane. (b) Typhoon. (c) Baguio. (d) Willy-willy.

Q. What causes the fog frequently associated with the frontal areas

between two air masses? Why are night conditions more conducive
to such fogs than day conditions?
A. It is caused by the vapor-producing contact of cold and warm air
masses. During the night additional surface cooling takes place
with corresponding increase of condensing effect in the warm mass
and consequent tendency to produce heavier low-lying fog.

Q. Is fog more common and dangerous along cold fronts or warm
fronts? Why?
A. Along warm fronts. Due to the warm moisture-laden air so often
passing over the cooler sea-surface, as, e.g., fog conditions on
the Newfoundland Banks from this cause.

Q. When water vapor condenses in a storm area and is precipitated
in the form of rain, snow, etc., what is the effect upon the temperature of the air?
A. The temperature is lowered.

Q. Which is lighter: (a) dry air; (b) moisture laden air?
A. (b) Moisture-laden air.

Q. What are isallobars? What is their value in constructing weather
maps and forecasting?
A. They are lines of equal change of barometric pressure in a cyclone, much the same as isobars which are lines of equal pressure itself.
    They are valuable for determining the direction of travel of the
cyclone and for estimating its rate of travel.

Q. In what direction do warm fronts usually move and what is their
average speed of movement?
A. Warm fronts tend to travel in the direction of the general circulation, which in temperate latitudes is usally in an E'ly and
slightly poleward direction. Their speed averages 500 miles per
day in summer; 700 miles in winter.

Q. In the Southern Hemisphere, in which semicircle of a tropical
cyclone would a vessel be if the wind shifted counterclockwise,
while she was hove to?
A. In the dangerous semicircle.

Q. In the Northern Hemisphere, how should a steam vessel maneuver in the dangerous semicircle of a tropical cyclone?
A. Bring the wind 4 points on starboard bow and make as much
way as possible; if obliged to heave to, do so with head to sea.

Q. Hove to in the Southern Hemisphere under tropical cyclone conditions with the barometer falling and the wind shifting clockwise,
what is the vessel's probable position relative to the center of the
storm, and what action should be taken if possible to avoid the

center of the storm?

A. Vessel is in the navigable semicircle. Bring the wind on port quarter and hold course indicated. If obliged to lie to, do so stern to sea. If under sail, heave to on starboard tack.

Q. Describe the use of a storm card or diagram of wind direction in maneuvering in a tropical cyclone area.

A. The storm card is a graphic representation of a cyclone in the hemisphere given. By means of the card, a given wind direction will indicate the bearing of the storm center, while a given shift of wind gives the vessel's position with relation to the storm's path or line of progression. This information is required in order to maneuver ship to advantage with the view of avoiding the storm's center.

Q. What weather conditions may result from the movement of a cold air mass over a warmer sea surface?

A. Low-lying fog or mist, density of which depends upon the degree of temperature difference between sea and air, and also the force of wind. In extreme cases, as in very cold air and light wind, a frost smoke or dense surface fog results, but with increase of wind will develop into wisps of vapor with improved visibility. In general, fog resulting from the conditions in question is thin and tenuous.

Q. If the smoke from the funnel does not rise, but lies horizontally, what atmospheric conditions are indicated?

A. High humidity or rainy conditions.

Q. What is the Bermuda high?

A. A subtropical area of comparatively high and constant barometric pressure, centered generally in the latitude of, but considerably farther eastward than, Bermuda. It is around this area, called the horse latitudes, that the general wind circulation of the North Atlantic revolves in a clockwise direction.

Q. What causes the fog frequently encountered off the grand banks of Newfoundland?

A. The warm moisture-laden southerly winds which blow over the cold waters of that region are the source of its notoriously prevalent fogs, especially during the summer months.

Q. How can a ridge of high mountains give rise to a depression?

A. During the warm season in light winds, when the land is heated on both sides of such ridge and the air rises as a heated nearly stationary mass of lowering pressure.

Q. What is a central area of high pressure called and in what direction do winds circulate around it in both the Northern and Southern Hemispheres?

A. A <u>high.</u> In the Northern Hemisphere circulation takes place about it in a clockwise direction; in the Southern Hemisphere, in an anticlockwise direction.

Q. What is a line called which connects all points on a weather chart that have the same reading of the barometer?
A. An isobar.

Q. What is the relation between wind direction and the direction of the isobars on a weather chart?
A. Wind direction takes up a direction roughly parallel with the isobars, or clockwise around the center of high barometric pressure and anticlockwise around the center of low pressure in the Northern Hemisphere; and anticlockwise around a high, clockwise around a low, in the Southern Hemisphere. Since the flow of air tends to run from a high to a low pressure area, wind direction departs from that of the isobar to a degree which increases with the distance of the latter from the center of pressure, appearing to flow somewhat spirally outward from a high, and inward toward a low, center of barometric pressure.

Q. Draw a sketch of the earth showing the location of high and low pressure belts and the general wind systems.
A.

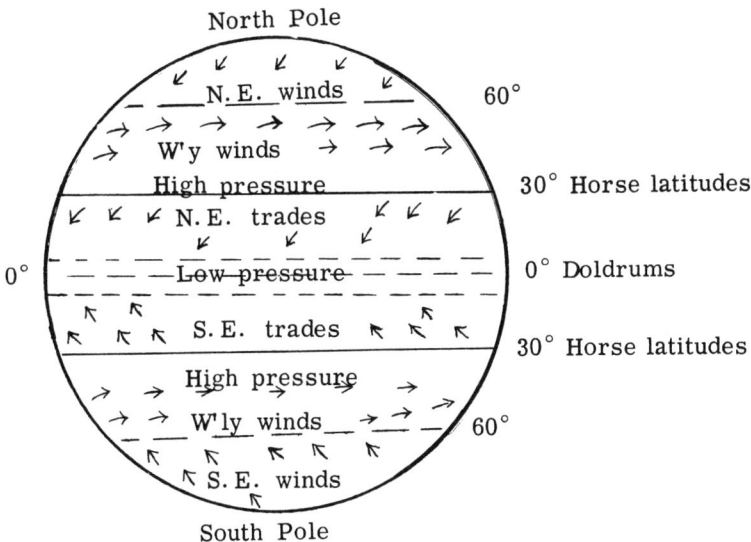

Q. What is the normal barometric pressure at sea level?
A. Normal barometric pressure is usually synonymous with standard atmospheric pressure at sea level, with a temperature of 59°F, or a barometer height of 29.921 inches.

Q. Where can detailed information about ocean winds and currents be obtained?
A. From the monthly <u>Pilot Charts</u> issued by the U.S. Navy Hydrographic Office.

Q. How do you determine the reliability of the ship's barometer, whether mercurial or aneroid?
A. According to whether its readings maintain a reasonable consistency, when repeatedly compared with a standard instrument. A varying error indicated in successive comparisons shows barometer's unreliability.

Q. State how Buys-Ballot's Law is used at sea in order to determine the approximate bearing of a storm center.
A. Facing the wind, storm center lies 8 to 12 points on observer's right hand in the Northern Hemisphere, or on his left hand in the Southern Hemisphere. At beginning of storm, allow 10 points in the leading half of storm to 12 in its rear; 8 points when storm has reached whole gale force.

Q. What is the dew point of the atmosphere and how it is determined?
A. Dew point is that temperature of the atmosphere at which its water content condenses. It may be determined from Tables 16 and 17 of <u>Bowditch</u>, given the difference between the dry and the wet bulb readings of a psychrometer.

Q. What is the distinction between tide and current?
A. Tide is periodic rise and fall of a body of water, while current is the horizontal movement, especially of the surface water, of such body.

Q. Hove to in advance of a tropical cyclonic storm, in what position would a vessel be with respect to the track followed by the storm center if: (a) The wind veered; (b) The wind backed; (c) The wind remained steady in direction and increased in force?
A. (a) Vessel is to right of storm track, or in the dangerous semicircle, if in the Northern Hemisphere; if in the Southern Hemisphere, in the navigable semicircle. (b) She is to left of storm track, or in the navigable semicircle, if in Northern Hemisphere; in the dangerous semicircle, if in Southern Hemisphere. (c) Vessel is in the path of storm.

Q. What are the dangerous and navigable semicircles of a tropical revolving storm in the Northern Hemisphere?
A. The dangerous semicircle is that half of the storm to the right of its track, assuming the observer to be looking in the direction of storm's advance. The navigable semicircle is that half to the left of storm's path. The first is called <u>dangerous</u> because its winds are stronger and tend to drive vessel into the storm's path;

the other is <u>navigable</u> because its winds are less violent and tend to blow vessel away from the storm.

Q. What are the indications of the approach of revolving storms?
A. Long swell from the storm's direction; barometer unsteady and starting to fall after being somewhat above normal; mares' tails or cirrus clouds increasing and appearing to converge in storm's direction, or that point of ominous heavy cloudbank on the horizon; barometer's rate of fall now increasing; cirrus gives way to cirro-stratus formation, followed by the heavier formations alto-stratus and strato-cumulus; frequent squalls begin accompanied by in-creasing rain and wind; barometer continuing to fall; sky becomes completely overcast and rain-squalls more frequent and violent.

Q. What is a warm front?
A. The leading edge of a mass of advancing warm air which is re-placing colder air.

Q. What does the size of waves depend upon?
A. Upon the volocity and duration of the wind raising them, and also upon its <u>fetch</u>, or straight distance it has traveled toward the area in question.

Q. What are the two reliable signs of field ice?
A. 1. <u>Ice blink,</u> or the white to yellowish glare appearing in the horizon and sky immediately above it. 2. An abrupt smoothing of the sea in a breeze and gradual lessening of swell, indicating ship is to leeward of ice field.

Q. Sketched here are vertical cross sections through two types of frontal systems. (a) What are fronts called when the warm air is aloft? (b) What type of such a front is <u>A</u> and what type is <u>B</u>?

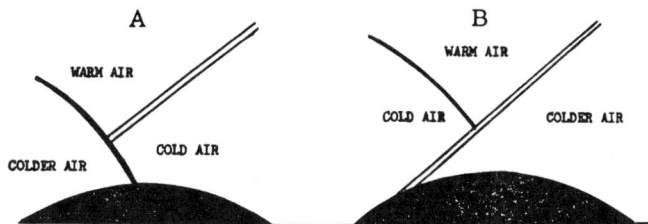

A. (a) Occluded fronts. (b) <u>A</u> is a cold occluded front; <u>B</u> is a warm occluded front.

20. NAUTICAL ASTRONOMY AND NAVIGATION DEFINITIONS

Q. What is:
Vernal equinox?
A. The point in the ecliptic through which the Sun passes in changing from South to North declination on or about March 21, or the instant of this occurrence.

Q. Conversion angle?
A. The angle between the rhumb line and the initial great circle course or bearing from one point to another.

Q. Hour circle?
A. A great circle of the celestial sphere passing through the poles.

Q. Logarithm?
A. The power to which a fixed number called the base must be raised in order to equal a given number. Thus, with 4 as the base, the logarithm of 64 is 3, since $4^3 = 64$.

Q. Nautical twilight?
A. Period of fading daylight between the sinking of the Sun below the visible horizon and his depression to not more than 12° below the celestial horizon.

Q. Time signal?
A. A signal marking a specified time, such as that given out by radio from an observatory for the purpose of providing an accurate check on ships' chronometers.

Q. Occultation?
A. Extinction of the light of a heavenly body by the intervention of another heavenly body; as, an occultation of Mars by the Moon.

Q. Solstice?
A. One of the two points of the ecliptic farthest from the celestial equator, or the instant the Sun reaches one of these points, thus attaining maximum declination.

Q. Meridional parts?
A. The length, in units of 1' of longitude at the equator, of an arc of a meridian between the equator and a given parallel of latitude on a Mercator chart.

Q. Prime meridian?
A. The meridian of 0° 0' 0", used as the origin for measurement of longitude; also called the Greenwich meridian, from the observatory through which it passes.

Q. Greenwich apparent time?

A. Greenwich hour angle of the true sun's center, expressed in time plus 12 hours, rejecting 24 hours if necessary; local apparent time at the Greenwich meridian.

Q. Greenwich mean time?
A. Greenwich hour angle of the mean sun, expressed in time units plus 12 hours, rejecting 24 hours if necessary; local mean time at the Greenwich meridian.

Q. Sidereal hour angle?
A. Angular distance of a point in the heavens, measured westward on the celestial equator, from the vernal equinox to the hour circle passing through such point.

Q. Apparent time?
A. Hour angle of the true sun's center, expressed in time units plus 12 hours, rejecting 24 hours if necessary; time based upon rotation of the earth relative to the apparent (true) sun.

Q. Polar distance?
A. Angular distance of a point in the heavens from either celestial pole.

Q. Amplitude?
A. Angular distance or arc of the horizon north or south of the true east or west point; as, W. 15° N., or E. 7° S.

Q. Diurnal circle?
A. The apparent daily path of a heavenly body.

Q. Sidereal day?
A. Duration of one rotation of the earth with reference to a star; or, elapsed time between two successive meridian passages of the vernal equinox. It is about 3m. 56s. shorter than a solar day.

Q. Circle of equal altitude?
A. A circle on the earth's surface passing through all points at which a heavenly body's altitude is identical at a given instant.

Q. Parallel of altitude?
A. A small circle of the celestial sphere parallel to the horizon, all points on which have the same altitude at a given instant.

Q. Most probable position?
A. Position of a vessel judged to be the correct one, when the exact position is not known.

Q. Greenwich sidereal time?
A. Westerly hour angle of the vernal equinox, as measured on the celestial equator, from the meridian of Greenwich. It is expressed in time units up to 24 hours.

Q. Define the term <u>magnitude</u> as it is employed in nautical astron-
omy.
A. Relative brightness of a celestial body. Stars up to magnitude
1.50 are called <u>first magnitude stars</u>; those from 1.50 to 2.50
are <u>second magnitude stars</u>; those between 2.50 and 3.50, <u>third
magnitude stars</u>; and so on to the sixth magnitude.

Q. What is meant when two celestial bodies are said to be in:
(a) Conjunction; (b) Opposition?
A. (a) Two celestial bodies are said to be in <u>conjunction</u> when having the same sidereal hour angle; especially said of planets.
(b) Two celestial bodies are in <u>opposition</u> when their sideral hour
angles differ by 180°; especially said of planets.

22. SIGNALLING BY INTERNATIONAL CODE FLAGS, FLASHING LIGHT AND SEMAPHORE; LIFESAVING, STORM AND SPECIAL SIGNALS

Q. What would be indicated by a black or green signal seen floating
in the air from a parachute about 300 feet above the water?
A. That a torpedo has been fired. Used to simulate a torpedo attack in special naval exercises, such as that of protecting a convoy.

Q. State the meaning of the following hoist in International Code
Flag Signalling:

(a)	(b)	(c)
Answering pennant	X	T
E	2	1
	1st	1st
	repeater	repeater
	0	0
		3rd
		repeater

A. (a) "Going to spell," or, "Letters which follow spell a word."
(b) "Bearing 220° true." (c) "Time 1100."

Q. When signalling by International Code Flags and using the code
flags or answering pennants to indicate a decimal point, is the
code flag included in determining which repeater or substitute is
to be used?
A. No. The answering pennant when used as a decimal point is to
be disregarded in determining which repeater to use.

Q. Describe how the International Code flags are used to signal
the position of the ship expressed in terms of latitude and longitude.
A. Each of the two groups indicating degrees and minutes of latitude
and longitude are signalled by 4 numerals preceded by and joined
with the letter P. Where it is desired to designate the latitude as
North or South, or the longitude as East or West, the appropriate

letter should be added after either group. (Thus, Lat. 46° 15';
Long. 58° 30'; is signalled: P4615   P5830; and where the designa-
ting letter is required, as in Lat. 00°15'; Long. 00° 10': P0015N
P0010W.)

Q. In sending a message to a vessel by Morse Code using flashing
light, how would you indicate that the message would be coded
from the International Code of Signals?
A. By the group indicator <u>PRB</u>.

Q. Name the component parts of a Morse Code message.
A. Call; identity; break sign; text; ending.

Q. Show exactly how you would signal the following times, using the
International Code flags: (a) Five minutes past midnight. (b) Six-
forty-five p. m. (c) Ten o'clock a. m. (d) Ten o'clock p. m.

A. (a) T	(b) T	(c) T	(d) T
0	1	1	2
1st. Rp.	8	0	1st. Rp.
2nd. Rp.	4	2nd. Rp.	0
5	5	3rd. Rp.	3rd. Rp.

Q. What signal, that may be transmitted by flashing light, is provided by the International Rules of the Road to indicate that a
vessel is in distress and requires assistance from other vessels
or from the shore?
A. <u>S O S</u>.

Q. When a vessel in distress in International Waters requires assis-
tance from the shore, what signals are provided by the Interna-
tional Rules of the Road for her to use?
A. A gun or other explosive signal fired at intervals of about a
minute.
  A continuous sounding with any fog-signal apparatus.
  Rockets or shells throwing red stars fired one at a time at
short intervals.
  The signals <u>S O S</u> made by radiotelegraphy or by any other sig-
nalling method using the Morse Code.
  The radiotelephony signal consisting of the spoken word, "Mayday."
  The International Code signal of distress, "N C."
  A square flag having above it or below it a ball or anything re-
sembling a ball.
  Flames on the vessel, as from a burning tar barrel, or oil
barrel, etc.

Q. What is indicated by an aircraft circling a vessel at least once,
then crossing the bow close at a low altitude, opening and closing
the throttle or changing the pitch of the propellers, and then flying away on a particular bearing?
A. The vessel is advised thereby of the need for her assistance.

She should alter course to steer in the direction in which the plane flew away.

Q. Describe the procedure for calling another vessel, or vessels, using the International Code flags.

A. If no signal letters are hoisted superior to the signal, it will be understood as being addressed to all ships within signalling distance; in all other cases, signal letters of ship or ships addressed are to be hoisted superior to the signal.

If it is not possible to determine signal letters of ship to which it is desired to signal, V H for "You should hoist your signal letters" should be hoisted first; at the same time ship will hoist her own signal letters. If this fails, then N M J must be hoisted for "I wish to signal to vessel or vessels (number indicated if necessary) on bearing indicated from me."

Q. Describe the procedure for answering flag signals.

A. Vessel addressed shall hoist the answering pennant at the "dip" upon seeing each hoist; then "close up" immediately signal is understood. The pennant is lowered to the dip as soon as the hoist is hauled down on the transmitting ship; hoisted close up again as next hoist is understood; and so on, until signal is completed.

Q. Describe the correct use of the erase sign and show how the erase sign is made in signalling by flashing light.

A. The erase sign, EEEEEEE, etc., indicates that the last word or group was signalled incorrectly. It is to be answered with the same sign. The transmitting ship will repeat the last word or group which was correctly signalled, and proceed with remainder of the message.

If the whole message is to be canceled, the erase sign must be made, followed by the ending sign, thus, EEEEEE   AR.

Q. For what purpose is the model verb "to glean" printed in all of its forms in the text of the International Code of Signals?

A. In order to circumvent an erroneous interpretation of a signal due to differences in the verb forms in different languages. By including in the signal the applicable affirmative, negative, or interrogative form of the model verb "to glean," no doubt should then exist as to the signal's intended meaning.

Q. What is the lifesaving signal indicating, "landing here highly dangerous"?

A. By day: Horizontal motion of a white flag, or arms extended horizontally. By night: Horizontal motion of a white light or flare.

Q. If you sighted several red parachute flares, no aircraft or surface vessels in the vicinity, what would be indicated and what should be your action?

A. The presence of a lifeboat or lifeboats whose occupants require immediate assistance. I would advise the master at once.

Q. How would you transmit the following procedure signals and signs in signalling by blinker light: (a) Space sign; (b) "Everything which follows in this message is to be repeated back word by word, as soon as received;" (c) Ending sign; (d) From; (e) "You are correct"?

A. (a) <u>II</u>, or space sign, is used to separate the signs <u>AA</u>, <u>AB</u>, <u>WA</u>, <u>WB</u>, from the identifying words or groups which follow them. It is also used to separate whole numbers from fractions. (b) The repeat sign <u>UD</u>. (c) <u>AR</u>. (d) <u>De</u>. (e) <u>C</u>.

Q. How do you complete a signal using flags?

A. Transmitting ship hoists the answering pennant singly, after the last hoist of the signal, to indicate message is completed. The receiving ship answers this in same manner as all other hoists.

Q. What are the meanings of the flag letters, <u>D</u>, <u>E</u>, <u>F</u>, <u>G</u>, when flown as single letter signals?

A. <u>D</u> = "Keep clear of me—I am maneuvering with difficulty." <u>E</u> = "I am directing my course to starboard." <u>F</u> = "I am disabled. Communicate with me." <u>G</u> = "I require a pilot."

Q. How would you signal the following message by International Code Flags?
    "Bearing 45 miles 90° true from Diamond Head, Hawaii." (The hoist for Diamond Head AEWN.)

A. 1st. Hoist: X   2nd. Hoist: 4   3rd. Hoist A
             0   5   E
             9   W
          1st. Rep.   N

Q. In signalling by blinker light, what is the sign for end of message and how is it answered?

A. <u>AR</u>, answered by <u>R</u>.

Q. How many flags are in an International Code Flag hoist used between a vessel towing and the vessel she is towing? How are towing signals made at night?

A. One flag. By flashing light.

Q. What is the meaning of the letter <u>W</u> when sent by the receiving ship during a communication by blinker light?

A. "I am unable to read your message owing to light being not properly trained or burning badly."

Q. In signalling by International Code Flags, what is the significance of signals consisting of: (a) Single-letter signals; (b) Two-letter signals; (c) Three-letter signals; (d) Four-letter signals?

A. (a) Messages of very urgent or very common use. (b) Urgent or important signals, mostly of distress and maneuvering, with a few general signals of common use. (c) General vocabulary. (d) Those commencing with <u>A</u> are geographical signals, or signify names of places; other 4-letter signals are those of ships, signal stations, etc.

Q. Four-letter signals beginning with the letter <u>A</u> are used for what type signals?
A. Geographical signals, or those indicating names of places.

Q. How are the code flags used to signal the chronometer time?
A. Vessel A hoists <u>D F J</u> for "I wish to get a rate for my chronometer. Will you give me a comparison?" Vessel B acknowledges with the answering pennant; then hoists <u>O Y Z</u> for "Greenwich Mean Time." Vessel A acknowledges with answering pennant. Vessel B, upon deciding the exact minute of G. M. T. to signal, hoists (for example) <u>T 1 5 3 0</u> for "15 hours 30 minutes"; and at exactly that instant sharply hauls down the signal. Vessel A acknowledges with answering pennant hoisted close up.

Q. Explain the use of amplifying phrases in International Code Signalling.
A. By the use of those phrases, in many instances the sense of a message will be clearer to the party addressed, and scope of the Code will be increased accordingly. Thus, the hoist <u>A G U</u>, denoting "The following is advice or a suggestion," followed by <u>G I E</u> for "I am flooding hold to extinguish fire," should be decoded "Suggest flooding hold to extinguish fire."

Q. How would you acknowledge the receipt of a code group in a coded message sent you by blinker light?
A. By repeating back such code group.

Q. If at sea you sighted an international orange buoy about three feet in diameter, what action should you take?
A. I would immediately inform nearest naval authority of its position. It indicates a submarine in distress on the bottom.

Q. What is the space sign used in signalling by Morse Code and for what purposes is it used?
A. <u>II</u> (.. ..), the space sign, is used to separate the signs <u>AA</u>, <u>AB</u>, <u>WA</u>, and <u>WB</u> from the identifying words or groups which follow them. It is also used to separate whole numbers from fractions.

Q. What is the meaning of the answering pennant over <u>G</u> in International Code Flag Signalling?
A. Code flag over <u>G</u> indicates the spelling of words is completed, and that signals which follow are to be looked up in the Code in the usual manner.

Q. What is the break sign in blinker signalling?
A. BT (— ... —).

Q. How are numbers sent when signalling by semaphore?
A. They are to be spelled out in words.

Q. How would you call a pilot by blinker light at night?
A. Send the call sign, AA AA AA, etc., to the pilot vessel or station. Upon receiving answer, TTTTT, etc., send "I require a pilot", or the code signal, P T.

Q. In sending a message by flashing light, how would you request the receiving ship to repeat back, word for word, the message?
A. By inserting letter G, signalled separately, at beginning of message.

Q. What distress signals would be appropriate for use in international waters during foggy weather?
A. A gun or other explosive signal fired at intervals of about a minute.
A continuous sounding with any fog-signal apparatus.
The signal S O S made by radiotelegraphy.
The radiotelephony signal consisting of the spoken word MAYDAY.

24. SEAMANSHIP

Q. Make a rough sketch of the standing lug lifeboat sail, as shown; name the edges, and corners, and describe briefly its construction.

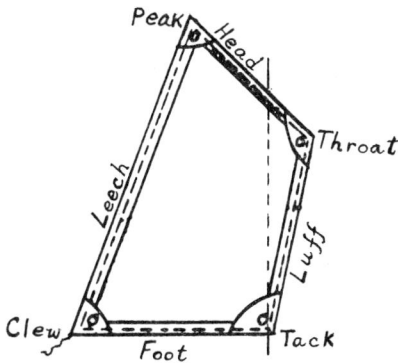

A. The sail is made of light canvas, usually with cloths parallel to the leech. It is strenghtened along its entire edge by the boltrope to which the canvas is strongly sewn, after being doubled back a few inches to form the tabling. Head of sail is secured to the yard, a cringle in its peak and another at the throat being provided to take the turns of the peak lashing (or head earing) and throat lashing, respectively.

This sail, the standing lug, is secured to its mast at the tack, or lower forward corner, by the tack lashing, and its sheet is secured to the clew cringle for this purpose at the after lower corner. A row of reef points usually is fitted parallel with the sail's foot, so that about one-third the hoist may be taken in, or reefed, during strong winds. It is hoisted by the halyard, which runs on a sheave set fore-and aft in the mast, the yard being secured close to the mast, at about one-third the yard's length from the throat, by means of a ring or traveler.

Q. In anchoring a vessel in fog, how might you determine the vessel's way through the water in order to have the vessel dead in the water or with minimum way on her when the anchor is dropped
A. Throw overboard a wad of paper, piece of wood, or other light object (a life buoy with a line would do) and observe vessel's way relative to such stationary object. If darkness prevents this, when vessel is dead in the water will be indicated by the wash of the backing propeller reaching about amidships.

Q. What precaution, with respect to way of the vessel, is necessary in anchoring in a strong current or tidal stream?
A. That vessel shall not be moving over the ground at more than a reasonable velocity, considering the probable danger to ground tackle if anchoring with too much way in that respect.

Q. In picking up the anchor, what information must the mate on the foc'sle head relay to the bridge in order that the engines may be used to minimize the stress on the windlass and chain?
A. He must indicate the lead of the cable, i.e., the direction in which the chain stretches out, or, as with a slack hawse, whether it lies up and down.

Q. What is the purpose of the stream and kedge anchors, that are carried by seagoing vessels?
A. Stream anchor is used where an anchor must be laid out, as from the stern, or for a breast, in congested waters. The kedge is used for moving ship as required when main engines are not available, or for setting out with a line attached for the purpose of hauling off a heavy anchor for extra security or for refloating the vessel.

Q. Describe in detail how merchant ships prevent water from entering the chain locker.
A. Oakum, old rope yarns, rags, etc., are stuffed tightly around the chain cable in the spurling pipes (or chain pipes leading into the locker) and then covered with a mixture of sand and cement. Older practice is to unshackle cable from anchors, drop it into the locker, plug and cover pipes with canvas.

Q. In addition to flooding the chain locker, what damage may be caused a vessel by taking water through the chain pipes?
A. Overflow may cause damage to ship's stores in forepeak, injure electric wiring, or, if locker is on after side of collision bulkhead, may flood bilges, damage hold ceiling and cargo in the forward hold.

Q. You are standing by the anchor windlass on the foc'sle head of a vessel proceeding in a channel. You receive an order to drop the anchor because the vessel has taken a sudden sheer toward another vessel or the shore. Describe how you would handle the anchor.

A. Let go by quickly releasing brake; then, as cable begins leading aft, easily apply brake so that paying out of cable is under control. Hold cable as required by orders from bridge.

Q. How would you embark passengers into a lifeboat when abandoning a vessel in rough weather?

A. Lower boat to embarkation deck; secure her against fore-and-aft motion by the painter and a sternfast, and against swinging against ship's side by frapping lines around the falls. See that all persons have put on their life belts. Members of the steward's department will assist in the orderly placing of passengers in boat. Then prepare to lower boat to water in accordance with the master's orders.

Q. What test is required by the Regulations each year where practicable in order to test the strength and efficiency of lifeboats and the gear for lowering them?

A. Each lifeboat shall be lowered to near the water and then be loaded with its allowed capacity, evenly distributed throughout the boat's length; then lowered into the water until afloat and released from the falls. In making the test, persons or deadweight may be used, total weight being at least equal to the allowed capacity of lifeboat, considering persons to weigh 165 pounds each.

Q. Where a lifeboat may be damaged in lowering by projecting obstructions or contact with the hull due to list, what provisions must be made to facilitate launching if the boat is 15 feet or more above the water when the vessel is light?

A. They shall be fitted with skates or other suitable means to facilitate launching against an adverse list of up to 15 degrees.

Q. Name the anchors carried by a seagoing vessel.

A. 2 Bowers, 1 spare Bower, 1 Stream, 1 Kedge. Vessels (powered) under 380 equipment tonnage require no spare Bower; those above 1070, no Kedge. Sailing vessels of any tonnage, all five.

Q. How is the required number and weight of anchors for a vessel determined?

A. According to the classification society's nominal value assigned each vessel, called her equipment tonnage, which closely approximates the vessel's gross tonnage.

Q. Illustrated is a sketch of a brake band assembly and compressor for a typical windlass. (a) Describe the care and inspection you would make in seeing that this equipment is in good condition for

its service. (b) The steel bar B, angled up into the central groove
of the wildcat, has what function?

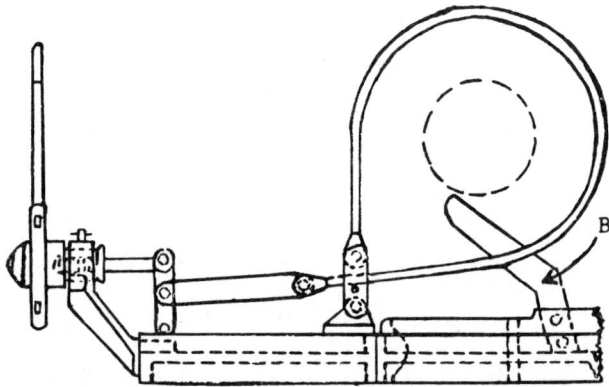

A. (a) Working parts should be kept lubricated, especially bearings
and screw threads of the brake wheel. Inspection should particularly include that for wear and tear or corrosion of connecting
bolts and the brake band. (b) B, sometimes called a stripper, prevents chain cable, as it is hove in, from jamming in the wildcat
and thus from heaping up beneath the latter, instead of falling
clear into the chain-locker pipe.

Q. Name the parts indicated on the anchor sketched.

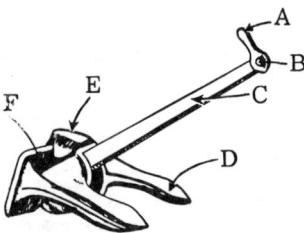

A. A. Ring. B. Ring-pin. C. Shank.
D. Fluke. E. Crown. F. Palm.

Q. Describe the methods that may be employed to move an anchored vessel to
avoid striking, or being struck by, other
vessels while swinging in a tide or wind
shift.

A. 1. By heaving in cable, as when ship
apparently will not clear another astern.
2. By slacking away cable, as when one anchored vessel swings
toward, or falls down on, the fore part of another. 3. By heaving
short at slack water, so as to reduce to a minimum the radius
through which ship will swing to the new tide. 4. By use of the
helm, as in a tideway, to sheer vessel as required. 5. By use of
both helm and engines to sheer vessel, come astern, or leave
anchorage berth altogether to avoid damage. 6. By a mooring line
from inshore quarter, as in a narrow waterway.

Q. With the wind and tide in opposite directions, what factors will
determine the manner in which a vessel will ride to her anchor?
A. Force of wind; velocity of current; magnitude of opposition to
wind force by ship's above-water structure; draft of vessel.

Q. Describe briefly how a sailing vessel is able to sail in the direction from which the wind is blowing.
A. By alternate tacks, or by sailing close-hauled, i. e. , as close to the wind direction as possible while keeping sails full, tacking, or turning into the wind, to sail on the other tack as necessary. Depending upon rig and underbody lines, a vessel will sail 4 to 6 points off the wind on each tack. She is on the port tack when sailing with wind before the port beam; on the starboard tack with wind before the starboard beam.

Q. What equipment for sewing canvas is required in a lifeboat?
A. A sailmaker's palm, needles, sail twine, marline, and a marlinespike, all contained in a ditty bag made of canvas.

Q. What is the purpose of canvas covers on lifeboat winches?
A. To protect them from the weather, from water during hosing down the deck, and from flying spray—chiefly against corrosion.

Q. What color is required for lifeboat sails?
A. Indian orange.

Q. What care should be given canvas aboard ships?
A. It should always be dry before stowing away, and should be stowed in a dry place, away from oils or grease of any kind.

Q. How many tarpaulins are required for hatches of a merchant vessel in ocean service?
A. Three.

Q. What is the minimum grade of material required for tarpaulins?
A. No. 4 waterproofed canvas.

Q. Where the shell of a lifeboat is liable to damage, wear, or corrosion from contact with chocks, how is the boat fitted to keep the possibility of such damage to a minimum?
A. In way of the chocks, filling pieces are fitted on the planking of a clinker-built boat, to provide a smooth and even surface against the chocks. In the case of carvel-built or metal boats, chocks usually are faced with heavy canvas.

Q. Where the shell of a lifeboat is liable to damage, wear, or corrosion from contact with chocks, what maintenance care should be taken by the officers and crew of the vessel?
A. The bearing surfaces should be kept clean or clear of accumulation of paint and, especially in the case of metal boats, should be kept free of corrosion, boats being lifted clear of chocks for proper drying of paint on both chock and bearing surface on boat.

Q. What protection is afforded aboard ships against flooding of compartments by water backing through scuppers, tank overflows, sanitary discharges, etc., below the freeboard deck?

A. By fitting to advantage a <u>clapper</u>, <u>non-return</u>, or <u>sea</u> valve, which allows a one-way flow only in such arrangements.

Q. What are the dangers that may be created by vent or sounding lines from a tank being damaged below the deck of a vessel in cargo holds or other spaces?

A. Cargo might be damaged by oil or water, as from a tank under pressure. An accumulation of gas of a harmful sort might arise through a damaged sounding pipe of a D. B. tank containing oil. A false sounding might be taken, as failing to discover rise of water in a well or hold compartment, with consequent damage to cargo or fittings, or serious adverse effect on ship's stability.

Q. What precautions must be taken to avoid harbor pollution when taking fuel oil or petroleum cargoes?

A. Ballast discharge valves should be tightly closed, and lashed if necessary. Mooring lines should be carefully tended and hose must be of proper length to allow for any motion of vessel. Scuppers should be plugged to stop any spill from going overboard. Hose should be in good condition and properly suspended. Drip pans under hose connections, vent pipes, etc. Sawdust, rags, and nonsparking tools available in case of spillage. Topping off tanks should proceed at a reduced rate, with care to prevent a spill. Hoses should be carefully drained before being disconnected.

Q. Where vessels are fitted with cowl type ventilators, what means must be provided for closing them in the event of storm or fire?

A. In the case of larger cowl ventilators, a shutter, or closing arrangement, is provided in the shaft; smaller cowls are removed and their shafts closed by fitted plugs with canvas covers over all.

Q. What is the importance of freeing ports on a vessel with solid bulwarks operating in a heavy sea?

A. So that heavy water may quickly run off the deck and thus reduce risk of damage to hatches, etc., or adversely affect vessel's stability status.

Q. What speed must a fully loaded motor lifeboat be capable of attaining?

A. A speed of at least 6 knots in smooth water.

Q. What quantity of fuel is required to be carried in a motor lifeboat?

A. Such quantity as is required for 24 hours continuous operation.

Q. In shifting a vessel forward on a pier as illustrated, would offshore headline <u>A</u>, inshore headline <u>B</u>, or inshore headline <u>C</u> provide the greatest pulling effect? Why?

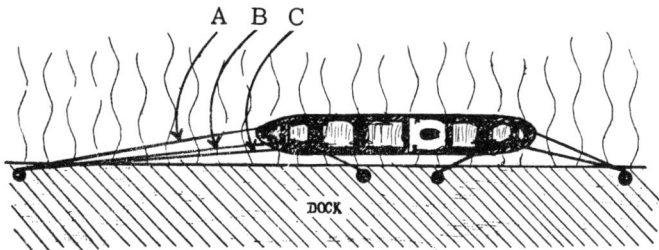

A. Inshore headline C, because its pull is nearer the fore-and-aft line than the others, and consequently will be least binding, or holding vessel against dock.

Q. Referring to the sketch: (a) What is the name and purpose of the figure illustrated? (b) Explain the meaning of the various lines and letters. (c) How is the marking placed on vessels?

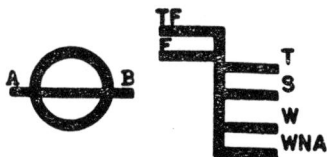

A. (a) Load lines or Freeboard marks. They mark the limit to which a vessel may be immersed by her load at the current season, or in the seasonal zone through which she must pass en voyage. (b) All lines are 1 inch in width and the upper edge of each is the true mark. The disc marks the vessel's mid-length between perpendiculars. Upper edge of line A B, the Summer load line or Freeboard mark in sea water, passes through the disc's center. A B names the Load Line assigning authority, American Bureau of Shipping.

T F = Tropical fresh, or limit of immersion in fresh water in a tropical zone. F = Fresh, or limit in fresh water when load limit is the Summer line. T = Tropical zone limit in sea water. S = Summer line, same as that through center of disc. W = Winter season limit in sea water. W N A = Winter North Atlantic, which is 2 inches below the Winter mark on powered vessels navi-gating in North Atlantic latitudes.

(c) On steel vessels they are cut in or center-punched on the plating; on wood vessels, cut into planking at least one-eighth inch. They are painted white or yellow on a dark ground, or black on a white ground.

Q. What is the required length of lifeboat falls?
A. They shall be of sufficient length to lower the boat to the light load line with vessel heeled 15 degrees toward the off side.

Q. If for any reason the boat falls were too short to enable a life-boat to be lowered into the water, what might be done?
A. If possible, give vessel the required heel; otherwise, rack off all parts of falls above lower blocks; unreeve hauling ends from upper blocks; bend on spare rope to falls; take the weight; cut away rackings; and lower away from any convenient bollard, bitts,

etc. If practicable, reduce weight carried in boat as required.

Q. Are provision and special equipment lockers of a lifeboat required to be watertight?

A. The Regulations require that "the locker shall be suitable for
the storage of the small items of equipment." The condensed milk
and hard bread are packaged in hermetically sealed cans, "in
compartments providing suitable protection." Also, the drinking-
water containers "shall be stowed in drinking-water tanks, lockers,
or other compartments providing suitable protection."

Q. What color should running light screens be painted?

A. Black.

Q. Describe the use of tricing lines on lifeboats suspended from
gravity davits when the boat is swung into the embarkation deck
for passengers to get into it. State why the frapping lines should
be passed before releasing the tricing line pelican hooks.

A. Tricing lines are used to haul in and secure boat close to ship's
side at the embarkation deck against rolling motion of the vessel.
When ready to lower away, frapping lines should be set up in
place, so that boat will remain thus steadied upon letting go the
tricing lines.

Q. When the vessel is moored to two anchors, does she require the
same amount of cable on each of the two anchors as when lying
at one anchor?

A. Ordinarily, yes. However, in shallow water where tidal conditions make it inadvisable that vessel should lie over her lee anchor, as during a low stage of tide, length of cable should exceed
vessel's length by at least 5 fathoms.

Q. How are lifeboats required to be numbered and marked?

A. They shall be numbered from forward aft, with odd numbers on
the starboard side. The numbers shall be plainly marked or painted in figures not less than 3 inches high, on each bow.

Q. What is the purpose of the footings in a lifeboat?

A. Also called foot waling, they serve as a floor and to protect the
boat's planking from injury.

Q. Describe briefly the operation of an electro-hydraulic steering
apparatus and the type of hand-operated emergency steering gear
that may be provided with it.

A. This steering apparatus operates by direct action of either of
twin hydraulic rams on the stout tiller at the rudder-stock head.
A special oil is used in the cylinders and the pumping unit, consisting of an electric motor operating a variable-stroke pump at
constant speed, is fitted with a pressure regulator to prevent over-
loading or stalling of the motor.

The emergency gear consists of a hand-operated pump which works on the same principle as the regular gear, but having a separate pair of hydraulic rams act upon the rudderhead arm, or tiller, on the after side of the rudderhead. The steering wheel is attached to and activates the pump as required by the helmsman.

Q. If you were in charge of a lifeboat: (a) How would you prevent it from swinging as the vessel rolled when the boat is at the embarkation deck? (b) How would you prevent it from swaying if the ship is pitching?
A. (a) Either by frapping lines around the falls, or by tricing lines, or both, to hold boat steady and close to ship.
(b) By boat's painter and a sternfast, both steadied taut and leading well forward and aft, respectively.

Q. Describe how a lifeboat should approach a wrecked vessel in rough weather to save passengers and crew and then return to her own vessel.
A. After leaving the rescuing ship, which would lie to windward of wreck as close as practicable to provide a lee, boat should bear away to approach wreck as close as possible on the lee side. The rescuing ship will proceed to leeward of wreck and boat will bear away with her load to make the lee side of her vessel.
During the rescue operation, a judicious use of oil will do much toward keeping down the sea.

Q. When moored to two anchors, how is a foul hawse prevented?
A. By maneuvering with helm or engines, or both, or kedging, so that vessel will swing with each turn of tide through the same semicircle.

Q. What scope of chain is used under normal conditions in anchoring?
A. Five times the depth of water.

Q. What anchor is normally used in anchoring?
A. The port bower anchor.

Q. What precautions to avoid pollution of coastal waters should be taken by a vessel pumping bilges, ballast, or oil overboard at sea?
A. Pumping should be confined, if possible, to such time as vessel is farthest from the coast. Where it is necessary to pump bilges or ballast containing oil, and the oil may pollute coastal waters, the discharge should be kept under constant observation. If discharge shows oil, the bilge or ballast water should be pumped into one of the vessel's tanks and disposed of in port as slops; or, such pumpings may be carried by the ship and discharged at sea when far enough from shore to cause no pollution to coastal waters.
In all cases, consideration must be given to currents which may

carry pumpings into coastal waters, even though vessel discharges the slops at an apparently safe distance from shore.

Q. What precaution must be observed when taking on water ballast to avoid danger of oil pollution, cargo damage, and structural damage to the vessel?

A. In a tanker, overflowing a tank should be avoided, as overflow would cause any oil floating on the incoming water to pollute the waters in the area. Where cargo is stowed adjacent to tanks being filled, as in dry cargo ships, bilges should be sounded frequently to check for any leakage into cargo space; also, tanks being filled should be checked to avoid putting unnecessary water pressure on the tank top.

Q. In the sketch shown: (a) What is the tension on a topping lift when the height of the kingpost above the boom gooseneck is 40 feet, the length of the topping lift span is 40 feet, and the boom forms an angle of 45° with the kingpost? (b) What is the thrust on the boom in the sketch when the weight of 1 ton is being lifted? Consider loss of efficiency due to friction as 10 percent at each block.

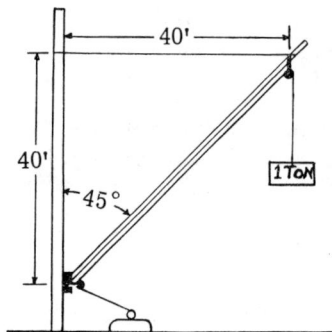

A. (a) Tension on span bears same ratio to the weight as length of span to height of kingpost; or, 40:40 = 1:1. Therefore, tension on the topping-lift span is 1 ton. (b) Thrust on boom bears same relation to the suspended weight as does the boom's length to height of the kingpost. (Length of boom = 40 sec 45° = 40 x 1.414 = 56.56 feet.) Thus, Thrust: 1 = 56.6:40, or Thrust = 56.6 ÷ 40 = 1.415 tons, to which must be added the tension on fall, which, as lifting 1 ton and overcoming friction of 10% in the head block, becomes 1 + .1, or 1.1 tons.
Therefore, Thrust on boom = 1.4 + 1.1 = 2.5 tons.

Q. A beam weighing one ton is to be lifted by a bridle sling, each leg of which forms an angle with the beam of 30° as shown in the sketch. What is the stress on each leg of the sling, when the weight of the beam is suspended from the sling?

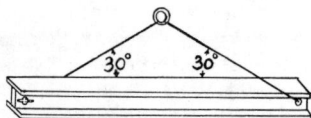

A. Each leg's vertical component of stress being half the beam's weight, or .5 ton, tension on leg is equal to .5 cosec 30°, or .5 x 2.0 = 1 ton.

Q. What is the minimum number of tucks in an acceptable thimble or eye splice in wire rope for use on cargo gear?

A. Three tucks and a halved tuck.

Q. What precaution must be taken in splicing nylon or other plastic type rope with a slippery surface and high elasticity?
A. Short and long splices must be stretched and tightly seized around the tucked strands' ends; eye splices stretched and served over entire splice.

Q. A weight of 3 tons must be lifted using one-half inch diameter wire rope with a breaking strength of 9.4 tons. A factor of safety of 5 is required. (a) Will doubling up the gear, that is, using a single sheave moving block, provide the necessary factor of safety, considering friction loss as 10 percent per sheave for each of two sheaves? (b) What strength must the shackle for the upper block have, using a safety factor of 5?
A. (a) B. S. of wire 9.4 tons ÷ Safety Factor 5 = 1.88 tons S. W. L. Weight 3 tons. Total friction to overcome by 2 sheaves = 3 × .20 = .6 ton. Total weight 3 + .6 = 3.6 tons. Stress on fall = 3.6 ÷ 2 = 1.8 tons. Therefore, the necessary Safety Factor is provided.

(b) Stress on hauling part of fall = 1.8 tons
Weight = 3.0 "
Stress on upper block shackle = 4.8 "
Safety Factor ×5
Strength of upper shackle =24.0 tons

Q. A vessel is loading cargo in a forward hold when it is noticed that the pipe running along the bilge to the forepeak is leaking water badly. The forepeak tank is full of water. What would you do to prevent damage to the cargo?
A. Close the valve at the collision bulkhead. (This valve is required installation and can be operated from the deck.)

Q. What care should be given mooring lines when ice and snow conditions are encountered?
A. Keep them well protected from the elements, as by covering them with canvas, in as dry a location as possible.

Q. What caution should be observed when navigating a power-driven vessel in shallow water?
A. She should proceed at reduced speed in shallow water, especially if deeply laden, because good steering will be difficult, slip of propeller greatly increased, and excessive squat may cause the after body to contact the bottom. Also, the suction effect must be guarded against when passing close to other vessels, and if in narrow waters, the displacement wave may incur damage to boats and other craft moored along shore. Both anchors should be ready at all times for letting go, in the event of vessel taking a sheer, as in a shallow channel, due to inequalities in depths of water.

Q. What are the two functions which paint used on a vessel's bottom must perform; i.e., what are the two types of paint used on a ship's bottom, and what is the purpose of each type?

A. The under coat or coats are for preservation of the metal, and so called anticorrosive paint. The outer coat, or antifouling paint, is for protection of ship's underbody plating against accumulation of marine growth (acorn and goose barnacles, slime, etc.)

Q. What precautions should be borne in mind by ship officers when maneuvering vessels powered with geared turbine drive?

A. It must be borne in mind that, since the backing power of geared turbines is rarely more than half their ahead power, the vessel's headway must be kept within correspondingly narrower limits than would be the case with reciprocating engines.

Q. In a limited space, why is it easier to turn a single right-handed screw ship to starboard than it is to port?

A. Because with engines going astern vessel's head swings to starboard (or throws stern to port). While going ahead with left rudder will more quickly cant ship to port, this advantage is more than offset by the starboard cant resulting from the necessary reversal of engines. Hence, starting vessel's turn with engines ahead and full starboard rudder (right rudder), then reversing engines with helm amidships, enhances her swing to starboard.

Q. Would you measure wire rope as A or B in the sketch?

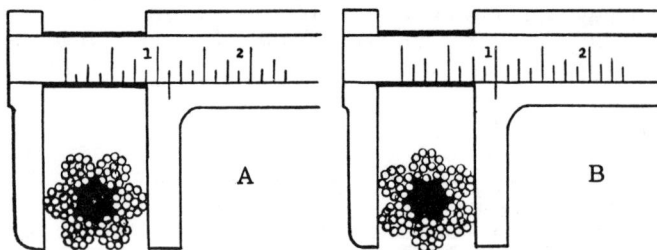

A. I would measure the rope as in A.

Q. What minimum factor of safety should be used with wire rope?

A. Where wire rope is subjected to jerks or sudden changes of stress, as in hoisting and lowering use, a minimum safety factor of 5 is considered proper. In the case of wire rope commonly worked at a nearly constant stress, a factor of 4 is sufficient. New wire is considered in both cases.

Q. Is the steering effect of a right-handed propeller greater going ahead or astern? Why?

A. When going astern. When vessel is moving ahead, much of the sidewise thrust of the screw is reduced by the wake current which

tends to increase pressure on the upper blades; while when moving astern, there is no wake current to lessen sidewise thrust,
the screw always turning in the mass of undisturbed water.

Q. Describe the instructions required to be posted in the steering
engine room.
A. These shall be posted in at least 1/2-inch letters and figures,
instructions relating in order the steps to be taken in changing to
emergency steering. Each clutch, gear, wheel, lever, valve, or
switch which is used in changing over shall be numbered or lettered on a metal plate or painted, so that the markings can be recognized at a reasonable distance. Instructions shall indicate each
clutch or pin to be in or out and each valve or switch to be opened or closed in shifting to any means of steering for which the
vessel is equipped. Instructions shall be included to line up all
steering wheels with rudder amidship before changing gears.

Q. Describe briefly the purpose of a main steam condenser, and
the consideration that a deck officer may be obliged to give it.
A. The condenser's purpose is to reconvert exhaust steam from the
main engine into water, while also increasing the engine's efficiency through the exhaust steam's back pressure being greatly
reduced upon entering the vacuum created by conversion of steam
to condensate, as in reciprocating and turbine engines. Since sea
water is circulated through the scores of small-diameter tubes in
reducing the surrounding steam to condensate, it is important to
prevent sand or mud, such as might be stirred up in shallow
depths, from entering the condenser. It is the duty of the officer
in charge of the deck to notify the engine room of such condition
of the water.

Q. Why do ships yaw badly in a following sea?
A. Each following sea has a prolonged impact upon vessel's after
end. Any irregularity in the wave's mass or its advance gives an
element of sidewise thrust which, multiplied by the distance from
amidships, results in a great slewing moment and a yaw is thus
produced.

Q. What methods are available to reduce yawing?
A. Altering course to bring sea a point or two on either quarter
has been found effective in moderate-sized ships; but more so by
an alert experienced helmsman who will anticipate the yaw with a
generous amount of counteracting rudder as vessel's stern lifts
to each oncoming sea.

Q. Describe the effect of wind on the steering and heading of a
vessel underway.
A. With wind nearly ahead or nearly astern, there is no effect on
steering from this cause. Depending upon the above-water structural area the vessel presents to the breeze, wind pressure having

a lateral component tends to steady the steering in that a lesser amount of helm is required. Where there is a preponderance of exposed surface at ship's after end, she will tend to steer into a side wind, but this effect might be offset by a markedly lesser draft forward. Conversely, a greater exposed area forward of amidships will cause vessel to fall off the wind; more so if draft forward is a few feet less than her after draft.

Q. What is the most likely damage that may occur to an ordinary merchant vessel when operating in floe-ice, or in areas where large logs or floating objects of like nature may be encountered?
A. Damage to the propeller.

Q. In the sketch the seamen are testing a rope to assure its safe working load. Each seaman exerts a force of 100 pounds. Is the stress on the line greater in case A or case B? Explain your answer, stating the total stress on the line in each case.

A   B

A. Stress is greater in case B. In A, two men are withstanding the pull of the other two; in B, the post is withstanding the pull of three men. Accordingly, stress on line in A is 200 pounds; on B, 300 pounds.

Q. What is the purpose of load lines on vessels?
A. In the interests of safety both of vessel and persons aboard, it is the limiting draft to which a vessel may be immersed, in order that her freeboard in the load condition will have reached the assigned minimum for a vessel of her class and construction navigating in a given seasonal zone on the high seas.

Q. How do you measure freeboard?
A. Freeboard is the distance measured vertically downward, at the side of the vessel amidships, from the upper edge of the deck line to the upper edge of the load line to which vessel is immersed, floating upright.

Q. When must the steering gear be tested by a licensed officer?
A. Not more than 12 hours prior to vessel's departure, on vessels making a voyage of more than 48 hours' duration; and at least once every week on all other vessels.

Q. Describe the devices used for the measuring of ullages.
A. A graduated vertical rod of wood or metal permanently fitted in

the hatchway. As used by hand, a graduated rod of light wood or metal having a floating disk at its lower end; or, a plumb bob and measuring tape.

Q. How should guys be positioned for maximum efficiency in securing a boom?
A. As far away from the boom, and as nearly opposed to the direction of stress exerted on the boom by the cargo fall, as is possible.

Q. How often must motors in motor-propelled lifeboats be operated?
A. For at least 5 minutes at every Fire and Boat Drill, which must be held at least once in every week.

Q. What equipment must be provided on gasoline-powered lifeboat motors to prevent fire caused by carburetor backfire, or danger because of gasoline dripping into the bilge?
A. Backfire flame arrester on carburetor; drip collector under carburetor; 2 hand fire extinguishers.

Q. How are motor-lifeboat gasoline tanks vented, i.e., what means are provided to prevent the gasoline becoming "airbound" in the tanks and not flowing to the fuel lines?
A. A vent pipe at highest point of tank, as installed under conditions of normal trim, to terminate in a "U-bend" as high above weather deck as practicable, and discharge end to be fitted with removable flame screens or flame arresters.

Q. Describe briefly the use of steam turbines as main propulsion units and the methods of connecting the engine to the shaft.
A. In the steam turbine, potential energy of steam is converted to kinetic energy by expansion in a nozzle or suitable passage from which the steam emerges at high velocity. This kinetic energy is, in turn, converted to mechanical energy for turning the propeller shafting by directing the steam jet against blades mounted on a rotor, which is enclosed in a casing containing the nozzles or stationary blades through which the steam is expanded or directed. The turbine is necessarily a high-speed unit, and its use in ship propulsion today is practically limited to the "geared turbine," in which the engine shaft engages the propeller shaft by a system of gears.
   Most merchant vessels' turbines operate at from 3000 to 6000 r.p.m. and are connected to propellers turning from 80 to 100 r.p.m. As it is therefore impracticable to make such a large reduction by using only one small gear to one large one, a double reduction is made, i.e., the driving gear drives an intermediate gear which, in turn, drives the last or propeller-shaft gear. The intermediate gear turns at about 700 to 1000 r.p.m. Most of these gears are of the spur or helical type, of which there are many modifications.

Q. What precautions should be taken in order to prevent kinking when using manila mooring lines on a windlass gypsyhead or a capstan?
A. The turns should alternately be taken in opposite ways at each heaving, i.e., right-handed, switching to left-handed, or vice versa, with each successive use on the capstan or gypsyhead.

Q. What is the purpose of the brake fitted on the steering gear of some vessels?
A. For the purpose of securing the quadrant, in the event of steering gear being disabled, until repairs or adjustments have been made.

Q. In what length of time should the steering engine be capable of putting the rudder hard over from one side to hard over to the other side?
A. In 30 seconds.

Q. Describe the factors affecting the steering effect of a right-handed screw propeller, when going ahead.
A. Assuming there is no side breeze, from a dead stop engines being started slow ahead, vessel's stern will swing to starboard (bow to port) with rudder amidships, and this effect will diminish as the way is increased. With increased engine speed the same tendency to cant to port continues to diminish, and at full speed usually disappears altogether. Reasons for this are: 1. While gathering way, the side thrust of the lower blades predominates over that of the upper blades, due to the surface broken water, thus swinging stern to starboard. 2. As vessel's way increases, the wake current tends to equalize the pressure on all propeller blades, and thus drive vessel straight ahead.

Q. What measures could you take to prevent a vessel pounding heavily in a head sea?
A. If it were impracticable to increase water-ballast weight and proceed on same course at reduced speed, I would bring the sea 3 or 4 points on either bow as the first leg of a series of tacks, using my judgment as to appropriate engine speed.

Q. Approaching a dock starboard side to, in a right-hand single screw steamer with moderate headway, what precautions should be taken, before backing, in order to prevent the bow from swinging in toward the dock when the engine is reversed?
A. Put rudder aport to give ship a small cant off from dock, in order to allow for a swing to starboard upon engine being reversed. (However, most vessels may be steered straight and brought to a stop without canting by putting rudder hard right as engines are started full astern.)

Q. Can the guys of a boom be so positioned that they need not be

slacked off or hove in when raising or lowering the boom?
A. Yes; provided that their lower ends are secured at same height
as the boom's heel, and in the same athwartship line.

Q. Describe the method of rigging booms where two topping lifts
are employed to eliminate guys.
A. Where the necessary span between topping-lift blocks at the
masthead is available, as in the distance between two Samson
posts, the two lifts are spread so as to form a bridle and so
eliminate necessity for guys.

Q. What is the proper method of placing cable clamps on wire rope?
Would you place the nuts used to fasten the "U" bolts all on the
same part of the rope, or would you stagger the clamps alternately?
A. All the nuts should be placed on the same side, i.e., on the
"live" or standing end of the wire.

Q. How would you turn the stern quickly to port in a twin-screw
vessel with sternway and both engines going full astern?
A. Go full ahead on the port engine.

Q. In making a hydro report on the sighting of a derelict, what
information would you endeavor to include?
A. Position in latitude and longitude; description, including rig,
approximate height above water, length, if awash, etc.; if any
wreckage or cargo seen floating in vicinity. Also weather conditions and approximate set and drift of current.

Q. If a guy is rigged as shown in the sketch, what is the effect?

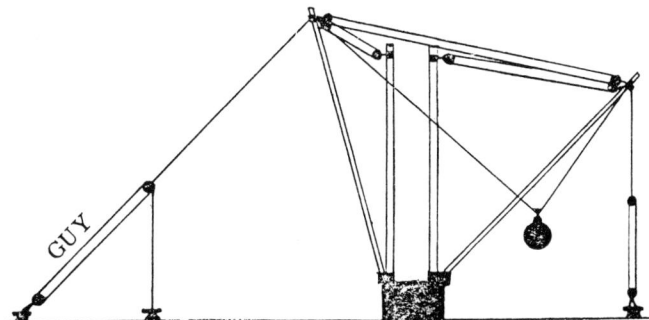

A. Strength of the guy tackle is lessened by approximately 1/2
strength of the hauling part, or the guy is reduced to about 5 6
of its strength.

Q. A 3-inch line has a breaking stress of 9000 pounds. Using a
safety factor of 5, what weight would you pick up with a threefold

tackle, considering loss of efficiency due to friction as 10 percent at each sheave?

A. With 6 parts at moving block, efficiency of tackle = 1.00 — .60 = .40%. Then (9000 x 6 x .40) ÷ 5 = 21,600 ÷ 5 = 4320 lbs.

Q. With a right-handed single screw backing, why is the stern forced to port?

A. Because of the side thrust by the lower blades in their travel from port to starboard, which greatly exceeds the opposing thrust of the upper blades, due to the broken surface water.

Q. How should hatch beam or pontoon slings be fitted for safety of personnel handling them?

A. Beam slings should be the two-legged bridle type, having sufficient length and properly sized hooks that they may be hooked on without a man climbing out on the beam to do so. Pontoon slings should have 4 legs and meet same requirements as beam slings. Hand lines should be attached to each leg of bridle slings, for use in preventing the pontoons, hatch beams, and strongbacks from swinging during removal.

Q. If a hook be straightened out, is it safe to bend it back and then return it to use?

A. No; the hook should be reforged to restore its probable loss of strength.

Q. What is the deck line on ocean and coastwise vessels?
   Note: This question refers to the load-line markings of a vessel.

A. The white line on a dark ground, or black line on a light ground, 12 inches long by 1 inch wide, whose upper edge marks the upper surface of the <u>freeboard deck</u>, or its continuance, at vessel's side, at mid-length between perpendiculars. The upper edge of this line is the datum mark from which the vessel's freeboard is measured.

Q. What is the maximum weight per draft permitted when loading explosives in accordance with the regulations?

A. 2400 pounds.

Q. Does a knot in a manila line increase or reduce the breaking strength of the line?

A. It decreases the strength of a rope by as much as 30%, depending upon the type of knot.

Q. Using the rule of thumb B $= \dfrac{C^2}{2.5}$, where $\underline{B}$ is the breaking stress in tons and $\underline{C}$ is the circumference, determine the breaking stress of a 3-inch manila line.

A. B = (3 x 3) ÷ 2.5 = 9 ÷ 2.5 = 3.6 tons.

Q. Using the rule of thumb formula B $= \dfrac{C^2}{2.5}$, where $\underline{B}$ is the breaking stress in tons and C is the circumference, find the size of manila rope to use to lift a 1-ton weight, when a factor of safety of 7 is required.

A. $\dfrac{B}{7} = 1 = \dfrac{C^2}{2.5 \times 7};$ $C^2 = 2.5 \times 7 = 17.5$; $C = \sqrt{17.5} = 4.18$, or size of rope required is 4-inch circumference.

Q. What is the required factor of safety for lifeboat falls?
A. A safety factor of 6, based on the maximum working load.

Q. If a force of 50 pounds is applied at point F of the luff tackle shown: (a) What is the weight that may be lifted at W allowing 10 percent friction loss at each sheave?   (b) If W is lifted one foot, how far must the line at F be pulled? (c) What stress is put on the padeye at point C when lifting W?

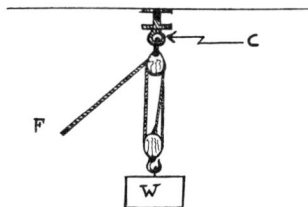

A. (a) Tackle lifts $(50 \times 3) - .30$ W lbs.
W $+ .30$W $= 150$, or 1.3W $= 150$ lbs.
W lifted $= 150 \div 1.3 = 115.4$ lbs.
(b) $1 \times 3 = 3$ feet.
(c) Approximately $50 + 115.4 = 165.4$ lbs.

Q. A manufacturer states that the breaking strength of his 3-inch circumference manila rope is 9,000 pounds. If you use this rope as a single whip cargo fall, what is the safe working load, using a factor of safety of 7?
A. B = 9,000 lbs.; S. W. L. = 9,000 ÷ 7 = 1286 lbs.

Q. On merchant vessels when using booms to handle heavy weights or delicate objects, how do you reduce dynamic stresses; that is, stresses due to change of velocity of the load, such as taking up fast on a load at rest, increasing speed of hoisting, or suddenly stopping?
A. In hoisting, by gently or handsomely accelerating the hoisting speed, and again easing the power as the load reaches maximum height; and in lowering, by braking or regulating the power to an easy stop.
    Experienced winchmen "get the feel" of a load and, as is required of them, avoid sudden jerks or stresses on the gear.

Q. Why is the hauling part of a heavy lift purchase usually led to the mast rather than directly to the winch?
A. Because with such lead both thrust on the boom and load on the topping lift are lessened by a considerable portion of the stress on the hauling part of the purchase.

Q. When is the tension of a topping lift at a maximum; i. e., at what angles with the mast is the heaviest stress put on the topping lift due to the weight of the boom and any weight being lifted?

A. The topping lift attains maximum tension when it makes the smallest angle with the mast.

25. CARGO STOWAGE AND HANDLING

Q. In discharging cargo into a lighter as shown, with only a small amount of drift on the boom, what care is necessary?

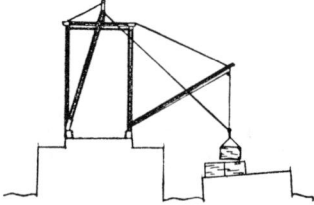

A. That the inboard fall is slacked away sufficiently to allow drafts to be landed as far inboard on the lighter as possible; also, that the lighter not be given a list by too much weight loaded on one side, so risking loss of cargo overboard.

Q. If 2,000 tons of iron ore with a stowage factor of 15 is stowed in a cargo hold of rectangular shape whose bottom is 50 feet long and 45 feet wide, what is the height of the center of gravity of the ore above the bottom of the hold?

A. $\dfrac{2000 \times 15}{50 \times 45} = \dfrac{30000}{2250} = 13.33$ feet = height of surface of ore, which, divided by 2 = 6.67 feet, or height of C.G. of ore.

Q. What type of tools should be used for opening and closing oil tank hatch covers?

A. Non-sparking tools.

Q. At what pressure should the oil discharge piping of tank vessels be tested?

A. 100 pounds per square inch.

Q. You are required to load wet logs in No. 4 lower hold and cases of canned goods in No. 4 'tween decks. What precaution would you exercise to avoid sweat damage to the canned goods?

A. The 'tween deck hatch should be secured against flow of moist air from the lower hold, and ventilation of 'tween decks and lower hold should be independent of each other.

Q. Describe the stowage of cement and the precautions necessary for protection of other cargo in the same hold with cement.

A. Cement in bags is given compact stowage, bags fore-and-aft; if in barrels, stow on end not more than 9 high. Requires good thickness of dunnage; must be kept dry. For protection against absorption of wet from moist cargo, if present, cement should be securely covered with tarpaulins. Other cargo in same hold also should be covered prior to loading the cement to protect it from dust damage. Cement must be handled carefully to avoid raising too much dust.

Q. Define: (a) Explosive range; (b) Fire point; (c) Flash point.
A. (a) Explosive limits of a mixture of a flammable gas with air; thus the mixture is an explosive one when, as with gasoline in air, its vapor is between 1% and 6% of the mass, or the "explosive range" of gasoline is 1 to 6%.
  (b) Temperature to which a flammable liquid must be raised so that its surface layers will take fire.
  (c) Temperature to which a flammable liquid must be raised to give off a flammable gas.

Q. Describe briefly how the amount of water below the oil in an oil tank may be determined.
A. In light oils or gasoline, if the brass sounding rod is carefully chalked before lowering into the tank, chalk will disappear upon contact with water, and depth of the latter is thus indicated.
  In any oil, a strip of litmus paper attached to the rod will show the water sounding by discoloration of the paper; or the litmus itself, if rubbed on the rod beforehand, will give same result.

Q. Define: (a) Inflammable liquid; (b) Combustible liquid.
A. (a) A liquid which gives off inflammable vapors when its temperature is 80° F. or below.
  (b) A liquid which gives off inflammable vapors only when its temperature is above 80° F.

Q. What precautions must be observed in the choice of wood for use as dunnage?
A. Care must be taken, as in the stowage of bagged flour, sugar, coffee, or rice, hides, marble, and certain other commodities, that dry clean spruce, pine, or fir is preferred to such woods as oak, mahogany, or redwood, since the latter are apt to leave damaging stains on the goods. Generally, it is good practice in carrying general merchandise, to use none other than the clean woods above noted.

Q. Describe the methods employed in the shipment of wet hides and the precautions necessary for good cargo turnout.
A. Wet hides, salted or pickled, are shipped in casks, bales, bundles, or loose, and in every case must be treated as wet and odorous cargo. They should be stowed apart, well away from goods that are liable to injury by moisture or tainting. Hides in bales, bundles, or loose must be kept from contact with vessel's metal parts. No dunnage wood of oak must be used. Loose wet hides are salted down in a lower hold or a deep tank, are laid on a dunnage-covered floor perfectly flat with hair side up, each layer being covered with salt and afterwards soused with strong pickle. Ample ventilation is required to throw off the strong odor and moisture, and to prevent deterioration of hides, and hatches should be removed as often as conditions permit to effect this most necessary precaution.

Q. Describe the precautions necessary in the stowage of essential oils.

A. Generally highly volatile, essential oils are apt to cause ignition of organic or finely divided material, such as cotton, waste, textiles, sawdust, and charcoal, when mixed with these. They should, therefore, be kept apart from foodstuffs, solvents, or textiles, and also, because of their pungent smells, away from tea, tobacco, flour, etc. This type of cargo should be stowed in an isolated place, where possible tainting or leakage damage is eliminated, as, e.g., in the fore- or the after peak, and kept under lock and key, such goods usually being greatly valued. Dunnage used in stowage should be disposed of, in case of future damage by tainting to foodstuffs or fine goods.

Note: "Essential Oils" is a term used to describe such oils as almond, attar of roses, clove, wintergreen, lavender, etc. which are used in perfumery and cooking.

Q. In loading adjacent tanks with dissimilar products; would you top off your second tank at level A, B or C? Why:

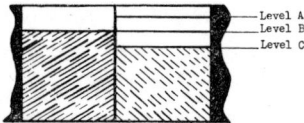

A. At level B; because any defect arising in the tightness of the bulkhead between tanks, or in that of the pipe line common to both, will cause little or no mixture of the products.

Tank 1   Tank 2

Q. How many gallons are there in a United States barrel?

A. 42 U.S. gallons or 35 imperial gallons.

Q. Prior to loading Grades A, B, or C cargoes, what precautions are necessary with respect to boiler and galley fires?

A. All fires and open flames under boilers and in ranges should, if possible, be extinguished, and in any event no such fires or open flames should be permitted in any compartment which is on, and open to, that part of the deck on which the cargo hatches and hose are located.

Q. With respect to the danger of fire and explosion of liquid petroleum cargoes, why are greater precautions usually necessary when loading than when discharging?

A. Because greater danger exists due to the presence of gases expelled from the cargo tanks during the loading.

Q. A locomotive weighing 32 tons is stowed on its 4 wheels, each of which has an area of one foot resting on the deck. (a) What is the load per square foot on the deck if the locomotive's weight is equally distributed on the 4 wheels? (b) If the deck capacity is 400 pounds per square foot, how could the weight be distributed?

A. (a) Locomotive's weight on each wheel is 32 ÷ 4 = 8 tons, or 16,000 lbs. per square foot.   (b) Bearing surface to be occupied is (16,000 × 4) ÷ 400 = 160 square feet. Weight could be distributed on heavy timbers covering an area of 8 × 20 feet, plus that required to support the timber used; and shoring up both the deck considered and that next below it would likely be necessary.

Q. What protection against fire is necessary where cowl deck ventilators feed directly into a magazine or a hold in which explosives are stowed?
A. Cowl deck ventilators, when fitted into or immediately adjacent to the magazine, shall be covered with a fine wire screen of not less than a 30 x 30 mesh at the weather end of the ventilator.

Q. On vessels carrying mail, is it permissible to break bulk prior to discharging of the mail in ports of the United States?
A. No; as provided by Revised Statutes 3988.

Q. Would you consider the stowage of boxed cargo better at A, making use of all possible space, or at B where the successive tiers are kept level? State your reason.

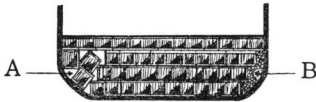

A. Better at B. Such compact stowage conforms to the important requirement of protecting cargo against damage by vessel's motion in a seaway; A stowage does not.

Q. A vessel preparing to load grain has four small hatches installed as sketched at A, B, C and D in her 'tween deck. What is their purpose?
A. These are trimming or wing hatches through which the men engaged as trimmers have access to the bulk cargo to be trimmed, such as coal or grain, in the lower hold. As here, they are used for wing feeders, where the hold is loaded with bulk grain. A boxlike construction of planks, or feeders, is built in each hatch to contain sufficient grain to replenish by gravity any space in the lower hold resulting from the vessel's motion or from shrinkage of the grain.

Q. When a hold is completely filled with loose grain in bulk, what quantity must be contained in feeders for that hold?

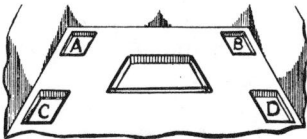

A. Not less than 2-1/2% and not more than 8% of the carrying capacity of the hold.

Q. How many long tons are there in 100 metric tons if a metric ton is .98421 long tons?
A. 100 x .98421 = 98.421 long tons.

Q. Explain what is meant by optional cargo and state the care necessary in the stowage of such cargo.

A. Optional cargo is a shipment that is to be discharged, according to the shipper's choice, at one of two or more ports. It will be necessary to regulate the stowage so that such shipments are at hand at any of the ports in question; or, at least, with the aim of reducing to a minimum the necessity of shifting other cargo.

Q. When trimmers are employed on bulk cargoes, what precautions should be taken to insure that none have been walled off by cargo in the hold?

A. Loading should be stopped when the hatchway is full until cargo is trimmed down. Then the men should be ordered out of the hold until the next "run" again fills the hatchway, and so on, until loading is completed.

Q. A vessel has a fresh water allowance of 8 inches. A hydrometer reading taken in a sample of water in which she is loading reads 1015. How far below her salt water draft may she load due to allowance for fresh water?

A. $8 \times \dfrac{1025 - 1015}{25} = 8 \times \dfrac{10}{25} = 8 \times \dfrac{2}{5} = \dfrac{16}{5} = 3$ inches.

Q. In stowing carboys of acid, which are not completely boxed, what is the maximum number of tiers permitted?

A. Carboys of such corrosive liquids must be stowed not more than two tiers high.

Q. Why is the top planking of bins constructed for deck cargo required to be of sturdy construction?

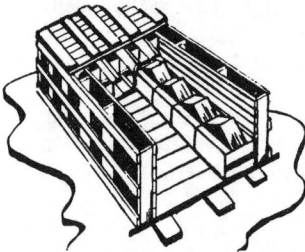

A. As cargo stowed in such bins usually is of the dangerous type, the goods must be thus adequately protected from possible crushing damage.

Q. You are required to supervise the stowage of two consignments of butter contained in cases as sketched. Describe the difference in the manner of stowage required for each lot.

A. Ordinary tier stowage for each, preferably with boxes lying fore-and-aftwise, but 1/2-inch battens or laths should be laid across each tier of B boxes, in order to provide air circulation through the mass.

Q. Your reading of a combustible gas indicator showed that less than 0.1 percent petroleum vapor was present in a tank that had been used for sour crude (containing hydrogen sulfide, H2S). Would you consider the tank safe as far as toxicity and explosibility are concerned?

A. As far as explosibility is concerned, yes; but, in the matter of toxicity, no. (Hydrogen sulphide can be fatal even if present in relatively small concentrations.)

Q. Describe the hazards that may be involved when working in tanks that have carried gasoline having a tetraethyl lead content.

A. In addition to hazards to be expected from petroleum gas, there is danger of lead poisoning, against which mechanical filter respirators should be used.

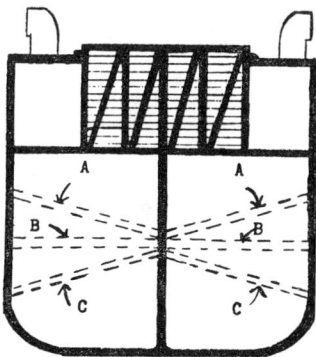

Q. Where shifting boards are rigged for a grain cargo: (a) Would you regard wooden shores A, B, or C as most efficient? (b) Why? (c) What compensation is made for inefficient positioning of shores?

A. (a) C shores. (b) Because least likely to be disturbed by ship working in a seaway; also, either C has more supporting value than the others during heavy rolling or if the vessel takes a heavy list. (c) An increase of the shifting boards' thickness in accordance with the rules.

Q. An oil hose has an inside diameter of 8 inches. What is the minimum radius to which the hose should be bent?

A. 8 feet, or 12 times its inside diameter.

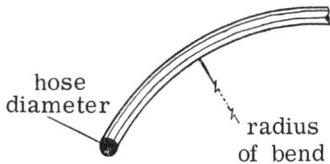

Q. When gas-freeing a tank vessel, what precaution must be taken with respect to vent lines, heating coils, steam smothering lines, and loading and discharge piping?

A. All must be cleaned and blown out free of gas.

Q. When a centrifugal pump is operating with a suction lift: (a) What care is necessary? (b) What is the maximum suction lift possible?

A. (a) To see it does not become "airbound."

(b) Theoretically, 34 ÷ specific gravity of liquid, in feet; practically, 22 ÷ spec. gravity, in feet.

Q. What means are required to evacuate the oil from a flooded pump room?

A. A cargo pump or a cargo-stripping pump may be used to pump out the oil via the bilge suction. (See valve illustration, next page.) The valve stem, as with steam-supply valves to pumps, is fitted with an extension rod for operation at deck level.

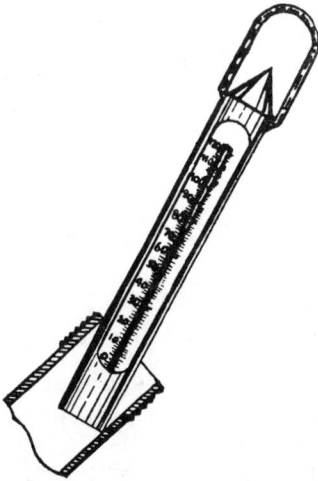

Q. Describe the proper manner of reading the thermometer shown, when determining the temperature of a liquid cargo.

A. The instrument should be kept upright while immersed as near as possible up to the mercury's height, which latter should be level with the observer's eye.

Q. When a vessel has a gas-free certificate reading "safe for men-safe for hot work": (a) What is the maximum vapor content in the tank's atmosphere? (b) What residues may be present in the tank?

A. (a) .2% by volume. (b) None.

Q. Why is a stop-check valve such as that sketched required to be fitted on a pump room bilge suction when the bilges are pumped by the cargo pumps or cargo stripping pump?

A. So that when the bilges are pumped out the suction line may be closed against entrance of oil or water via such pumps.

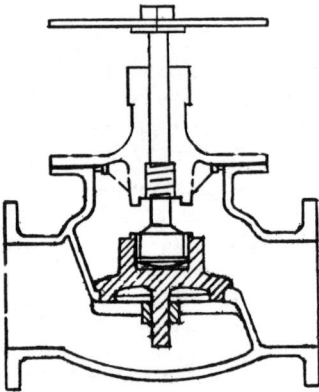

Q. A vessel loads frozen ice cream which comes aboard packed in dry ice. What precautions would be necessary in stowing and discharging such cargo?

A. Since "dry ice" is solidified carbon dioxide, which returns to its gaseous state as it melts, the amount of oxygen present may become decreased. Accordingly, both during stowage and prior to discharge of such cargo, the compartment concerned should be thoroughly aired and continuously ventilated.

Q. What are the three necessary conditions that must be maintained in a refrigerated compartment in order to have good cargo turnout?

A. Cleanliness of cargo space; proper stowage; constant refrigeration.

Q. Why is it important that the ventilation ducts in pump rooms extend below any floor plates so that air is circulated through the lowest part of the pump room?

A. Because petroleum vapors are heavier than air and tend to settle in the lowest parts of any space, as below the floor plates indicated.

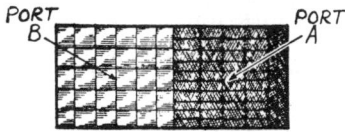

Q. After the bales for port <u>A</u> had been discharged at that port, how would you protect the cartons for port <u>B</u> against damage from the rolling or pitching of the ship enroute to port <u>B</u>, if shoring material was not at hand?

Note: The separation between <u>A</u> and <u>B</u> is thwartship.

A. Rearrange the stowage by breaking down the first 3 tiers to form at least 4 tiers in compactly laid equal steps, sloping into the space vacated by the bales.

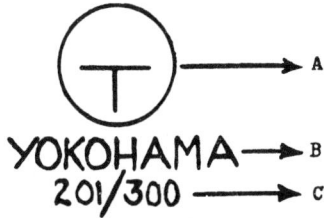

Q. If a case is marked as sketched, what is the meaning of <u>A</u>, <u>B</u>, and <u>C</u>?

A. (A) Shipper's identifying mark on cases of this consignment. (B) Port of delivery. (C) Consecutive numbers of the 100 cases in the shipment. This case will be assigned one of these numbers.

Q. What are the duties of the senior deck officer during oil transfer operations?

A. (a) Supervise the handling of cargo system valves. (b) Start transfer of cargo slowly. (c) Observe hose and connections for leakage. (d) Observe operating pressure on cargo system. (e) Observe rate of loading for the purpose of avoiding overflow of tanks. (f) Observe conditions in pump room at frequent intervals.

Q. A vessel is fitted with insulating mats which enable her to make a refrigerated space in the square of a 'tween deck whose wings and ends are refrigerated. In using such mats, would you consider the tightness of the bottom mats or the top mats of the space as being more important?

A. Tightness of bottom mats is more important, because surface-cooling ventilation is available on top, but not below, the space indicated.

Q. What inspection is required prior to making repairs involving riveting, welding, burning, etc., on a tank vessel?

A. After the tanks and pipe lines have been cleaned and made ready, a certified chemist enters tanks and inspects them. If found to be cleaned to his satisfaction, and if the gas content is 0.2% or less, a certificate is issued stating the tanks in question are <u>Safe for Men and Fire</u>.

Q. What provisions are made in the bilge system of a vessel to protect the pipes from becoming clogged or the pumps being damaged?

A. The bilge-suction line in each bilge or well is fitted with a rosebox or strum for the purpose of straining out any loose matter in the bilge water.

Q. How can the possibility of clogging the bilge suction be reduced when carrying granular cargo such as grain, coal, rock ballast, etc?

A. By making the limber boards tight, as by laying separation cloths, or by nailing strips over, or temporarily caulking, the seams.

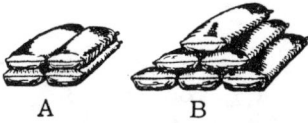

A   B

Q. In supervising the stowage of bagged cargo in a hold: (a) When would you stack the bags as in A? (b) When as in B?

A. (a) When the commodity requires all possible ventilation. (b) When thorough ventilation is not important.

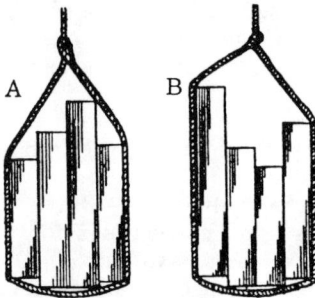

A   B

Q. In supervising the discharge of delicate crates from a cargo hold, would you sling them as in A or B? Why?

A. As at A. Because in B the placing of taller packages outside of the shorter ones results in a crushing stress which is practically absent in A.

Q. The deep tanks of a vessel hold 500 tons of fresh water. How many tons of coconut oil with a specific gravity of 0.93 could be stowed in these deep tanks?

A. $\dfrac{.93}{1.00} = \dfrac{C}{500}$; $C = \dfrac{.93 \times 500}{1.00} = 465$ tons coconut oil.

Q. A vessel reserves 30' × 60' of the deck area of a hold for 300 tons of machinery parts stowing at 30 cubic feet per ton. How high will the consignment of machinery stow?

A. 300 × 30 = 9000 ft³ reserved for machinery on a floor 30' × 60', or 1800 ft² Therefore, 9000 ÷ 1800 = 5 feet high, machinery will stow.

Q. In carrying horses, many remote from the water barrel get an insufficient supply of water owing to the laziness of attendants; how can you detect this?

A. The animals will whinny, become restless and feverish, and will not eat their fodder.

Q. Would you stow cylinders containing compressed gases adjacent to the side of a ship?

A. Cylinders of non-flammable gases must be stowed no closer than 3 feet to ship's side; flammable gases not less than 8 feet.

Q. Referring to the sketch: (a) When is shoring used in the 'tween deck of a vessel? (b) What is the purpose of the carlings indicated by <u>B</u>?

B

A. (a) When a deckload or a piece of heavy cargo requires greater support than that afforded by the upper deck itself.

(b) They are for stiffening and additional support to the deck plating, and also, as fitted snugly between the beams, act as stiffeners to the latter, in the sense of holding them to their work.

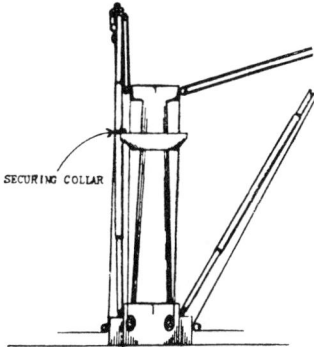

SECURING COLLAR

Q. When the topping lift is up and down in the stowed position of the boom, how would you take the weight off the securing collar in order to release it? See illustration.

A. Ease up the cargo fall and all other gear fast to the boom. Set taut the bull rope, or single wire or manila led from boom nearly in way of the securing collar, through a block at the cross-trees and thence to the deck (not shown in sketch).

Q. When empty drums or barrels have been used to hold dangerous goods, what precautions must be taken in order to ship them empty, without restrictions?

A. In order to avoid being classed as dangerous cargo, such empty containers must be certified to have been thoroughly cleaned; any that have carried dangerous liquids or volatile toxic products must be perfectly tight before shipment.

Q. How should plate or sheet glass be stowed?

A. It should be stowed on edge and athwartship, preferably in a 'tween deck, and in the square of the hatch, if possible, so that handling to the wings may be avoided. With properly marked side uppermost, the cases or crates should lie supported along their entire length, and well chocked off against movement of the vessel, preferably by using suitable cargo.

Q. How would you stow cargo parcels in order that the markings are readily found?

A. "Marks and numbers up," to quote the old rule. Stowage should conform to the desideratum of having the markings on every package meet the eye as discharge of the cargo proceeds.

Q. The bilge drain wells of a hold are located in the after end. Would it be preferable to stow drums of liquid latex in the forward or the after end of this hold?

A. They should be stowed in the forward end of this hold. Better to have any leakage of latex coagulate in the open, than to plug the bilge suction, if allowed access to the wells in the liquid state.

Q. What practice is frequently followed to eliminate danger of contamination or tainting by odorous or liquid commodities?

A. A specially isolated hold or compartment is reserved for stowage of such cargo.

Q. Oxidizing materials such as chlorates, nitrates, or peroxides must not be stowed in the same compartment with certain types of cargo. Name at least two such types.

A. Combustibles and acids.

Q. In securing deck cargo as illustrated: (a) What is the purpose of angle iron A and wooden capping B? (b) How may the wedges used for tightening the braces as at C be prevented from working loose?

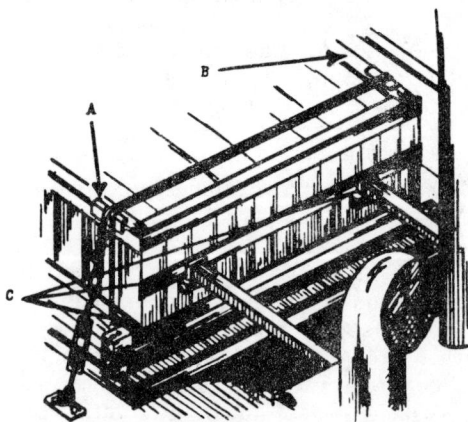

A. (a) As a bolster or chafing piece, A protects the case against pressure of the lashings. B generally strengthens the case and stiffens its edges against slinging or lashing stresses.
(b) By nailing their butt ends to the reinforcing piece.

Q. How may 'tween deck drains in a cargo hold be checked to determine if they are functioning properly?

A. By observing how freely the water, as poured from a bucket or other handy receptacle, is carried into the hold bilge or well.

Q. Why is it important that 'tween deck drains be in good condition?
A. So that any leakage from the cargo or condensation from ship's plating, etc., may be carried off to the bilges and thus avert possible damage to dry cargo.

Q. How should bilges or drain well strainers be prepared for stowage of bulk cargoes?
A. They must be protected against entrance of the loose cargo and consequent probable clogging of the strainers. This is done by laying canvas over the limber boards, nailing strips of wood over the seams, or temporarily caulking each seam or crevice through which cargo might find admission.

Q. How many board feet of dunnage would you estimate to be in a stack which is 5 feet high, 5 feet wide, and 12 feet long?
A. $\dfrac{t'' \times b'' \times L'}{12} = \dfrac{60 \times 60 \times 12}{12} = 3600$ board feet.

Q. Before proceeding to the next port, what measures to prevent overcarriage should be taken upon completion of discharge of a partial cargo?
A. A complete inspection of the cargo remaining aboard should be made with the objective of determining with certainty that all cargo for the present port has been landed.

Q. Describe the conditions that must be observed in the stowage of corrosive liquids.
A. Corrosive liquids must be stowed in such manner that the containers may be easily observed. They must be well separated from foodstuffs and cargo of an organic nature, especially flammable solids and oxidizing materials. When stowed on deck and vessel has explosives on board, engine-room space must separate these two types of cargo. Also, if given deck stowage, any leakage from corrosive liquids must drain into a scupper leading directly overboard.

Q. Why type of nails are required for the inside sheathing of a magazine for explosives? Why?
A. Only copper or cement-coated nails. So that the possibility of sparking through friction or shock may be eliminated when in contact with such cargo.

Q. Define: (a) Weight cargo. (b) Measurement cargo. (c) Ad valorem cargo.
A. (a) Goods having a stowage factor of 40 or less.
   (b) Goods stowing at more than 40 cubic feet per long ton.
   (c) Goods carried at a freight rate according to their value.

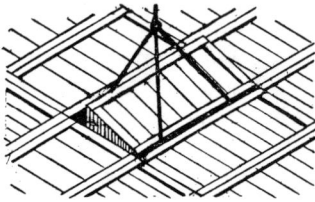

Q. When heavy crates or boxes of cargo are tightly stowed as illustrated, how may breaking out the first box be facilitated for the longshoremen in the port of discharge?

A. Arrange the stowage so that the last 1 or 2 cases will be in the hatch square, or as near thereto as possible, and leave their slings undisturbed.

Q. What precautions to prevent theft are usual at sea when carrying precious metals or bullion?

A. Usually such valuable shipments are carried in a strongroom located where easily observed and guarded at all times. Perhaps no safer practice exists than that of placing precious metals in a strongbox or other lockup at the bottom of a trunk hatch, and then filling the hatch with baggage not wanted on the passage.

Q. What stowage is required for motion picture films with a nitro-cellulose base?

A. Such films usually are packed in individual metal containers put up in cases. They should be kept in a cool place, readily accessible for throwing overboard in case of fire.

Q. A hold of a vessel has a bale capacity of 60,000 cubic feet. Would it be feasible to stow 300 tons of baled kapok in this hold if 10 percent were allowed for broken stowage? The stowage factor of kapok is 188.

A. The hold lacks the capacity required for the proposed stowage by 2040 cubic feet, since stowage bulk = 300 x 188 x 1.10 = 62040 cu. ft.

Q. What type portable lights and lighting fixtures should be used in locations where an explosion or fire hazard may exist due to flammable gases or vapors, combustible dust, or easily ignitible fibers or materials producing combustible dusts?

A. The light bulbs must be enclosed in gastight lamp covers. Only special approved equipment may be used for such dangerous conditions, regular extension cords and lights being prohibited. Regulations for Tank Vessels require lighting only by the use of approved explosion-proof, self-contained, battery-fed lamps.

Q. What is the minimum thickness of timber that may be used for grain shifting boards?

A. 2-inch boards.

Q. Describe the work performed by the National Cargo Bureau and its surveyors with regard to cargo stowage.

A. It provides an agency for formulating recommendations to the government as to regulations for safe stowage of dangerous goods;

works to achieve uniformity of safety standards in cargo stowage; supplies information to the shipping industry on problems of transportation of the thousands of marketed commodities; and offers the industry a low-cost cargo-loading inspection service of any loading operation.

Its surveyors, upon finding a cargo loaded as satisfactorily stowed, issue a certificate to the effect that cargo is safely stowed both with respect to the cargo itself, adjacent cargo, the ship, and crew.

Q. What precautions are necessary in the stowage of calcium carbide?

A. Reject all containers in bad condition; stow in a dry place away from corrosives, oxidizing materials, flammables, and explosives. Recommend 'tween-deck stowage, close to square of hatch. Ventilate well and stow nothing over it.

Q. In securing deck cargo, why is tomming, as shown at B, preferable to shoring, as shown at A?

A. Because B withstands the lifting action of any heavy water that may be shipped; A does not.

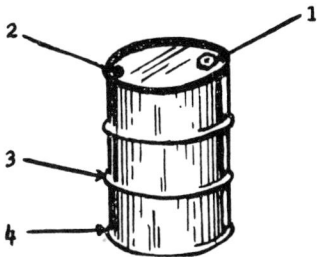

Q. Name the numbered parts of the drum illustrated.

A. 1. Bung. 2. Vent. 3. Hoop. 4. Chime.

Q. How would you fight a calcium carbide fire?

A. Shut off all ventilation to the compartment and open the CO_2 supply. If CO_2 not available, turn on the steam smothering line. Use no water. Keep CO_2 or steam supply going, if possible, even if fire appears to have been extinguished, until arriving in port, when all should be in readiness for removing hatches and disposing of the cargo. Ventilate compartment thoroughly before allowing men to enter.

Q. What precautions are necessary for a cargo of cotton?

A. Chiefly those against fire. While transferring cotton, fire hoses should be ready for immediate use and barrels of water with buckets kept ready at hand near the hatches. "No smoking" should be rigidly enforced. Galley funnel and smokestack to be screened against the spark hazard. Keep cotton away from the slightest contact with oil or grease, and hence apart from any oily or greasy cargo. Cover all ventilator cowls with wire gauze. Check all electric fixtures and connections in cargo spaces against sparking. Reject loading of wet bales. Protect against rust by covering all iron parts of ship in contact with cargo by burlap or mats.

Consult the Rules Governing Loading of Cotton issued by the New York Board of Underwriters for full information regarding the risks involved when stowing cotton with certain other goods.

Q. Describe the precautions necessary when a cargo hold is partially filled with loose grain in bulk.
A. If grain occupies not more than one-third the hold's capacity, no shifting boards are required. If over one-third the hold is filled, shifting boards as for a full hold are required. In both cases, however, the grain must be leveled off and overstowed by bagged grain, bales of cotton, or suitable general cargo of such mass or amount as to secure the bulk grain from shifting. Over the bulk grain, a floor of 2 thicknesses of boards placed fore-and-aft and athwartships must be laid; the lower boards to be spaced not more than 4 feet apart, the upper ones not more than 4 inches apart.

Q. When deck cargo is stowed above the bulwarks and closer than 8 inches to the side of the vessel, how would you eliminate the need for longshoremen hanging over the side to secure guys?
A. I would rig good pendants or strops to reach from the guys' usual securing points to clear the deckload.

Q. When cargo is being handled which is injurious or irritating to eyes, respiratory passages, or lungs, what precautions should be taken to safeguard personnel working in the area?
A. Provide maximum ventilation in enclosed spaces before handling such cargo. If toxic effects continue, provide personnel concerned with gas masks or other appropriate respiratory equipment.

Q. Describe the care required in order to carry a cargo of bagged sugar.
A. Sugar should be stowed to allow for sinkage, so that bags may clear stringer plates, beams, etc., and not be sheared in two or otherwise badly damaged. Especially with raw or semi-refined sugar, great care should be taken to reduce condensation to a minimum by observing principles of proper ventilation; cargo tends to heat in warm weather. Keep sugar free of contact with ship's iron, which latter should be covered with burlap or matting. Precautions against fire are most important, as sugar may be ignited by sparks and the resulting blaze is among the most difficult to extinguish. Before discharging, hatches should be left fully open and maximum ventilation given the hold, so that men may not become gassed by fumes commonly present due to fermentation in warmer temperatures.

Q. What precautions should be observed in stowing burlap bags or cargo packaged in burlap?

A. Keep it away from vegetable oils, especially linseed oil and turpentine, on account of danger of spontaneous combustion. Carriage of burlap in any form in same compartment as turpentine is considered dangerous practice. Some kinds of this material are classed as Dangerous Goods and of the same order as cotton with respect to its stowage. Hand hooks should not be allowed in handling.

Q. How would you load a cargo of iron ore?

A. Load all holds at same time, if possible, with about two-thirds the cargo in lower holds and one-third in 'tween decks, and running the major portion into the middle holds and a lesser portion into the end holds. Trim the ore well into the wings and thus distribute the weight, while tending to make vessel's motion easier in a seaway.

Q. Describe the precautions necessary in the carriage of vegetable oils in bulk.

A. Tanks must be thoroughly clean and, where edible oils are carried, there must be present no metallic or bituminous paint, or other covering. Tanks should be isolated from ship's pumping and filling system by blank flanges. Where the oil requires heating in order to facilitate its transfer, care must be taken to adhere to shipper's instructions as to limit of temperature in the process.

Q. When dangerous cargoes are loaded: (a) What disposition must be made of damaged or leaking packages? (b) Where should such damaged packages be repaired or recoopered?

A. (a) They shall not be accepted on board any vessel for transportation or storage; but if restored or repaired to the satisfaction of the owner or master, they may be accepted. Damaged containers which it is not feasible to restore, however, shall be refused and promptly reported by the owner or master to the Coast Guard or corresponding authority in a foreign port.

(b) If discovered as damaged on board, they should be landed and repaired in an approved place.

Q. How would you make a lee side for a lighter while lying at anchor?

A. Run a mooring line from about amidships or a little farther aft, on same side as the anchor in use, and make it fast to the anchor cable outside the hawsepipe. Heave taut the line and slack away cable until ship's head falls off at the required angle for a lee.

Q. How would you stow on deck carboys containing corrosive liquids?

A. Stow not more than 2 tiers high, on planks, in a sheltered place, always accessible, and near to a scupper which leads directly overboard. If explosives are loaded, corrosive liquids must be separated from them by the engine-room spaces. Use wire lashings, if required.

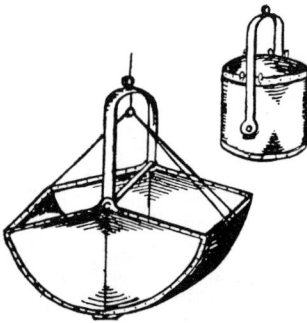

Q. When mechanical equipment, such as that sketched, is used to discharge bulk cargoes: (a) What damage to ship's structure can be caused and how is it averted? (b) In the event that damage is noted, what measures should be taken by the ship's officers?

A. (a) While hatch coamings, hold ladders, etc., may suffer minor harmful knocks, material damage may occur to ship's tank tops, if not protected by hold ceiling of sufficient thickness against the heavy shocks commonly accompanying use of such equipment.

(b) With recovery for damage to ship in view, the facts should be noted in ship's log, with names of witnesses, after calling attention of the responsible cargo operator or stevedore to damage incurred.

Q. What type of cargo may be handled by the method of single whip and skid, as illustrated?

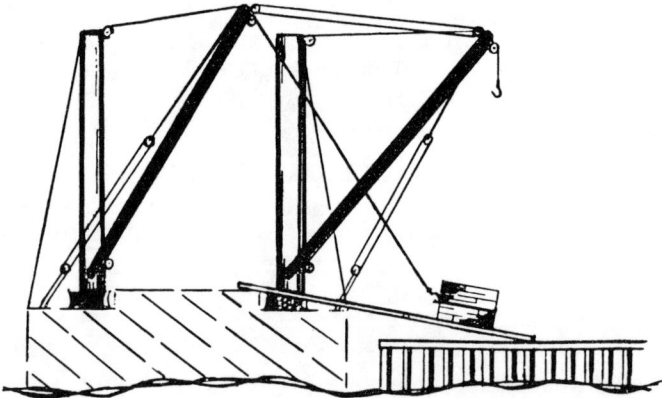

A. Bales of cotton, hay, jute, etc., or such resilient goods.

Q. In the event that leakage occurred from carboys of corrosive liquids stowed on deck, what steps should be taken?
A. Find the faulty carboys and throw them overboard. Hose down the leakage and resecure. Use wire lashings.

Q. What is the meaning of the term "on deck protected" as applied to dangerous cargoes?
A. A stowage term, meaning that such goods are to be carried on

the open weather deck, protected from the elements by awnings
and dunnage.

Q. Given a dry bulb temperature of 75° and a wet bulb temperature
of 62.5°, find: (a) Relative humidity. (b) Dew point.
A. (a) Table 16, Bowditch: Entering with 12.5° difference, between
dry and wet bulb temperatures, and 75° dry bulb temperature,
gives 49% relative humidity.
(b) Table 17, Bowditch: Entering with values as above, gives
dew point 54° (F.).

Q. Define an inflammable solid.
A. A solid substance, other than an explosive, that is liable, under
conditions incident to transportation, to cause fires through friction, absorption of moisture, or spontaneous chemical change.

Q. Define an oxidizing material.
A. Any substance that yields oxygen readily and so stimulates the
combustion of organic material.

Q. What care is necessary during the voyage when transporting a
cargo of explosives or other dangerous articles?
A. In addition to the requirement that stowage and discharge shall
be supervised by a licensed officer, in accordance with regulations
prescribed by the Coast Guard in Explosives or Other Dangerous
Articles on Board Vessels, the following must be complied with:
Frequent inspections of cargo, especially during bad weather, to
insure the goods are carried with safety, having in view the possible damage by shifting cargo, spontaneous heating, or leaking
or sifting containers. Such inspections should be duly logged, with
details of corrections made to dangerous conditions discovered, if
any.
Also, temperature readings of compartments concerned shall be
taken at proper intervals and recorded in ship's log. Any rise
noted in consecutive readings should urge increased frequency of
inspections.

Q. Would you use dark or light colored tarpaulins or awnings to
protect compressed gases in cylinders from direct rays of sun?
Why?
A. Those of light color. Dark-colored canvas becomes heated to a
much greater temperature than the other, due to its comparatively
poor reflecting power.

Q. When a vessel is carrying inflammable liquid cargo on deck or
in the holds, what precaution must be taken to warn of the danger?
A. Signs printed INFLAMMABLE VAPORS. KEEP LIGHTS AND
FIRE AWAY. NO SMOKING shall be posted at each way of approach to such cargo when stowed on deck, and in the vicinity of
cargo-hold ventilators when stowed in the holds. The letters shall

be painted on a white ground in a bright red color, and shall be not less than 3 inches in height.

Q. What signals must be displayed by a tank vessel during transfer of bulk cargo?

A. When alongside a dock, a red flag by day and a red electric light by night shall be hoisted so as to be visible from all sides. While at anchor, the red flag only shall be displayed.

Q. When a tank vessel is fast to a dock during transfer of cargo, what warning must be given persons approaching the gangway?

A. One or more placards showing, in letters not less than 2 inches high, the following:

WARNING
NO OPEN LIGHTS
NO SMOKING
NO VISITORS

Q. What precautions must be taken against operation of the radio equipment when Grades A, B, or C liquids are being transferred?

A. A sign shall be placed in the radio room warning against use of equipment, except by permission of the senior deck officer.

Q. Why are vessels engaged in the carriage of refrigerated cargoes usually painted white and provided with wooden decks over the refrigerated spaces?

A. The vessels' wood decks provide substantial additional insulation against the sun's heat, while their white-painted sides, through their property of reflecting the sun's rays, greatly reduce the steel's capacity for conducting heat to the holds.

Q. If a ship drydocks while carrying refrigerated cargo, what steps must be taken if the refrigerating plant must be operated?

A. Since a continuous supply of cool water is required for the condenser, immediate steps must be taken to connect the plant with the shore line.

Q. A vessel has two similar reefer spaces, one holding apples with a specific heat of .90, the other holding smoked bacon with a specific heat of .50. Both boxes are kept at 35° F. If the refrigeration machinery is shut down, which box will lose its temperature most rapidly? Which will require the longer time to cool down from a temperature of 70° F., using the same machinery and the same power?

A. The bacon box will lose more rapidly. The apple box will take longer to cool down.

Q. Name at least two types of refrigerant gases used on merchant vessels and describe the hazards that they can create.

A. Ammonia: danger is always present of pungent asphyxiating fumes, as from an uncontrolled leak.

Freon 11: destructive to packing containing rubber and will also dissolve oils or grease; dries up the skin.

Q. State the purpose of gratings in refrigerated compartments and describe in detail how you lay them.
A. To keep cargo from contact with the usual metal deck, and to provide through air circulation under the cargo. The gratings are laid with their bearers athwartship, so that any leakage or condensation may run directly to side of compartment and into the drainage pipes.

Q. Would you use the gratings for stowage of high density cargo of a general nature in a refrigerated compartment which is thoroughly insulated?
A. No; I would remove gratings and use dunnage.

Q. Show (by means of a sketch if desired) how you would determine the maximum length of steel pipe that could be loaded.
A. Where pipe is to be loaded in a lower hold, the measurement taken from starboard forward corner of 'tween-deck hatch coaming to port after corner of lower-hold coaming, plus this measurement extended to meet the hold ceiling (or a bulkhead or a block of other cargo), will indicate such maximum length.

Q. A vessel loads 2,000 tons of cargo using ten gangs of longshoremen, ten hours each: (a) What is the rate of loading per gang hour? (b) If each of the above gangs is composed of 15 men, what is the rate in tons per man hour?
A. (a) 2000 ÷ (10 x 10) = 2000 ÷ 100 = 20 tons per gang hour.
   (b) 20 ÷ 15 = 1.333 tons per man hour.

Q. Why should insufficiency of packing or use of poor packaging material be noted on an exception report?
A. In order to record, as protection of the vessel's interests, the evidence required to defeat a possible claim by consignee against ship for damage incurred while goods were in vessel's care.

Q. When inflammable liquids are stowed on the deck of a vessel, what precautions are mandatory in order that fire-fighting equipment is immediately at hand?
A. At least 1 fire hose shall be stretched out ready for instant use and 1 or more fire extinguishers shall be at hand at all times.

Q. What precautionary measure is usual on merchant vessels to warn longshoremen or other workmen against using the ship's booms to lift weights in excess of their safe working load?
A. On each boom "Safe Working Load" in tons is marked in conspicuous letters.

Q. In loading ore, would you permit each hold to take its full complement before the others are started?

A. No. As far as practicable, loading should be, roughly, with even distribution of the weight fore-and-aft, completing and trimming ship with somewhat less weight toward the ends.

Q. How is the stowage factor for a commodity determined from the measurement and weight?

A. 2240 lbs., or 1 ton, divided by the weight of 1 unit of the cargo in question, determines the number of units in 1 ton. Then the cubic measurement of a unit multiplied by the above quotient will give the stowage factor; or F = (2240 × unit cubic) ÷ unit weight.

27. DETERMINATION OF AREA AND VOLUME

Q. Find the volume of a cone 30 feet in height, whose base is 40 feet in diameter.

A. $\dfrac{.7854 \; d^2 h}{3} = \dfrac{.7854 \times 40 \times 40 \times 30}{3} = 12566.4$ cubic feet.

Q. A hold is 25 feet wide and 12 feet deep. If you stow 165 tons of cargo against the forward bulkhead, how far aft will it extend, allowing 45 cubic feet to a ton?

A. $\dfrac{165 \times 45}{25 \times 12} = \dfrac{99}{4} = 24\text{-}3/4$ feet.

Q. The diameter of a smokestack is 10 feet and its height 40 feet. (a) What is its surface area in square yards? (b) Find how much it would cost to give it one coat of paint if 1 gallon of mixed paint costs 3 dollars and covers 70 square yards.

A. (a) $\dfrac{3.1416 \times 10 \times 40}{9} = 139.6$ sq. yds.   (b) $\dfrac{140 \times 3}{70} = \$6.00$.

Q. Find the number of square yards of canvas required to make a trysail, the luff being 40 feet, the foot 30 feet. The foot is at right angles to the luff. How much would the canvas cost at 37 cents per linear yard, the width of sail canvas being 2 feet?

A. $\dfrac{40 \times 30}{9 \times 2} = \dfrac{1200}{18} = 66.67$ square yards.

   Lineal yard = 2/3 square yard. So, 66.67 ÷ .6667 = 100 lineal yds., and cost = 100 × .37 = $37.00.

Q. A rectangular plate is 24 feet 6 inches long and 8 feet 9 inches wide. What is the area of the plate?

A. 24.5 × 8.75 = 214.375 square feet.

28. LIFESAVING APPARATUS AND FIRE-FIGHTING EQUIPMENT

Q. Describe the stowage of the water which is required to be carried in lifeboats on ocean and coastwise passenger vessels.

A. For each person the lifeboat is certified to carry, 3 quarts of drinking water consisting of 9 approved hermetically sealed containers per person. These shall be stowed in drinking-water tanks, lockers, or other compartments providing suitable protection.

Q. May a lifeboat which is certified to carry 65 persons be fitted with an approved type of hand propelling gear?
A. Yes; such lifeboat shall be either motor-propelled or fitted with an approved type of hand-propelling gear.

Q. How often are drills with the line-throwing appliance required to be held aboard ocean passenger vessels?
A. At least once in every 3 months.

Q. How often must fire and boat drills be held?
A. At least once in every week, and in the case of a passenger vessel making a voyage of more than 1 week's duration, drill shall be held before leaving port and at least once a week thereafter.

Q. Describe the method of firing the mounted line-carrying gun.
A. The gun shall be actually fired, using 2-1/2 ounces of powder and the regular service projectile with any flexible line of proper size and length suitably faked or laid out.

Q. Adrift in a motor lifeboat from an ocean passenger vessel, what equipment could you utilize to signal or attract an airplane or vessel?
A. By day: A floating orange smoke signal; a signalling mirror. By night: One or more red hand flares; one or more red projected parachute flares or rocket-propelled parachute flares; searchlight (if class A motor lifeboat). By day or night: Radio installation (if class A motor lifeboat).

Q. How should lifeboat chocks on passenger vessels be fitted in order to facilitate the launching of the boats?
A. In such manner that the boats may be swung out without lifting them from the chocks.

Q. How often must fire and boat drills be held aboard ocean passenger vessels?
A. At least once in every week, and, when the voyage is to occupy more than 1 week, before leaving port also.

Q. How often must life floats and buoyant apparatus be cleaned and thoroughly overhauled?
A. At least once in every year.

Q. Describe the use of the mechanical firing attachment required for the line-carrying (Lyle) gun.
A. The attachment is designed to fire a .22" caliber blank cartridge into the powder charge down through a hollowed bolt screwed into the priming hole of the Lyle gun. Its trigger mechanism is cocked,

a cartridge inserted, and firing takes place by a pull on a lanyard.

Q. Describe the stowage and method of securing life floats and buoyant apparatus aboard ocean passenger vessels.
A. They shall be stowed in such manner as to be readily launched, and life floats more than 400 lbs. in weight shall not require to be lifted before launching. The lashings securing life floats and buoyant apparatus to the vessel shall be such as may easily be slipped. They may be stowed one above the other, but not more than 4 high and kept apart by suitable distance-pieces; also, means shall be provided to prevent them from shifting.

Q. How must the emergency lights on a passenger vessel be marked?
A. With a letter "E" at least 1/2 inch high.

Q. When lifeboats are damaged and repairs are necessary, what is the procedure before making such repairs?
A. Advance notice must be given to the Officer in Charge, Marine Inspection. When emergency repairs are made, notice shall be given that officer as soon as practicable.

Q. Describe the stowage of the following equipment in a lifeboat aboard an ocean passenger vessel: (a) Hatchets. (b) Oil, illuminating. (c) Oil, storm.
A. (a) Hatchets shall be attached to boat by individual lanyards and be readily available for use, 1 at each end of boat.
(b) 1 quart of illuminating oil kept in a metal container.
(c) 1 gallon carried in a suitable metal container constructed to permit a controlled distribution of the oil on the water, and so arranged that it can be attached to the sea anchor.

Q. In lifeboats aboard ocean and coastwise passenger vessels: (a) How many spare bulbs and batteries for the flashlight are required to be carried? (b) How long may the batteries remain in the flashlight or be used as spares?
A. (a) 3 spare cells (or 1 3-cell battery) and 2 spare bulbs.
(b) Not beyond the serviceable date appearing on the cell or its jacket.

Q. What license or certification must be held by persons appointed as first and second in command of each lifeboat and life raft carried aboard ocean passenger vessels?
A. Such persons must be either a licensed deck officer, an able seaman, or a certificated lifeboatman.

Q. Who is charged with the appointment of persons to command lifeboats and life rafts?
A. The master of vessel concerned.

Q. May articles not required by the regulations be stowed in a

lifeboat aboard ocean passenger vessels?
A. No; unless such can be stowed so as not to reduce the seating capacity or space available to the occupants, and so as not to interfere with the boat's seaworthiness or overload the davits or winches.

Q. How many life lines are required to be fitted on an ocean cargo vessel's lifeboat davit spans?
A. Two life lines.

Q. How many life lines are required to be fitted to an ocean passenger vessel's davit spans?
A. Two life lines; but 4 are required on emergency boats' davit spans.

Q. How many life lines are required to be fitted to an ocean passenger vessel's davit spans for the emergency boats?
A. Four life lines.

Q. How often must valves and other appliances necessary to make a compartment watertight be operated to meet the passenger vessel requirements?
A. At least once in every week that vessel is navigated. If voyage is to exceed 1 week in duration, such valves shall be operated before vessel leaves port.

Q. Describe the provisions carried as life-raft equipment aboard ocean or coastwise passenger vessels and the stowage thereof.
A. 2 lbs. hard bread or its equivalent for each person the raft is certified to carry. The provisions shall be packaged in hermetically sealed cans of an approved type, which shall be stowed in compartments providing suitable protection.

Q. What lifeboatage is required on ocean cargo vessels?
A. Sufficient lifeboats on each side of the vessel to accommodate all persons on board.

Q. How many service lines are required as equipment for the line-throwing appliance carried aboard ocean cargo vessels?
A. Four service lines.

Q. What is the service use limit of the rockets carried as equipment for a line-throwing appliance?
A. Four years from date of manufacture.

Q. When passenger vessels are fitted with watertight doors in the subdivision bulkheads, may these be kept open at sea?
A. They shall be closed, except when necessarily opened for working purposes, and in such cases always shall be ready to be immediately closed.

Q. State the type, number and location of fire extinguishers required to be provided for emergency power plants and emergency
fuel tanks aboard ship.

A. For emergency power plant, 1 CO_2, 15-lb. size, located outside
the space in vicinity of exit, subject to approval of Officer in
Charge, Marine Inspection. For emergency fuel tanks, none required.

Q. Describe the combination letter and number symbol used to
classify hand portable fire extinguishers carried aboard ocean
passenger vessels.

A. The letter indicates type of fire the extinguisher is used against,
thus: A is for fires in ordinary combustibles, where quantities of
water or solutions containing large percentages of water are of
first importance; B is for fires in flammable liquids, greases,
etc., where a blanketing effect is essential; and C for fires in
electrical equipment, where use of a nonconducting extinguishing
agent is most important.

The roman number denotes the size, I for the smaller, and II
for the larger, of the two extinguishers considered as of the hand
portable type.

Q. Whenever a vessel, moored to a waterfront facility, is without
power to operate its fire pumps, what measure should be taken
to provide water for fire-fighting purposes?

A. Vessels over 1000 tons gross shall have at least 1 shore connection to her fire main available to each side of the vessel, in
an accessible location. Suitable cut-out valves, check valves, and
adapters shall be provided as necessary, in order to have available at a moment's notice a water supply in ship's fire main.

Q. State the three methods by which fire spreads and what should
be done to prevent this in combating fires on board vessels.

A. Fire spreads by radiation, conduction, and convection. Radiation
of the fire heat is destroyed by a cooling agent, as the commonly
used fog-spray, or by CO_2. Spread of fire by conduction is fought
by wetting and cooling, as with water; by wetting, cooling, and
smothering, as with fog; by smothering and cooling, with fog-foam;
or by smothering with foam, CO_2, steam, or sand. Spread by
convection is that which takes place when portions of liquids and
gases heated to a greater degree than the rest of their mass become lighter and move upward into cooler portions. These heated
gases may be carried by drafts to ignite combustibles at some
distance away. Cooling and smothering are called for here, as
effected by fog, CO_2, foam, or fog-foam; or cooling by water itself.

Q. What are the requirements governing the number and location of
fire hydrants aboard ocean passenger vessels?

A. Fire hydrants shall be of sufficient number and so located that any part of the vessel, other than main machinery spaces, accessible to passengers and crew, and all cargo holds may be reached with at least 2 streams of water from separate outlets, at least 1 of which shall be from a single length of hose. In main machinery spaces, excepting shaft alleys containing no assigned space for stowage of combustibles, every part shall be capable of being reached by at least 2 streams of water, each from a single length of hose from separate outlets.

Q. At annual inspections, what is done to the carbon dioxide (CO_2) cylinders in a CO_2 fire-extinguishing system? When are the cylinders replaced and when must they be recharged?
A. They are weighed to detect any possible loss of gas. Cylinders are replaced if found excessively corroded or faulty beyond immediate repair. Recharge of cylinders is required if weight loss exceeds 10% of weight of charge.

Q. Must a fire hose remain connected to its hydrant at all times? If not, under what conditions may it be disconnected and where must it be stowed?
A. Yes; excepting that, on open decks where hose is exposed to heavy weather, or where hose may be liable to damage from handling cargo, it may be temporarily removed from its hydrant and stowed in an accessible nearby location.

30. RULES AND REGULATIONS FOR INSPECTION OF MERCHANT VESSELS

Q. What is a licensed officer's duty in assisting marine inspectors of the Coast Guard?
A. He shall point out all defects and imperfections known to him in the hull, equipments, boilers, or machinery of his vessel; he also shall report to the Coast Guard at earliest opportunity all accidents or happenings resulting in injury to his ship, her equipments, boilers, or machinery.

Q. In the logbook: (a) When are entries to be made: (b) What is required if an entry is not made on the same day as the occurrence? (c) Can an entry be made more than 24 hours after arrival in port, of any occurrence previous to arrival in port?
A. (a) As soon as possible after the occurrence indicated.
   (b) It shall be made and dated so as to show the date of the occurrence, and of the entry respecting it.
   (c) It may not.

Q. If your vessel is equipped with lifesaving apparatus over and above that required by the Merchant Marine Inspection, is it necessary to give the same care to the upkeep of this extra gear that you give to the required equipment? Give the reason for your answer.

A. Yes; the spirit and intent of the Rules governing Marine Inspection demand that all lifesaving equipment on board meet with certain standard requirements.

Q. What is the Oil Pollution Act and the penalty for its violation?
A. Officially termed the "Oil Pollution Act, 1924," it prohibits generally the discharge of oil into the coastal waters of the United States from any vessel, except in case of emergency imperiling life or property or unavoidable accident. Such offense is punishable by a fine not exceeding $2500 or not less than $500, or by imprisonment for not more than 1 year or not less than 30 days, or by both such fine and imprisonment; and such offender, if a licensed officer, may suffer suspension or revocation of his license. The vessel involved shall be liable for the pecuniary penalty specified in the Act.

Q. Name some of the records which may be required as evidence by a hearing board in the event of a marine casualty or accident.
A. Rough deck log; rough engine log; official log; gyro course recorder; gyro error log; compass deviation record; master's night order book; chart indicating ship's course, etc.; carpenter's tank and bilge sounding record.

Q. What does the law state with regard to the rating of the man at the wheel in narrow and crowded waters or in low visibility?
A. In such waters, none below the rating of Able Seaman may take the wheel.

Q. What data does the certificate of inspection contain, by whom is it issued and how long is it issued for?
A. It certifies that the particular vessel, with respect to her structure, boilers and their appurtenances, piping, main and auxiliary machinery, electrical installation, and, also to her lifesaving appliances, fire-detecting and extinguishing equipment, and other equipment which are listed, is in satisfactory condition and fit for the service for which she is intended. It also indicates that the vessel complies with the Federal Communications Commission's requirements in her radio installation, including fixed and portable radios for lifeboats.

The certificate is issued by the Officer in Charge, Marine Inspection, as authorized by the Coast Guard District Commander, who, in turn, is directly responsible to the Commandant, U.S. Coast Guard. It is issued for 1 year from date of completion of inspection.

Q. Name some of the information which may be found on a Certificate of Inspection.
A. Number of boilers and description of main machinery; number of fire hoses and portable extinguishers; hold fire-detecting and

extinguishing equipment; number and capacity of lifeboats and life rafts; life preservers, life buoys; number of W. T. bulkheads; compasses, and navigational equipment.

Q. What devices are required by the regulations to warn the passengers and crews of vessels in the event of emergency?
A. Ringing of ship's bell, blasts of ship's whistle, and general alarm bells, or other means in addition to these which will provide positive and certain notice of an existing emergency.

Q. What stations on a vessel must be connected by voice tube or telephone?
A. Navigating bridge or pilothouse and the engine room.

Q. What is the penalty for failure to promptly report a collision with aids to navigation to the Merchant Marine Inspectors?
A. Suspension or revocation of license.

Q. How does the officer or lifeboatman in charge of a boat know if the men assigned report to the proper boat and are familiar with the duties assigned on the station bill?
A. He should hold a roll call, which should check with the Station Bill, and the men should be questioned individually as to their familiarity with the duties assigned them.

Q. If a vessel sights people in danger of being lost at sea, is the master legally obliged to assist them if he may do so without serious danger to his own vessel, crew, or passengers?
A. Yes.

Q. Where the crew of a vessel assists in saving life from a vessel in distress and are thereby unable to assist in saving property, are they entitled to salvage?
A. Yes.

Q. What are the emergency signals used for the following: (a) Fire alarm. (b) Dismissal from fire stations. (c) Boat station or boat drill. (d) To lower boats. (e) To stop lowering boats. (f) Dismissal from boat stations.
A. (a) A continuous rapid ringing of ship's bell for not less than 10 seconds, supplemented by continuous sounding of general alarm bells for not less than 10 seconds.
   (b) General alarm sounded 3 times, supplemented by 3 short blasts of ship's whistle.
   (c) A succession of more than 6 short blasts followed by 1 long blast of ship's whistle, supplemented by a similar signal on general alarm bells.
   (d) 1 short blast of ship's whistle.
   (e) 2 short blasts of ship's whistle.
   (f) 3 short blasts of ship's whistle.

Q. What information is required on a Notice of Casualty?
A. Name and official number of vessel involved; owner or agent; nature and probable cause of casualty; locality in which it occurred; nature and extent of injury to persons and damage to property.

Q. By whom must instruments, machines, and equipment connected with the safety of life be approved before they may be used on board ship?
A. Commandant, U.S. Coast Guard.

Q. What would you do in the matter of handling the crew and advising and handling the passengers in time of emergency?
A. I would see that the members of the crew assigned to the various stations under my charge were acting in an orderly manner and that the passengers were properly directed or advised with the objective of avoiding unnecessary panic or confusion. What is expected of the crew as a matter of duty, and of the passengers as providing for their own safety, as the objectives of the Fire and Boat Drills, I am obliged to execute, as an officer under the master's authority, in orderly disciplined procedure.

Q. How shall spaces or lockers containing equipment for the use of the emergency squad be marked?
A. They shall be marked EMERGENCY SQUAD EQUIPMENT.

Q. Describe the method of electrical bonding mandatory for vessels transferring liquefied petroleum gases and which is usually employed for vessels transferring inflammable or combustible liquids.
A. A bonding cable, which is connected to the shore pipe line and provided with a switch, is bolted while the switch is open to a bright metallic part of ship's hull or cargo line within a few feet of the hose connection. Switch is then closed, so that any stray currents are grounded and cargo hose may be connected or disconnected in safety. When hose has been disconnected, switch is again opened and cable is removed from ship.

Q. What is the rule regarding unnecessary whistling within any harbor limits of the United States and what is the penalty for its violation?
A. Unnecessary sounding of ship's whistle is prohibited within any harbor limits of the United States. Any licensed officer who authorizes or permits such unnecessary whistling is subject to suspension or revocation of his license.

Q. What is the penalty for flashing, or causing to be flashed, the rays of the searchlight into the pilothouse of a passing vessel?
A. Revocation or suspension of offender's license or certificate.

Q. How are fire and boat drills to be conducted?
A. The drills shall be conducted as if an actual emergency existed.

All hands must report at their respective stations and be prepared
to perform their duties as specified in the Station Bill; and passengers shall be encouraged to fully participate in the drills, and
also shall be instructed in use of life preservers.

Q. What is the penalty for any licensed officer who shall authorize
or permit the carrying of any light, electric or otherwise, not
required by law, that will in any way interfere with distinguishing
the signal lights?
A. Revocation or suspension of his license.

Q. When should the vessel's drafts be taken and entered in the logbook?
A. Before departing from her loading port or place for a voyage by
sea.

Q. What does the law state in regard to the rating of the lookouts?
A. That "no boy shall be placed on the lookout except for the purpose of learning."

Q. When a vessel is in port and the power plant is to be shut down
or made inoperative for a period, what precautions must be taken?
A. In addition to properly mooring and securing the vessel, the law
requires that, in vessels over 1000 tons gross, there shall be at
least 1 shore connection to the fire main available to each side
of the vessel in an accessible location. Suitable adapters, cut-out
valves, and check valves shall be provided in order to assure
free flow of shore supply of water on board.

Q. In port, what information for use in emergency should be immediately available for duty officer, watchmen, and other operating personnel?
A. Location of nearest telephone, with call numbers of port captain,
marine superintendent; of nearest fire alarm; of water-supply valve
and hose connections to fire main from dock (if alongside with no
power); of all controls to fire extinguishing system or systems on
board; of any explosives or dangerous cargo; and of general contents of ship's holds, deep tanks, and double-bottom tanks; also,
number and identity of persons on board.

Q. Define the term flame arrestor as it is used in the Tanker Regulations.
A. "Any device or assembly of a cellular, tubular, pressure, or
other type used for preventing the passage of flames into enclosed
spaces."

Q. Define the term flame screen as used in the Tanker Regulations.
A. "A fitted single screen of corrosion-resistant wire of at least
30 by 30 mesh, or 2 fitted screens, both of corrosion-resistant
wire, of at least 20 by 20 mesh, spaced not less than 1/2 inch

or more than 1-1/2 inches apart. "

Q. How would you mark the manual control for automatic fire dampers in ducts passing through main vertical zone bulkheads of passenger vessels?
A. In red letters at least 1/2 inch high, VENTILATION FIRE DAM-
PER, with the open and closed positions similarly marked.

Q. What is the purpose of a pressure vacuum valve required on
many types of tank vessels and what care should it receive?
A. For automatic regulation of pressure or vacuum in enclosed
spaces. It should be frequently tested, and maintained in good
working order.

Q. How must entries be made in the official logbook?
A. Every entry shall be signed by the master and by the mate or
some other member of the crew, and it shall be made as soon as
possible after the occurrence indicated. If not made on same day
as the occurrence noted, it shall be made and dated to show both
the date of the occurrence and that of the entry respecting it; but
in no case shall such entry be made more than 24 hours after
vessel's arrival of her final port of the voyage.

Q. How often shall the motor or hand-operated propelling gear of
a lifeboat be operated and how long each time?
A. The motor of each motor-propelled lifeboat shall be operated in
both the ahead and astern positions for not less than 5 minutes at
least once in each week. Hand-propelled lifeboats shall be operated at each Fire and Boat Drill.

Q. When a fire watchman fails to follow his prescribed route, or
to record each station within the specified time, what action must
be taken?
A. Such offense must be the subject of a logbook entry setting forth
the day and time of the failure in question, with names of witnesses and/or evidence such as the patrol-clock record. The offender
is thus made subject to proceedings by the Coast Guard with respect to suspension or revocation of his certificate.

Q. Why should fire extinguishers not be stowed in passenger and
crew quarters when the extinguishing medium is kept under pressure?
A. In order to avert possible injury to persons in the event of explosion of a defective extinguisher of such type.

PART II. CHIEF MATE

1. LATITUDE BY POLARIS

Q. On 1 September, 1959, in D. R. Longitude 51°-06' West, Polaris was observed at evening twilight to have a sextant altitude of 47°-30' and a bearing of 359°.5 by gyro-compass. The chronometer read 10h-45m-24s. The chronometer was 1m25s fast. The sextant index error was 1'.5 off the arc. The height of eye was 25 feet. Required: Latitude at time of sight and gyro-compass error.

A.

Chron.	22h 45m 24s	
Error	− 1m 25s	
G. M. T. , Sept. 1,	22h 43m 59s	

G. H. A. Aries at 22h	=	310° 18. 9'
Corr. for 43m 59s	=	11° 01. 6'
G. H. A. Aries	=	321° 20. 5'
Long. W.	=	51° 06. 0'
L. H. A. Aries	=	270° 14. 5'

True Az.	=	001.3°
Gyro	=	359. 5°
Gyro Error	=	1. 8° E.

Polaris h_S	=	47° 30. 0'
I. E.		+ 1. 5
Dip		− 4. 9
Refr.		− 0. 9
h_0	=	47° 25. 7'
Const.		−1° 00. 0'
		46° 25. 7'
a_0	+ 1	25. 9
a_1	+	0. 6
a_2	+	0. 9
Latitude	=	47° 53. 1' N.

3. FIX OR RUNNING FIX

Q. Enroute from Spain to Milwaukee, in D. R. Latitude 46°-10' North and Longitude 26°-05' West, three (3) celestial bodies were observed. Given the following information on the celestial bodies, determine ship's position. (Candidates may use any method.)

Body	Observed Altitude	Greenwich Hour Angle	Declination
SATURN -------	19°-24'. 9	60°-07'. 8	17°-30'. 5 S.
MOON(L. L.) ---	13°-19'. 9	321°-49'. 2	05°-45'. 2 S.
ARCTURUS ----	37°-29'. 4	441°-34'. 9	19°-24'. 6 N.

A. Saturn:

G. H. A.	60°	07. 8'	(Solution by Ageton's method)
Long.	26	05. 0 W.	
L. H. A.	34	02. 8 W.	A 25190
Dec.	17	30. 5 S.	B 2060 A 52166
			A 27250 B 7288 B 7288 A 27250
K	20°	50. 5' S.	........A 44878
Lat.	46	10. 0 N.	
K − L	67	00. 5	.... B 40827
H_c	19	17	.... A 48115 B 2507
H_0	19	24. 9	Z = N 145. 5° W A 24743
		7. 9' toward	360. 0
			Z_n = 214. 5° (P. L. 124-1/2/304-1/2°)

Moon:	G. H. A.	321° 49. 2'				
	Long.	26 05. 0 W.				
	L. H. A.	295 44. 2				
		360 00. 0				
or		64 15. 8 E.	A 4536			
	Dec.	5 45. 2 S.	B 219	A 99918		
			A 4755	B 35314	B 35314	A 4755
	K	13° 03' S.	. . . . A 64604			
	Lat.	46 10 N.				
	K — L	59 13	. . . . B 29091			
	H$_C$	13° 07'	. . . . A 64405		B 1148	
	H$_O$	13 20		Z = N 113° E A 3607		
		13' toward		Z$_n$ = 113° (P. L. 23°/203°)		

Arcturus:	G. H. A.	441° 34. 9'				
	Long.	26 05. 0 W.				
	L. H. A.	415 29. 9				
		360 00. 0				
or		55 29. 9 W.	A 8401			
	Dec.	19 24. 6 N.	B 2541	A 47843		
			A10942	B 20122	B 20122	A 10942
	K	31° 53' N.	. . . . A 27721			
	Lat.	46 10 N.				
	L — K	14 17	. . . . B 1364			
	H$_C$	37 34	. . . . A 21486		B 10094	
	H$_O$	37 29. 4		Z = N 101. 3° W	A 848	
		4. 6' away		360. 0		
				Z$_n$ = 258. 7° (P. L. 169°/349°)		

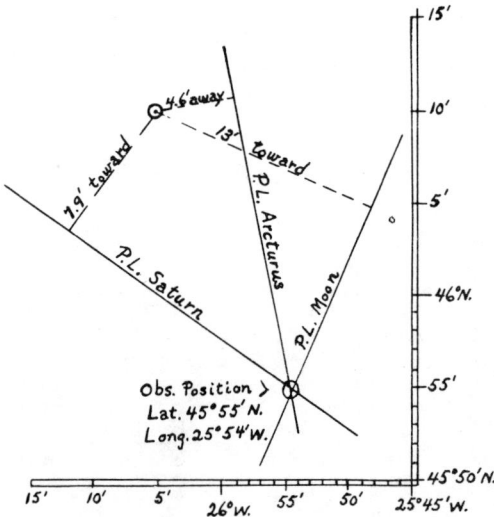

Q. The following 3 sextant altitudes of planets were obtained on
2 March, 1959. The height of eye was 57 feet, the sextant index
was 2'.0 on the arc in all observations. Given:

	Venus	Jupiter	Mars
	Observation #1	Observation #2	Observation #3
Planet sext. alt.-----	2°-09'.6	12°-47'.6	46°-13'.3
Bar. pressure ------	30.5 in.	1030 mb.	30.0 in.
Temperature -------	80° F.	28° Celsius	52° F.
		(Centigrade)	

Required: The observed altitudes.

A.

	Venus - Obs. 1	Jupiter - Obs. 2	Mars - Obs. 3
H_S	2° 09.6'	12° 47.6'	46 13.3'
I. E.	− 2.0	− 2.0	− 2.0
	2 07.6	12 45.6	46 11.3
Dip	− 7.4	− 7.4	− 7.4
	2 00.2	12 38.2	46 03.9
Refr.	−18.2	− 4.2	− 0.8
H_a	1 42.0	12 34.0	46 03.1
Temp & Bar	+ 1.2	+ 0.2	0.0
H_O	1 43.2	12 34.2	46 03.1

Q. The following 3 sextant altitudes of stars were obtained. The
height of eye was 64 feet; the sextant index error was 2'.5 off the
arc in all observations.
Given:

	Observation #1	Observation #2	Observation #3
Star sext. alt. -----	3°-56'.7	15°-21'.6	60°-01'.3
Bar. pressure -----	30.5 in.	990 mb.	30.0 in.
Temperature-------	12° F.	(−) 15° Celsius	63° F.
		(Centigrade)	

Required: The observed altitudes.

A.

	Star - Obs. 1	Star - Obs. 2	Star - Obs. 3
H_S	3° 56.7'	15° 21.6'	60° 01.3'
I. E.	+ 2.5	+ 2.5	+ 2.5
	3 59.2	15 24.1	60 03.8
Dip	− 7.8	− 7.8	− 7.8
	3 51.4	15 16.3	59 56.0
	− 12.1	− 3.5	− 0.6
H_a	3 39.3	15 12.8	59 55.4
Temp & Bar	− 1.6	− 0.4	0.0
H_O	3 37.7	15 12.4	59 55.4

Q. Given:

	No. 1 Mars	No. 2 Saturn	No. 3 Jupiter
Date -----------	26 April, 1959	7 September, 1959	29 May, 1959
GMT -----------	05h -38m-27s	14h-08m-58s	22h-38m-17s
Long.-----------	16°-23'.0 West	48°-56'.0 East	5°-57'.0 West

Required: The meridian angle and declination of the planet in each of the 3 cases. Indicate whether the planet is east or west of the meridian in each case.

A.

	Mars - 1	Saturn - 2	Jupiter - 3
GMT	Apr. 26, 5h 38m 27s	Sept. 7, 14h 08m 58s	May 29, 22h 38m 17s
GHA	188° 34.3'	285° 23.8'	343° 00.5'
Corr.	+9 36.8	+2 14.5	+9 34.3
	198 11.1	287 38.3	352 34.8
Long.	16. 23.0 W.	48 56.0 E.	5 57.0 W.
LHA	181 48.1	336 34.3	346 37.8
	360 00.0	360 00.0	360 00.0
Mer. Ang. =	178° 11.9' E.	23° 25.7' E.	13° 22.2' E.
Declination..	24° 47.5'N.	22° 40.5' S.	18° 08.9' S.

4. STAR IDENTIFICATION

Q. On 20 January, 1959, at Latitude 7°-09' South, Longitude 112°-15' West, a morning star observation is taken at 12h-48m-39s GMT of a star whose corrected altitude is 40°38'.2, and whose azimuth is 118°.9 True.

Required: The name of the star.

Candidates may use any method of solution. Show all work.

A.

G.M.T. Jan. 20d 12h 48m 39s		Z_n 118.9°	
G.H.A. Aries	299° 07'	180.0	
corr.	12 12	Z_S 61.1	Log hav 9.4113
	311 19	H_0 40° 38'	" cos 9.8802
Long.	112 15 W.	Lat 7 09	" " 9.9966
L.H.A. Aries	199 04		Log hav 9.2881
L.H.A. Star	47 55 E.		Nat " 1941
	246 59	L — H 33° 29'	" " 0830
	360 00	90 — D 63 31	Nat hav 2771
S.H.A. Star =	113 01	90 00	
	Star's Dec. = 26° 29' S.		

Star having nearest position to that indicated is Antares, as given on page 269, Nautical Almanac, 1959.

Z_S	61.1°	Log sin 9.9422
H	40° 38'	" cos 9.8802
D	26° 29'	" sec 0.0481
Star's L.H.A.	= 47° 55'	Log sin 9.8705

5. CHART NAVIGATION

Q. How does a great circle course appear on a polyconic chart?
A. As a curved line with its convexity toward the nearest pole.

Q. How are the latitude and longitude of a point found on a gnomonic chart?
A. By reference to the meridians and parallels in the immediate vicinity of the point.

Q. How is the true bearing determined between any two points on a large scale polyconic chart?
A. By the angle which a straight line representing the bearing makes with the meridian at or near mid-distance between the points.

Q. How is the distance measured on a polyconic chart?
A. By the scale along any parallel or along the central meridian.

Q. Describe the usual method for using a gnomonic chart to determine the great circle course for a ship.
A. A straight line drawn between departure and destination points lays out the great circle track. If such track appears a satisfactory one, a number of points along the route are plotted on the Mercator chart as a succession of destinations to be reached by rhumb courses. Course and distance on each leg are found by measurement on the Mercator chart.

Q. Can any chart representation of the earth's surface preserve all of the following properties: (a) The true shape of physical features. (b) Correct angular relationships. (c) Equal areas, or the representation of areas in their correct relative proportions. (d) True scale values for measuring distances. (e) The representation of great circles as straight lines. (f) The representation of rhumb lines as straight lines.
A. It cannot, excepting the case of a small area such as a harbor, all large-scale projections of which become practically identical.

Q. What is the principal feature of Mercator projection charts that makes them desirable for marine navigational use?
A. That courses and bearings are represented by straight lines.

Q. Does a Mercator projection chart correctly picture the shape of an area? Explain your answer.
A. No. With increase of distance from the equator the charted area suffers distortion by expansion at a progressive rate which very closely agrees with that of the values of secants of the latitudes considered.

Q. Are all charts oriented so that north is shown at the top of the sheet? Explain your answer.

A. No. While it is customary to orient Mercator and polyconic charts in that manner, a few of these may be drawn obliquely, as in the case of a large-scale chart featuring a coastline running in a N. E. and S. W. direction. Also, a gnomonic chart is not so oriented because the parallels appear thereon as arcs of concentric circles or, as in the case of a chart of the polar regions, wholly or partly as complete circles.

Q. State in detail how you would make use of depth curves on nautical charts to assist you in fixing your position.

A. A depth curve may be used as a line of position, crossed with a bearing of a terrestrial object or another line of position obtained from a celestial observation; or it may be advanced with course and speed of ship to intersect another such curve. It also may be followed to advantage, where an echo-sounding instrument is used, as in making the entrance to a port, until an abrupt change in depth occurs or a bearing, by radio or otherwise, of a known object is obtained.

Q. A ship X checks her position using a sextant to determine angles D and E between points A and B, and B and C, respectively. How accurate would you consider the position thus determined when plotted with a three arm protractor?

A. Since the circles passing through A, B, and X and B, C, and X coincide, position of X is indeterminate. X may occupy any place on the arc A-X-C in the conditions noted.

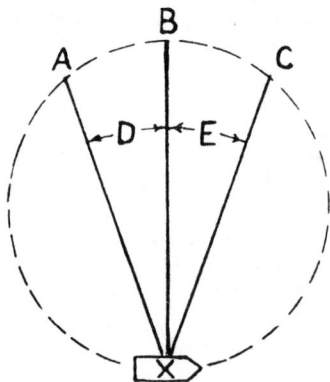

Q. State three methods by which, without obtaining the precise position, the navigator may assure himself that he is clear of any particular danger.

A. 1. By observing that vessel is outside the danger bearing, or compass bearing indicating limit of approach to the danger. 2. By keeping on, or toward the proper side of, a position line indicated by two known objects in range, or in line with each other. 3. By either a horizontal or a vertical danger angle observed by sextant as that which clears the danger.

Q. How would you determine your position by a chain of soundings?

A. By marking on tracing paper vessel's course and distances run between soundings, according to scale of chart in use. The tracing paper is then laid over the chart and moved so as to match observed soundings as noted with those given on chart, with the paper always kept closely oriented to the charted course.

Q. What is meant by the figures 1:200,000 on a chart?
A. It is the natural scale of the chart and expresses the ratio of 1 unit (as 1 inch) of distance as charted to that of 200,000 such units on the earth's surface.

Q. For what type navigation would a chart with 1:200,000 on it be suitable?
A. For a general chart, or one intended for coastwise navigation outside outlying reefs and shoals.

Q. Convert 7-1/2 meters into feet.
A. 1 meter = 3.28 feet; therefore 7-1/2 meters - 7-1/2 × 3.28 = 24.6 feet.

Q. State the purpose and describe the use of hachures on charts.
A. Hachures indicate the direction and extent of steep slopes, as those of the banks along a coast line. The length of the lines indicates height of the slope, and the purpose of these is to show the appearance of the coast as viewed from seaward.

Q. What is the length of a nautical mile?
A. 6076.1 feet; or 1852 meters; or 1.15 statute miles.

Q. State what navigational aids are indicated by the symbols below.

A. (a) Lighthouse and airport light beacon. (b) Lightship. (c) Beacon. (d) Marker or landmark. (e) Lighted buoy. (f) Fairway or mid-channel buoy. (g) Buoy, any type. (h) Black buoy. (i) Buoy having horizontal stripes, red or black.

Q. A vessel with a speed of 10 knots is proceeding through a current setting NE true with a drift of 6 knots. (a) What course should be steered to make good a course of NW true? (b) What speed will the vessel make on this course?

A.
(a) 278° true.
(b) 8 knots.

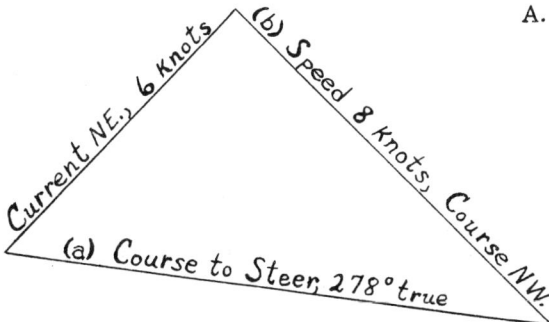

Q. Two vessels are in Latitude 50° North. They are 400 miles apart when they obtain radio direction finder bearings of each other. (a) Would they bear east or west from each other precisely on the uncorrected radio bearing? (b) Would the bearings of one differ from the other by precisely 180°?
A. (a) No.   (b) No.

Q. Sketched is a marine type radio direction finder loop antenna. Why is it important that the insulator and gasket noted by <u>A</u> be kept in good condition and clean from paint and other material?

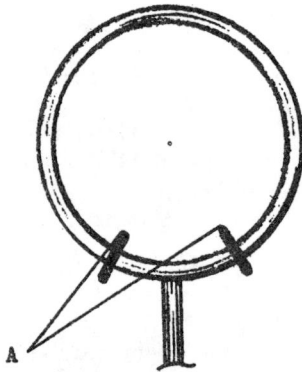

A. It is necessary to shield the loop in order to prevent it from acting as an ordinary antenna, thereby introducing errors. However, if the metal shield were not broken, it would be a shorted turn, which also is not desirable. The insulator inserted in this break in the shield must be kept free of paint in order to preserve its effectiveness. Painting would impair the insulator's purpose and likely harm the waterproofing gaskets.

Q. Would you use Mercator sailing or Middle Latitude sailing for a distance of 600 miles or more? Explain your answer.
A. Mercator sailing, in order to eliminate the error arising at such distances due to the assumption that departure made good is measured on the mid-latitude parallel between the points considered.

Q. What accuracy can be expected normally with bearings furnished by shore radio direction finder stations?
A. To within 2° on either side of the bearing given, if distance of station is less that 150 miles.

Q. How would you regard bearings by shore radio direction finder stations which were described, as doubtful, approximate or second class?
A. These should be disregarded, unless they give warning of an impending danger, in which case they should be used, but with extreme caution.

Q. For courses near 090° or 270°, why is the use of the Mercator sailing formulas not normally desirable?
A. Due to the rapidly increasing differences of tangent and secant values for courses approaching 90° and 270°, large errors are likely to ensue unless both the data given and the solution are

rigorously precise. Hence the formulas are considered incompatible with safe and practicable navigational procedure.

Q. When is great circle sailing most advantageous?
A. When both departure and destination points differ greatly in longitude and not greatly in latitude of the same name, the track being free of obstructions, such as ice, land, or prevailing bad weather.

6. COMPASS DEVIATION

Q. Enroute from Philadelphia to Liverpool, in D. R. Latitude 42°-00' North and Longitude 50°-00' West, an azimuth of the star γ (Gamma) Ursa Minoris was observed. The following data was obtained.

Compass Bearing of Star	Greenwich Hour Angle	Declination of Star
28°-00' psc	255°-55'. 6	71°-59'. 1 N.

Variation for the locality was 24°-36'. 0 West

Required:The true azimuth and deviation of standard compass.

Candidates may use any method of solution.

A. G. H. A. of star   255° 55. 6'
    Long. W.   50   00. 0
                    205   55. 6
                    360   00. 0

t	154 04. 4 E.	Log hav 9. 9776 ...	Log sin 9. 6408
1	42° 00' N.	" cos 9. 8711	
d	71 59 N.	" cos 9. 4904	cos 9. 4904
		" hav 9. 3390	
		N hav 2183	
1 - d	29 59 ...... N	" 0669	
90 - h	64° 34'...... N	" 2852	
h =	25 26 .... sec 0. 0443		

                    Z_n = 8° 37'   Log sin 9. 1755
              Compass = 28   00
              Comp. error = 19   23 W.
              Variation = 24   36 W.
              Deviation = 5° 13' E.

11. PILOTING

Q. Your vessel is steering 283° True, a light is sighted bearing 219° p. s. c. , variation 23° East, deviation 1° East. On what compass bearing must the light be again observed so that the run between bearings will equal the distance off when the light bears 193° True?
A. Course 283° true, comp. error 24° E, gives 259° as course p. s. c. 1st. bearing p. s. c. is then 40° on bow. Table 7, Bowditch, under "Difference between Course and 1st. Bearing" 40°, find Factor 1. 00 in 2nd. column abreast 79°. 259° − 79° = 180° p. s. c.

Note: Problems may be given pertaining to piloting which are under other titles in this book.

Q. On course 104° p. g. c., gyro error 1° West, a light is sighted bearing 113° p. s. c., variation 23° East, deviation 1° West. On what gyro bearing must the light be observed so that the run between bearings will equal the distance off when the light bears 194° p. g. c. ?

A. 1st. Bearing 113° p. s. c., comp. error 22° E., gives 135° true; gyro error 1° W gives 1st. Bearing as 136° p. g. c., or 32° on bow. Table 7, Bowditch, gives Factor 1. 00 abreast 59° on bow as 2nd. Bearing, or light must be observed on 104° + 59° = 163° p. g. c.

Q. On course 283° True, a light is sighted bearing 228°p. s. c., variation 23° East, deviation 3° East. On what bearing must the light be observed so that the run between bearings will equal the distance off when the light bears 167° p. s. c. ?

A. 1st. Bearing 228° p. s. c., comp. error 26° E. gives 254° true, or 29° on bow. True Course − 26° E = 257° p. s. c. With 1st Bearing 29° on bow, Factor 1. 00 is found in Table 7 abreast 51° on bow as 2nd. Bearing. Course 257° p. s. c. − 51° = 206° p. s. c.

Q. A ship is steering 101° p. g. c., variation 23° East, deviation 3° West, which is 82° p. s. c. A light is sighted bearing 129° True. On what gyro bearing must the light be observed so that the run between bearings would equal the distance off when the light bears 191° gyro?

A. Course 82° p. s. c., comp. error 20° E, gives true course 102° and gyro error 1° E. 1st. Bearing 129° true = 27° on bow. Table 7, with 27° on bow as 1st. and 46° as 2nd. Bearing gives 1. 00 as Factor. 102° + 46° = 148° true as 2nd Bearing = 147° p. g. c.

Q. It is desired to avoid coming closer than within 0. 8 miles of a light listed as 110 feet above high water level. Determine the proper vertical danger angle in this case and state how you would use it.

A. D = . 56h ÷ v', or . 8 = (. 56 × 110) ÷ v' = 61. 6 ÷ v'. Therefore, v', or number of minutes in the vertical danger angle, = 61. 6 ÷ . 8 = 77', or angle is 1° 17'. (Also see Table 9, Bowditch.)

As light is approached, measure by sextant the vertical angle subtended by the lantern's center and the shore line (limit of high water). As long as the angle does not exceed 1° 17', vessel will come no closer than . 8 mile from the light.

12. AIDS TO NAVIGATION

Q. How are arcs of visibility and limits of a light given in a light list?

A. Arcs of visibility or obscured sectors of lights are given in degrees, in a clockwise direction from seaward toward the light, or as observed from a vessel.

Q. From what reference point is the height of a light measured?

A. Level of mean high water.

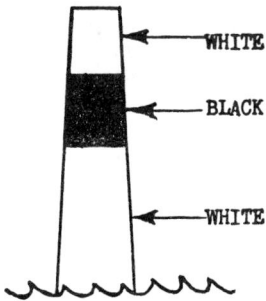

Q. What is indicated by the white and black alternate horizontally banded buoy sketched?

A. The buoy marks a fishing-net area.

Q. Describe how light phase characteristics are assigned to buoys in the lateral system of buoyage of the United States.

A. Port and starboard hand buoys, regularly flashing, occulting, or quick-flashing. Mid-channel buoys, short-long flashing. Buoys marking junctions or obstructions that may be passed on either side, interrupted quick-flashing.

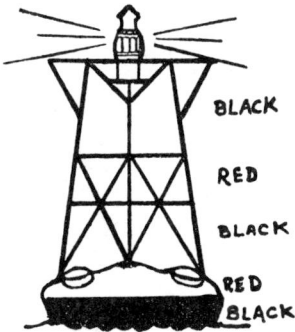

Q. Entering from seaward you sight the black and red horizontal band buoy shown. (a) Which side is best to leave it on in passing? (b) What number would you expect it to have? (c) What color light would you expect it to show? (d) What light phase characteristic would it likely have? (e) Sketch the chart symbol for the buoy.

A. (a) Port side. (b) No number; it may be lettered. (c) White or green. (d) Interrupted quick-flashing. (e)

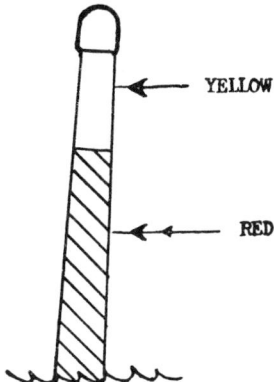

Q. A buoy painted yellow and red as illustrated is used in what system of navigational aids?

A. In the marking system for the intracoastal waterways.

Q. What action should be taken if a light is found to be extinguished or any other defect is noted in its operation?

A. If in U.S. territory, such defect should be reported by the most prompt means available to the Commander of the U.S. Coast Guard District concerned.

Q. How may the color of a light be affected by atmospheric conditions?
A. A white light may take on a reddish hue.

Q. What is the purpose of international numbers assigned to major seacoast lights in the Light List?
A. To facilitate identification, reporting of defects, etc., when vessels are in foreign waters.

13. SPEED BY REVOLUTIONS

Q. Propeller pitch 17.7 feet, revolutions per day 81,630, calculate
the day's run allowing 6 per cent slip.

A.
$$\text{Day's run} = \frac{81630 \times 17.7 \times (1.00 - .06)}{6076.1} = 223.5 \text{ miles.}$$

	81630	Log	4.91185
	17.7	"	1.24797
	.94	"	9.97313
			6.13295
	6076.1	"	3.78363
Run =	223.52	"	2.34932

15. INSTRUMENTS AND ACCESSORIES

Q. Do Loran sky wave corrections represent the exact amount of
correction necessary or are they merely average correction values?
Explain.

A. They represent average correction values for converting sky wave
readings to the equivalent ground wave readings. With increase of
distance from transmitting station such corrections become more
accurate due to the lesser effect on the sky wave path by changes
in density or height of the ionosphere. Use of sky waves at distances less than 250 miles from either master or slave station is
not recommended.

Q. Are Loran sky waves as reliable and accurate for navigational
purposes as ground waves?

A. No.

Q. What precautions must be borne in mind in celestial navigation
or piloting, when the navigator uses lines of position that cross
at small angles?

A. That small errors in plotting, in actual observation of a bearing, or in the calculated azimuth result in relatively large errors
in the vessel's charted position.

Q. Where is the most unfavorable area for obtaining a line of position from a pair of Loran transmitters?

A. Near or along the base line extension.

Q. Describe the factors which influence the accuracy of a fix obtained by using Loran lines of position.

A. Accuracy of a Loran fix depends upon that of each line of position and the angle at which the lines intersect. Factors governing
accuracy of position lines are proper synchronization of signals;
vessel's position with relation to transmitting stations; uncertainty
of signals' travel time where sky waves are employed; observer's
skill in making the readings; alignment of the indicator; incorrect
geographical position of transmitters; and errors in plotting position lines.

Q. Explain briefly how the 180° ambiguity in radio direction finder bearings may be resolved.

A. The sense antenna's output is the same intensity with signals from any direction. If this output is exactly equal to maximum output of the loop, it will cancel the output from one side and double that from the other, since polarity in the two sides is opposite. With such an arrangement a single minimum signal results, and the 180° ambiguity is thus removed.

Q. If a ship's radio direction finder is fitted with a quadrantal error compensator, will it be affected by changes made in the set or its surroundings?

A. The changes indicated will have no less effect on the insturment's accuracy on that account.

16. MAGNETISM, DEVIATION AND COMPASS COMPENSATION

Q. Name and describe the functions of A, B, C and D in the sketch shown.

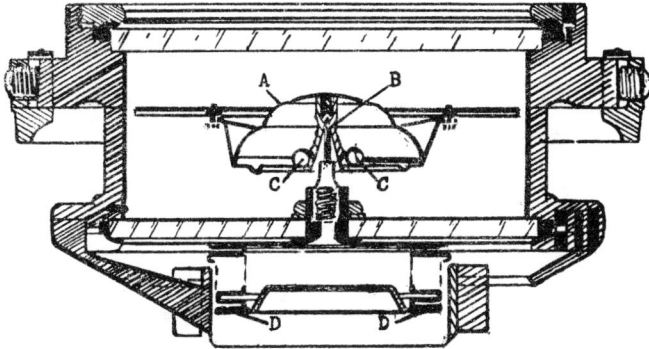

A. A = Central float or air chamber which floats card and its magnets in liquid-filled bowl, with objective of providing freest possible movement of card-float-magnet assembly by reducing friction on pivot to a minimum. B = Pivot having a hard tip (usually of iridosmium) on which rests the jewel bearing in center of card-float-magnet assembly. C = Magnets which are set in the card's N. — S. line to give compass its direction-indicating power. D = An expansion bellows which provides for effect of temperature change in the fluid, keeping the bowl full.

Q. Using the Napier diagram shown at top of page 110:
(a) Determine the magnetic course when steering 271° by compass.
(b) Determine the compass course to steer to make a magnetic course of 260°.

A. (a) "Depart by dotted, return by plain." 271° comp. gives 251°
mag.
  (b) "Depart by plain, return by dotted." 260° mag. gives 280°
comp.

Q. At what point in a bar magnet is the attraction greatest?
A. At and near its ends.

Q. If an unmagnetized soft iron bar is brought near a compass, how
should it be held to exert the maximum effect?
A. Vertically, with either its upper or its lower end in the E. - W.
line indicated by the card.

Q. What is meant by dip (also known as magnetic inclination, or
magnetic latitude)?
A. Angle of depression which lines of force of earth's magnetic
field make with the horizontal; or, angle which a freely suspended
bar magnet in the N. - S. magnetic line makes with the horizontal
at a given magnetic latitude.

Q. In adjusting the magnetic compass, is it best to place fewer
magnets very close to the compass or more magnets farther away
from the compass? Explain your answer.
A. More magnets farther away. Fewer magnets close to the compass tend to disturb the symmetry of the magnetic field at the
compass. Especially in higher latitudes, and where magnets must
be placed with their poles red to red or blue to blue with relation
to the compass-card magnets, the closer correcting force reduces
directive power of the latter and hence the instrument's efficiency.

Q. On what magnetic heading of the vessel is the maximum deviation caused by induced magnetism in vertical soft iron?
A. On East or West.

Q. Where is there no induced magnetism in vertical soft iron?
A. At the magnetic equator.

Q. Would you regard <u>A</u>, <u>B</u>, <u>C</u> or <u>D</u> in the sketch as representing
correct placing of the iron in a Flinders bar holder? Why?

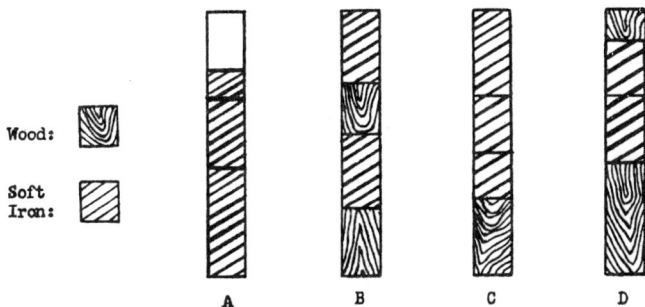

A. <u>C</u>. Because it satisfies the required conditions of being a homo-
geneous bar (soft iron) and having its upper end properly set with
respect to the compass-card's magnets.

Q. What is the effect of a change of latitude on uncorrected deviation due to permanent magnetism?
A. Deviation will increase due to decrease of compass-needle's
north-seeking power with increased magnetic latitude, or distance
from magnetic equator; i.e., with decrease of horizontal component of earth's total magnetic force.

Q. Why is it desirable: (a) To check a compass adjustment on opposite cardinal headings to that of initial placement of correctors;
(b) To check the quadrantal sphere positions at an adjacent inter-
cardinal heading from that of initial positioning; (c) To <u>halve</u> any
errors found in each instance?
A. (a) and (b). Because the adjustment may have corrected a constant deviation such as that caused by an inaccurate azimuth mirror,
a faulty value of the variation, a calculation error, or an incorrectly placed lubber line. (c) Since a constant deviation may have
been corrected as noted in (a) and (b), its value in each instance
will appear doubled. In <u>halving</u> the deviation thus observed, a constant deviation (or, more correctly, the constant component of
total deviation) remains uncompensated, as it should be.

Q. How would you correct easterly quadrantal deviation on a SW
heading?
A. With ship's head S.W. magnetic, move the quadrantal spheres
toward the compass until deviation disappears; i.e., until ship's
head by compass coincides with her magnetic heading. Then secure the spheres. (Each sphere should be kept exactly the same
distance from center of the compass-card throughout the operation.)

Q. If the westerly deviation increases on westerly headings as the
vessel steams south, what adjustment should be made in the Flin-
der's bar?

A. Reduce the Flinders bar's length or remove it altogether. This condition indicates, in north latitudes, an overcompensation by Flinders bar and an under-compensation by fore-and-aft magnets.

If vessel reaches the magnetic equator, where vertical induction is nil, compass may be corrected by the magnets for error due to permanent magnetism on W'ly (or E'ly) courses. Upon a subsequent substantial change of latitude, deviation arising on these courses may then be corrected by Flinders bar. Thus the bar will be adjusted for any future latitude change.

Q. How would you correct your compass for westerly error due to permanent magnetism?
A. With ship's head East magnetic, use fore-and-aft magnets, blue pole forward. With ship heading North magnetic, use thwartship magnets, blue pole to starboard. Place ship on the opposite headings and remove half the error remaining, if any.

18. TIDES AND CURRENTS

Q. What is meant by the term vulgar establishment of a port?
A. Average interval, expressed in hours and minutes, between time of transit (upper or lower) of full or new moon and next high water.

Q. What is the diurnal range of the tides?
A. Difference in heights of high and low water on a given day or a number of consecutive days; where tide is chiefly diurnal, difference in heights of mean higher high water and mean lower low water.

Q. What causes the difference in height between two successive high waters of the tides?
A. This difference, called diurnal inequality, is attributed to the effect of the moon's position in declination. When, e.g., she has a high declination, the tide wave following her upper transit will attain greater height than that following lower transit, except at places on or near the equator. This is explained by the moon's attraction occurring in a direction oblique to the plane of the equator. The upper transit, or higher tide, being about 180° different in longitude from that of the lower transit, it follows that the earth's rotation brings about alternate high and higher high waters each half lunar day.

Q. How would you determine the time of high and low water for a locality not listed in the Tide Tables?
A. To the local time of the moon's transit (upper or lower) as determined from G.M.T. of transit given in the Nautical Almanac, add the mean high water lunitidal interval or establishment of the port, as usually given on a chart of port concerned. To the result, which is time of high water for the day in question, add or subtract 6 hours, 13 minutes, or a fourth lunar day, for time of low water.

Q. Define the term <u>lunitidal interval</u> and state the various types of
lunitidal intervals that may occur.

A. Interval of time between upper or lower transit of the moon and
a particular phase of the tide—generally the next high water.
Mean high water lunitidal interval or <u>establishment of the port;</u>
<u>high water full and change</u> (H W F & C) or <u>vulgar establishment.</u>
The last terms denote, respectively, the average elapsed time in
a whole month from the moon's upper or lower transit until next
high water and the same elapsed time on days of full and new
moon only.

Q. At Longview, on the Columbia River (Lat. 46°-06' North and
Long. 122°-58' West) on 21 October 1959: (a) What is the time and
velocity of the maximum PM ebb current? (b) What is the direction
and the average velocity of the ebb current at this point? (c) Under
what conditions would tabulated data of the Current Tables be in-
applicable to this position?

A. 21 Oct. , 1959, max. ebb Gray's Harb. Ent. 0653   Vel. 1. 9 kts.

Time diff.   +540   Ratio   . 7

max. ebb Longview . . . . 1233 . . . .   1. 3 kts.

(a)   or 0. 33 p. m.

(b)   315° true, 2. 0 kts.

(c)   During freshets

Q. At Newburg, New York (Lat. 41°-30' North and Long. 74° -00'
West) on 29 July, 1959: (a) What is the time and velocity of maximum PM ebb current? (b) What is the average velocity of the ebb
at this point? (c) In what period of the year might you expect values other than those tabulated in the Hudson River?

A. 29 July, 1959, max. ebb Narrows   0801   Vel. 1. 6 kts.

Time diff.   415   Ratio   . 6

max. ebb Newburgh 1216   . 96

(a)   or 0. 16 p. m. . . . . . . or   1. 0 kt.

(b)   1. 1 kts.

(c)   In autumn, winter, or spring

Q. At the Columbia River Entrance (N. Jetty) on 4 February, 1959:
(a) What is the time and height of PM low water? (b) What is the
mean range of tides for this locality? (c) What is the diurnal range
of tides for this locality? (d) What is the range of PM tides at
this locality?

A. 4 Feb. , 1959, Low Water Astoria 1726. . . . . . . Ht. — 0. 4 ft.

Time diff. — 115   Ht. diff. — . 1

L. W. Columbia R. Entrance   1611 . . . . . . Ht. — . 3

(a)   or   4. 11 p. m.   H. W. Ht.   7. 0

(b)   6. 0 ft.   diff.   — . 5

(c)   7. 6 ft.   H. W.   6. 5 ft.

(d)   6. 5 — (— . 3) = 6. 8 ft. range

Q. At Godthaab, Greenland on 4 July, 1959: (a) What is the time
and height of AM low water? (b) What is the range of AM tides
for this date at this locality?

A. 4 July, 1959, Low Water Argentia   0052   Ht.   0. 2 ft.
                              Time diff. − 46   Ratio   2
              L. W. Godthaab   0006   . 4
    Ht. H. W. 4. 0   (a)   or   0. 06 a. m.   +1. 5
    Ratio   2   Ht.   1. 9 ft.
                8. 0   (b)   9. 5 − 1. 9 = 7. 6 ft. range
              + 1. 5
                9. 5

19. OCEAN WINDS, WEATHER AND CURRENTS

Q. What is the meaning of the term dew point?
A. It is the temperature of the atmosphere at which its water content condenses.

Q. What is a hygrometer?
A. An instrument for measuring the relative humidity and thence the dew point of the atmosphere.

Q. What do the following named instruments measure? (a) Hygrograph. (b) Psychrometer. (c) Thermograph. (d) Barograph.
A. (a) Relative humidity of atmosphere.
    (b) Relative humidity of atmosphere.
    (c) Continuous record of temperature.
    (d) Continuous record of atmospheric pressure.

Q. What is an isotherm?
A. On weather maps, a line joining all places having the same air temperature.

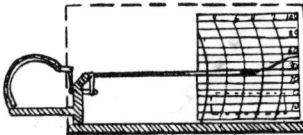

Q. Referring the the sketch: (a) What is the name of the instrument, used to record temperature? (b) State how the bimetallic element causes changes in temperature to be recorded.
A. (a) Thermograph. (b) The pen-arm is linked to the bimetallic bow so as to be moved according to variations in curvature of the bow caused by changes of temperature. The bow consists of two metals of different expansion coefficients, and so opens with a rising temperature due to the greater expanding rate of its inside metal, which tends to straighten it; conversely with decreasing temperatures.

Q. What is saturation? Explain in full.
A. The word signifies "state of being full," as applied to the atmospheric humidity condition. In the term saturation point, we indicate the air as being filled to capacity with moisture, or a relative humidity of 100% prevails.

Q. Convert (—) 15° Celsius (Centigrade) into the temperature Fahrenheit.

A. $F. = \frac{9}{5}C + 32 = \frac{-15 \times 9}{5} + 32 = -27 + 32 = +5°$ Fahrenheit,

or the same as found in Table 15, Bowditch.

Q. Describe the type of precipitation associated with the approach of a warm front and a cold front.

A. With the warm front approaching an area in which temperature is above freezing, a steady rain of considerable duration may be expected; or, if below freezing conditions prevail, precipitation will begin with rain, changing to sleet and snow. With the cold front, the clouds of which approach rapidly as compared with those of the warm front, precipitation takes the form of heavy rain slowly diminishing and of comparatively short duration.

Q. How is the barometric pressure at sea level indicated on a weather map at sea and on a ship's report (the symbol PPP designates the pressure on the standard form for reports)?

A. According to the height of the mercury column in a barometer, which also may be shown on an aneroid barometer, as expressed in inches, millimeters, or millibars.

Q. What is the sea-water pressure at 100 fathoms depth?

A. Pressure in lbs. per in.^{2} is .444 times the depth in feet. At 100 fathoms, or 600 feet, $P = 600 \times .444 = 266.4$ lbs. per in.^{2}

Q. How is atmospheric pressure expressed in meteorology; i.e., in what units is it measured?

A. In inches, millimeters, or millibars, each of which indicates the graduations of the mercury column in a mercurial barometer.

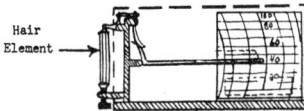

Hair Element →

Q. Explain how the hair hygrograph records the humidity.

A. A number of strands of human hair are set under tension so as to move the pen-arm as required when shrinkage or stretching of the hair takes place. Shrinkage occurs in dry air; stretching, with increase of humidity.

Q. Explain how the temperature, pressure, and volume of gas are related. State in words or in mathematical notation the gas laws.

A. At constant temperature, volume of a gas varies inversely as its pressure, or $P \times V = C$, i.e., pressure times volume is a constant. Also, the pressure increases proportionately with rise in temperature, or the ratio of pressure to temperature is a constant, or $P \div T = C$. With a given volume, the relation of pressures at different temperatures may be expressed as $P_1 : P_2 = T_1 : T_2$.

Q. How is the pressure affected by the passage of a front?
A. Pressure decreases with passage of a warm front and increases with that of a cold front.

Q. Define: (a) A bar. (b) A millibar.
A. As indicating atmospheric pressure: (a) 14.50 pounds per square inch; or 29.53 inches mercury; or 1000 millibars. (b) .001 bar; or 0.0145 pound per square inch; or 0.0295 inch mercury.

Q. What is a gradient?
A. Decrease or increase of a quantity with distance in a given direction.

Q. What is advection fog?
A. That common type of fog formed when warm, moist air blows over a cold surface and is cooled below its dew point; or, when cold air blowing over a warm surface, as that of the sea, absorbs and becomes "clouded" with excess moisture.

Q. What is an air mass?
A. Extensive body of air within which temperature and moisture conditions are uniform in any horizontal plane.

Q. How does a body of air acquire characteristic properties?
A. A body of air is a mixture of nitrogen, oxygen, some other gases in lesser quantity, and a single, changing ingredient termed water vapor. It is the presence of the last-named element in varying quantity which gives the air its descriptive term dry or moist, its value ranging from nearly zero to 30 parts per 1000. Air above a desert may be characterized as warm and dry, over the tropical ocean as warm and moist; that over a cold area may be cold and dry, while its passage over the sea changes it to cold and wet. Cold air holds little water compared with warm air's great capacity. Hence a body of air acquires its characteristic properties by its amount of water vapor held in suspension and its temperature.

Q. What are the phenomena, characteristic of the passage of a cold front, which are associated with wind shifts?
A. Rapidly moving clouds, usually of the alto-cumulus and cumulus type, forming in a squall line, with a few brief showers; strong, shifting, gusty winds which settle down in a N.W. direction (in N. Hemisphere); barometer rising sharply with clearing weather.

Q. What is the Wave period?
A. The time interval between passage of successive wave crests at a stationary point.

Q. How is the Wave period determined?
A. Period in seconds = $\sqrt{}$ (Length of wave $\div$ 5.12).

Q. What is the name of the cloud type which gives rise to halos of the sun and moon?
A. Cirro-stratus.

Q. How is alto-stratus distinguished from cirro-stratus and nimbo-stratus?
A. Cirro-stratus is a high cloud of thin, whitish or veil-like milky appearance, and nimbo-stratus is the low, dark, typical rain cloud which gives steady or intermittent precipitation but not showers, while alto-stratus is a cloud formation of middle height having a grayish or bluish gray appearance, covering the sky as a sheet or a fibrous veil.

Q. Name six atmospheric processes which cause air to be cooled below its dew point, thus causing condensation and clouds.
A. Passage of a cold front; passage of a warm front; passage of cold air over a warm surface of sea or land; passage of warm air over a cold surface; rising warm air from a heated area, in a more or less saturated condition, being cooled in lowering temperatures aloft; warm air in horizontal motion being suddenly deflected upward by a land elevation.

Q. What sequence of cloud types is characteristic of the approach of a warm front?
A. Cirrus, cirro-stratus, cirro-cumulus, alto-stratus, stratus or strato-cumulus.

Q. What are the signs that may indicate the proximity of ice?
A. Scattered pieces of ice floating about; an abrupt smoothing of sea or gradual lessening of swell; appearance of ice-blink, or yellowish glare in the sky above an ice field, becoming whitish if clouds are present; presence of many birds and seals; marked drop in temperature if ice is to windward; at night, in clear weather, the sky along the ice is markedly lighter than the rest of the horizon.

Q. What is a lead in ice?
A. A widened crack or opening in an ice field affording passage for a vessel.

Q. What are the causes of packing of compact slush, or packing of hummocked-ice?
A. Pressure of one or more floes against another, as by a continuous breeze or by a current; also by pressure of a floe against fast ice, or that along a shore.

Q. How should an ice field be entered?
A. Enter from leeward, if possible, at slow speed and at right angles with the ice edge, avoiding projecting tongues. If an offshore wind is blowing, work toward shore for a probable lead or opening. In any case, look for the weakest ice or any open water

that will carry ship in the general direction of her course. Get all possible information on the extent and movements of ice in the area before attempting to navigate through the often deceiving floe or field.

Q. Why is it standard procedure to rig for towing before reaching ice, when vessels are to proceed in an ice convoy?

A. So that, in the event of passage through ice becoming difficult, each vessel may be ready for prompt assistance by the accompanying ice-breaking vessel, or a "mutual tandem" tow of entire convoy may be arranged.

Q. How are ships moored to ice?

A. By ice anchors and hawsers. The ice anchor is a stockless, single-fluked hook which is embedded in the ice. Though not as convenient, any anchor of suitable weight with its flukes set in a hole made for the purpose will be found satisfactory.

Q. What precautions should be taken by a vessel that is drifting with engines stopped during the night or during a period of poor visibility in an area where icebergs are prevalent?

A. Keep a sharp lookout alow and aloft; listen for sounds of cracking and noise of pieces of ice falling into water; watch for floating pieces; be specially alert if sea suddenly lessens or air temperature falls; if visibility is very poor, sound ship's whistle at intervals for a possible echo from a berg; if vessel is radar-equipped, use the system fully, but do not wholly rely upon results.

Q. What influence has the earth's rotation on air currents moving from a position of high pressure to a position of relatively low pressure?

A. They are diverted from a direct path toward the right in the Northern Hemisphere and toward the left in the Southern Hemisphere.

Q. When a vessel transmits a radio message advising of a tropical storm, is the vessel liable for the cost of the message?

A. No; such message is free of cost to all ships concerned.

Q. How are messages concerning storms preceded when transmitted by radiotelegraphy?

A. By the signal TTT Storm.

Q. What information should be included in a message from a vessel warning of a tropical storm?

A. The message should begin with a warning statement indicating there is good reason to believe a tropical storm is making up or approaching, or an ominous disturbance is apparent. Then should follow the G. M. T., date, and ship's position; barometric pressure and tendency during past three hours; true wind direction and force; squall and precipitation notes; state of sea and description of swell with direction from which it comes; true course and speed of ship.

Q. How may swells indicate the approach of a tropical storm?

A. An unusually long swell coming from the direction of the storm may set in two to three days before arrival of a cyclone. It grows heavier with the storm's approach.

Q. How does the appearance of a tropical cyclone, as depicted by the isobars drawn on a weather map, differ from the appearance of an extratropical cyclone originating in the middle latitudes?

A. They are much more circular in shape, especially toward the center. Those of extratropical cyclones are less symmetrical, often partly oval or otherwise distorted from the circular, but as they grow older the circular pattern usually develops.

Q. Can storms with gale winds occur under anti-cyclonic conditions with rising barometers? Explain your answer.

A. No, since the high pressure area is one of outflowing winds of small force which represent the diffusion of a slowly settling air mass from aloft. In anti-cyclonic conditions a rising barometer indicates only lighter winds and clearing skies.

Q. The maximum height of storm waves can be approximated by the formula:

$H = 1.5 \sqrt{F}$ where H is the height in feet and
F is the fetch in nautical miles

Using this formula, determine the maximum height of storm waves that may be encountered when a gale is blowing from a direction in which the coastline is distant 64 miles.

A. $H = 1.5 \sqrt{F} = 1.5 \times \sqrt{64} = 1.5 \times 8 = 12.0$ feet max. height of waves.

Q. In stormy weather at sea, is the direction in which the waves are moving always the same as the direction of the wind? State the reasons for your answer.

A. No. Where a shift of wind occurs, the sea will continue its direction until "beaten down" by that arising from the new wind. Often a continued swell, or remains of the old sea, may run for some hours as a cross sea.

Q. In which semicircle of a tropical cyclone would a vessel be if the wind shifted clockwise while she was hove to in the Northern Hemisphere?

A. In the dangerous semicircle.

Q. In the Southern Hemisphere, how should a steam vessel maneuver if she is on the storm track in front of the center of a tropical cyclone? Answer in full.

A. Run with wind 2 points on port quarter. Hold course and make as much speed as possible. If vessel makes bad weather of it, slow down but continue until wind shifts to right and weather improves.

Q. Hove to in the Northern Hemisphere, under tropical cyclone conditions the barometer is rising and the wind is shifting counter-clockwise. What is the vessel's probable position relative to the center of the storm and what action should be taken to leave the storm area as rapidly as possible?
A. Ship is in the rear quadrant of navigable semicircle. Bring the wind on starboard quarter, or as near the beam as possible if sea conditions permit, and proceed until weather clears up.

Q. Explain the value of synoptic charts of weather conditions for maneuvering of vessels in extratropical storms.
A. In that the information conveyed indicates the path or trend of bad weather conditions along the vessel's track, and consequently advises the navigator of any necessary departure from his proposed route in order to avoid extremely hazardous or delaying effects of such storms.

Q. Describe a tropical cyclone.
A. A violent storm originating in a tropical area, characterized by high velocity winds spirally rotating about a center of very low barometric pressure, accompanied by almost continuous rain. The whole circulating mass moves along at from about two or three miles per hour to as much as thirty, in a westerly direction at its beginning and usually recurves to the eastward in from Latitude 25° to 30°. Its winds reach a velocity of 150 miles per hour in many cases.

Q. What are foehn and chinook winds?
A. The term given to winds which, having encountered a mountain barrier and lost a large proportion of their moisture in the ascent, blow down the leeward side of the high land being reheated in the descent by compression. The general term for such wind is foehn; in the Rocky Mountain region it is called chinook. A warm dry wind, it may blow with any force, from that of a gentle breeze to a gale.

Q. State the three elements which compose the pressure tendency.
A. Amount of change in barometer readings; whether change is up or down; and time elapsed between observations.

Q. How is the pressure tendency determined: (a) With a barograph; (b) With a barometer?
A. (a) By noting the change of pressure in a given period of time, as indicated by the pen-mark on the rotating chart. (b) By noting the amount of fall or rise in a given elapsed time.

Q. A vessel discharging cargo at anchor observes an approaching

Q. A vessel discharging cargo at anchor observes an approaching thunderstorm. A flash of lightning is followed after 12 seconds by thunder. Six minutes later another flash of lightning is followed in 8 seconds by thunder after the second flash of lightning. How much time does the vessel have to rig rain tents or cover the hatches before the storm reaches her?

A. Sound travels at approximately .18 mile per second.
At 1st obs. storm is 12 x .18 = 2.16 miles off.
At 2nd obs. storm is 8 x .18 = <u>1.44</u> miles off.
In 6 minutes storm travels <u>.72</u> mile.
Then .72:1.44 = 6:x; x = (1.44 x 6) ÷ .72 = 12 minutes to reach.

Q. What is the effect of the earth's rotation on the direction of current?

A. It deflects the set, or direction of flow, toward the right in the Northern Hemisphere and toward the left in the Southern Hemisphere, by an angle varying from about 15° in shallow coastal areas to about 40° in the oceans.

Q. Under certain conditions in the Northern Hemisphere it may be assumed that the current sets 30° to the right of the direction in which it is driven by the wind, and its velocity is 2 percent of the wind velocity. (a) Basing your answer on the foregoing statement, estimate the direction and velocity of the current that may be expected if the wind is from the east at 35 knots. (b) Using the direction and velocity of the current estimated in (a), find the course to steer to make good a course of 210° if the speed of your vessel is 12 knots. To solve this problem, consider current only, disregarding any other factors that may be involved.

A. (a) Wind E. = 90°. Set = 90 + 180 + 30 = 300°. Vel. = 35 x .02 = .7k.
(b) In this case the current sets 90° to right of course to be made good; so that, using Traverse Tables, with 12 as D. Lat. and .7 as Dep., gives course 3-1/2°. Then 210° — 3-1/2° = 206-1/2° course to steer.

Q. Give a general description of <u>Buys-Ballot's</u> Law.

A. In the Northern Hemisphere, if one faces the wind, center of low pressure lies somewhat behind the right hand, and center of high pressure lies somewhat before the left hand.
In the Southern Hemisphere, if one faces the wind, center of low pressure lies somewhat behind the left hand, and center of high pressure lies somewhat before the right hand.

Q. What is a cold front?

A. The intersection with the horizontal of the advancing frontal surface of a mass of cold air.

Q. The direction of the wind in a cyclone is south. State the probable bearing of its center from the ship in the Southern Hemisphere.

A. The bearing would be 8 to 10 points to left of wind direction, or between E. and ENE.

Q. The three sketches below show the symbols used on printed weather maps to represent cold fronts, warm fronts, and occluded fronts at the surface. (a) What type front is represented by sketch No. 1? (b) What type front is represented by sketch No. 2? (c) What type front is represented by sketch No. 3?

A. (a) Cold front. (b) Occluded front. (c) Warm front.

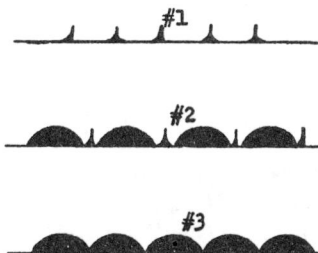

Q. Describe cirro-stratus clouds.

A. Very high clouds of whitish appearance, often completely covering the sky, sometimes taking the form of a tangled web of feathery streaks, but generally, a thin, milky veil which does not blur the outline of the sun or moon.

Q. What is an occlusion in an extratropical cyclone?

A. In the last stages of the extratropical cyclone, the closing of its warm sector by an overtaking cold front which races about the system's center. The warm air is thus totally displaced by the cold throughout the system.

22. SIGNALLING BY INTERNATIONAL CODE FLAGS, FLASHING LIGHT, LIFESAVING, STORM AND SPECIAL SIGNALS

Q. State precisely how you would express the following times using coded international code flag signals: (a) 3:18 a.m. (b) 7:56 p.m. (c) 11:01 a.m. (d) 11:01 p.m.

A.

(a) T	(b) T	(c) T	(d) T	
0	1	1	2	
3	9	1st R.	3	
1	5	0	0	
8	6	2nd R.	1	(R. = Repeater)

Q. How many flag hoists should be shown at a time.

A. One only as a rule. Where a situation demands expedient action, any number of hoists may be shown, but each must be plainly set apart from the others and displayed in the order indicated in Article 69 of the Code Book.

Q. You are on a ship constructed with twin screws and have lost both propellers. The flag signal TH means "I have lost my propeller." In signalling another vessel, how could you assure that he understands you have lost both propellers?

A. The hoist TH, followed by CIH which means both.

Q. When a vessel is in distress and has sent a radio telegraph message requesting assistance, what measure would be taken to insure that rescue craft can obtain her precise position and shortest course to take in order to assist her?

A. Approximately 10 minutes after sending out the original distress signal, vessel should transmit slowly on the distress frequency <u>MO</u> and her own call sign for 3 minutes. Also, after sending out the distress signal she should transmit 2 dashes each of approximately 10 seconds' duration, followed by her call sign, in order to permit direction-finder stations to obtain her bearing; such procedure to be repeated at frequent intervals, as necessary.

Q. What radio distress signal is provided so that a vessel may obtain assistance from other vessels even though such vessels may not have a radio operator on watch at the time the distress signal is transmitted?
A. This signal, which is provided for actuating the auto-alarm required on such vessels, consists of a series of 12 dashes sent in one minute, the duration of each dash being 4 seconds and the interval between dashes, one second.

Q. What pyrotechnic equipment must be provided on United States merchant vessels on the high seas for the purpose of indicating that they are in distress and require assistance from other vessels or the shore?
A. Twelve approved hand-held, rocket-propelled, parachute, red flare distress signals kept in a portable watertight container within the pilothouse or on the navigating bridge.

Q. If you sighted a red flare at sea, suspended by a small parachute about 300 feet above the water, with no vessels or aircraft in the vicinity of the flare, what does the signal indicate, and what action would you take?
A. This indicates a ship's boat or raft requiring assistance. I would head for the location noted with the aim of rescuing or assisting the persons involved.

Q. If an aircraft flies over your ship and circles, then crosses close ahead at a low altitude opening and closing the throttle, or changing the propeller pitch, and then heading away in a particular direction, what action would you take?
A. I would alter course to proceed in the direction last taken by the plane. His action indicates assistance is required by some surface craft or ditched plane.

Q. If, after a period, the aircraft crosses the wake close astern at a low altitude, opening and closing the throttle, or changing propeller pitch, what would this indicate?
A. It would indicate that the assistance of the surface craft thus signalled to was no longer required.

Q. What is indicated by the one-flag signal <u>U</u> or the letter <u>U</u> by blinker light?
A. "You are standing into danger."

Q. What does <u>PRB</u> mean when it is received as the first group in the text of a message sent by flashing light?

A. It indicates that the message which follows consists of code groups from the <u>International Code of Signals.</u>

Q. State the function of the model verb "glean".

A. It is to circumvent any error in interpreting a code signal which may be caused by differences in the verb forms of different languages. By including, where necessary, the applicable affirmative, negative, or interrogative form of the verb "glean," no doubt should exist as to the meaning of the signal.

Q. If you are receiving a message in Morse code, which is being transmitted by sound, what procedure should you follow when a word or group is missed?

A. Receiving vessel should immediately make the repeat sign <u>UD</u>, upon which the transmitting ship will cease signalling and then go back a few words or groups and continue the message.

Q. If at sea you sighted a buoy 3 feet in diameter and painted yellow, what action must you take?

A. This is a buoy released from a submarine on the bottom unable to surface. I would at once advise naval authorities of the position and time of sighting such buoy.

Q. What are the warning signals displayed in inland waters of the United States by Coast Guard vessels while handling or servicing aids to navigation?

A. Displayed from the yard arm: By day, 2 orange and white vertically striped balls in a vertical line not less than 3 feet or not more than 6 feet apart. By night, in a position where they may best be seen, 2 red lights in a vertical line not less than 3 feet or not more than 6 feet apart.

24. SEAMANSHIP

Q. Why is great care necessary in inspecting preformed type wire rope, when this is used for cargo falls, topping lifts, slings, guys, or other gear on a ship?

A. Because wear and tear effects on this rope are much less noticeable than in regular lay rope. Its outer wires wear thinner before breaking, and broken ends of these do not protrude as in other rope.

Q. Describe in detail how you would attach a wire rope socket.

A. Measure from end of rope the length of basket of socket. From this point serve with 3 seizings. Cut out hemp center, if any, and open out all strands. Separate all wires and straighten them out. Cleanse all with kerosene oil from ends to first seizing and wipe dry. Then dip wires for 3/4 their length in a solution of 1/2 muriatic acid and 1/2 water. (Use no stronger than this and be careful it touches no other part of the rope.) Dip wires long enough to be thoroughly cleaned and wipe dry. Bunch ends together, secure with a whipping, and slip socket over them; then cut whipping and distribute wires evenly in basket and flush with its top. Place fireclay around bottom of basket (socket) and pour in molten zinc. Use only high grade zinc, preferably heated not above 830° F. (Do not use babbitt or other antifriction metal.) Remove all seizings except the one nearest socket. Cool slowly.

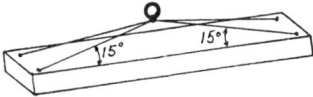

Q. What would be the effect of a wire rope fall jamming in a sheave of the purchase of a jumbo boom when lowering a weight?
A. The purchase would cease to function and both the fall and the block in which the jamming has taken place would suffer injury. This would call for replacement of the purchase as quickly as possible.

Q. A pontoon weighing 2,000 pounds is to be lifted by a four-legged bridle sling, each leg of the sling forming an angle of 15 degrees with the top of the pontoon as indicated in the sketch. What is the stress on each leg of the sling when the weight of the pontoon is suspended from it? (Refer to sketch above.)
A. 2000 ÷ 4 = 500 lbs. sustained by each leg. Stress on each leg varies as the cosecant of the angle leg makes with the horizontal. Therefore, 500 x cosec 15° = 500 x 3.86 = 1930 lbs. stress on each leg.

Q. What circumference of manila line would be required for a lifeboat fall rove off through two triple blocks if the weight of the boat is 4,000 pounds, the gear of the boat 1,050 pounds, and the capacity 30 persons?

Hint: The weight of each person by regulations is considered 165 pounds. The factor of safety required by regulations is 6. Use the formula $B = C^2 \times 900$ for computing strength of manila line, where B is breaking strength in pounds, C is circumference. Friction is considered at 10 percent loss per sheave.

A. Boat   4000 lbs.
   Gear   1050
   Persons 30   4950
   Total   10000
   Each davit   5000

Allowing 10% friction for each sheave in purchase, or 6 x 10 = 60% total friction, or 5000 x 1.60 = 8000 lbs. stress on each davit; and, since there are 6 parts at the moving block of each tackle, 8000 ÷ 6 gives the working stress of rope required.

So, with a safety factor of 6, for size of rope we have:

$$\frac{B}{6} = \frac{C^2 \times 900}{6} = C^2 \times 150 = 1333 \text{ lbs. (working stress)}$$

$$C^2 = 1333 \div 150 = 8.89$$

$$C = \sqrt{8.89} = 2.98,$$

or 3-inch circ. rope.

Q. Why is extra care necessary when winding wire rope for the purchase and topping lift of a heavy lift boom on winch drums?

A. To avoid any sudden stresses caused by slipping of riding turns and consequent injury to wire, the falls should be wound on drums with each turn laid snugly against its neighbor.

Q. Referring to the sketch: (a) With a gun tackle purchase made fast to the hauling part of a single whip as shown, how much weight at W may be lifted with a force at F of 100 pounds, allowing 10 per-cent friction loss at each sheave? (b) To lift W 3 feet, how far must the line at F be pulled? (c) What stress is put on the pad eye at C when lifting the weight?

Blocks and Tackles

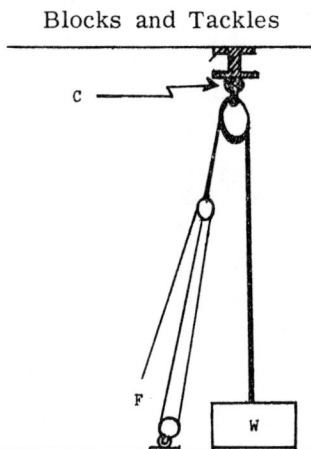

A. (a) Theoretically, P : W = 1 : 3 = 100 : 300. Friction considered as 10% for each sheave, then W = 300 — 30% = 300 — 90 = 210 lbs.

(b) W is lifted in the ratio of 1 foot to each 3-foot pull on tackle, or 1 : 3 = 3 : F. Therefore F = 3 × 3 = 9 feet.

(c) Tackle pulls 300 — 20% = 240 lbs. and W lifted is 210 lbs. Therefore, stress at C = 240 + 210 = 450 lbs.

Q. In the selection of correct thickness of grain shifting boards, what is the governing factor?

A. Length of the unsupported span of boards.

Q. In the selection of the correct rectangular cross section or diam-eter of timbers to be used as shores for grain shifting boards, what are the governing factors?

A. Length of shore and area of boards to be supported.

Q. What size of wire rope and shackles is the minimum allowed to be used for staying grain shifting boards?
A. 3-inch circumference wire and 1-inch shackles.

Q. Where must shores used for bracing grain shifting boards be bridged?
A. Where shores are 24 feet or more in length.

Q. What action must be taken if the drum of an electric winch rotates to pay out the wire under the stress of a load while the switch is in the off position?
A. Apply the mechanical foot brake which is provided for such event.

Q. What is the minimum thickness of wood to be used for hatch boards on weather deck hatches?
A. Two and three-eighths inches.

Q. What is the minimum number of tarpaulins required for covering hatches, and what is the minimum grade of the material to be used?
A. 2 tarpaulins. Waterproofed No. 4 cotton or No. 6 hemp canvas.

Q. In a steel lifeboat, what parts of the boat's structure give it longitudinal strength?
A. Keel, stem and stern posts, and gunwale with side-benches combined; also the boat's entire skin plating.

Q. What care must be taken when aluminum fittings are used on steel vessels in salt water service?
A. To guard against corrosion of the fittings by "galvanic attack" due to proximity of the steel.

Q. How do you rig an anchor buoy and how should it be handled for safety and efficiency when dropping or raising a bower anchor?
A. Make fast the buoy rope by its tail of chain or wire to the crown or an arm of the anchor; hang and lightly stop both buoy rope and buoy outside ship's rail, so that, as anchor is dropped and cable payed out, the line and buoy will be carried clear. Length of buoy rope should be about 5 fathoms greater than depth of water. When raising the anchor, before heaving it home in the pipe, buoy rope should be hauled aboard by a boat hook and thrown clear of possible injury by being jammed by the anchor, or else taken in from the anchor altogether.

Q. Describe the construction of the detachable links used to join shots of chain and the procedure of connecting and disconnecting shots.
A. The detachable link replaces the connecting shackle at each 15 fathoms of cable and in size and shape differs very little from an

ordinary stud link. It is made to allow insertion or withdrawal of
its neighboring end links of adjacent shots of chain, in connecting
and disconnecting shots, through the opening in its side formed by
removal of the detaching arrangement. This arrangement consists
of twin fittings shaped to set together and form both the stud and
the removable part of the link, the whole being locked by a simple
system of intermeshing lugs secured and keyed by a tapered pin
driven down through, and into the seat of, the stud.

Q. Within what length of time should a properly operating steering
engine be able to put the rudder from hard over on one side to
hard over on the other side with vessel going full speed ahead?
A. Such engine should be capable of shifting the rudder from hard
over on one side to hard over on the other in 30 seconds.

Q. In the event of a fireroom fire, what provisions are available
to shut off the fuel pumps?
A. They shall be provided with means of control from a readily
accessible position outside the boiler room which shall always be
accessible in the event of fire occurring at location of pumps.

Q. In anchoring in deep water, what precaution should be taken?
A. The anchor should be backed out to within a few fathoms of the
bottom, so that, in view of the unusually heavy weight of cable
payed out, proper control of the wildcat by the brake may then
be facilitated.

Q. Why must you avoid twists in the chain between the wildcat and
the anchor, when the anchor is hove tight and in the hawse pipe?
A. Because the twisted chain sets a damaging stress on both the
wildcat and the chain itself; also, it is probable a severe twist
will jam the anchor in the hawsepipe, and links fail to set properly
in riding chock.

Q. How is the wear on a shot of chain cable determined?
A. By inspection of the links and measurement of the chain's elon-
gation.

Q. How should the bitter end of anchor cables be secured in the
chain locker and why should it be so secured?
A. It should be passed through a heavy ringbolt at bottom of locker,
and its end link secured to the deckhead, preferably by a slip hook.
In this way the bitter end may be cast loose without trouble or delay, should it be necessary to slip the cable.

Q. When a vessel is moored with two anchors down, how may she
insure swinging the right way with the change of the tide?
A. Give her a sheer with the helm at last of the tide, so that
change of tide may catch her on the proper quarter; or, if this
fails, use the engines and helm as required.

Q. What could be the result of swinging the wrong way on a vessel moored with two anchors in a tideway?

A. A "cross" in the hawse, or one cable leading over the other, would be the result. Continued swings in the wrong direction would add further crosses or "turns" in the cables.

Q. If a draft of 1,000 pounds of cargo be lifted with the sling sketched here, what is the compressive stress on the spreader shown?

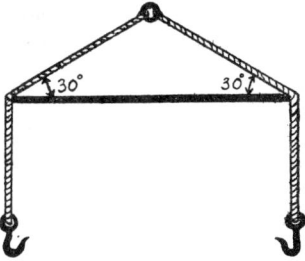

A. If a perpendicular from the ring to mid-point of spreader represent the magnitude of 1/2 the weight to be lifted W, or 500 lbs.; then 1/2 the spreader's length gives magnitude of 1/2 the thrust T.

Then,

$1/2W \div 1/2T = \tan 30°$, or $W \div T = \tan 30°$, and

$T = W \div \tan 30° = W \cot 30° = 1000 \times 1.732 = 1732$ lbs.

Q. A vessel displacing 8,000 tons making 5 knots brings up on her anchor in one hundred feet. The chain has a breaking strength of 320,000 pounds. Will the stress on the chain exceed the breaking strength?

Note: Use formula

$$F = \frac{W}{g} \times \frac{V^2}{2S}$$

where F = stress in pounds

W = displacement of the vessels in pounds

G = acceleration due to gravity, 32.16

V = speed in feet per second

S = distance in which the vessel is stopped.

A. $V = \dfrac{5 \times 6076}{3600} = 8.44$ ft. per sec. $V^2 = 8.44 \times 8.44$

$F = \dfrac{8000 \times 2240 \times 8.44 \times 8.44}{32.16 \times 2 \times 100} = \dfrac{1276503000}{6432} = 198,461$ lbs.

Therefore, the chain's breaking strength exceeds its stress by 121,539 lbs.

Q. Describe the effect of wind on a vessel backing.

A. In a fresh breeze, a vessel will tend to back into the wind's eye, regardless of propeller-canting action or number of screws. In moderate winds, I would expect a right-handed single-screw vessel going astern to take such direction as will bring the wind between 4 points of the starboard quarter and the starboard beam. In maneuvering, backing with wind on port side, vessel's head will rapidly cant to starboard, especially if draft is light; with wind on starboard side, she should cant little or nothing.

Q. Are there any rules which specify the size of mooring lines which a vessel must use?

A. Yes; the classification societies provide for the initial outfit of mooring-lines in their rules. For example, according to Lloyd's Tables, a powered vessel of 13,000 tons' load displacement and having an Equipment Numeral 37195 is required to have, in addition to certain anchors and chain cable, a 120-fathom, 5-inch wire towing hawser; two 90-fathom, 8-inch manila or 2-3/4-inch wire hawsers; and 2 warping lines of 7-inch manila or 2-1/2-inch wire.

Q. Rescuing a man overboard at sea, describe the "Williamson turn".

A. Put helm hard over to throw ship's stern away from man. Hold rudder hard over until ship is swinging, then steady her on a course approximately 60° from original course. When ship heads on a new course, swing rudder hard over on other side until she is on 180° from original course. Original speed is maintained until vessel is steady on this reverse course.

Q. Bringing up on her anchor chain at 3 knots, will a vessel exert a greater stress on her chain in light or loaded condition? Why?

A. In the loaded condition, due to her greater momentum. Momentum, or quantity of motion, is always proportional to the mass times the velocity.

Q. Describe a fire warp and how it is used.

A. A flexible wire rope led in the direction which will best heave ship away from her berth, in case of fire either on the dock or on board. It usually is led to the outer corner of wharf or dock, from forward if vessel is heading in, or from aft if heading out. By heaving on the warp, vessel will move clear of berth and then may either anchor or be assisted by a tug.

Q. On a vessel where it is necessary to stow the chain in the locker, prescribe the precautions necessary to avoid injury to the men tiering the chain.

A. Provide men with chain hooks; warn them of the danger of chain tumbling on their legs if not promptly tiered, and thus the necessity of calling out if chain is coming in too fast. In larger ships, one of the men should use a whistle for signalling the deck to stop heaving in, etc. Chain lockers are notorious for harboring petroleum gas: be wary of this danger also.

Q. What care should be taken to prevent eye injury or other injuries to a man while handling the brake of a windlass in letting go the anchor?

A. Use goggles for eye protection against flying particles from the cable; also, see that ample clear deck space is provided about after side of windlass and that chain pipes are clear.

Q. A vessel is moored stern to a quay, bow anchored to two anchors with a slight spread. Both anchor cables and lines are taut. A strong wind comes up athwart the mooring as illustrated. How may the leads of the lines and cables be improved?

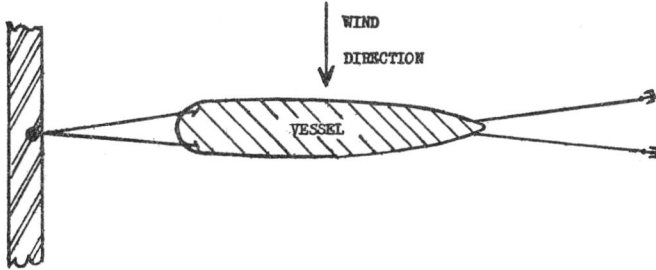

A. If there is room to leeward, run another line to windward from the port quarter, heave in the slack and make fast. Then slack away evenly on all stern lines and on port anchor cable, and also on the starboard cable if necessary. Hold all when stress on both lines and cable is sufficiently eased. Vessel may be hove back to her original berth when wind abates, or shifts to advantage.

Q. How should a windlass be fitted to prevent injury to personnel while engaging or disengaging the wildcat, handling lines, etc.?
A. With an efficient safety pawl or a cable stopper to prevent anchor and cable from running out in case of accidental loosening of windlass brake.

Q. The after holds of many vessels are sounded from the shaft alley. Why are these sounding pipes fitted with spring-loaded self-closing valves?
A. So that, if holds are flooded, the shaft alley may be protected against water entering through such pipes; or, conversely, should the alley become flooded, entry of water into holds may be prevented.

Q. When a vessel is fitted with a gangway that does not have self-adjusting treads, how do you protect people from injury to their legs by slipping through the steps when the gangway is nearly horizontal?
A. By placing and securing planks of sufficient width along and over the steps, with footing pieces across them if necessary.

Q. What may be the result of permitting a centrifugal or rotary pump to run dry when pumping inflammable or combustible oils?
A. Heating and/or sparking which may result in fire or an explosion.

Q. In washing the holds of a freight vessel the strainers become plugged and it is impossible to pump out the water by means of the bilge pump. A portable pump is rigged on deck, 35 feet above the tank top of the hold and hose lead both down the hold and over the side, but the pump fails to pump the water out of the hold. Under these circumstances, what would you do to pump out the water?

A. Lower pump to a point where good suction may be obtained. Then the discharge may be forced up the hose and overboard.

Q. On a deeply loaded vessel in heavy weather taking green seas aboard, what prevents water going into the tanks through the gooseneck vents on deck?

A. In older vessels plugs of wood or small hinged covers secured by butterfly nuts were used to close such vents. More modern fittings of this kind are equipped with ball checks designed to float upward and automatically stop ingress of water reaching up to vent's mouth.

Q. What inspection and maintenance would you give gooseneck vents?

A. Gooseneck vents fitted with ball checks should be examined frequently to see that they are working efficiently, and a schedule for overhauling them should be maintained, especially where vents leading to fuel tanks require their fire screens to be kept clean and in order.

Q. What is the purpose of equalizing valves fitted where tanks are divided by a longitudinal bulkhead? How would you maintain such valves and in what position should they be kept?

A. They are for allowing the liquid to flow from one side of tank to the other, independent of the cargo line, as when the liquid is to be leveled off or "equalized" to a common depth. Such valves should be kept closed until actually required to be opened. However, they should be frequently checked for efficient working and maintained in good order.

Q. Describe the precautions which you would regard as necessary for personnel engaged in painting with spray guns.

A. Protection for the face and eyes by a suitable mask; also, the hands and arms should be properly protected. If spray gun is used in an enclosed space, ample ventilation must be provided.

Q. Describe the precautions necessary in painting with red lead or lead-based paints.

A. In order to guard against possible lead poisoning, good ventilation is necessary in enclosed spaces, and the skin must be protected from a continued contact with such paint. If a spray gun is used, a good protective mask is most necessary for the painter.

Q. Describe briefly the usual procedure followed in cleaning and gas-freeing oil tanks.

A. This usually is done by the Butterworth cleaning machine, which is lowered into the tank after the latter is steamed. The machine is simply a revolving nozzle which throws a continuous stream of hot water around the tank. Beginning at the top, it is lowered in 5-foot stages as the work progresses, the slops being kept pumped out and overboard at sea, or to shore if in port, until tank is clean and gas free.

Q. When seamen are working upon a mast near radio transmitting antennae, what precautions should be taken?

A. See that no radio transmission takes place while men are so engaged. Have the radio operator understand the situation and be guided accordingly.

Q. What precautions should be observed to prevent shock of personnel, when portable electric lights or appliances are used?

A. That the cables and all parts of the portable lamps are in good order and efficiently insulated.

Q. In taking bunker oils, or loading or discharging oil cargo, what precautions should be taken to prevent harbor pollution in the event of a spill on deck?

A. Be prepared to stop oil transfer at a moment's notice. Plug all scuppers on the working deck. Have buckets and nonsparking scoops at hand for gathering up the spill.

Q. If through an accident, oil is spilled into harbor waters, how can pollution be minimized?

A. Arrest the flow at once by plugging scuppers and gathering up the spilled oil from the deck. Dry up the deck with sawdust.

Q. What precautions are advisable when padeyes, cleats, lashings, or other fittings are so located on the decks that personnel may trip or stumble over them in the dark?

A. Where practicable, have the area providing a required passageway sufficiently lighted. Failing that, rope off the passage area in such way as personnel may walk clear of obstructions.

Q. Why is a reciprocating or rotary type pump normally employed for stripping tanks of liquid?

A. Because such pumps are capable of maintaining a suction under severe conditions, as when required to pump oil which contains sand or sediment, or possesses a high viscosity, in the stripping process.

Q. Describe how planks used for staging should be tested in order to determine that they are strong enough to carry their load with an ample safety factor.

A. Support the plank on deck so that it bears near each end and let as many men stand upon it as will make up the necessary weight test.

Q. To determine if a tank is gas free: (a) What instrument is used? (b) In circumstances where a gas chemist is unavailable, what precautions must be observed in using such instruments?
A. (a) A combustible gas indicator. (b) Tests should be taken at various levels and locations in the tank. Such tests are satisfactory for determining whether the tank is safe for men to enter it, but should not be so considered for use of an open flame, such as a torch used in welding, etc. In the latter case a chemist's certificate must be secured before repairs may be carried out.

Q. What precautions should be taken when personnel are obliged to traverse decks over the top of deck cargo?
A. Efficient means to prevent falling overboard or into a "well," as the space left around a winch, or stumbling over cargo, lashings, etc., in the dark. Guard rails or lifelines, spaced not more than 12 inches apart vertically, and to a height of at least 4 feet above the cargo, should be fitted. Cargo should be stowed sufficiently level for gangway purposes.

Q. What is the <u>carrier</u> bearing fitted on most modern vessels at the rudder?
A. It is the bearing which supports the rudder's weight. Similar to the thrust bearing on a propeller shaft, rudderstock has one or more shoulders or collars, either shrunk on or forged, which bear upon the corresponding landings in a casting or built-up casing encircling the stock and containing the necessary lubricant. Usually the arrangement is a continuation of the stuffing box through which the rudderstock enters the hull.

Q. If a vessel is moored as sketched, with a camel well aft between the ship and dock, what would be the effect of heaving on the head lines with the stern line taut?

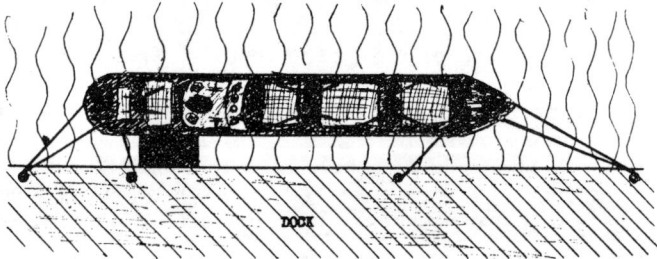

A. Each after line would be subjected to an unusually heavy stress due to the great leverage moment indicated; and, especially in way of the forward end of the camel, a straining, if not damaging, pressure would be delivered to the vessel's side structure.

Q. Referring to the sketch: (a) When buffer springs are fitted on a quadrant type steering gear, why is it important that the quadrant be free to move on the rudder stock? (b) Under what circumstances would you use a key in the keyways marked B?

Note: Tension and compression on springs exaggerated in sketch for clarity.

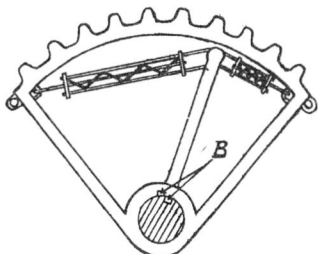

A. (a) So that the purpose for which such springs are fitted may be served, viz., absorption of shocks to the steering gear caused by seas surging or striking against the rudder. (b) When vessel is navigated in comparatively smooth water, as in a harbor, a river, etc.

Q. What materials are usually employed for rudder gudgeon bushings and how is the bushing clearance determined?

A. Lignum vitae, bronze, and sometimes a soft steel. Inside diameter of bushing should be a little greater than that of the pintle. For average-sized vessels this is three thirty-seconds of an inch when bushing is installed.

Q. Describe the methods used to repair leaking rivets.

A. Leaking rivets may be calked, or have their edges closed up by a calking tool; hardened up, or hammered, as in the original riveting process, in order to expand them for effectual watertightness (or oiltightness); or sometimes welded to the pierced metal. If found slack and not sound, they should be replaced.

Q. What precautions should be observed when using carbon tetrachloride fire extinguishers, or when employing carbon tetrachloride for cleaning purposes?

A. Pump the liquid directly into the flame. If in an enclosed space, retire immediately to avoid asphyxiating fumes from the liquid, unless a gas mask is used. If used for cleaning purposes, see that plenty of fresh air or good ventilation is present.

Q. How could you stop a leak caused by a rivet dropping out of the shell below the water line?

A. Drive a tapered hardwood plug in the hole.

Q. A crack appears on an internal bulkhead of a vessel at sea. What measure could you take to stop the crack from lengthening?

A. Bore a half-inch hole through the plate to meet the crack at its lengthening end. The hole may then be plugged with a softwood spile, a cork, or the like.

Q. When oil is discovered in a vessel's bilge wells at the time soundings are taken, what steps should be taken to prevent oil pollution of coastal waters?

A. Do not pump out bilges while in such waters, unless to prevent their overflow into the hold. In the latter event, a portion only should be pumped out, so that the oil will remain (on top of the water) until vessel again is outside coastal waters and free to discharge all bilge drainage.

Q. In replacing strainer plates for hold bilge suctions, what is the amount of plate that must be perforated with holes for the water to pass through?
A. Such amount that the total open area (perforation) is not less than 3 times that of the suction pipe.

Q. In washing out holds or in circumstances where it is feared the nature of the cargo will tend to clog the strainer plates should pumping water be necessary, what precautions might be taken to insure that the water will flow into the well?
A. Keep limber holes free during the washing process by passing a small line (or preferably a small chain) along the bilge and through each hole. A sharp pull back and forth at frequent intervals will ensure free flow to well.

Q. What markings are required on the trick wheel in a vessel's steering engine room, in order that any possible misunderstanding of orders may be averted, should it be necessary to have a man steering from there directed by orders from outside?
A. "At all steering stations there shall be installed a suitable notice on the wheel or device, or in such other position as to be directly in the helmsman's line of vision, to indicate the direction in which the wheel or device must be turned for right rudder and for left rudder."

Q. Why must indiscriminate welding of padeyes or other fittings on a vessel's structure be avoided, even when no fire hazard is involved?
A. Because such weldings may interfere with the geometric continuities in vessel's structure, thus inviting the likelihood of fractures resulting from probable concentrations of stress at the welds.

Q. What precautions with respect to the bilge wells and strainers would you take on a vessel prior to taking 3 feet of sand ballast in the lower hold?
A. Provide ample protection against admission of such material into bilges, as by covering limber boards with old canvas, temporary calking, nailing slats over cracks, etc.

Q. When spray painting is being done in a compartment, what precautions must be taken against fire or explosion?
A. Allow no smoking. Have ready at hand a portable fire extinguisher (not a tetrachloride one). Provide good ventilation. Forbid use of a torch or any open flame or sparking tool in the vicinity.

Q. Describe the specifications for wedges to be used in battening hatches.

A. Wedges are to be made of a tough wood, having a taper of not more than 1 to 6, and to be not less than 1/2 inch thick at the toe.

Q. Describe the specifications for battening bars to be used on hatches.

A. Bars are to be of steel and have a width of 2-1/2 inches and a thickness of not less than 3/8 inch.

Q. What number of locking bars is required for hatches?

A. Locking bars are required for every section of hatch covers.

Q. In painting decks, what precautions should be taken against creating a slipping hazard for personnel working about the deck?

A. Rope off area being painted, providing as necessary a temporary gangway for leading personnel clear of painted surface. Have the location plainly marked or placarded with the warning Wet Paint.

Q. Where a vessel is fitted with a positive means for closing a nonreturn valve above the freeboard deck, what notice is required?

A. Such valve control must be identified as to its service by a suitable name plate, and also fitted with an indicator to show whether the valve is open or closed.

Note: Candidates for Chief Mate's Licenses may be asked questions on ship construction similar to those in the Master's Examination in connection with the subject of seamanship.

25. CARGO STOWAGE AND HANDLING

Q. A vessel loading grain has the feeder constructed in the square of the hatch. The distance from the feeder to a bulkhead is 30 feet as sketched. What precaution is required by the grain regulations?

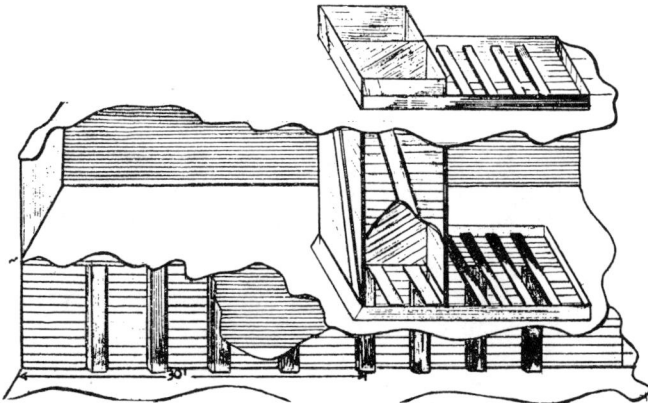

A. Since the distance in the lower hold between bulkhead and hatchway feeder exceeds 25 feet, a wing feeder on each side of the 'tween deck also must be provided to feed the hold. If there are no 'tween deck openings for such wing feeders, then 4 tiers of bagged grain must be laid on the bulk grain, extending from the bulkhead to within 25 feet of the hatchway feeder.

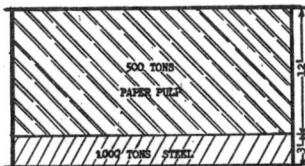

Q. What is the height of the center of gravity of the hold shown? (The hold has rectangular form).

A. Height of C. G. of paper above base = $3 + 1/2(12) = 9$ feet,
Height of C. G. of steel above base = $1/2(3)$ = 1-1/2 feet;
Moment of C. G. of paper about base line = 500×9 = 4500 ft. -tons,
Moment of C. G. of steel about base line = $1000 \times 1\text{-}1/2 = 1500$ ft. -tons;
Moment of C. G. of hold about base line = $1500 \times H$ = 6000 ft. -tons;
Height of C. G. of hold = H = $6000 \div 1500 = 4$ feet.

Q. Three hundred tons of one-half inch steel plate with a stowage factor of 7 are stowed across the bottom of a cargo hold measuring 60 feet by 40 feet. At what height is the center of gravity of the parcel of cargo above the inner bottom? How could you raise the height of the center of gravity and facilitate discharge?

A. $\dfrac{300 \times 7 \times 1}{60 \times 40 \times 2}$ = .44 ft. height of C. G. above inner bottom.

While raising the C. G., in order to allow a burden of no more than 450 lbs. per sq. ft. on inner bottom, for a shortened fore-and-aft measurement, L, of the bulk, we have

$\dfrac{300 \times 2240}{L \times 40}$ = 450; whence, L = $\dfrac{300 \times 2240}{40 \times 450}$ = 37.3 ft.;

and, for height to which the mass will stow,

H = $\dfrac{300 \times 7}{37.3 \times 40}$ = 1.41 ft., and C. G. is now .70 ft. above inner

bottom. Thus, the C. G. is raised .70 — .44 = .26 ft.; but, for a further rise in the C. G., and for facilitating discharge, heavy, evenly laid dunnage should be placed between, at most, every 2 tiers of plating.

Q. A vessel loads a bulk cargo which may shift under bad weather conditions. She is not required by regulations or accepted stowage rules to provide shifting boards. What precautions may be taken to minimize danger?

A. Erect shifting boards nevertheless and, in addition, if any general cargo is available, stow it over the bulk up to the deckhead. Where the bulk may occupy an entire hold, have it properly trimmed up to the beams.

Q. How can you estimate the tendency to shift of a bulk commodity?
Discuss the factors that may influence the tendency of a cargo to
shift.

A. Tendency of a bulk cargo to shift may be estimated by the value
of the material's angle of repose, or angle which the sides of a
heap poured upon a level surface make with the horizontal, about
23° in the case of wheat, 31° for fine sand, 39° for dry earth,
40° to 45° for gravel, etc. But while a list of 23°, with a load
of bulk wheat, for example, may not disturb the grain in smooth
water, the effects of a vessel's motion in a seaway will considerably lessen such angle of repose, especially so as the height of
grain's surface is increased from the center about which vessel
rolls. This greater swing or disturbing force administered by
vessel's roll also tends to start in motion that part of the bulk
farthest from the midship fore-and-aft line.

Thus, in heavy weather, good seamanship demands that adequate
protective measures shall have been taken to preserve vessel's
stability against the effect of a displaced center of gravity due to
shifting of cargo.

Q. Slabs of copper are to be loaded each of which is 12 inches wide,
12 inches long, and 4 inches high. Each slab weighs 110 pounds.
How high might this commodity be stowed in a 'tween deck whose
allowable load per square foot is 450 pounds?

A. One square foot is occupied by each slab weighing 110 pounds;
so that 450 ÷ 110 = 4+ slabs weighing 450 pounds. The slabs being
each 4 inches high, then 4 slabs × 4 = 16 inches, or the height
the consignment may be stowed.

Q. How would you stow citrus fruit packed in the type of crate
illustrated?

A. Stow crates athwartships on flat
side, or on end bulge to bulge and
back to back, with dunnage strips
laid along and over each tier; but in
any case aim to have space between
bulges in line with the air movement
in compartment. Place at least 3 inches dunnage, or gratings, on floor
for good air circulation, and keep at
least 6 inches space above cargo. Avoid
deep stowage, but if 6 boxes or more
high, build a false floor at about the
middle tier.

Q. What are three basic methods of protecting personnel when stowing radioactive materials?

A. (a) Keeping cargo at a safe distance from personnel. (The radiation varies inversely as square of the distance.)

(b) Limiting time of exposure of men handling such materials.

(c) Stowing the material in such manner that other cargo which may act as a shield is interposed between the source of radiation and crew members or others who are on board the vessel for a lengthy period.

Q. A lot of special cargo on a pier is to be loaded. You examine one of the identical cartons of the lot which is marked as sketched. (a) What is the purpose of the marking?

(b) What is the total cubic space the consignment will occupy?

Note: 22/25 on the carton sketched indicates this to be the 22nd piece of a total of 25 pieces or cartons of the lot.

A. (a) This is a shipper's mark for identifying the pieces constituting a particular consignment of goods.

(b) $\dfrac{14 \times 16 \times 18 \times 25}{1728} = \dfrac{175}{3} = 58.3$ cubic feet.

Q. Why is cargo stowed in 'tween decks, on decks, and in the wings of the hold more likely to shift than cargo in the lower hold?

A. Because those locations partake of a greater velocity in the rolling motion — often in the case of a stiff ship, beginning with a marked suddenness amounting sometimes to a jerk — due to their comparatively great distances from the center about which vessel rolls.

Q. What precautions would you observe in order to assure proper readings from a combustible gas indicator?

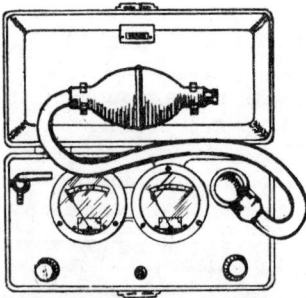

A. Samples of the air must be taken from various parts and at various heights in the compartment concerned, since distribution of gas may follow no regular pattern, although in an undisturbed tank or other confined space heaviest concentration of petroleum gas is found at lowest levels.

Q. What precaution is advisable when bulk cargo is stowed in the 'tween decks?

A. The bulk should be leveled off and topped with same cargo in bags, or other suitable boxed or bagged cargo, and shifting boards should be erected in any case. (It should be noted here that, excepting oats and cottonseed, no grain in bulk other than that carried in feeders is allowed to be carried in the 'tween decks.)

Q. What is the principle of operation of a combustible gas indicator?
A. A sample of the air is drawn or pumped from the space concerned through a length of small tubing into the instrument, where
   it flows over a hot platinum wire of an electrical circuit from two
   small dry cell batteries. This detector unit is balanced against the
   filament of a small electric light bulb burning in an inert gas. Combustible gas in the sample burns easily in the presence of platinum
   detector filament, which heats up during the combustion according
   to amount of gas burned. Wire's resistance is thus increased and
   causes electric current to become unbalanced, which, in turn,
   causes a movement of the pointer on the electrical meter. This
   movement is directly proportional to the amount of combustible
   gas concentrated in the air sample.

Q. Three compartments of equal volume as sketched are available
   to carry a cargo of quick-frozen fruit on a long voyage. The only
   point that must be considered is the economy of refrigerating plant
   operation during the voyage. Which of the three would you select?
   Explain your answer.

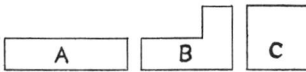

A. Compartment A, because air circulation through the mass, and consequent effective maintenance of the required temperature, is accomplished
with least mechanical effort.

Q. A cargo of gasoline has a coefficient of expansion of .0006 per
   degree Fahrenheit. If this cargo is loaded at a temperature of
   60° F., and cargo temperatures up to 74° F. are anticipated on
   the voyage, how many barrels would you leave out in a tank whose
   capacity is 10,000 barrels, in order to allow for expansion?
A. Let x = number of barrels to be loaded; then .0006(74 — 60) x =
   .0084x = barrels expansion from 60°. Therefore, 1.0084x = 10,000
   barrels, and x = 10,000 ÷ 1.0084 = 9916.7 barrels to be loaded; or
   10,000 — 9916.7 = 83.3 barrels to leave out.
   (As commonly computed, 10,000 × .0084 = 84 barrels)

Q. When a vessel which is fitted with heating coils in her tanks is
   carrying light fuel such as kerosene or gasoline, what precautions
   should be taken to eliminate any possibility of contaminating boiler
   feed, inspection tanks, heating pipe lines, etc.?
A. A back pressure of 50 to 60 lbs. per sq. in. should be maintained through the heating system in order to prevent the possibility of any leakage entering the coils. Inspection tanks should
   be opened at frequent intervals to ascertain whether or not any
   oil or impurities have entered the system, and if necessary, renew or clean the filters.

Q. When carrying chilled beef suspended from hooks in the overhead of a refrigerated compartment, where is the center of gravity of the compartment?

A. At a height above its deck approximately equal to that of the rails from which the beef is suspended.

Q. What care is necessary in the successful carriage of chilled beef suspended from hooks? How should such beef be stowed?
A. A first requisite is that temperature of the compartments should vary no more than half a degree from that at which the beef is to be carried (usually 28-1/2° to 29-1/2° F.) as directed by the shipper.

The meat must be kept from contact with brine pipes and hung well clear of the deck. While stowage should be compact enough to prevent undue chafing as vessel rolls, care must be taken not to interfere with the necessary circulation of air. Hung from fore-and-aft rails at the deckhead, usually one height of beef is stowed; but sometimes two heights, of which the upper consists of hind quarters and the lower, fore quarters, are hung, the latter by chains of appropriate length. Plenty of room beneath the meat must be left for air circulation.

Q. Describe briefly the automatic controls used in refrigerated compartments to regulate temperature and humidity.
A. Temperature control is largely effected by thermostats within the cargo space. These thermostats control starting and stopping of the compressors. Humidity is regulated by controlling the difference in temperatures of coils and chamber atmosphere, and by regulating the admission of outside air.

Q. What check is advisable by the cargo officer and/or refrigerating engineer on automatic temperature and humidity controls?
A. They should be checked at regular intervals by means of a portable mercury thermometer and a hygrometer. A maximum-minimum type of thermometer mounted in the refrigeration space may be used to detect temperature fluctuations.

Q. What shipping papers relating to the cargo are required on board a loaded tanker or vessel towing such a vessel, and what information must be afforded by such papers?
A. She shall have on board a bill of lading, manifest, or shipping document giving name of consignee and delivery point, approximate quantities of each kind and grade of cargo, and for whom or whose account cargo is being handled. In the case of unmanned barges being towed, an entry in the logbook of the towing vessel covering the above-noted information shall be considered as complying with this requirement.

Q. Would you permit scaling of the deck or hull adjacent to a hold where cargo is being worked? Why?
A. No; because the din of scaling hammers would interfere with the stevedores' work, possibly resulting in a serious accident due to misunderstanding of signals by voice or whistle. Efficient cargo handling could not be expected amid such disconcerting conditions.

Q. How would you load <u>A</u>, 50 feet long and 5 feet deep, into hatch <u>B</u> which is 45 feet long? Answer in detail.

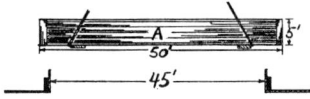

A. If width of hatchway will allow, turn <u>A</u> obliquely, or cornerwise, and lower away; if not, lengthen one leg of sling so that the object may be dipped under hatch coaming at one corner, while just clearing the coaming at the other, or opposite, corner. Then heave or haul the low end into the hold space, while lowering away to clear the coaming.

Q. Describe the precautions you would take to protect passengers from injury on vessels working cargo.

A. Have the spaces in way of moving cargo fenced or roped off; permit no passengers to loiter about the hatchways or, if necessary, anywhere on the working deck; and place appropriate danger notices at all possible approaches to such forbidden areas.

Q. A vessel has a dead-weight carrying capacity of 5,000 tons and a cubic capacity of 300,000 cubic feet. How much of each of the following commodities should she load to be full and down to her marks?

(Lead—Stowage Factor, 18; Cotton—Stowage Factor, 80)

A. Let L = weight of lead, and C = weight of cotton; then

$$L + C = 5,000 \text{ tons, and } 18L + 80C = 300,000 \text{ cu. ft.}$$
$$\underline{18L + 18C = 90,000 \text{ cu. ft.}}$$
$$62C = 210,000 \text{ cu. ft.}$$

C = 3387.1 x 80 = 270,968 cu. ft. C = 210,000 ÷ 62 = 3387.1 tons
L = 1612.9 x 18 = 29,032 cu. ft. L = 5,000—3387.1 = 1612.9 tons
Total = 300,000 cu. ft. Total = 5000 tons

Lead, 1612.9 tons or 29,032 cu. ft.; cotton, 3387.1 tons or 270,968 cu. ft.

Q. Describe briefly the dangers that may arise when carrying goods of a hygroscopic nature.

A. Hygroscopic materials, such as grain of all sorts, soft woods, jute, cotton, paper, sugar, and others of animal or vegetable origin, are those which will absorb or give off moisture (water vapor) under some humidity conditions in the immediate atmosphere. Hence, there are hygroscopic cargoes which, although in apparently dry condition when loaded, may absorb enough moisture from other substances in their vicinity to result in heating or odor damage or tainting to themselves. Also, such cargo, when more or less saturated, may cause similar damage by giving off its water vapor to other innocent substances stowed in same compartment. Spontaneous heating, mold, odor damage, and tainting are common effects of near stowage of "wet" and "dry" goods, especially where rising temperatures and faulty ventilation may occur.

Q. What are the requirements for a general average?

A. A general average act occurs only when any extraordinary sacrifice or expenditure is intentionally and reasonably made or incurred for the common safety, or for the purpose of preserving from peril the property involved in a common maritime adventure. Ship, cargo, and freight (in the course of being earned) are required to contribute proportionately in making good the loss incurred for the common safety.

Q. What inspection of cargo equipment is required by the master of a vessel prior to loading explosives?

A. The master or other person in charge of the vessel shall ascertain by examination the condition and working order of all slings, tackle, baskets, boxes, crates, chutes, mattresses, and other equipment for use in loading the explosives, whether or not such gear is supplied by the vessel.

Q. Is the master of a vessel empowered to reject the equipment for loading explosives furnished by a contracting stevedore?

A. Regardless of ownership of any or all equipment, if not in safe working condition, the master or other person in charge of the vessel shall prohibit its use in transfer of explosives to or from the vessel; and during the necessary close observation of the gear in transfer operations, should there be noted any defect or damage to such gear, replacements or repairs shall be effected immediately.

Q. A vessel has a dead-weight carrying capacity at load displacement of 10,500 tons. Fuel, water, and stores require 1,500 tons. Her cubic capacity is 500,000 cubic feet. What is the average stowage factor of a cargo that she could carry that would put her "full and down"?

A. D. W. capacity   = 10,500 tons
　 fuel & stores   =   1,500 tons
　 cargo capacity   =   9,000 tons
　　Average stowage factor = 500,000 ÷ 9,000 = 55.55

Q. Describe at least two methods employed on vessels for determining the relative humidity in a cargo hold.

A. By means of a psychrometer or hygrometer, which consists of two thermometers, one having a dry bulb, the other a wet one, the latter being so called from its covering wick that is kept inserted in a small receptacle of distilled water. Comparative rate of evaporation, as shown in the difference in readings of the thermometers, is the basis for determining relative humidity by the use of tables covering every probable temperature condition.

　　Also, by the hair hygrometer, which gives a continuous record of the degree of saturation of the air. Based upon the peculiar ability of human hair to react to the wetness and dryness of the air, its many strands of the hair are kept under tension by a small spring. Shortening takes place in dry air, lengthening in nearly saturated air, and such variations are registered through the movement of a pointer, to which is attached the recorder-pen on a revolving time-graph.

Q. When stowing a commodity which is very dense, such as pigs of lead or flasks of mercury, what precautions should be taken to avoid structural damage to the ship?

A. Such cargo should be given lower hold stowage where possible, but in any case care must be taken to distribute the weight so that local concentration of more than that allowed per surface unit may be avoided. If 'tween deck stowage is required, shoring up the beams from next deck below will be necessary, if the weight is found to exceed the deck's allowed supporting capacity, notwithstanding that cargo is spread over the widest possible area. Dunnage should be freely used to both chock off and separate the pigs or flasks, with the view of preventing any movement of the cargo during heavy weather.

Q. How is a cargo vessel loaded in order that she may have quick dispatch at several ports of discharge?

A. Cargo for each port should be so distributed that as many hatches as possible (and side-doors, if any) may be worked simultaneously. Where possible, cargo loaded in any compartment for different ports should be kept distinctly separated and accessible according to order of discharge.

Q. Outside air has a dry bulb temperature of 70° and a relative humidity of 70 percent. Would there be any danger of condensation if a cargo with a surface temperature of 65 degrees is ventilated with outside air? (a) Would you consider sweat likely on the side of a ship with a sea water temperature of 38°, an air temperature in hold of 54° dry bulb, and 45° wet bulb? (b) Would you ventilate if outside air was 60° dry bulb, 52° wet bulb?

A. No, since the dew point under the conditions noted would be 60°. (a) No; the dew point is 35° in these conditions. (b) No; this would unnecessarily increase the relative humidity about 10% and so the dew point to 45°.

Q. A vessel with a beam of 50 feet has a freeboard of 10 feet on her high side and a list of 5°. What is her mean freeboard if the low side is not accessible to measure the freeboard?

A. Increase of freeboard due to 5° list = $1/2B \times \tan 5° = 25 \times .087 =$ 2.17 ft. Difference between freeboard observed and that due to list, or $10 - 2.17$, gives mean freeboard, 7.83 ft., or 7 ft. 10 in.

Q. What precautions would you take to avoid excessive strain on your vessel while loading bulk cargo?

A. Have loading operations arranged so that the weight will be distributed as evenly as possible throughout vessel's length as the work proceeds. Final trimming of a weighty cargo should taper off toward ship's ends, i.e., so that the continuity of stress due to weight shall not abruptly terminate at either extremity of hold spaces.

26. CHANGE IN DRAFT DUE TO DENSITY

Q. A vessel loads a full cargo at a dock where the hydrometer floats at 1012. To what draft will she have to be loaded so as to draw 23 feet, 6 inches, when she gets to sea?

A.
$$1012 : 1025 = 23.5 : D. \quad D = \frac{1025 \times 23.5}{1012} = 23.8 \text{ ft., or } 23 \text{ ft. } 9\text{-}1/2 \text{ in.}$$

Q. How would you determine the applicable load line for a port?
A. First find from ship's load-line certificate the maximum draft allowed for the particular region or regions and the season in which the vessel is to be navigated; then ascertain the additional allowance (or lesser freeboard allowed) for density of the water, if below that of sea water; and also, in the case of a considerable distance from the port to the high seas, determine any allowance for consumption of fuel and water until leaving the sheltered area.

Q. Determine the displacement in sea water of a vessel which has a loaded draft of 24 feet, length along the load water line of 450 feet, beam at the load water line of 56 feet, and a block coefficient of .8.

A.
$$\text{Displacement} = \frac{450 \times 56 \times 24 \times .8}{35} = 13,824 \text{ tons.}$$

Q. How would you determine the load line in fresh water for a vessel loading to Winter or Winter North Atlantic Load Line?
A. Such load line is above the W or the WNA mark at a distance equal to the allowance for fresh water, or that measured vertically from top edge of Summer mark (S) to top edge of Fresh water mark (F). In other words, the freeboard for W or WNA is lessened by the allowance for fresh water given in the load-line certificate.

28. LIFESAVING APPARATUS AND FIRE-FIGHTING EQUIPMENT

Q. What precautions would you take in handling boats equipped with releasing gear which operates under tension (Rottmer gear)?
A. The lever for releasing the hooks should be secured in proper position and painted the required bright red; also, the persons assigned to such lifeboats should be cautioned against interfering with the lever, which must be marked "DANGER—LEVER RELEASES HOOKS."

Q. Where passenger vessels are fitted with loud-speaker systems, how often do the regulations require that the system be tested?
A. At least once every week.

Q. How often must the emergency lighting and power system be operated and inspected? State the test required for internal combustion engine-driven generators and storage batteries on passenger vessels.

A. At least once in each week. Internal combustion engine-driven emergency generators shall be operated under load for at least two hours at least once in each month that vessel is navigated. Storage batteries for emergency lighting and power systems shall be tested at least once in each six-month period that vessel is navigated.

Q. How often must watertight doors in subdivision bulkheads be operated on passenger vessels?
A. At least once in each week that vessel is navigated.

Q. How often must watertight doors in subdivision bulkheads be inspected on passenger vessels?
A. At least once in each week that vessel is navigated.

Q. Describe the lowering of lifeboats at the vessel's annual inspection.
A. Each boat is lowered near to the water and there loaded to its allowed capacity, evenly distributed throughout the length; lowered to float in the water and released from the hooks. Either persons or dead weight may be used in making the test, but total weight must at least equal boat's capacity, considering persons to weigh 165 pounds each.

In the case of gravity davits, it shall be shown that each boat can be swung out and lowered from any stopped position by releasing the winch brake alone. Use of force to start the davits or the winch will not be permitted.

Q. What is the total weight used for weight-testing lifeboats and davits at annual inspection?
A. It shall be at least equal to the allowed capacity of boat, considering persons to weigh 165 pounds each.

Q. On cargo vessels of over 500 gross tons on international voyages, when the lifeboat deck is more than 30 feet above the light load line, what do the regulations require for launching a boat in the hours of darkness?
A. That there be readily and continuously available approved illumination, from the vessel, of lifeboats when alongside and in process of, or immediately after, being launched.

Q. Do the Passenger Vessel Regulations permit the dismantling of lifeboats or rafts for maintenance work at sea or when passengers are aboard?
A. No; the Regulations require that the lifeboats, life rafts, life floats, and buoyant apparatus shall be "available for immediate

use at all times when vessel is being navigated, and, insofar as reasonable and practicable, while vessel is not being navigated. "

Q. Sketched here are three typical fire-alarm system thermostats. (a) Describe briefly what causes such thermostats to actuate an alarm. (b) When the system is de-energized or the power on it fails, how is the officer on watch alerted? (c) How are such thermostats tested?

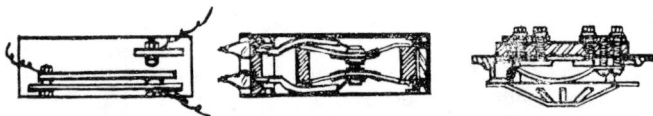

A. (a) They are activated by difference in thermal expansion of two dissimilar metals. Heat causes opening (or closing) of an electric contact by this action.

(b) A small current flowing through a high resistance circuit activates a bell.

(c) By using a portable hand light as a source of heat, replacing usual guard and globe with a sheet-metal shield and noting the time required to activate the thermostat. If this differs materially from the average, thermostat should be suspected of being defective.

Q. In ordering or purchasing equipment for lifesaving purposes aboard ship, how would you determine if they were approved by the Coast Guard?
A. By consulting the nearest Officer in Charge, Marine Inspection, or the Coast Guard District Commander having jurisdiction.

Q. What markings are required on passenger vessels to direct the passengers to their lifeboat embarkation stations?
A. The sign TO BOATS in at least one-inch letters above an arrow of appropriate dimensions, installed in passageways, stairways, etc., throughout the vessel, so that from any location normally accessible to passengers or crew, including fire doors in stairway enclosures and main vertical zone bulkheads, and all closed watertight doors in subdivision bulkheads, the direction of shortest route to follow will be apparent. Also, near the exits to embarkation deck similar signs shall be placed to indicate boat stations nearest each exit; thus, above a conspicuous arrow, "TO BOAT STATIONS NOS. 1, 3, 5" (or "2, 4, 6").

The notices shall be printed in any other language in addition to English, or other action taken to achieve the same purpose, where languages appropriate to the vessel's service must be considered.

Q. Can life preservers be laundered or repaired, and if so, under what conditions?

A. Only such minor repairs as will maintain their efficiency may be effected. All other repairs or alternations must be examined and approved by Coast Guard Merchant Vessel Inspection.

Life preservers may be laundered as required, but C. G. Inspection should be advised, so that the necessary examination of this equipment may be arranged for upon such cleaning being completed.

Q. A vessel has a beam of 60 feet. The distance from the davit span to the light water line is 40 feet. What is the required length of the life lines fitted to the davit span?

A. Since lifelines must be of such length as will reach the water at lightest sea-going draft, with vessel listed 15° either way, then length of lines = $40 + (60 \div 2)$ tan $15° = 40 + (30 \times .268) = 40 + 8.04$, or 48 feet.

Q. How may you determine if cleaning oils, disinfectants, and waxes are approved for use aboard vessels?

A. It must be stated on the container's label, or on a separate label, or be etched or stamped on each container, that the article is <u>certificated for use as stores on board vessels.</u>

Q. How are persons in the engine or fire room warned of the release of carbon dioxide gas?

A. By an approved audible alarm which is automatically sounded when the gas is admitted to such spaces.

Q. How are passenger vessels required to mark lifeboat stations on the embarkation deck?

A. By signs in 3-inch letters, as, LIFEBOAT STATION NO. 1, placed on deck beams or suspended athwartship from overhead. If there is insufficient head room or no overhead structure at a station, a similar sign shall be permanently installed where readily seen.

Q. What precautions do the Regulations for Passenger Vessels prescribe with respect to painting?

A. An excessive number of coats will be discouraged, unless noncombustible paint is used. Nitrocellulose or other highly flammable or noxious fume-producing paints or lacquers shall not be used.

Q. How often must the fuel tanks be emptied and the fuel changed in motor lifeboats carried aboard passenger vessels?

A. At least once in every year.

Q. How often must all life floats be cleaned and thoroughly overhauled?

A. At least once in every year.

Q. Is it permissible to use fire hose for washing down the decks?

A. No; fire hose shall be used for no other purpose than fire drills and fire extinguishing.

Q. On a vessel where passengers are carried who do not speak
English, what precautions are required by the regulations with respect to notices, directional signs, etc. ?

A. All stateroom notices, directional signs, etc., shall be printed,
in addition to English, in languages appropriate to the service in
which vessel is engaged, or other action may be taken to achieve
the purpose desired.

Q. What is the maximum temperature that should be permitted in
the compartment where carbon dioxide cylinders are stowed?

A. 130° F.

Q. What provisions against the danger of fire must be provided on
vent outlets from oil tanks?

A. Vent outlets shall be fitted with a single screen of corrosion-
resistant wire of at least 30 x 30 mesh, or with two screens of
at least 20 x 20 mesh spaced not less that 1/2 inch or no more
than 1-1/2 inches apart.
Satisfactory means must be provided for closing such vents without damaging the screens.

Q. On passenger vessels, how frequently must the smoke inlet for
the fire detecting system in the cargo hold be examined? How
would you smoke-test the system for fire detection in the hold?

A. At least once in each 3 months. Tests are made in each hold
or compartment by actually submitting the smoke from a burning
piece of paper, a special smoke-pot, etc., to the uptake inlet.

Q. Are galvanized nozzles and couplings acceptable for use on United States merchant vessels?

A. No; all nozzles shall be of good grade bronze or equivalent
metal, and couplings must be of brass, bronze, or other equivalent metal.

Q. The Passenger Vessel Regulations state : "all parts of the fire
main located on exposed decks shall either be protected against
freezing or be fitted with cutout valves and drain valves so that
the entire exposed part of such piping may be shut off and drained
in freezing weather." (a) Assume that you have the night duty on
a passenger vessel in a northern port in freezing weather. A rub-
bish fire breaks out on the open foredeck. State in detail what
steps you might have to take to make effective use of your fire
hose. (b) What precautions must be taken with respect to cut-off
valves in non-freezing weather?

A. (a) It might be necessary to use a part of the fire main which
has been cut out and drained. This would require closing the drain
valves and opening the cut-out valve (or valves). Then stretch out
the necessary hose and, if desirable, order the engineer in charge
to increase water pressure in the line.
(b) They should be sealed or secured in the open position.

Q. On a vessel fitted with smoke detecting apparatus for the holds and deep tanks where liquid and dry cargo may be alternately carried, what precautions must be taken when liquids are carried?

A. In each case a valve must be installed between the hold or tank and the detecting cabinet, so that the line may be closed when liquids are carried. Where a smoke-detecting system is combined with a fire-extinguishing system, operation of such valve must not affect the operation of such extinguishing system.

Q. How is the radio operator of a tanker warned against the use of his equipment while inflammable cargo is being transferred?

A. A sign must be placed in the radio room warning against use of radio equipment during transfer of Grade A, B, or C inflammable liquids, except by permission of senior deck officer.

Q. In discharging CO_2 into a paint locker of small size with a watertight door battened down and a mushroom ventilator screwed down tight, what precautions should be borne in mind?

A. Suitable means shall be provided for relieving excessive pressure which may accumulate within the locker when carbon dioxide is injected.

Q. What do the regulations prescribe with respect to openings of spaces protected by a CO_2 fire-extinguishing system? Why should a CO_2 system differ from a steam system with respect to such openings?

A. Means shall be provided for closing all openings to such spaces from the outside. Relatively tight doors, shutters, or dampers are required for openings to lower portion of the space, while the upper portion is required to be so constructed that it may be closed off either by permanently installed means or by use of canvas or other material normally carried on the vessel.

Because CO_2, when released to a compartment, rapidly expands to 450 times its stored volume, and, being heavier than air, it fast settles down and over the lower part of the space. Thus, with the objective of quickly smothering a fire, every opening leading to the space must be closed off tightly in order to stop both leakage of CO_2 and any air currents which would disturb its blanketing effect. As differing from steam in this respect, CO_2 must be closely confined to the space in which it is released in order to avoid its accumulation elsewhere and so present the danger to personnel of asphyxiation.

Q. On a ventilation duct passing through a main vertical zone bulkhead of a passenger vessel, how could you determine in case of fire whether the automatic damper had functioned properly?

A. Such damper is fitted with a visible indicator which shows whether it is opened or closed.

Q. At what temperatures do automatic fire dampers operate to close passenger ship vent ducts? In locations such as the galley, what temperature is permitted?
A. They are designed to operate at approximately 165° F. in normal locations; in locations such as galleys, at approximately 212° F.

Q. How would you inspect the ventilation duct dampers for necessary maintenance and repairs?
A. By removing the hinged or bolted plate in each duct, which is installed for access to the damper.

Q. How may a person unfamiliar with a passenger vessel find the location of fire-fighting equipment and means of ingress as quickly as possible if the vessel is over 1,000 gross tons or on international voyages?
A. By consulting the general arrangement plans required to be permanently exhibited for the guidance of the officer in charge of the vessel. These plans show for each deck the various fire sections limited by fire-retardant bulkheads; particulars of fire detecting, manual alarm, and fire-extinguishing systems; fire doors and means of ingress to different compartments; and ventilating systems, including positions of dampers and identification of fans serving each section.

Q. What regulations govern making alterations, repairs, or operations involving riveting, welding, burning, etc., in or on the boundary of oil tanks, oil lines, or oil heating coils?
A. In accordance with the Rules and Regulations for Tank Vessels currently in effect for new construction, insofar as is possible. Minor alterations or repairs shall be in accordance with regulations in effect at time vessel was contracted for or built but, where possible, in accordance with regulations for new construction.

Q. Describe the precautions against fire from electrical cables and lighting fixtures that you would take in cargo holds.
A. Before taking in cargo, inspection of holds should include examination of all lighting fixtures and cables, and renewals or repairs where necessary should be effected at once. Where cargo is of a type likely to cause damage to the fittings, frequent inspections should be made in the course of cargo transfer. Hold lights should be switched off immediately after hatches are closed.

Q. What publication sets forth the regulations for transportation of explosives or other dangerous cargoes?
A. Explosives or Other Dangerous Articles on Board Vessels issued by U.S. Coast Guard under the designation C G - 187.

Q. What is the duty of the master of a vessel carrying dangerous goods when the containers in which these goods are packed develop leaks during the voyage?

A. He may dispose of such faulty goods by jettisoning or otherwise destroying or rendering them innocuous, or may carry them to the nearest port, whichever course in his judgment provides maximum safety for ship and personnel. If damaged or leaky containers are brought into port, delivery shall not be made to consignee directly or indirectly. A report must be made to the nearest Officer in Charge, Marine Inspection, with request as to disposition of the goods. A report also must be made covering disposal of any dangerous goods carried as cargo during the voyage.

Q. What amount of carbon dioxide is required aboard merchant vessels fitted with the CO_2 type of extinguishing system?
A. The amount in pounds required for each cargo space shall be equal to the gross volume of the space in cubic feet divided by 30. For machinery spaces, paint lockers, tanks, etc., amount required for each shall be equal to gross volume divided by the appropriate factor given in the Regulations.

Q. On vessels fitted with mechanical exhaust ventilation over galley ranges, what precautions should be taken to prevent fire in vent ducts? Explain your reasons.
A. In addition to the automatic and manual dampers required in the vent ducts for closing off passage of air in event of fire, galley vent ducts should be protected against entry of sparks or flame by a fine-meshed wire screen. Such screen should be periodically removed and cleaned, and the ducts also should be kept in clean condition. The hazard of an oily or fatty deposit in the vents or on the screens due to their close proximity to the galley range demands such precautionary measures.

29. SHIP SANITATION

Q. What measures should be taken to insure that men handling food are free from communicable diseases, and take sanitary precautions while performing their duties?
A. They should have a thorough physical examination once a year and an inspection for communicable diseases at frequent intervals between such examinations. A carrier of typoid or other communicable disease for obvious reasons should never be permitted to handle food, dishes, or eating utensils. Any crew members signed on without examination should not be assigned to duty in steward's department until they have passed a thorough medical examination.

Steward's department workers above all others should be impressed with the need to reduce communicable disease. They should be scrupulously clean in their bodies and clothing and should form the habit of washing their hands with soap and water before preparing food and after each trip to the head. The hands should be thoroughly dried before returning to the galley.

Q. What type of toilet seats must be provided for the use of the crew?

A. Open front type that automatically lift up when not in use.

Q. What provisions for the protection of the crew are required on vessels trading in areas where insects are a problem?
A. By the fitting of suitable screens to ventilating skylights, air-ports, ventilators, and doors to uncreened spaces and the open deck, or by other methods.

Q. How should hose used for filling potable water tanks be stowed, and what care should be taken in handling such hose?
A. It should be stowed preferably near the potable water filling line in an easily accessible closed cabinet, which should be clearly marked POTABLE WATER HOSE ONLY. Or, if not stowed in this way, its ends should be capped with appropriately attached threaded metal fittings to minimize contamination of inside surface.
   The hose should be handled so that its ends never are dropped or dragged in contaminated water or in any other way harmfully exposed to unsanitary treatment.

Q. What is the purpose of the check valve shown on a pier's water connection used for connecting a ship's fire line to a shore supply of water pressure?

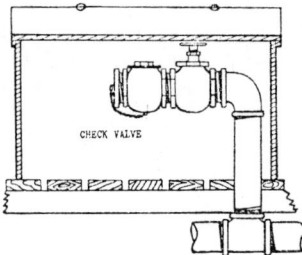

CHECK VALVE

A. So that, in the event of pressure building up in ship's fire main to exceed that in the shore line, any impurities may not enter the latter.

Q. How should potable water piping be marked?
A. It should be suitably stenciled, painted or striped with 6-inch bands of light blue paint at fittings, on each side of partitions, decks, and bulkheads, and at intervals not exceeding 15 feet in all spaces except quarters, dining rooms, saloons, and other public places where the interior finish would be marred. Either the bodies of valves installed in that part of the potable water system which is marked should be painted light blue or the valve wheel should be appropriately labeled.

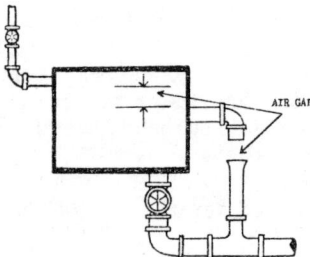

AIR GAP

Q. Why is an air gap, such as that illustrated, required in sinks, wash basins, tubs, trays, washing machines or other similar receptacles that may be connected to a potable water supply?
A. So that the displaced air in the waste pipe may not be retarded, and the water flow consequently hampered, when contents of receptacle are released.

Q. How would you detect the presence of rats on board your vessel?

A. By marks of their destructive gnawing habits, which are never confined to a single package of edible cargo or stores; by their nestings in corners in the holds, near storerooms, etc.; by their droppings which may be found in almost any location, but especially where the rat may find the necessary moisture for subsistence, such as condensation on piping or other metal surfaces, food refuse, etc.

Q. Describe the four methods which may be employed to prevent rat infestation of a vessel.

A. By use of rat guards properly placed on all mooring lines, together with the watchful closing of all side doors or other openings which admit passage of rats, while vessel is alongside.

By ratproof construction, in which passage through wood partitions, bilges, ducts, air openings, etc., is prevented by strong wire mesh.

By fumigation, which is done by release of a deadly gas, usually hydrocyanic, throughout entire vessel, all openings being closed.

By trapping, in which a sufficient number of traps are set in appropriate places.

30. RULES AND REGULATIONS FOR INSPECTION OF MERCHANT VESSELS

Q. How often must the lifeboat crew of a passenger vessel be exercised in their duties in the lifeboats, i.e., rowing, and operating hand-propelling gear in the water?

A. At least once in every 3 months.

Q. How often must each lifeboat of a passenger vessel be lowered to the water?

A. At least once in every 3 months.

Q. What members of the crew, if any, are not required to exercise at the oars?

A. Female members, if any.

Q. Where must copies be posted of the placard Instructions for the Use of the Gun and Rocket Apparatus for Saving Life from Ship Wreck as Practised by the United States Coast Guard?

A. In the pilothouse, engine room, and in crew's quarters of all vessels.

Q. What is the minimum standard for natural or artificial lighting in spaces where the crew is regularly employed or quartered?

A. That it will be possible on a clear day to read print such as that of an ordinary newspaper in any part of the clear working space.

When it is not possible to provide adequate natural lighting, artificial lighting may be accepted on the same basis.

Q. What color paint must be used in crew spaces?
A. Interior sides and deckheads of crew spaces shall be coated with enamel, paint, or other material light in color.

Q. What persons are excluded from the pilothouse and bridge of vessels under way? What persons may be allowed on the bridge under the responsibility of the Master?
A. All persons not connected with navigation of the vessel; but, upon the responsibility of the officer in charge, the following may be allowed: U. S. Coast Guard inspectors, licensed officers of vessels, apprentice pilots, officers of U. S. Coast Guard, Navy, Coast and Geodetic Survey, and Engineering Department of the U. S. Army, or Maritime Administration personnel.

Q. Describe the signalling lights required on vessels over 150 gross tons, both for new and existing vessels.
A. For vessels contracted for on and after November 19, 1952, a device which produces a narrow, high-intensity beam of light suitable for daylight communication at speeds up to 9 words per minute. Axial candlepower of beam shall be not less than 60,000, with a total divergency of approximately 6 degrees. The lamp shall be fitted with a suitable sighting arrangement capable of directing the beam on the receiving station. It may be operated by keying current through the lamp, by moving shutters, or by other approved means. It may be either a fixed unit mounted above the wheelhouse, a semi-fixed unit for quick mounting at either side of navigating bridge, or a portable unit. Fixed and semi-fixed lights to be energized from ship's emergency power and lighting system; portable lights from a storage battery capable of operating the units 2 hours continuously without recharging.
  For existing vessels built after November 19, 1952, an efficient lamp with a Fresnel lens and high-speed bulb operated by a waterproof key, fitted with a suitable condenser. Lamp shall be permanently fixed above the bridge and so connected that it may be operated from the emergency power source.

Q. What certificate is accepted as prima facie evidence of compliance with the Rules and Regulations for Bulk Grain Cargo?
A. Certificate of loading issued by the National Cargo Bureau, Inc.

Q. Must the station bill set forth the duties and duty stations of apprentices, beauty parlor operators, horse tenders, or workaways? Explain.
A. Yes. Each member of the crew is assigned special duties and a duty station for the various emergencies. The duties, as far as possible, shall be comparable with the regular work of the individual.

Q. State in detail the requirements of the regulations with respect to drills with line-throwing appliances?

A. The master is charged with the duty of drilling his crew in the use of such appliance, including the actual firing of the projectile and line at least once in every three months. The service line provided may not be used for drill purposes, but any flexible line of proper size and length, suitably faked or laid out, shall be used with the projectile at each drill.

Q. What vessels are required to have an emergency squad? Do the regulations permit other than required vessels to have such a squad?
A. Passenger vessels in which the size of crew permits. Yes.

Q. What are the duties of the emergency squad?
A. The squad shall be specially trained in use of all emergency and rescue equipment and should be made generally familiar with the vessel and fundamentals of damage control.

Q. What is the signal for the assembling of the emergency squad?
A. Such signal is left to the discretion of the master, providing it shall not conflict with any general alarm of navigational signal.

31. LAWS GOVERNING MARINE INSPECTION

Q. Should the master of a vessel fail to produce logbooks, advance sheets, slop chest invoices, or accounts requested by the shipping commissioner, is he liable to penalty? Would a mate or other member of the crew be liable for such a failure?
A. Yes; he is liable to a penalty of not more than $100 for each offense, and may be further punished for contempt of process of court.
   Yes; any member of the crew called upon in such matter is liable for same penalty.

Q. What is the law concerning time off duty for licensed officers before taking charge of a watch on sailing day?
A. The master, owner, agent, or other person having authority shall not permit an officer of any vessel to take charge of the deck watch upon leaving or immediately after leaving port, unless such officer has had at least 6 hours off duty within the 12 hours immediately preceding time of sailing.

Q. In the event of any collision with a light ship, buoy or other aid to navigation, what is the duty of the person in charge of the colliding vessel?
A. The person in charge of such vessel shall report the accident to the nearest Officer in Charge, Marine Inspection.

Q. What penalty is provided by the law for failure to maintain the crew quarters in a clean and sanitary condition and failure to pro-vide and maintain the proper plumbing and mechanical appliances?
A. Such vessel's certificate of inspection shall be withdrawn and shall not be reissued until the faulty condition has been corrected.

The master or other licensed officer of the vessel who is responsible for such improper condition of the vessel shall be subject to a penalty of not more than $500.

Q. What is the duty of the master of a vessel with respect to an alien stowaway and to what penalty is he liable for failure to perform such duty?

A. He must detain on board, or at any place designated by an immigration officer, any alien stowaway until such person has been inspected; he also must detain stowaway on board, or in another designated place after inspection, if ordered to do so by an immigration officer; and, when required by an immigration officer, he shall deport such stowaway either on his own vessel or another, at the expense of his own vessel.

Failure to perform such duty with respect to each stowaway subjects the master to a payment of $1,000 to the collector of customs.

Q. Whenever possible, who must sanction the engagement of a seaman in a foreign port?

A. A U.S. consular officer.

Q. Where must the tonnage and official number of every documented vessel be placed?

A. Carved or otherwise permanently marked on the vessel's main beam.

Q. What ratings may be filled by a seaman holding a merchant mariner's document endorsed able seaman?

A. Any unqualified rating in the deck department and as a lifeboatman.

Q. What is the penalty for maltreatment of crew?

A. A fine of not more than $1,000, or imprisonment for not more than 5 years, or both.

Q. What is the penalty for shipping a man not holding a merchant mariner's document issued by the Coast Guard?

A. A fine of $100 for each offense.

PART III. MASTER

1. LATITUDE BY POLARIS

Q. On 26 August, 1959, in D. R. Longitude 36° -10'West, Polaris was observed at <u>evening twilight</u> to have a sextant altitude of 23° - 25' and a <u>bearing of 001°</u> by gyro-compass. The chronometer read 21h-26m-40s. The chronometer was 1m-50s slow. The sextant error was 1'.0 on the arc. The height of eye was 30 feet.

Required: The latitude at time of sight and the gyro-compass error.

A. Chron.   21h 26m 40s H_s 23° 25.0'

Chron.	21h 26m 40s		H_s	23° 25.0'		
Error, slow	+ 1 50		I. E.	− 1.0		
G. M. T. 26 Aug.	21 28 30		Dip	− 5.3		
G. H. A. Aries	289° 21.6'		Refr.	− 2.2		
corr.	+ 7 08.7		H_o	23 16.5		
	296 30.3		Const.	− 1 00.0 *		
Long. W.	36 10.0		a_o	+ 1 33.8 *		
L. H. A. Aries =	260 20.3		a_1	+ .3 *		
Z_n Polaris	000.8° *		a_2	+ .9 *		
Gyro	001.0°		Latitude =	23° 51.5' N.		
Gyro error	.2° W.					

*(Nautical Almanac Corrections)

3. FIX OR RUNNING FIX

Q. Enroute from Pago Pago, Samoa to San Francisco, in D. R. Latitude 2°-47' South and Longitude 161°-19' West, three celestial bodies were observed.

Given the following information on the celestial bodies, determine the ship's position.

Body	Observed Altitude	Greenwich Hour Angle	Declination
DENEBOLA------	57°-54'.4	188°-30'.4	14°-48'.9 N.
VEGA ----------	09°-48'.9	86°-25'.4	38°-44'.7 N.
SATURN(Planet)--	56°-24'.9	130°-34'.2	17°-20'.3 S.

A. G. H. A. Denebola   188° 30.4'

Long. W.	161 19.0			
L. H. A. , W.	27 11.4	L hav	8.74224	From Azimuth Tables.
Lat. D. R. , S.	2 47.0	L cos	9.99949	H. O. 71, Z_n = 304°.
Dec. N.	14 48.9	L cos	9.98532	Through point lying
		L hav	8.72705	304°, 4.4', from D. R.
		Nat Hav	05334	Position, draw Posi-
L - D	17 35.9	Nat hav	02340	tion Line in a 214°
	32° 10'.....	Nat hav	07674	and 34° direction.
	90			
H_c	57° 50'			
H_o	57 54.4			
	4.4' toward			

G. H. A. Vega	86° 25. 4'		
Long. W.	161 19. 0		
L. H. A. , E.	74 53. 6	L hav	9. 56783
Lat. D. R. , S	2 47. 0	L cos	9. 99949
Dec. N.	38 44. 7	L cos	9. 89206
		L hav	9. 45938
		Nat hav	28800
L - D	41 31. 7	Nat hav	12569
	80° 03. 5'. . . .	Nat hav	41369
	90		
H_c	9° 56. 5'		
H_0	9 48. 9		
	7. 6' away		

From Azimuth Tables. H. O. 71, Z_n = 50°. Through point lying 230°, 7. 6', from D. R. Position, draw Position Line in a 320° and 140° direction.

G. H. A. Saturn	130° 34. 2		
Long. W.	161 19. 0		
L. H. A. , E.	30 44. 8	L hav	8. 84685
Lat. D. R. , S.	2 47. 0	L hav	9. 99949
Dec. S.	17 20. 3	L hav	9. 97980
		L hav	8. 82614
		Nat hav	06701
L - D	14 33. 3	Nat hav	01605
	33 30. 0	Nat hav	08306
	90		
H_c	56° 30. 0'		
H_0	56 24. 9		
	5. 1' away		

From Azimuth Tables. H. O. 71, Z_n = 118°. Through point lying 298°, 5. 1', from D. R. Position, draw Position Line in a 208° and 28° direction.

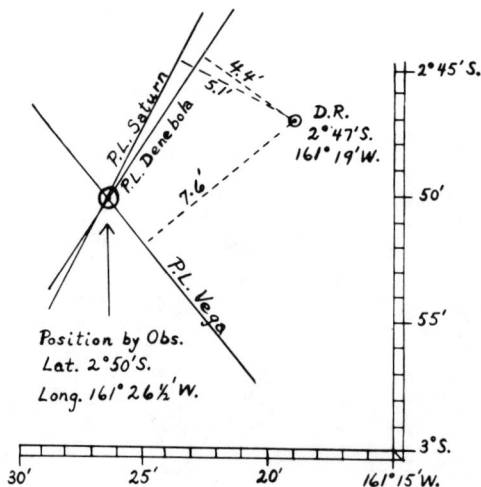

Position by Obs.
Lat. 2°50'S.
Long. 161° 26½'W.

D.R.
2°47'S.
161°19'W.

4. STAR IDENTIFICATION

Q. On April 17, 1959, in Latitude 41° 16' South and Longitude 92° 38' East, a morning observation is taken at 22h 28m 28s G. M. T. of a star whose corrected altitude is 54° 28' and whose azimuth is 297° true.

Required: Identify the star.

A.

G. M. T.	16 Apr.	22h 28m 28s	
G. H. A.	Aries, 22h,	174° 17. 7'	
Corr.		+7 07. 0	
		181 24. 7	
Long. E.		+92 38. 0	
L. H. A. Aries		274 02. 7	
		360	
S. H. A. Ship		85 57. 3	
Approx. L. H. A. star		33 30	W.
Do. S. H. A. do.		119 27	

From H. O. 214: Under LAT. 41°- DECLINATION SAME NAME AS LATITUDE, Altitude 54° 28' and Azimuth 117° (Z_n 297°) indicates an H. A. of very nearly 33. 5° and a Declination of 19. 5° S. Consulting the Star List, page 268, Nautical Almanac, we find <u>Beta Scorpii</u> to be the star in question.

Q.

Given:	No. 1	No. 2	No. 3
Date -------	7 January, 1959	31 May, 1959	23 September, 1959
GMT -------	01h-17m-23s	11h-47m-02s	20h-02m-20s
Longitude---	58°-20'. 0 West	149°-49'. 0 East	20°-39'. 0 West

Required: The Meridian Angle, Horizontal Parallax, and Declination of the Moon in each of the three cases. Indicate whether the Moon is East or West of the Meridian in each case.

A.

	No. 1	No. 2	No. 3
G. M. T.	8 Jan. 01h 17m 23s	31 May 11h 47m 02s	23 Sept. 20h 02m 20s
G. H. A. Moon	210° 28. 5'	50° 23. 1'	226° 23. 1'
Corr.	+ 4 08.9	+11 13. 4	+ 33. 4
	+ 1. 7	+ 11. 6	+ . 5
	214 39. 1	61 48. 1	226 57. 0
Long.	58 20. 0 W.	149 00. 0 E.	20 39. 0 W.
L. H. A. Moon	156 19. 1 W.	210 48. 1 W.	206 18. 0 W.
or		360	360
Mer. Angle	....	149° 11. 9 E.	153 42. 0 E.
Dec.	18° 38. 1' S.	2° 00. 7' N.	17° 42. 8' N.
Corr.	—. 4	+ 7. 5	+. 1
Dec.	18° 37. 7' S.	2° 08. 2' N.	17° 42. 9' N.
Hor. Par.	59. 3'	54. 8'	54. 2'

Q. Given:	No. 1	No. 2	No. 3
	Venus	Jupiter	Saturn
Date -------	2 January, 1959	14 May, 1959	15 August, 1959
GMT -------	3h-47m-22s	9h-25m-45s	23h-02m-19s
Longitude---	123°-47'.0 West	165°-23'.0 East	88°-38'.0 West

Required: The Meridian Angle and Declination of the Planet in each of the three cases. Indicate whether the planet is East or West of the Meridian in each case.

A.	No. 1	No. 2	No. 3
	Venus	Jupiter	Saturn
G. M. T.	3 Jan. 03h 47m 22s	14 May 09h 25m 45s	15 Aug. 23h 02m 19s
G. H. A.	210° 07. 6'	130° 40. 4'	37° 45. 3'
Corr.	+11 51. 2	+ 6 27. 5	+ 34. 9
	221 58. 8	137 07. 9	38 20. 2
Long.	123 47.0 W.	165 23.0 E.	88 38.0 W
Mer. Angle	98° 11. 8' W.	302 30.9 W.	50 17.8 E
		or 57 29.1 E.	
Dec.	22° 24. 1' S.	18° 34. 4' S.	22° 37. 0' S.
Corr.	− .4	0. 0	0. 0
	22° 23. 7' S.	18° 34. 4' S.	22° 37. 0' S.

Q. The following 3 sextant altitudes of the moon were obtained. The height of eye was 61 feet and the sextant index error was 2'.5 on the arc in all observations. Given:

			(Upper Limb)
	Observation No. 1	Observation No. 2	Observation No. :
Moon sext. alt. -----	6°-17'.8	23°-26'.2	46°-42'.8
Bar. Pressure -----	29.2 in.	980 mb.	30.4 in.
Temperature-------	51° F.	0° Celsius	80° F.
		(Centigrade)	
Hor. Parallax ------	55'.5	61'.2	57'.9

Required: The observed altitudes.

A.	Obs. No. 1	Obs. No. 2	Obs. No. :
H$_S$ Moon's L. L.	6° 17. 8' ...... L. L.	23° 26. 2' ......U. L.	46° 42.
			− 2.
Index Error	− 2. 5	− 2. 5	− 7.
Dip	− 7. 6	− 7. 6	
App. alt.	6 07. 7	23 16. 1	46 32.
			− 30.
			0
Press. & Temp.	+ .2	− .1	+ 49
Par. & Refr.	+ 59. 7	+1 01. 4	+ 3
	+ 2. 2	+ 9. 2	
H$_O$ Moon's Cent.	7 09. 8	24 26. 6	46 55

Q. The following 3 sextant altitudes of planets were obtained on 6 February, 1959. The height of eye was 18 feet, the sextant index error was 2'.5 off the arc in all observations. Given:

	Saturn Observation No. 1	Jupiter Observation No. 2	Venus Observation No. 3
Planet sext. alt. -	7°-56'. 7	15°-37'. 9	21°-17'. 7
Bar. Pressure --	29. 0 in.	1000 mb.	30. 0 in.
Temperature----	(—) 5° F.	33° Celsius (Centigrade)	52° F.

Required: The observed altitudes.

A.

	Saturn Obs. No. 1	Jupiter Obs. No. 2	Venus Obs. No. 3
H_S	7° 56. 7'	15° 37. 9'	21° 17. 7'
Index Error	+ 2. 5	+ 2. 5	+ 2. 5
Dip	— 4. 1	— 4. 1	— 4. 1
App. alt.	7 55. 1	15 36. 6	21 16. 1
Press. & Temp.	— . 8	+ . 3	0. 0
Par. & Refr.	— 6. 6	— 3. 4	— 2. 4
H_O	7° 47. 7'	15° 33. 5'	21° 13. 7'

5. CHART NAVIGATION

Q. What chart would you use to locate the earth's magnetic equator?
A. An isomagnetic chart which gives the magnetic inclination or dip in all parts of the world, as H.O. Chart 1700, for a certain epoch or year.

Q. A vessel at 60° South Latitude is 300 miles due West of a radio beacon. Determine graphically, by use of the conversion angle formula:
   conversion angle = 1/2 difference longitude x sine Middle Latitude, or by table, the bearing that would be obtained by the use of a radio direction finder.
A. 300 miles W. of radio beacon × sec 60° = 300 × 2.000 = 600' = 10° 00' D. Long. Entering Table 1, Bowditch, in "Latitude of Receiver 60°, Same Name," under Latitude of transmitter 60°, find Correction 4.3° abreast of D. Long. 10°. Radio bearing therefore would be 90° + 4.3°, or 94.3°.

Q. When a scale is given for a Mercator chart, to what part of the chart is it generally applicable?
A. To the mean latitude of the charted area. The latitude scale is also the scale of distance on such chart, and a unit of such scale is taken abreast of the area considered.

Q. How is distance measured on a polyconic chart?
A. By a straight line joining the points considered. The correct distance scale is along any parallel or along the central meridian of the chart.

Q. Make a rough sketch showing how the charted island with contours indicated would appear at positions A and B in profile.

(contour interval— 200 feet)

A.

A   B

Q. The distance between two points on a polyconic chart of the Great Lakes is 100 statute miles. How long would it take a vessel making 15 knots to traverse the distance?

A.
$$\text{Hours} = \frac{100}{1.15 \times 15} = \frac{4}{.69} = 5.8, \text{ or } 5 \text{ hrs., } 48 \text{ mins.}$$

Q. Describe how you use a gnomonic chart to determine a composite Great Circle Track with a limiting latitude.

A. Lay off a straight line (arc of a great circle) from point of departure, tangent to the limiting parallel (small circle indicating highest latitude desired to navigate), and another straight line from point of destination, also tangent to the limiting parallel.

If required to transfer this composite track to a Mercator chart, various points are selected, say at each 200 miles, along the route and laid off as with great circle sailing.

Q. Name the type of Gnomonic Chart sketched.
A. A Polar Gnomonic Chart.

Q. How does a rhumb line appear on a polyconic chart?
A. A slightly curved line having its convexity away from the pole.

Q. After laying down a straight line between two points on a polyconic chart, how would you determine the course?

A. The course is indicated by the angle which such straight line makes with the meridian of the mean longitude of the points in question.

Q. Positions X and Y are determined by using the three arm protractor to plot the angles measured by the sextant between shore
objects A and B, and B and C. Should position X or Y be considered more reliable? Why?

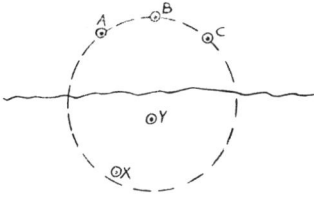

A. Position Y is the more reliable.
Since vessel's position is located at
the intersection of two circles, viz.,
one passing through A, B, and Y,
the other through B, C, and Y, position Y is satisfactorily defined in the
conditions noted, while X is so close
to being on the identical circles passing through A-B and B-C that the
point may not be definitely established.

Q. Give the meaning of the following symbols as shown on a chart:

A. A sunken wreck not dangerous to surface navigation. General
current setting in the direction indicated at 2 knots velocity. A
sunken rock considered a danger to navigation.

6. COMPASS DEVIATION

(Azimuth—Moon)

Q. Enroute from Honolulu, Hawaii to Manila, Philippine Islands, in
D. R. Latitude 22°-27' North and Longitude 175°-20' East, an azimuth of the Moon was observed. The following data was obtained
at the time of observation:

Compass Bearing of Moon	Greenwich Hour Angle	Declination of Moon
81°-00' psc	107°-29'.8	2°-51'.3 N.

Variation for the locality was 9°-00'.00 East
Required: The true azimuth.
The deviation of the standard compass.

A. G. H. A. Moon   107° 29.8'   From Azimuth Tables, H. O. 71,
   Long. E.   + 175 20.0   Lat. 22° 27' same name as Dec.,
   L. H. A.   282 49.8 W.   True Azimuth = 92° 18'
              or   77° 10.2' E.   Comp. Bearing = 81° 00'
               =   5h 08m 41s   Comp. Error   = 11° 18' E.
                                         Variation   = 9° 00' E.
                                         Deviation   = 2° 18' E.

9. MERCATOR SAILING

Q. By Mercator sailing, find the true course and distance from a
point in the proximity of Cape Race in Latitude 46°-18' North and
Longitude 52°-35' West to Diamond Shoal Light Ship in Latitude
35°-05'.3 North and Longitude 75°-19'.7 West. Show all work.

A. From Lat. 46° 18' N.   M. P.   3124. 7   Long.   52° 35' W.
   To   "   35 05.3 N.   2237. 1   "   75 19. 7 W.
       D. Lat = 11 12. 7   M. D. L. = 887. 6   D. Long = 22 44. 7
               = 672. 7' S.   = 1364. 7' W.

   Tan Co = D. Long ÷ M. D. L.
   1364. 7   Log   3. 13503   Dist. = D. Lat × sec Co
    887. 6   "   2. 94822   672. 7   Log 2. 82782
   56° 58' L tan   10. 18681 .... L sec   0. 26342
   Course = 237°   Distance = 1234 miles   1233. 8   Log 3. 09124

10. GREAT CIRCLE SAILING

Q. Enroute from New London, Conn. to São Luiz, Brazil, a vessel
leaves point A at Latitude 41°-06' North, Longitude 71°-42' West
for point B at Latitude 01°-17' South, Longitude 44°-55' West.
   Find:
       Great Circle Distance.
       Great Circle Initial Course.
       Great Circle Final Course.
       Great Circle Latitude of Vertex.
       Great Circle Longitude of Vertex.
       Great Circle Longitude of Equator Crossing.
       Great Circle Course at Equator.

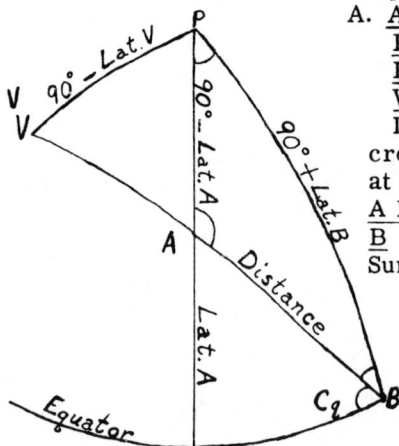

A. A B = G.C. Distance
   P A B = G.C. Initial Course
   P B A = G.C. Final Course — 180°
   V   = Position of Vertex
   Long. V — 90° = Long. of Equator
   crossing; 180° — (90° — C_q) = G.C. Course
   at Equator crossing.
   A Lat. 41° 06' N.   Long. 71° 42' W
   B   1 17 S.   44 55 W
   Sum = 42° 23'   APB = D. Long. 26 47 E

For the Distance A B: For the Initial Course:
Hav A B = hav (Lat A + Lat B) + hav θ   (Sin PAB = sin APB. sin PB)
(hav θ = cos Lat A. cos Lat B. hav APA)   sin AB
Lat A   41° 06'   L cos 9. 87712   APB 26° 47'   L sin 9. 65381
Lat B   1° 17'   " cos 9. 99989   PB   91° 17'   " sin 9. 99989
APB   26° 47'   " hav 8. 72950   AB   48° 52'   " csc 0. 12310
                    N hav   04041   PAB 143° 16'   " sin 9. 77680
        42° 23'   "   " 13067   or Initial Course =   143. 3°
A B   48° 52' .... "   " 17108
or Distance = 48° 52' × 60 = 2932 miles.   (PAV = 180° — 143° 16')
                                              = 36° 44'

For the Final Course:
$(\text{Sin } 180° - PBA = \dfrac{\text{Sin } APB. \cos \text{Lat A}}{\sin AB})$

APB	26° 47'	L sin 9.65381
Lat A	41° 06'	" cos 9.87712
AB	48° 52'	" csc 0.12310
PBA	26° 48'	" sin 9.65403

Final Course = 180° — 26° 48'
       or 153.2°

For G.C. Course at Equator:
Since Lat V = angle C_q,
Course = 180° — (90° — 63° 13')
      = 90° + 63° 13'
      = 153° 13'
or Course at Equator = 153.2°

For Lat. of Vertex:
$(\text{Cos Lat V} = \cos \text{Lat A}. \sin PAV)$

Lat A	41° 06'	L cos 9.87712
PAV	36° 44'	" sin 9.77677
Lat V	63° 13' N	" cos 9.65389

For Long. of Vertex and
    Long. of Equator Crossing:
$(\text{Cot } APV = \sin \text{Lat A}. \tan PAV)$

Lat A	41° 06'	L sin 9.81781
PAV	36° 44'	" tan 9.87290
APV	63° 52'	" cot 9.69071

Long. A 71° 42' W.

Long. V 135° 34' W. Vertex
         90° 00'

Long.   45° 34' W. Equator
               Crossing.

Q. From Farallon Island, L.H., San Francisco, at Latitude 37°-42' North, Longitude 123°-00' West, to San Bernardino Island L.H., in the Philippine Islands, at Latitude 12°-45' North, Longitude 124°-17' East. Find: Great Circle Distance; Great Circle Initial Course; Great Circle Final Course; Great Circle Latitude of Vertex; Great Circle Longitude of Vertex.
    The Latitude of Three Points Whose Longitudes Differ 5°, 10°, and 15°, Respectively, from that of the Vertex.

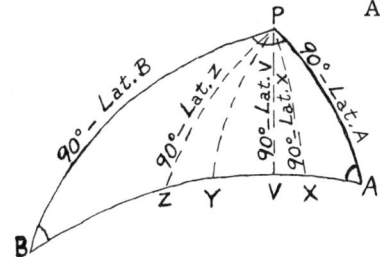

A.   A B = G.C. Distance
360° — PAB = G.C. Initial Course
180° + PBA = G.C. Final Course
 90° — PV   = Lat. of Vertex
APV   = Long. of Vertex - Long. A
 90° — PX = Lat. of a point X
 90° — PY = Lat. of a point Y
 90° — PZ = Lat. of a point Z

For the Distance A B:
By cosine-haversine formula)

PA	112° 43'	L hav 9.84079
Lat A	37° 42' N.	" cos 9.89830
Lat B	12° 45' N.	" cos 9.98916
		hav 9.72825
		N hav 53488
Lat	24° 57'	" hav 04666
B	99° 23'	" hav 58154

or Distance = 99° 23' × 60
          = 5963 miles.

A	Lat.	37° 42' N.	Long. 123° 00' W.
B		12° 45' N.	124° 17' E.
D.	Lat.	24° 57'	247° 17'
			360° 00'
			APB 112° 43'

For the Initial Course:
$(\text{Sin } PAB = \sin APB. \sin PB. \csc AB)$

APB	112° 43'	L sin	9.96493
Lat. B	12° 45'	" cos	9.98916
AB	99° 23'	" csc	0.00585
PAB	65° 46'	" sin	9.95994
360° 00'			

294° 14' or Initial Course = 294.2°

For <u>Lat. of Vertex</u>:

(Cos <u>Lat V</u> = cos <u>Lat A</u>. sin <u>PAB</u>)

Lat A	37° 42'	L cos 9.89830
PAB	65° 46'	" sin 9.95994
Lat V	43° 49' N	" cos 9.85824

For <u>Long. of Vertex</u>:

(Cot <u>APV</u> = sin Lat A. tan <u>PAB</u>)

Lat A	37° 42'	L sin 9.78642
PAB	65° 46'	L tan 0.34667
APV	36° 21'	L cot 0.13309
Long A	123° 00' W.	
Long V	159° 21' W.	

For <u>Lat. of point Y</u>:

(Tan <u>Lat Y</u> = cos 10°. tan <u>Lat V</u>)

VPY	10° 00'	L cos 9.99335
Lat V	43° 49'	" tan 9.98206
Lat Y	43° 23' N.	" tan 9.97541

For the <u>Final Course</u>:

(Sin <u>PBA</u> = cos <u>Lat V</u>. sec <u>Lat B</u>)

Lat V	43° 49'	L cos 9.85827
Lat B	12° 45'	" sec 0.01084
PBA	47° 43'	" sin 9.86911
	180° 00'	
	227° 43' or <u>Final Course</u>.	
	= 227.7°	

For <u>Lat. of point X</u>:

(Tan <u>Lat X</u> = cos 5°. tan <u>Lat V</u>)

VPX	5° 00'	L cos 9.99834
Lat V	43° 49'	" tan 9.98206
Lat X	43° 42' N.	

For <u>Lat. of point Z</u>:

(Tan <u>Lat Z</u> = cos 15°. tan <u>Lat V</u>)

VPZ	15° 00'	L cos 9.98494
Lat V	43° 49'	" tan 9.98206
Lat Z	42° 50' N.	" tan 9.96700

11. PILOTING

Q. In piloting a vessel through a curved section of a tidal river, where would you find the deepest water and the most rapid current?

A. Nearer the concave bank; with a sharper curve in river, the channel would lie closer to such bank.

Q. Name some of the factors you would consider in selecting a good anchorage site.

A. Strength of current; range of tide; nature of holding ground; depth of water; shelter afforded by land; radius of swing about anchor; facilities for communication with shore, by boat or signal.

Q. Describe a method of finding distance from an isolated object which is within a moderate distance, such as an islet or a vessel, over which the horizon may be seen.

A. By use of the angle of depression, or the angle measured vertically downward by sextant between the horizon and waterline of object or vessel. Table 22, <u>Bowditch</u>, "Dip of the Sea Short of the Horizon," gives the required distance as that corresponding to angle of depression observed at a given height of eye.

Q. Heading east on a dark night, you are a mile and a half north of a light which is located on the east end of a reef with no other aids to navigation visible. An outlying shoal lies two and a half

Note: Problems may be given pertaining to piloting which are under other titles in this book.

miles to the eastward of the light. With no appreciable current
and no range finder available, describe how you would round the
light, passing between the reef and the outlying shoal and maintaining the same distance off the light, until on a course of south-
east for open water.

A. Bring the light on the starboard beam, keeping it on that bearing until vessel has swung to South. Light would then be bearing
West; so the passage is cleared and course is altered to S. E.

Q. How may the sextant be used in order to round a lighthouse in
the daytime so as to maintain a constant distance off the lighthouse
until on a desired change of course?

A. Determine the vertical angle of lighthouse which corresponds to
required distance off. Then round the light so as to maintain such
angle by sextant equal to, or a little less than, the predetermined
value, until the desired change of course is reached.

Q. When making a landfall, if soundings should fail to agree in a
general way with those shown on the chart and a marked departure
from the characteristic bottom shown on the chart is noted, what
should be done?

A. Stop and take way off vessel at once. If a careful recheck of
courses and distances leading to this situation fails to indicate
the necessary corrective procedure, then remain stopped until
ship's true position is ascertained. Assuming no radio bearings
are available, no celestial observations, no recognizable landmarks
in sight, a passing vessel might be hailed or signaled for the necessary information. Failing the last expedient, and if depth of water is too great for anchoring, keep vessel in safe soundings until
her position is fixed by any reliable means, regardless of time
thus necessarily consumed in the interests of safety.

Q. Describe the use of depth contours (curves of equal depth) in
navigation.

A. Such curves are used as lines of position in that they show the
directions of loci of equal soundings. During thick weather, a
depth contour often may be followed as leading to a desired point,
as in making port. A radio bearing crossed with a depth contour
is used as a fix. Generally, their chief value lies in showing the
regularity or otherwise of coastal depths, thus simplifying the
navigator's work in keeping his vessel in consistently proper soundings.

12. AIDS TO NAVIGATION

Q. How would you estimate the power of a light whose candlepower
is not given?

A. In clear weather, a light may be estimated as high-powered,
medium-powered, etc., by its degree of brilliancy upon its appearance over the horizon at its geographic range; it may be estimated
as low-powered when not visible beyond its luminous range.

ORANGE

WHITE

ORANGE

WHITE

ORANGE

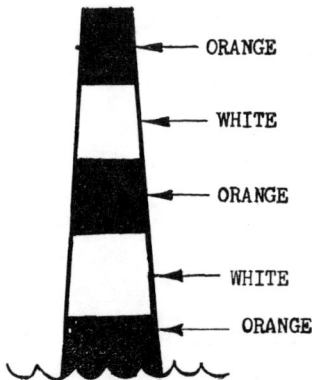

Q. Referring to the sketch: (a) What
type buoy is the orange and white
horizontally banded buoy shown, and
for what purpose would it be placed?
(b) How would such a buoy be indicated
on a chart?
A. This is a <u>spar</u> buoy placed for a
special purpose, which usually is indicated on chart. (b) ◖ <u>W Or</u>

Q. How do you obtain information about
foreign buoyage?
A. From the Sailing Directions covering the coasts in question, or from a
publication of the International Hydrographic Bureau entitled "Systems of
Maritime Buoyage and Beaconage adopted by Various Countries."
Such publications may be obtained by application to the U.S. Navy
Hydrographic Office, Washington, D.C.

13. SPEED BY REVOLUTIONS

Q. If the engine speed necessary to reach port at a designated time
is 12.6 knots and the pitch of the wheel is 13.6 feet, how many
revolutions per minute would have to be turned up?
A. $\text{Revs.} = \dfrac{12.6 \times 6076}{13.6 \times 60} = 93.8$, or 94 revolutions per minute.

14. FUEL CONSERVATION

Q. While turning up 90 revolutions per minute, a steamer consumes
8 barrels of fuel oil per hour. If it is determined that only 7
barrels of fuel per hour is available to reach port, how many
revolutions per minute shall the engines turn?
A. If R = revolutions required, then $8:7 = 90^3 : R^3$, and $R^3 = (90^3 \times 7)$
$\div 8$, or $R^3 = 729,000 \times 7 \div 8 = 91125 \times 7 = 637,875$.
Log R^3 = log 637875 = 5.804736
Log R = 5.804736 $\div$ 3 = 1.934912 = log 86.08, or 86 revolutions.

Q. A vessel has sufficient fuel to steam 760 miles at her normal
speed of 11 knots. If she has 915 miles yet to run on the same
amount of fuel, what speed must she reduce to?
A. Since consumption varies as speed squared times distance covered, and fuel consumed equals fuel remaining, then, if S = reduced speed,
$$\frac{11^2 \times 760}{915} = S^2 = \frac{121 \times 760}{915} = 100.5$$
whence, $S = \sqrt{100.5} = 10$ knots.

Q. A vessel has a trip 4,010 miles to make and leaves port with
1,010 tons of fuel. After running 2,500 miles at her normal speed

of 14 knots, the engineer reports he has only 270 tons of fuel remaining. At what reduced speed must you steam in order to reach your destination with 20 tons of fuel remaining?

A. 1010 — 270 = 740 tons fuel used at 14 knots;
   270 — 20 = 250 tons fuel to complete the passage;
   4010 — 2500 = 1510 miles to complete the passage;
   then, since fuel consumption varies as speed squared times the distance covered, we have,

$$\frac{740}{250} = \frac{14^2 \times 2500}{S^2 \times 1510}, \text{ from which } S^2 = \frac{250 \times 196 \times 2500}{740 \times 1510};$$

$$S = \sqrt{\frac{25 \times 196 \times 250}{74 \times 151}} = 10.47 \text{ knots.}$$

15. INSTRUMENTS AND ACCESSORIES

Q. Where, in the area covered by a pair of loran stations, may the most accurate lines of position be obtained?
A. Along the base line between the stations.

Q. Where, in the area covered by a pair of loran stations, are the least accurate lines of positions available?
A. Near the base line extensions.

Q. Why is loran known as a hyperbolic system of navigation?
A. Because the lines of position indicated on the Loran chart are hyperbolas, or lines connecting all points of equal difference of distance between two fixed transmitting stations.

Q. Within what distance from the transmitting station is the use of skywaves not to be relied on for obtaining a loran line of position?
A. Within about 250 miles.

Q. When a first sky wave and ground wave are matched, what precautions must be observed to obtain a line of position?
A. That the signals are identified correctly and the error avoided of using the wrong wave or failing to detect the true leading edge in the scope.

Q. Describe how the deviation of a radio direction finder is determined and how it is compensated.
A. Deviation is determined by comparison of the observed relative radio bearing with the correct relative bearing of the transmitting station. Thus, with relative bearing as observed by direction finder and correct relative bearing as observed by pelorus or gyro indicated as 48° and 46°, respectively, deviation is 2° Westerly. This is compensated by adjusting the cam arrangement so that the instrument will indicate 46° as the correct relative bearing. A calibration table of deviations is made up for directions of the incoming radio bearings relative to the ship's head.

16. MAGNETISM, DEVIATION AND COMPASS COMPENSATION

Q. If the easterly deviation increases on westerly headings as the
vessel steams north, what adjustment should be made in the Flinders bar?

A. Flinders bar should be increased in length by an amount which
will correct such increase in deviation.

Q. How would you correct westerly quadrantal deviation on a SW
heading?

A. By placing the quadrantal correctors in the fore-and-aft line, as
opposed to their usual position in the athwartship line, and setting
them at the appropriate distance from center of compass card, as
found by experiment.

Q. Does the heeling magnet, once adjusted, require change as the
vessel sails from one magnetic latitude into another? Explain your
answer.

A. Since the heeling error is caused chiefly by the vertical component of induced magnetism in soft iron, which increases with
the magnetic latitude, any material change in the latter necessi-
tates a new adjustment, and a change from N. to S. magnetic
latitude would require the magnet to be reversed, because of change
of polarity in the induced magnetism.

Q. If your compass card appears to be magnetically "frozen" on a
heading of 090° on all headings of the vessel, how would you adjust to correct this condition?

A. Assuming the fault is not with the compass itself, remove all
magnets and correctors from the binnacle and proceed to properly
compensate the compass.

Q. How would you detect and correct retained magnetism in the
soft iron spheres?

A. Rotate each sphere through 180° without altering its distance
from center of compass. If compass heading changes, sphere has
retained some magnetism. This may be corrected by tapping
sphere with a hammer when its blue pole is toward the north, or
by heating it to a dull red and cooling it slowly.

Q. Discuss the effects on the deviation of a compass when a vessel
stays on one course for several days, particularly in rough seas,
or lies at a dock on one heading for a lengthy period, or fails
to follow a reversal sequence in securing the degaussing equipment.

A. The effect on the compass deviation due to such conditions may
be summed up in the old rule that "the deviation hangs to the last
course."

During the period of unchanged heading, vessel is subjected to
an induced magnetism in her soft iron from the earth's field, which
results in an abnormal deviation upon first substantial change of

heading, attaining a maximum value for a change of 90°. Thus,
if vessel steers for a lengthy period approximately East magnetic,
she will attain, in northern latitudes, a polarity which is red to
port and blue to starboard of the fore-and-aft midship line. Then,
upon change to a northerly course, the polarity indicated will
cause an abnormal E'ly deviation, or will "hang to the last course."

Similarly, it may be shown that such a change from any heading
of lengthy duration adheres to the rule noted; however, the deviation observed upon such change of course rapidly decreases with
time occupied on the new heading.

Q. How would you test a magnetic compass for sensitivity?
A. Using a small magnet, draw the North point 2 degrees to either
side; then, removing the magnet, note with a magnifying glass its
exact position upon return to rest, as checked by the lubber line.
Repeat by drawing to the other side, and note result. Satisfactory
sensitivity is indicated, in a well-made compass, if card comes
to rest within one-sixth of a degree (as the mean of the two tests)
of its original position.

Q. How would you detect and correct retained magnetism in the
Flinders bar?
A. Hold each piece vertically with one end near and level with the
compass card, on its east or west side, and note the compass
reading. Then invert the piece of bar and again note compass
reading. If the reading differs, magnetism is retained in the bar
piece.

A small amount of magnetism may be removed by holding the
piece in the line of force of earth's field, with its blue pole toward north, and tapping one end gently with a hammer; but in
any case the surer treatment is to heat the bar to a dull red and
allow it to cool slowly.

Q. What sources of magnetism other than the vertical induction
from the earth's field may influence the action of the Flinders
bar?
A. From the mutual induction between the various correctors themselves; also, by induction from compass needles, fore-and-aft
and thwartship magnets, and heeling magnet.

Q. Given a compass and its Flinders
bar corrector arranged in alternate
positions as sketched. In which position will the Flinders bar exert the
greatest effect on the compass. Why?
A. Position A; because one of the bar's
poles or points of greatest magnetic
intensity is posed to exert its maximum effect. In B, compass
card is abreast of bar's neutral magnetic zone, or nearest its
polarity dividing line, and thus results in little or no effect.

Q. If a heeling adjuster or vertical force instrument is not available, how would you place the heeling magnet when adjusting the compass?
A. Place it at full distance down its tube, red pole up in northern latitudes, blue pole up in southern latitudes.

Q. How would you correct your compass for an easterly error due to permanent magnetism when the vessel is on an easterly heading?
A. By placing one or more of the fore-and-aft magnets in the binnacle, red pole forward, at such distance from compass card as will correct the error, and at that side of the midship line in which lie the opposite poles of any thwartship magnets in use.

17. CHART CONSTRUCTION

Q. Construct a small area plotting sheet for 59 degrees to 61 degrees North Latitude, allowing 3 inches for each degree of latitude.
A.

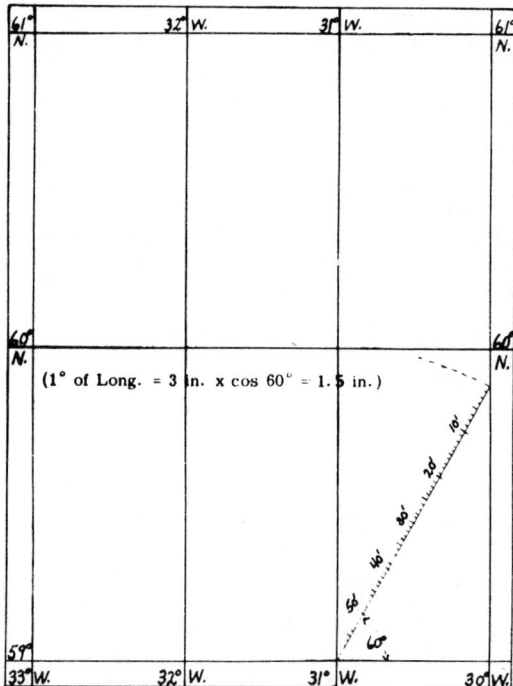

Q. Construct a Mercator chart, or a small area plotting sheet, for Latitudes 35 degrees North to 37 degrees North and Longitudes 157 degrees 30 minutes East to 158 degrees 30 minutes East. Use a scale of 2-3/8 inches to 1 degree of longitude and label latitude and longitude properly.

A.

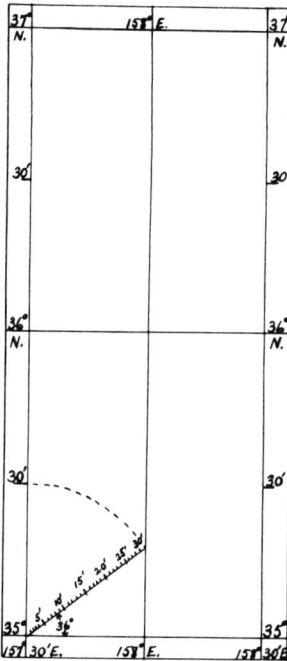

(In these charts, minutes of longitude are measured as perpendicular distance from the bordering meridian indicated to the appropriate number on the latitude and distance scale, shown as a slanted graduated line.)

18. TIDES AND CURRENTS

Q. At South End Woods Hole, Vineyard Sound-Buzzards Bay, (Latitude 41°-31' North and Longitude 70°-40' West): (a) What is the time and velocity of maximum AM flood current on 5 January 1959? (b) In what direction does the flood current flow at this point and what is the average velocity?

A. South End, Wood's Hole, 5 January, 1959.

(a) Cape Cod Canal, max. flood   0208   Velocity 4. 1 k.
                    constant + 140   ratio   . 4
     Wood's Hole, max flood   0348 . . . . vel. 1. 64 k

(b) 135° at average velocity 1. 5 kt.

Q. At Grindstone Island, Petitcodiac River, New Brunswick, Bay of Fundy: (a) What is the time and height of a. m. high water on 6 April, 1959? (b) What is the mean range of tides for this locality? (c) What is the spring range of tides for this locality? (d) What is the range of a. m. tides for this locality on 6 April, 1959? (e) What peculiar tidal phenomena may mariners encounter in this area?

A. Grindstone Id. , New Brunswick, Bay of Fundy, 6 April, 1959.

(a) St. John, N. B. , high water   1042   height 24. 8   ft.
                    constant + 19   ratio   1. 56
     Grindstone Id. , high water   1101   height 38. 7   ft.

(b) 32 feet.   (c) 36. 5 feet.   (d) Ht. of high water   38. 7 ft.
                                              Ht. of low water   5. 7 ft.
                                              Range of A. M. tide   33. 0 ft.
(e) The bore, or surge of flood tide about 2-1/2 hours before
high water, reaching 3-1/2 to 5 feet in height at springs.

Q. East of the Statue of Liberty in Upper Bay of New York: (a) Determine the time of a. m. slack high water on 10 April, 1959.
(b) What is the duration of slack water when a current less than
0. 1 knot can be expected?
A. East of Statue of Liberty, New York, 10 April, 1959.
   (a) H. W. slack, 9 April, 2255, at the Narrows, N Y. Harbor.
              constant + 55
                          2350
      H. W. slack, 10 April, 1109, at the Narrows, N. Y. Harbor.
              constant + 55
                          1204
   There is, therefore, no A. M. slack high water on 10 April.
   (b) By Table 4, Tide Tables, 12 minutes duration of slack.

Q. State what is meant by the diurnal inequality of the tides, and
describe the reasons why this phenomenon occurs.
A. A difference between the height of the two successive high waters
or low waters occurring in the tidal day (about 24 hours, 48 minutes).
   It is caused by the moon's changing position in declination. When
at low declination, the moon's attraction is nearly in the plane of
the equator, and an evenly distributed tide wave over all latitudes
results. As our satellite increases in declination, then a higher
high water and a lower high water alternately follow because the
moon's attraction now is in a direction oblique to the equator. A
place in north latitude, therefore, will now experience a higher
high water shortly after the moon's upper transit and a succeeding
high water of lesser height shortly after the moon's lower transit.
This difference is the diurnal inequality.

Q. Describe what is meant by a bore.
A. The banking up or surging of the incoming tide which occurs in
some estuaries. As the progressive tide-wave enters shallowing
water it is retarded by bottom friction and its front increasingly
steepens, until it develops into a foaming agitated wall of several
feet in depth, so forming the bore.

Q. What is meant by the term: high water lunitidal interval, establishment of the port, and vulgar establishment?
A. High water lunitidal interval is the elapsed time between the
moon's upper or lower transit and the next high water at a given
place.
   Establishment of the port is the average lunitidal interval,

usually determined from daily observations throughout one month. Vulgar establishment is the average lunitidal interval on days of full and new moon.

Q. Define: (a) The mean range of the tide. (b) The spring range of the tide. (c) The diurnal range of the tide.

A. (a) Difference in the heights of mean low water and mean high water.

(b) Difference in the heights of mean low water spring tides and mean high water spring tides.

(c) Difference between the lowest height and highest height of tide level on a particular day, or the average of such measure over a given period.

Q. Referring to the Current Diagram in the Atlantic Coast Current Tables, determine the time interval within which a 10 knot vessel should pass Overfalls L/V in order to go upstream with flood current to Chestnut Street, Philadelphia on the morning of 16 November, 1959.

A. Low water slack being at 0405, 16 November, 1959, at Overfalls L/V, vessel's best time to pass inward would be between 0405 and 0605.

Q. If, at the same time, a tidal current is setting north at 1.0 knot, and a wind-driven current is setting east at 1.0 knot, what is the resultant direction and velocity of current that may be expected from the combination of the two currents?

A. 045° at 1.4 knots.

Q. In a tidal strait, such as the English Channel, in which high and low water occur, respectively, at each entrance at about the same hour, at what location in such body of water would you expect (a) the greatest current velocity? (b) the greatest tidal range? (c) the least tidal range?

A. (a) At about its mid-length.
   (b) At its extreme ends.
   (c) At about its mid-length.

19. OCEAN WINDS, WEATHER AND CURRENTS

Q. Can a wet bulb thermometer ever properly read higher than a dry bulb?

A. No.

Q. How may the wet bulb temperature be determined in freezing weather?

A. Since freezing conditions render correct wet bulb readings impracticable, use of the hair hygrometer is resorted to, which instrument gives direct readings of the relative humidity.

substance to change its state at the boiling or freezing temperature; in changing from a liquid to a solid, or vice versa; or in
changing a liquid to a gas, or vice versa.

Q. What action does the Weather Bureau take when comparison indicates that a barometer is defective?
A. Replacement by a new or accurate one will be recommended, or
if ship is listed as a weather observation vessel, a reliable instrument will be supplied at public expense.

Q. What are supercooled water droplets?
A. Water droplets having a temperature below freezing.

Q. Convert 20° Celsius (Centigrade) into the temperature Fahrenheit.
A. $F = \frac{9}{5} C + 32 = \frac{9 \times 20}{5} + 32 = 36 + 32 = 68°$ Fahrenheit, or the
same value given in Table 15, Bowditch.

Q. Name three corrections that must be applied to readings of the
mercurial barometer, and explain why each correction is required.
A. For instrument error, as determined by comparison with a
standard barometer provided by U.S. Weather Bureau.
     For height above sea level and mean temperature throughout
such height, in order to reduce station readings to a standard
level for comparison purposes, as in synoptic weather charts,
(Table 11, Bowditch).
     For temperature, to reduce readings to the standard tempera-
ture of 32° F. (Table 13, Bowditch).
     For gravity error, to reduce readings to the standard sea-level
gravity at latitude 45-1/2°, for which the instrument is calibrated
(Table 12, Bowditch).

Q. How should a barometer be installed? Give the factors that
should be considered in determining a proper location for this instrument.
A. A barometer should be installed as a fixed accessory to a vessel's navigational equipment. Its position should be carefully selected as that in which it will be most readily accessible for reading, while being free from local disturbance or vibration, such
as the slamming of doors or engine tremors, and from sudden
changes of temperature. To give satisfactory service, a barometer,
whether mercurial or aneroid, should receive the care and attention demanded by the best chronometer.

Q. What is an isallobar?
A. A curved line on a weather chart joining all places having the
same change of barometric pressure in a standard interval (usually
3 hours), during passage of a cyclonic or anticyclonic wind system.

Q. If a surface temperature is 90° F. and the wet adiabatic, or pseudo-adiabatic, lapse rate is 1° F. for each 300 feet, what is the temperature of cirrus-type clouds at 21,000 feet altitude? In what form would the water vapor be present in such clouds?

A. Decrease of temperature = 21,000 ÷ 300 = 70°; therefore, temperature of cloud is 90 — 70 = 20° F.

Water vapor in the cirrus cloud is in the form of ice crystals.

Q. What are the factors that determine the stability characteristics of a body of air?

A. Stability of a mass of air depends entirely upon the lapse rate, or change in temperature per unit increase of height, which is governed by the temperature and degree of humidity at various levels.

Q. When is a body of air known as unstable?

A. When the lower layers of an air mass are much warmer than the upper layers, a portion of the air is forced to rise and will be warmer than the surrounding air as it rises. Thus vertical currents are set up with the cooling of the rising air and warming of that falling to take its place. In these conditions there is said to be a steep temperature gradient or maximum lapse rate.

Q. When is a body of air known as stable?

A. When there are no marked differences of temperature in the successive layers, or lapse rate is at a minimum. Any ascending air, in this condition, will cool to a lower temperature than that of the surrounding mass and so will fall back to its original level.

Q. Does the greatest vertical development of cumulo-nimbus clouds occur in the tropics or in high latitudes? Explain the reason for your answer.

A. In the tropics, because stronger upward air currents due to greater surface temperature hasten the ascent of water vapor to greater heights.

Q. Define the following types of New Ice: (a) Ice-crystals (Frazil crystals); (b) Slush (sludge); (c) Pancake ice; (d) Ice-rind.

A. (a) The small particles of ice, sometimes called spicules which first appear on the water in the freezing process.

(b) The initial stage in the freezing of sea water, appearing as a greasy substance having a scum of icy crystals on its surface.

(c) A collection of "pancakes," or pieces of newly formed ice which are approximately circular and several feet in diameter; the initial stage of the ice floe.

(d) A thin glossy crust of frozen slush on a quiet sea surface.

Q. When is the ice coverage at a minimum in Arctic waters?

A. Average minimum coverage occurs in August.

Q. A powered vessel can traverse ice covering up to what proportion of the sea surface without ice breaker assistance?

A. A nearly total coverage of comparatively light ice may be easily traversed, while heavier conditions require the presence of leads or lanes of clear water and so may not exceed a covering of about 90%. The proportion of ice covering, in other words, depends upon the thickness and regular formation or otherwise.

Q. What consideration must be given to draft when a vessel it to operate in ice?

A. Vessel should be trimmed slightly by the stern, or not more than two or three feet.

Q. In operating in ice, what precautions must be observed with respect to speed? If necessary to strike the ice, what part of the ship should encounter the blow?

A. Operate at slow speed, so vessel may be in full maneuvering control. Strike the ice, if necessary, head on; let the stem take the blow.

Q. Operating a vessel in ice, where could extra lookouts be stationed to help avert propeller damage? Why is an immediate stop shaft order necessary when ice appears near the propeller?

A. Extra lookouts should be placed aloft as vessel proceeds, so that timely notice may be given the bridge of heavier rafting, "closing in" conditions, spurs, etc., or of favorable leads ahead or on either bow. Propeller should be stopped upon heavy pieces of ice being passed close to the quarter, in order to avert danger of damage to blades. When maneuvering, it is good practice to place lookouts on the after deck armed with lengthy poles by which heavy pieces of ice may be pushed clear of propeller.

Q. What precautions must be observed when anchoring in ice?

A. Endeavor to anchor in a position in which ice pressure will not "nip" the vessel. If there is land to windward, work as close thereto as possible, and, if anchoring is necessary due to darkness, fog, etc., place vessel head to wind before doing so. Pay particular attention to rudder and propeller, being sure that no heavy ice gets in the way upon leaving the berth. If necessary, use a charge of dynamite to loosen ice around ship's stern in order to get a start from the berth.

Q. When it is necessary to back down in ice, how should the rudder be handled for maximum protection from damage?

A. In this maneuver, rudder should be kept amidships, so that no undue side pressure or shocks may endanger the steering gear.

Q. In order that other vessels may be apprised, what obligation is imposed by the 1948 Convention for the Safety of Life at Sea upon every shipmaster who encounters dangerous ice at sea?

A. He must communicate such information by all means at his disposal to ships in the vicinity, also to the proper authorities at first point on the coast with which he can communicate. The message should be transmitted as a broadcast, but its form is not obligatory.

Q. What precaution, with respect to speed, is imposed by the 1948 Convention for Safety of Life at Sea upon the master of every ship when ice is reported on or near his course?
A. He is bound to proceed at a moderate speed or to alter his course so as to get well clear of the danger zone.

Q. What duty is imposed by the International Convention for the Safety of Life at Sea, 1948, on the master of every vessel who encounters a tropical storm?
A. He is bound to communicate information of having met with such storm by all means at his disposal, in the form of a broadcast, to all ships in the vicinity and to send it to the first point on the coast to which communication can be made, with the request that it be transmitted to the appropriate authorities. Such message, giving ship's position, may be transmitted in plain language (preferably English) or by means of the International Code of Signals (Radio Section).

Q. After a vessel has transmitted a warning of a dangerous storm, what subsequent transmissions are desirable?
A. At least every 3 hours, as a broadcast to all ships in the vicinity, ship's position, weather and sea conditions experienced, including direction and force of wind and any change therein; height of barometer and whether falling or otherwise; and precipitation.

Q. What publication, containing information of the storm advisory services from whom weather information may be obtained by radio, is required to be carried by U.S. Merchant Vessels?
A. Hydrographic Office Publication No. 206, Radio Weather Aids.

Q. Why does wind at 2,000 or 3,000 feet above sea level blow nearly parallel to the isobars, whereas the wind at sea level is inclined toward the low pressure area?
A. In its flow toward the center of low pressure, the wind takes up a direction which is the resultant of its tendency to flow directly into the low pressure center and to partake of a quasi-circular path around that center due to the rotatory motion of the earth.
In the case of the wind at 2,000—3,000 feet elevation, it is comparatively unhampered in its nearly circular flow and thus only a slight spiral indraft toward the center results, as seen in its direction being nearly parallel with the isobars. At the surface, however, the frictional resistance encountered by the moving air retards its flow in the circular path and enhances that directly toward the low pressure center. Thus, in the latter case,

the wind blows at a greater angle from the isobars toward the center.

Q. What is the effect of a decrease in the depth of the water on storm waves rolling in from the open sea?

A. Bottom friction slows down the waves' velocity, with the result that successive waves "bank up" and become shorter and steeper as depth decreases, finally dissipating in the breaker or surf stage. The direction of waves usually is at right angles to the depth curves so that their advance, as a rule, is directly toward the beach, no matter what their deep-water direction in the storm.

Q. Describe synoptic conditions that are associated with origin of tropical cyclones.

A. A low pressure area appears with warm, moist winds, overcast sky, and increasing precipitation, usually in the form of rain-squalls, begins, with decreasing visibility. Barometer, which may have been acting erratically and even above normal, begins falling rapidly, wind and frequency of squalls increase, sea increases, and storm takes on a circular formation with a center of from 5 to 20 miles in diameter in which only light, variable winds and little precipitation are present. Heavy lightning continues throughout.

Q. How may merchant vessels obtain an analysis of the weather map, showing pressure centers and fronts, when no facsimile equipment or teletype is aboard?

A. By plotting the synoptic weather observations from the scheduled broadcasts on a sheet of tracing paper laid over a small scale chart of the region concerned. Pressure; wind direction and force; precipitation; front information; etc., are indicated at each observation point. The map may then be completed by drawing the isobars, or curved lines joining all places having equal barometric pressure. By comparison with a similar map drawn at next broadcast of data, expected progressive conditions at ship's place may be determined.

Q. Explain how mountainous terrain adjacent to the seacoast can cause strong local winds of gale force.

A. Through being "dammed up" on the windward side of such terrain, wind is spilled over and down the other side, sometimes with hurricane force, as the williwaw of Magellan Strait, the mistral of Gulf of Lyons, or the bora of the Adriatic.

Q. How may the probability of encountering gales on an ocean passage for a given period of time be determined?

A. By consulting the U.S. Hydrographic Office Pilot Chart for the month and region in question.

Q. (a) What is meant by the length of a sea wave?
(b) Define the Wave period.
A. (a) Distance, usually expressed in feet, between the crests of two successive waves.
(b) Elapsed number of seconds between passage of two successive wave crests over a fixed point.

Q. If the quantity "square root of sea wave length, L, divided by 5.12" gives the wave period, P, find length of a wave having a period of 11 seconds.
A. $\sqrt{(L \div 5.12)} = 11$, or $\sqrt{L} \div \sqrt{5.12} = 11$;
then $\sqrt{L} = 11 \times \sqrt{5.12} = 11 \times 2.26 = 24.86$, and
$L = 24.86^2 = 618$ feet, length of wave.

Q. The maximum height of storm waves can be approximated by the formula:
$H = 1.5\sqrt{F}$ where:
H is the height in feet and
F is fetch in nautical miles.
Using this formula, determine the maximum height of storm waves that may be encountered when a gale is blowing from a direction in which the coastline is distant 400 miles.
A. Height = $1.5 \times \sqrt{400} = 1.5 \times 20 = 30$ feet.

Q. Swells from ocean waves generated by storms move at a velocity 1/2 that of the individual waves. If the individual waves move at a speed of 40 knots, how long would it take the swell to reach the observer 400 miles away?
A. Speed of swell = 40 ÷ 2 = 20 knots; therefore, time in hours to reach observer = 400 ÷ 20 = 20 hours.

Q. In which semicircle of a tropical cyclone would a vessel be if the wind shifted clockwise while the vessel was hove to in the Northern Hemisphere?
A. In the left, or dangerous, semicircle.

Q. In the Southern Hemisphere, how would a steam vessel maneuver in the dangerous semicircle of a tropical cyclone?
A. She should bring wind on the port bow, hold course, and make as much way as possible; if obliged to heave to, do so with head to sea.

Q. How may you: (a) Estimate the bearing of the center of a tropical cyclone? (b) Estimate the probable path of a storm?
A. (a) In the Northern Hemisphere, center of storm lies 10 to 12 points to right of the wind, the latter value prevailing in rear of storm. Near the storm's front, center will bear 8 to 9 points to the right. In the Southern Hemisphere, allow 10 to 12 points to left of wind, with the latter value prevailing in storm's rear.

Center lies 8 to 9 points to left of wind near front of storm.

(b) By heaving to and noting change in bearing of storm's center, coupled with changes in barometer reading. Use of a storm diagram, showing the isobars as concentric circles, is recommended for this problem. Successive plotting of the storm center's bearing and the changes in barometric height between observations will indicate vessel's position with respect to storm's path, and thus the approximate direction in which storm is traveling. Where the center's bearing has no appreciable change while barometer continues falling, with increasing wind force, vessel is then in the storm's path, or its progressive direction is that opposite its bearing.

Q. Hove to in the Northern Hemisphere under tropical cyclone conditions, the barometer is falling and the wind shifting clockwise. What is the vessel's probable position relative to the center of the storm and what action should be taken if possible to avoid the center of the storm?

A. Vessel is in the dangerous semicircle. In a powered vessel, bring wind on starboard bow, hold course, and make as much way as possible. If obliged to heave to, do so with head to sea. In a sail vessel, put ship on starboard tack and make as much way as possible; if necessary to heave to, do so on starboard tack.

Q. State the precautions that should be taken in the event it becomes necessary to ride out a tropical cyclone at an anchorage.

A. Have main engines ready to move; their use will be required to reduce stress on anchor cables. Give ship a sheer and drop second anchor before paying out more cable on the first, i.e., have as little difference as possible in lengths of cable veered. As wind increases, pay out cable to have as much of it as possible lying on the bottom. Secure cables in riding chocks, also everything movable about deck, placing extra lashings on boats, rafts, booms, etc.

Q. What is one method of predicting the probable area within which a tropical cyclone can be expected to move within 24 hours from the time at which it is reported?

A. If in deep water, by the direction of long swell generated by the storm. Also, by distribution of atmospheric pressure over the region concerned. As storm will follow a path of least resistance, it may be expected to move into the area having lowest height of barometer.

Q. What is the intertropic convergence zone?

A. Approximately the doldrums, or equatorial region between the converging trade winds, birthplace of the tropical cyclone.

Q. Your vessel is proceeding toward a stationary thunderstorm at 15 knots. If you saw a flash of lightning and 10 seconds later heard thunder, how long would it take before you entered the storm

A. Time in minutes = distance in feet ÷ speed in feet per minute

$$= (10 \times 1117) \div \frac{15 \times 6076}{60}$$

$$= \frac{10 \times 1117 \times 60}{15 \times 6076} = 7.35 \text{ minutes.}$$

Q. How would you estimate the probability of encountering fog on an ocean passage?
A. By consulting the U.S. Navy Hydrographic chart for the month and ocean in question.

Q. (a) What is advection fog? (b) What is barber?
A. (a) Common type of fog formed by warm moist air blowing over a cold surface and is cooled below its dew point; or by cold air over a warm surface, as that of the sea, absorbing and becoming clouded with excess moisture.
   (b) Low-lying rising vapor, or foggy condition, resulting from a freezing wind over comparatively warm water.

Q. Under certain conditions in the Northern Hemisphere it may be assumed that the current sets 30° to the right of the direction of which it is driven by the wind and its velocity is 2 per cent of the wind velocity. (a) Basing your answer on the foregoing statement, estimate the direction and the velocity of the current if the wind is from the west at 50 knots. (b) Using direction and velocity of current estimated in (a), find the course to steer your vessel to make good a course of 030°, if the speed of your vessel is 10 knots. To solve this problem, consider current only, disregarding any other factors that might be involved.
   A. (a) Wind West drives current 90° + 30° = 120°; velocity 2% of 50 = 1 kn.
      (b) or, at 10 knots, course to steer = 024°.

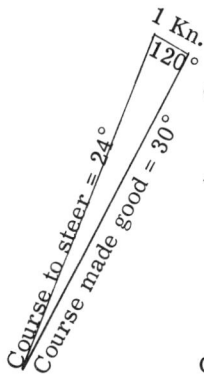

Q. How is the information concerning the direction and velocity of ocean currents obtained for Pilot Charts and Current Charts of the oceans?
A. It is obtained from U.S. Navy Hydrographic Office's collection of data resulting from its own surveys and research in oceanography, also from public and private institutions and persons in all parts of the world, including the records of cooperating naval and merchant vessels.

Q. In using information concerning current from a Pilot Chart or Current Chart, what consideration should be borne in mind with regard to possible differences between the actual current experienced and that shown on the chart?
A. That the duration, force, and direction of a different prevailing

wind, as a departure from average wind conditions indicated on
Pilot Chart for the season, may result in a considerable deflection
of prevalent current indicated on both Pilot and Current Charts for
the locality concerned.

Q. Currents shown on Pilot Charts and Current Atlases are resultant
currents. (a) What is the meaning of the term resultant? (b) How
would you assess the probability of your vessel encountering the
particular conditions indicated by the current information on the
chart?
A. (a) The single force, velocity, etc., which in effect is equal to
two or more given values, or components, of such elements.
   (b) By estimation of the degree of departure, if any, of actual
conditions from those average conditions given in the Pilot Chart.

Q. The distance between two ports on the Great Circle track is
3,000 miles, but the track traverses areas where adverse currents
whose average velocity is 1 knot can be anticipated. An alternate,
Mercator course of 3,400 miles in length between the ports traverses areas where a favorable current averaging 1 knot can be
expected. With the length of time required for the passage as the
only consideration, determine which track is preferable for: (a) A
vessel whose speed is 10 knots; (b) A vessel whose speed is 15
knots; (c) A vessel whose speed is 20 knots.
A. (a) 3000 ÷ 9 = 333.3 hours   3400 ÷ 11 = 309 hours
   (b) 3000 ÷ 14 = 214.3 "   3400 ÷ 16 = 212.5 "
   (c) 3000 ÷ 19 = 158   "   3400 ÷ 21 = 162   "

        Therefore, preferable track for (a) = Mercator;
                                         (b) = Mercator;
                                         (c) = Great Circle.

20. NAUTICAL ASTRONOMY AND NAVIGATION DEFINITIONS

Q. The earth actually rotates 366-1/4 times in a year, but the sun
crosses the meridian only 365 times, making the year consist of
365-1/4 solar days. What causes the apparent loss of one rotation?
A. This is caused by the extra rotation made by the earth's orbital
motion. Were the earth to stand still in her orbit, each star and
also the sun would cross a given meridian at the same time each
day. But, since the radius vector from the sun must line up with
the plane of the meridian at each successive noon, the earth will
have "stolen" a daily increment of about 59 minutes of arc (3 min.
56 sec. of time) of an annual additional rotation, thus completing
366 turns on her axis in all.

Q. At what rate per hour is Greenwich Observatory, in Latitude
51°-28'.6 North, being carried around the earth's axis?
A. Since the Observatory is carried 15° x 60 = 900 minutes of
longitude each hour, and the relation of D. Long. to Dep. = 1 to
cos. Lat., rate per hour = 900 x cos. Lat. = 900 x .623 = 560.70

nautical miles per hour (Table 6, Bowditch, gives 562.71, based on Clarke's spheroid of 1866).

Q. State two of the three factors which cause apparent time to differ from mean time.
A. 1. Variation in speed of the earth in her orbit.
   2. Variation of earth's rate of rotation.
   3. Obliquity of the ecliptic.

Q. How must the lines of position of bodies with altitude (H_O) from 86° to 90° be plotted? How are such position lines advanced?
A. With a radius of 90° — H_O, and center as body's geographical zenith position at instant of observation, an arc of a circle is described. This is the line of position. It is advanced in same manner as an ordinary position line, or in the direction of course and distance run between observations.

Q. Distinguish between superior and inferior planets.
A. Superior planets are those whose orbits lie farther from the sun than the earth's orbit; inferior planets, as Mercury and Venus, have their orbits nearer the sun.

Q. Define precession of the equinoxes.
A. The slow westward displacing of the intersecting points (equinoxes) of ecliptic and equinoctial, due to a tilting of the earth's axis in a reeling swing, such as may be observed in the spinning of a top.

Q. What is right ascension?
A. Arc of the equinoctial between the hour circle of vernal equinox and hour circle of a point on the celestial sphere, measured eastward from vernal equinox and expressed in hours, minutes, and seconds, 0 to 24 hours.

Q. What is the ecliptic?
A. A great circle of the celestial sphere, or path through which the sun appears to move in the heavens in the course of a year.

Q. Define: (a) Aphelion; (b) Perihelion; (c) Apogee; (d) Perigee.
A. (a) Point in the orbit of a planet lying farthest from the sun.
   (b) Point in the orbit of a planet lying nearest the sun.
   (c) Point in the moon's orbit farthest from the earth.
   (d) Point in the moon's orbit nearest the earth.

Q. What is precession?
A. Change in the position of the axis of a spinning body, as a gyroscope, when acted upon by a torque.

22. SIGNALLING BY INTERNATIONAL CODE FLAGS
AND FLASHING LIGHT.
LIFESAVING, STORM AND SPECIAL SIGNALS

Q. What are the signals for vessels and aircraft in distress on the
water which are provided by the International Rules of the Road?

A. (a) A gun or other explosive signal fired about every minute.

  (b) A continuous sounding with any fog-signal apparatus.

  (c) Rockets or shells, throwing red stars fired one at a time
at short intervals.

  (d) The group . . . — — —. . . . made by radiotelegraphy or other
method.

  (e) The spoken word Mayday sent by radiotelephony.

  (f) International Code distress signal indicated by N C.

  (g) A square flag having above or below it a ball or anything
resembling a ball.

  (h) Flames on deck, as from a burning tar barrel, oil drum, etc.

  (i) A rocket parachute flare showing a red light.

Q. Describe the care necessary when using the ship's whistle for
sending Morse Code messages by sound.

A. Avoid the possibility of ships in the vicinity mistaking or being
confused by such signals. Reduce the length of signals as much
as possible, especially in poor visibility conditions. Single-letter
signals only should be used, except in extreme emergency, never
any other in frequented navigational waters.

Q. Show precisely how you would signal the following: (a) Bearing
due North; (b) Five minutes past midnight; (c) Latitude 3° North;
(d) Longitude 86°-07' West.

A. (a)		(b)	(c)	(d)
X or X		T	P	P
3	J	0	0	8
6	U	1st Repeat	3	6
0	G	2nd Repeat	1st Repeat	0
		5	3rd Repeat	7
			N	

Q. What signals are provided by the International Rules of the Road
for an aircraft to indicate that she is in distress and requires
assistance?

A. Any of the signals listed in Rule 31, International Rules of the
Road, for use of a vessel or seaplane in distress. (See answer
to second question under SIGNALLING.)

Q. What information should be included in a distress message sent
by radio?

A. Ship's position; course and speed, if making way; nature of trouble; whether medical assistance is required; whether ship needs a tow.

Q. Who is responsible for control of distress traffic over the air-waves when a distress message has been sent?
A. The vessel in distress, or another vessel which learns distressed ship is unable to control such traffic; or vessel in distress may delegate control to a particular vessel. The latter may, if circumstances demand it, also delegate control to another ship (or aircraft).

Q. What are the signals used in radiotelegraphy and radiotelephony for distress, urgency, and safety traffic, respectively; and what is the purpose of these types of signals?
A. Distress signal in radiotelegraphy is S O S, repetition of which usually precedes the signal for actuating auto-alarms consisting of 12 dashes, each of 4 seconds' duration with 1 second between them, sent in 1 minute. That in radiotelephony is the word "Mayday."
  These signals indicate that sending station is endangered by some mishap or is threatened with disaster, and so requests immediate assistance.
  Urgent signal in radiotelegraphy is X X X; in radiotelephony, the word "Pan." This indicates calling station has an important message to transmit concerning safety of a vessel or aircraft, or of a person or persons on board or within sight.
  Safety signal in radiotelegraphy is T T T; in radiotelephony, the word "Saycuritay." This indicates station is about to transmit a message concerning safety of navigation or giving out meteorological warnings.

Q. What is the duty of a vessel's officers upon encountering any vessel or aircraft at sea displaying or transmitting any of the distress signals provided by the International Rules of the Road?
A. The master is bound to proceed with all speed to the assistance of persons in distress, informing them, if possible, he is doing so. If unable to do so, he must enter in the logbook the reason for failing to proceed to assist such persons.

Q. How is accurate reception assured when numbers are transmitted by flashing light?
A. By spelling out the numbers; for example, 486 as "four eight six".

23. STABILITY AND SHIP CONSTRUCTION

Q. Given the following data:

	Weight Tons	Vertical Center of Gravity Feet	Longitudinal Center of Gravity(from forward perpendicular Feet
Light Ship (including crew and stores)-------------	4,000	27	250
No. 1 hold -------------	1,000	25	75
No. 2 hold -------------	2,000	22	125
No. 3 hold -------------	1,000	24	175
No. 4 hold -------------	2,000	23	325
No. 5 hold ------------	500	25	375
Fuel oil and water ------	500	15	200

Displacement: 11,000 Tons.

Vertical distance from keel to metacenter at displacement of 11,000 tons is 26 feet.

Moment to trim one inch at displacement of 11,000 tons is 1,000 ft/tons.

Mean draft at displacement of 11,000 tons is 25 feet.

Longitudinal Center of Buoyancy at displacement of 11,000 tons is 223.6 feet from the forward perpendicular (at level trim).

Free surface correction is .7 foot.

Required: Metacentric height corrected for free surface.

The forward and after drafts (assuming the tipping center is located at the mid-length of the vessel).

A.

	Tons	Vert. c.g.	Vert. moment	Long. c.g.	Long. moment
Light ship	4,000	27	108,000	250	1,000,000
No. 1 hold	1,000	25	25,000	75	75,000
" 2 "	2,000	22	44,000	125	250,000
" 3 "	1,000	24	24,000	175	175,000
" 4 "	2,000	23	26,000	325	650,000
" 5 "	500	25	12,500	375	187,500
Fuel, water	500	15	7,500	200	100,000
	11,000		267,000		2,437,500

Vert. C.G. $= \dfrac{267,000}{11,000}$ Long. C.G. $= \dfrac{2,437,500}{11,000}$

       $= 24.27$ feet $= 221.6$ feet from F.P.

K M $= 26.00$ "   Long. C.B. $= \underline{223.6}$ "   "   "

F.S. corr. $= \underline{-.70}$ or L.C.G. $= \underline{2.0}$ ft. for'd of T.C.

G M $= \underline{1.03}$ feet

       Ch. of trim $= \dfrac{2 \times 11,000}{1,000} = 22$ in. by head.

Mean load draft = 25 ft. 00 in.	25 ft. 00 in.
1/2 trim = $\underline{+11}$	$\underline{-11}$
Calculated draft = $\underline{25}$ ft. 11 in. F.	$\underline{24}$ ft. 01 in. A.

Q. How are double-bottom tanks tested for tightness?
A. They are subjected to a head of water in a pipe extending above
tank to the height required for such test, after tank has been completely filled.

Q. What is the total upward force on a double-bottom manhole cover
of 200 square inches of area when fresh water to a height of 20
feet above the tank top is standing in the sounding pipe?
  Note: Fresh water weighs .433 pounds for a column one foot
high and one inch in area at the base.
A. .433 $\times$ 20 $\times$ 200 = 1732 lbs. upward force.

Q. A vessel concerned with her stability at departure checks it by
lifting with her booms a total of 40 tons, with the boom heads 50
feet from the center line. The clinometer is then carefully read
and shows a list of 5°. At the same time, the ship's displacement
is 8,000 tons including the suspended weights. (a) What is her
GM corresponding to this condition? (b) If the 40 tons is stowed
25 feet below the boom heads, what will the GM be?
A.
Shift of CG $= \dfrac{40 \times 50}{8,000} = .25$ ft.

(a) GM = .25 $\times$ cot 5° = .25 $\times$ 11.43 = 2.86 ft.

(b) $\dfrac{40 \times 25}{8,000} = \dfrac{1}{8} = .125$ ft. GM shift; 2.86 +.12 = 2.98 ft. GM.

Q. Why is it desirable that the valve-operating rods on tank vessels be made of solid rod rather than of pipe or other hollow
material?
A. Chiefly to provide ample material to allow for weakening in
event of corrosion. A holed hollow valve-rod also could provide
an outlet for gas, besides suffering much strength loss.

Q. How are the decks of tank vessels fitted to prevent leakage of
gas or vapor where valve-operating rods pass through?
A. Each valve-rod leads through a packing gland or stuffing box in
the base of a standard which confines and stiffens rod's working
end.

Q. On a vessel at sea it is desired to check the metacentric height
by employing the empirical formula:
$$T = \frac{.44\,B}{\sqrt{GM}}$$
. . . . where B is the vessel's beam of 50 feet and T is the full
period of the vessel's roll which was carefully timed and an average value of 15 seconds obtained.
  Required: The GM as given by using the formula.
  Note: Full period means starboard to port and back to starboard, or "period of double roll."
A. $T = \dfrac{.44B}{\sqrt{GM}} = \dfrac{22}{\sqrt{GM}}$; $\sqrt{GM} = \dfrac{22}{T} = \dfrac{22}{15} = 1.47$;

GM = 1.47^2 = 2.16 feet.

Q. With the cross curves shown below, draw the curve of statical stability for a displacement of 10,000 tons and a KG of 19 feet. Show all work.

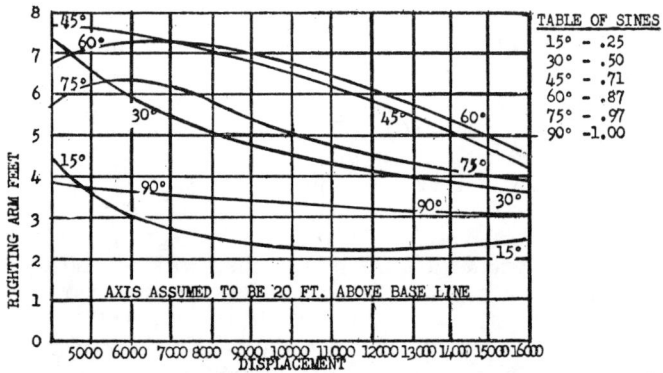

A. GM = GZ ÷ sin heel:

GZ at 15° heel = 2.3 ft.   2.3 ÷ .25 = 9.2 ft. GM
   " 30°   = 4.6 "   4.6 ÷ .50 = 9.2 "
   " 45°   = 6.5 "   6.5 ÷ .71 = 9.2 "
   " 60°   = 6.7 "   6.7 ÷ .87 = 7.7 "
   " 75°   = 5.0 "   5.0 ÷ .97 = 5.2 "

KG now being 19 ft., new GM = old GM + 1.

GZ = new GM x sin heel:

   at 15°: 10.2 × .25 = 2.6 ft.   at 60°: 8.7 × .87 = 7.6 ft.
    " 30°: 10.2 × .50 = 5.1 "   " 75°: 6.2 × .97 = 6.0 "
    " 45°: 10.2 × .71 = 7.2 "

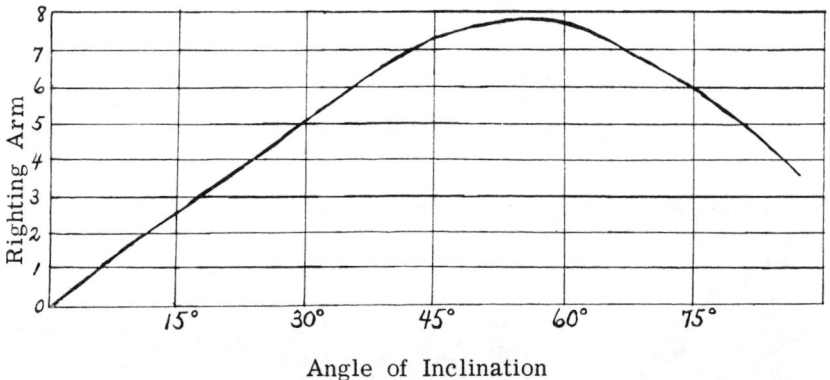

Angle of Inclination

Q. What is the purpose of blow-out plugs in the longitudinal bulkheads of refrigerated spaces on vessels?

A. These are for relief of an unsymmetrical flooded condition, in which water pressure "blows out" plugs, thus providing means of leveling the water in such emergency, while ordinarily maintaining effectiveness of bulkheads.

Q. Shown below is a statical stability curve. Copy this curve and show the loss of righting arm due to the center of gravity being 2 feet off the center line. Indicate the angle to which the vessel will list and the righting arm remaining at 45° angle of inclination.

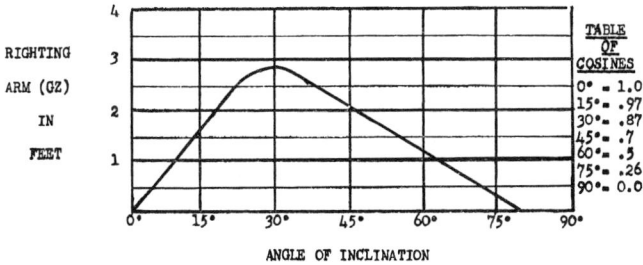

RIGHTING ARM (GZ) IN FEET

TABLE OF COSINES
0° = 1.0
15° = .97
30° = .87
45° = .7
60° = .5
75° = .26
90° = 0.0

ANGLE OF INCLINATION

A. Inclining Arm at 15° heel = 2 × cos 15° = 2 × .97 = 1.94 feet.
   "   "   at 30° heel = 2 × cos 30° = 2 × .87 = 1.74 feet.
   "   "   at 45° heel = 2 × cos 45° = 2 × .71 = 1.42 feet.
   "   "   at 60° heel = 2 × cos 60° = 2 × .50 = 1.00 foot.

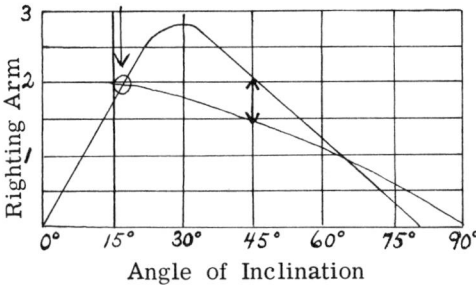

Angle of Inclination

Arrow indicates the angle to which vessel will list, or, 17° nearly. Righting arm remaining at 45° heel = 2.1 − 1.4 = .7 foot.

Q. A vessel of 6,000 tons displacement carries two slack tanks of carbon tetrachloride (sp. gr. 1.6). The tanks are each 40 feet long and 25 feet wide. What is the reduction in metacentric height due to free surface with vessel in sea water (sp. gr. 1.025)?
Note: The reduction in metacentric height due to free surface may be determined by the formula $\frac{rlb^3}{12\,V}$ where: r is the ratio of the specific gravity of the liquid in the tank to the specific gravity of the liquid in which the vessel is floating.
$\frac{lb^3}{12}$ = moment of inertia of tank. V = displacement volume.

A. $\dfrac{1.6 \times 40 \times 25^3 \times 2}{1.025 \times 12 \times 6000 \times 35} = \dfrac{1.6 \times 40 \times 15625 \times 2}{1.025 \times 12 \times 210,000} = \dfrac{50.0}{64.575}$;
or, reduction in GM = .77 foot.

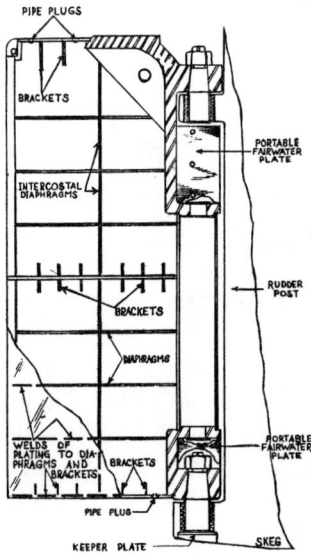

PIPE PLUGS
BRACKETS
INTERCOSTAL DIAPHRAGMS
BRACKETS
DIAPHRAGMS
WELDS OF PLATING TO DIAPHRAGMS AND BRACKETS
PIPE PLUG
KEEPER PLATE
PORTABLE FAIRWATER PLATE
RUDDER POST
PORTABLE FAIRWATER PLATE
BRACKETS
SKEG

Q. Referring to the sketch: (a) Why are the fairwater plates for the rudder made portable? (b) What materials are usually employed for rudder gudgeon bushings?

A. (a) So that, when repairs necessitate rudder being lifted or removed, fairwater plates may be taken off.

(b) Lignum vitae, bronze, and sometimes soft steel.

Q. What is meant by ceiling of a hold?

A. Wood flooring over the double-bottom tank tops; also, the inside planking of a sailing ship (wood built).

Q. What are limber holes?

A. Holes cut through the floor-plates next the shell plating, along the outside of a margin plate or next to a keelson, for draining water, as condensation, leakage, etc., into a well or to the bilge suction.

Q. What are lightening holes?

A. Circular or oval holes cut in web frames, floor-plates, hatch beams, etc., for lightening the weight without reducing the strength of such members. Usually such holes in floor-plates are made large enough to allow passage for a man.

Q. What provisions are necessary for the local increase in stress on a deck at hatch corners and other openings?

A. Carlings, or short stiffener-beams, are fitted around the openings. Where these support the ends of interrupted beams, they usually are called "headers."

Q. Why are the center girders, side keelsons, or other internals of a similar type welded by intermittent welds as sketched, rather than continuous welds when they are not required to be oil or watertight?

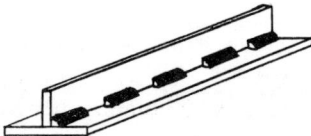

A. Because by this method the welding process subjects the material to much less heat, thus allowing faster progress in the work and reducing the tendency to set up distortions or undue stresses in the metal. With a continuous weld, necessary delays for cooling the metal render the method less economical with no more efficient results.

Q. What causes slight "ripples" between floors characteristic of the bottoms of welded vessels?

A. The uneven distribution of heat during the welding process. The heated area is resisted in expanding by the relatively cool surrounding area, and wavy distortion results.

Q. Referring to the sketch: (a) With a vessel in loaded condition and level trim, use the floodable length curve corresponding to this condition and determine if the vessel will sink when No. 1 and No. 2 holds are flooded if their permeability is estimated to be 63 percent. (b) Discuss briefly the effect of the trim by the head or stern, lighter displacement, and variation from given permeability when using the curve.

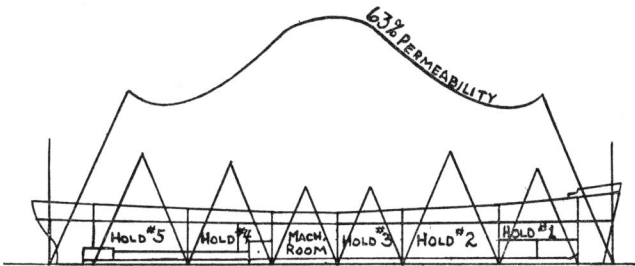

A. (a) Vessel will sink under conditions noted, because apex of the triangle which has length of Nos. 1 and 2 holds as its base lies without, or above, the given curve.

(b) Important influences on the floodable length must be taken into account, chief of which is the ratio of freeboard and sheer to draft. A cargo vessel of little sheer and floating at load draft, for example, may afford a much shorter floodable length, particularly toward her ends, than when in the light condition. For this reason, curve should be drawn for the load condition as that in which flooding danger is at its worst. Variation from limit of permeability indicated in the curve, beside ratio of depth to length, reserve buoyancy, and fineness coefficient, is also a serious consideration, as, for example, in the assumed case of a vessel having a similar curve to that illustrated loaded to her marks with pig iron.

Q. In checking a sliding watertight door for closeness of fit in the closed position, how would you make the check and what should be regarded as the maximum allowable clearance?

A. Check with a feeler gauge between door and frame. Clearance should be under .003 inch.

Q. How should the wedges be adjusted on a watertight door?
A. So that the door, when closed, fays evenly against frame, with all wedges delivering a uniform pressure.

Q. When vessels are fitted with flatplate keels, how are they fitted internally so that they have vertical rigidity in the keel structure?
A. Along its center line is fitted a strong vertical plate, called a center keelson or vertical center keel, which in turn is fitted fore-and-aft to the midship strake of tank top's plating, or, in tank vessels, simply strengthened at its upper edge by heavy angles.

Q. Describe briefly the causes of the stresses that frames must withstand.
A. Inward pressure of the water against shell; dry-docking, grounding, or pounding in a heavy sea; deck loads and stresses set up by cargo posts and masts with their supported weights; heavy concentrated loads such as engines, dead weight cargo, etc.; racking stresses from rolling and lurching in a seaway.

Q. What section of the regulations contains the minimum strength requirements for a vessel's framing?
A. That section concerned with the assigning of load lines, or "Load Line Regulations."

Q. Where bilge piping of a passenger vessel runs through a box or a duct keel as illustrated, what provisions are required to prevent flooding of the holds in case of bottom damage?

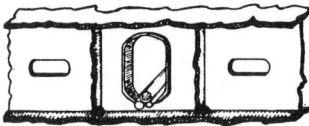

A. A nonreturn valve shall be fitted to the end of the bilge suction pipe in the compartment which it serves.

Q. When testing bottom on new construction or repairs, why must a slight leak or "weep" be regarded as more serious in a welded vessel than in a riveted vessel?
A. Because it is likely that a crack is developing, which, due to present "locked up" stresses in the metal, unlike the riveted job, may turn out to be a serious fracture.

Q. In dry-docking a vessel not in level trim, what stability and local pressure problems may be encountered in: (a) a graving dock; (b) a floating dock.
A. (a) Especially with a vessel having small GM, or a "tender" ship, care must be taken to place the bilge blocks progressively as keel lands at ship's deeper draft end, because as vessel's weight begins to rest on keel blocks, her GM begins to lessen. For this reason, placing of bilge blocks should be nicely timed to follow immediately upon vessel's landing on keel blocks, working along toward ship's lighter end.

(b) In addition to the foregoing precaution, that of guarding against possible variation in dock's buoyancy throughout its length should be observed; for example, a more buoyant section of dock could bring excessive lift upon a section of vessel's length having the same characteristic, which might result in a serious bending stress in her structure.

Q. What is meant by the faying flange of a frame in riveted construction?
A. The flange which is in flat contact with the plating.

Q. How has welded construction changed the methods of constructing ship framing?
A. Welding has changed riveting framing by eliminating the following: the faying flange which was riveted to shell plating; the need for beveling frames at curving parts of shell near vessel's ends; butt straps; hole-punching.

Q. On the sketch shown, identify A and B.

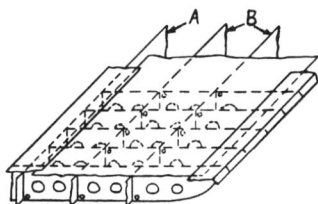

A. A. Vertical center keel.
   B. Intercostal side girders, or longitudinals; also, side keelsons.

Q. What is the purpose of the bilge keels?
A. To increase vessel's resistance to rolling.

Q. Do bilge keels affect a vessel's stability?
A. Only in that they considerably reduce the angle of roll.

Q. In repairing broken cleats for battens, what is the preferred method of attachments to frame, A or B?
A. B.

Q. Why is it important that the dockmaster of a floating drydock be informed of a vessel's trim when the vessel is being drydocked?
A. Because he then may trim dock so as to have keel blocks as nearly as possible parallel to ship's keel, which lends toward safer and simpler procedure.

A   B

Q. What is the function of side keelsons or longitudinal intercostals in the double bottom of a vessel?
A. To stiffen both shell and tank-top plating and to keep the floorplates to their work.

Q. Why is longitudinal framing usually employed for tank vessels and transverse framing used on freighters?

A. In disposing of needless decks and double-bottom tanks, with corresponding greater weight of material, found in the transverse system, the tanker gains considerable advantage in her greater dead weight carrying capacity. Also, to compensate for loss of longitudinal strength by dispensing with decks, inner bottom, etc., with the increase in size of tank vessels the longitudinal framing system became a necessity.

Q. Why are frames usually welded to shell plating with intermittent rather than continuous welds?

A. Because the continuous weld is capable of setting up irregular or locked-up stresses in the metal which tend to produce a "wavy" surface on the plating, where sufficient time for cooling is not allowed. Economy in time therefore is its advantage, while producing equally efficacious work as the slower "continuous" weld.

Q. In the illustration is a deep web frame with longitudinal frames passing through the slots. Why should the corners of the slot be rounded in one case and holes drilled in the other case?

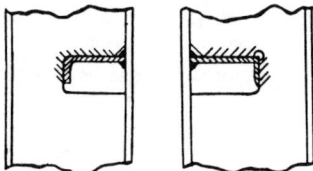

A. In both cases a rounded corner is thus formed with the objective of averting a starting notch for a crack in the web.

Q. How are the frames of a vessel numbered in usual practice?

A. From forward; frame No. 1 is next abaft the stem.

Q. Where is the spacing between frames measured, i.e., does the distance along the shell plating between frames necessarily represent the frame spacing?

A. Spacing of frames, which depends upon vessel's Transverse Number (breadth + depth), is closer toward bow and stern. In general, spacing is a few inches more for two-thirds vessel's length, as centered at midship point, than toward each end.

Q. Describe the reasons why vessels constructed with welded frames are more susceptible to impact damage in docking, etc., than vessels of riveted frame construction.

A. Local concentrations of stress in the welded area may be "released" and a crack appears; or, "locked-up" stresses in the metal, set up by sharp differences of temperature between weld and worked material, result in a brittle condition unknown to the riveted frame.

Q. Sketched here are various arrangements of the shell plating on the frames employed in ship's construction. (a) Name the arrangements. (b) Which arrangement is used most often in modern shipbuilding? (c) Why?

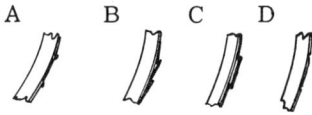

A. (a) A = double joggled. B = clinker. C = in-and-out. D = flush. (b) D. (c) Reduces weight; eliminates plate and frame joggling, and liners; provides smoothest hull surface; with modern welding practice, gives practically 100% of plates' tensile strength at seams and butts.

Q. What is the meaning of the term sheer of a vessel as applied to determination of a ship's load line?
A. Excess of vertical distance of freeboard deck above base line at bow or stern over that measured at midship point. Sheer usually is much greater forward than aft.

Q. How is the quality of steel regulated for use in the construction of merchant vessels?
A. According to the requirements of the interested classification society. Standards of tensile strength, ductility, hardness, toughness, and fatigue strength have been adopted according to actual tests of structural material. Verification tests of steel used in various parts of the vessel during building, as made by the society's surveyor, serve to check the quality of metal required by the rules.

Q. Why is the flat keel plate normally the heaviest plate on a vessel's bottom?
A. Because of its place as farthest removed downward from vessel's neutral axis, it is the principal bottom longitudinal strength member and accordingly must sustain great tensile and compression stresses. Also, in conjunction with the vertical center-plate keel, it must bear up vessel's weight on keel blocks when in dry dock.

Q. What is the effect of rectangular openings such as hatches on deck stresses? Why should such areas be checked carefully by deck officers following heavy weather?
A. Continuity of longitudinal strength, particularly in an upper deck, is interfered with by such openings, and it is possible that this disturbed status may not have been completely compensated in the structural arrangement provided for that purpose. Accordingly, it is desirable that the area in vicinity of deck openings be carefully examined for cracks, buckling, etc., developing in a spell of heavy weather.

Q. On passenger vessels, in what direction must the doors of public spaces, corridors, stairway enclosures, etc., open?
A. They shall open in the direction of escape, where practicable.

Q. Why are certain longitudinal seams riveted on vessels which
would otherwise be all welded in construction?
A. Such seams as juncture of sheer strake and deck stringer plate,
via gunwale angle bar, are riveted as crack arrestors in that this
change to riveting breaks failure continuity in the structure, as a
possible crack in shell plating, ascribed to release of pent-up stresses in welded areas.

Q. Why are most modern welded vessels built with flush butts and
seams?
A. Because the welding process involved gives practically full strength
of plates at their joints; liners, butt straps, and joggled plating or
framing are eliminated; the smooth hull surface reduces frictional
resistance to ship's speed; and corrosion spots or areas are reduced to a minimum.

Q. Name valves A, B, C, and D and briefly state the purpose of
each.

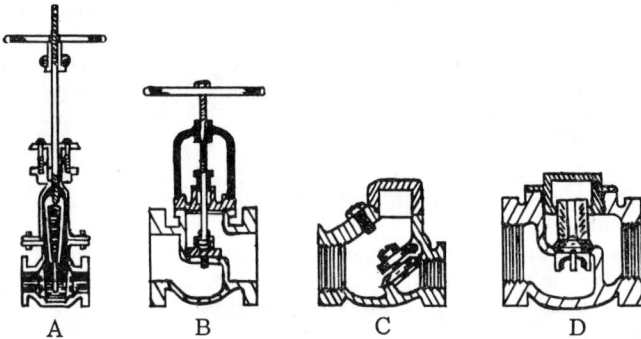

A   B   C   D

A. A = gate valve. B = throttle or control valve. C = swing check
valve. D = lift or floating check valve.
    A is for completely opening or closing a line. B is for control-
ling exact flow, as in loading a tanker. C is for nonreturn flow,
effected by drop or swing of check upon release of pressure from
within or pressure arising from without, as in a boiler-feed line.
D, in larger piping, is to prevent return flow, as in a fresh-
water supply line from shore to ship.

Q. What is the usual method used to distinguish the strakes and
plates of a ship?
A. Shell plating strakes are lettered from keel outward and upward,
with individual plates in each numbered from the stem; thus, on
port side of keel first strake is P A and first plate in the strake

is marked **P A 1**, and on starboard side, **S A 1**. Interrupted strakes, as those disappearing in a <u>stealer</u>, are marked according to usage in the particular shipyard. Deck plating begins with the midship strake marked M; thence successive strakes toward wings are marked <u>A</u>, <u>B</u>, <u>C</u>, etc., with each plate in each strake numbered from forward; thus P C 3 identifies 3rd plate from forward in 3rd strake to port of midship strake. Plating of deckhouses is similarly marked.

Q. How is worn or corroded plating checked for thickness?
A. By drilling a hole or holes as required and gauging the metal.

Q. The type stress being exerted on the rivet shown is known as
. . . .

A. Shearing stress.

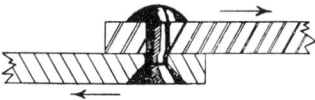

Q. What precautions to detect leakage of steam coils should be taken when it is necessary to heat a liquid cargo in order to reduce its viscosity at discharge? What dangers could arise from coil leakage?
A. The inspection tanks of the heating system should be opened at frequent intervals to ascertain whether or not any oil or impurities have entered the return steam line. Coil leakage could cause damage to boilers through entering into the engine-room feed and filter tank, for which reason the loofah sponges or other filter material should be maintained in proper condition in inspection tanks at all times.

Q. What is the maximum vapor pressure permitted on a tank, unless that tank has been constructed as an unfired pressure vessel?
A. Four (4) pounds per square inch.

Q. What is the purpose of pressure-vacuum relief valves?
A. For controlling excape of gas, as that generated by petroleum, from a tank. The valve is set to operate at a pressure of 2 to 3 lbs. per square inch.

Q. In dry-docking a vessel, what precautions are usually taken to insure that the keel plate is properly painted in the way of the keel blocks?
A. When paint has dried, relief blocks are set and wedged up between those first laid down, thus allowing removal of the latter to complete the work.

Q. Is the longitudinal center girder of a vessel's keel structure or are the floors normally built intercostally? Why?
A. No; because such construction would violate the important principle of maintaining continuity of strength in the chief members of the structure.

Q. Why is the longitudinal center girder of a vessel's keel structure usually built solid when fuel oil or water is carried in the
double bottom?

A. In order to limit the free surface area of a liquid carried and
its effect on vessel's GM. One-fourth the reduction in GM results
when a free surface occurs in a tank thus divided, as compared
with the through tank. Also, stresses and shocks set up in such
divided tank, when partly filled during heavy weather, are similarly
reduced by the barrier effect of the solid center girder.

Q. If it became necessary to put a hole in the beam in order to
support a chain fall for lifting a weight, in what part of the beam
would you place the hole?

A. As near the beam's neutral axis as possible, or approximately
in its middle line.

Q. What precautions should be taken with respect to shape if a hole
is burned out with a cutting torch instead of being drilled?

A. Hole should be reamed out so as to provide a clean continuity
of the cut or bearing surface.

Q. Discuss briefly the stress that may be put on a ship's structure
by heating when steaming tanks or heating liquid cargoes to reduce
their viscosity.

A. All structural parts in contact with the heated liquid will suffer
expansion in direct ratio to rise in temperature, and if this were
not qualified by irregularity in the heat distribution, it is likely
that little or no ill effects would result. However, the cooling of
the passing sea water upon vessel's shell plating in way of tanks
leaves an elongating stress on the weather deck and upper sides
which might prove to be the source of cracks developing downward
from the sheer strake. In every vessel using the tank-heating process, the great differential in temperature of underwater and
above-water structure brings a complication of stresses to bear
which generally is evidenced by at least considerable distortion of
the deck plating.

Q. What local strength is usually added to a vessel in areas such
as illustrated?

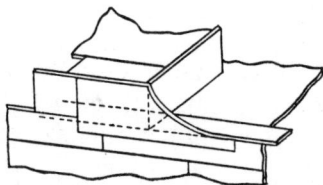

A. Continuity of longitudinal strength by
bridging the juncture or "break" indicated.

Q. How must the edges of thick plates
be prepared for welding? Why?

A. They are chamfered into a V-shaped
cross section. This is to provide ample space for the molten filler metal
to be built up and fused with the connected parts at each successive
pass.

Q. When a vessel is to be drydocked where the dock master is unfamiliar with the vessel, what information must be made available
to him?

A. He should be provided with vessel's docking plan, in which are
shown all transverse bulkheads, engine and boiler spaces, and sea
connections. Also with the plan several cross-sectional views of
ship's hull should appear, so that the blocking may be correctly
placed. He also should be informed of ship's double-bottom tank
condition, i.e., tanks that are full, empty, or contain certain
weight of water or oil.

Q. Describe briefly two or more methods employed to reduce the
rolling of ships.

A. 1. By bilge keels. These are vertically fitted fins along the turn
of the bilge on each side of ship, extending from about 1/4 to 3/4
her length at her widest part, and varying in depth from 1 to 3
feet. They act simply as a brake to reduce the amplitude of roll.

2. By anti-rolling tanks. These produce an opposing moment
against direction of roll by the flow or admission of water to the
low side, timed to exert maximum counter heeling effect as vessel begins a new roll.

3. By gyroscope stabilizer. In this method, a heavy gyroscope
rotor is made by a pilot gyro to precess in the opposite direction
to that which would result from vessel's roll.

4. By stabilizer, or anti-rolling, fins. These are, in effect,
vertical rudders which are installed to be projected from each
side of the hull, just above turn of the bilge, when ship gets under way. By gyroscope control the fins are pointed upward on the
downward roll and vice versa. Vessel's ahead motion sets up an
equal pressure on each fin, thus producing a couple to resist each
roll.

Q. On the web frame illustrated, what is A, B and C?

A. A = the web of frame. B = stiffening
flange. C = bracket.

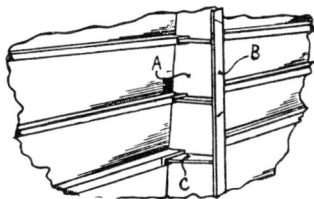

Q. Where the bilge keels of vessels are
welded directly to the bilge plating,
what precaution must be taken at
welded plate butts to eliminate notch
effect and danger of cracks?

A. That the welding, which usually is
intermittent along bilge keels, be kept
from contact with that of all plating butts. No local irregular
stresses then will be set up in the butts, which might otherwise
result in cracks in the metal.

Q. Why does the plating thickness of a vessel vary from one part
of the vessel to another?

A. Because its thickness is governed by the stresses the plating is required to withstand. Thus, the garboard, bilge, and sheer strakes are heavier than all others in the shell, because called upon to endure great longitudinal tensile and compressive stresses, situated as these are at maximum distance from ship's neutral axis. The principle of providing heavier metal to withstand greater stress is adhered to throughout construction.

Q. What is the purpose of the frame scallops illustrated, at joints in plating?

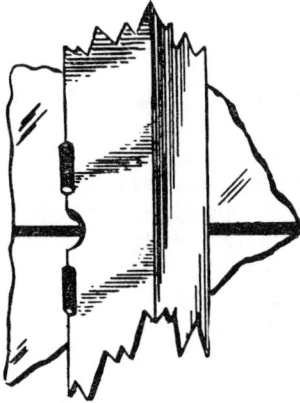

A. To prevent buckling of the web, and so a tension on plating seam, due to heating of frame at the welds.

Q. Describe panting stresses and name the structural features of vessels designed to resist these stresses.

A. Panting stresses arise from the fluctuating pressures of heavier waves against the bows, which cause the shell to pant, or work in and out, as vessel drives ahead. To resist such stresses, panting stringers bridge the frames from abaft collision bulkhead to ship's stem and are united at the latter point by breast hooks, triangular-shaped plates which stiffen the whole girder or stringer arrangement. A closer spacing of frames and an increase of shell-plating thickness is also provided here, and larger vessels are fitted with extra transverse members in the form of panting beams. Also, solid deep floors usually are fitted at each frame.

Q. Why is the caulk welding of riveted seams as shown here usually avoided?

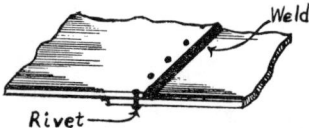

A. Because the welding process is likely to produce distorting stresses which may cause strain in the riveting and eventual lack of tightness in the seam.

Q. What circumstances or conditions might make a gas-free certificate invalid and make hot work or other repairs dangerous in or near a tank?

A. In the case of a tank having very rusty sides, the gas liberated from the rust may render tank unsafe in a few hours after having been found gas free.

Q. What is a stealer plate?

A. Where, owing to reduced breadth of plating toward vessel's ends, two strakes may be conveniently merged into one, such single strake is termed a <u>stealer</u>, perhaps because it reduces the number of strakes by one.

Q. What is meant by an A-60 bulkhead?
A. One capable of preventing passage of flame or smoke for 1 hour, and so insulated that average temperature on its unexposed side would not rise more than 250° F., or at any one point more than 325° F. within 60 minutes.

Q. Name the types of rivets shown in the sketch.

A. <u>A</u> = pan head. <u>B</u> = button head. <u>C</u> = steeple head. <u>D</u> = countersunk head. <u>E</u> = cone head. <u>F</u> = tap rivet.

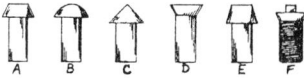

Q. Why are most seagoing vessels constructed with a smokestack which has an outer casing and an inner smoke pipe?
A. Casing confines heat radiating from smoke-pipe to an upward flow; provides an uptake for fireroom ventilation; also presents a shipshape appearance through being kept clean and painted without heat interference.

Q. On the drawing of one propeller and shaft of a twin screw vessel as shown, state the name and purpose of <u>A</u>, <u>B</u>, and <u>C</u>.

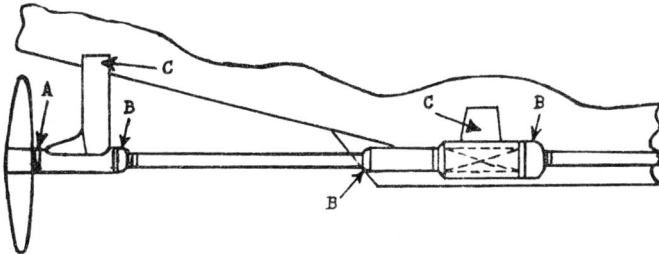

A. <u>A</u> = Rope guard, for preventing a fouled hawser from jamming between propeller and shaft-bearing tube.
   <u>B</u> = Streamline fittings over ends of shaft-bearing tubes to ease passage of the latter through the water.
   <u>C</u> = Propeller-shaft struts, brackets, or stays, for securing propeller-shaft arrangement in position.

Q. How is leakage of petroleum or vapors prevented where valve stems must pass through a tank top?
A. Valve stems pass through a stuffing box or packing gland fitted in tank top.

Q. When zinc, magnesium or iron anodes are fitted on a ship, should they be insulated or left in metallic contact with the steel of the hull? Why?

A. They should be left in direct contact with steel; because, while the anodes protect the steel in the galvanic flow to, say, a bronze propeller, they also protect the steel in the action set up between steel and anode. The anode being electropositive to both steel and bronze, it therefore would detract from full protection of the steel to insulate such anode.

Q. What strength requirements are put upon a vessel by deep draft?
A. Increased longitudinal strength, as in keel, bottom plating, and sheer strakes, also upper deck stringers; increased transverse strength, as in frames, beams, and bulkheads.

Q. What is meant by floodable length as applied to a vessel?
A. That part in the length of ship's hull, centered at a given point in the latter, which may be flooded to a given degree of permeability while ship remains afloat.

Q. What three (3) strakes usually are the most highly stressed part of the ship's structure because of longitudinal bending moment?
A. Keel plate with garboard strake, bilge strake, and sheer strake.

Q. Illustrated is the standard shipboard cable. What two functions are performed by the braided metal armor?

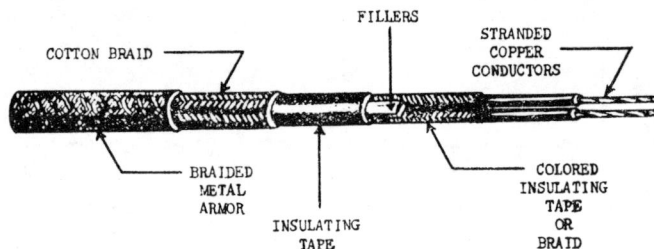

A. As cable's chief protection against outside injury, and as a shield against leaks of current.

Q. What are cant frames and where are they used?
A. Frames set in the structure obliquely to the fore-and-aft line. They are commonly used to shape and support the overhanging counter in an elliptical or rounded stern, being bracketed to the aftermost transom floor.

Q. In making alterations or repairs, in assigning tasks in various areas of the vessel, and in stowing cargo or quartering passengers, what precautions required by the regulations with respect to means of escape must be borne in mind?

A. Care must be taken to provide at least two means of escape; that at least one of these shall be independent of watertight doors; that the two means of escape shall be as far apart as practicable, so as to lessen the possibility of one incident blocking both escapes.

Q. What are the requirements of the regulations with respect to rails of vessels?
A. Rails or equivalent protection must be installed near the periphery of all weather decks accessible to passengers and crew. Space between rail courses shall not exceed 18 inches.

Excepting the case of small vessels other than passenger vessels, where rails at least 36 inches high are required, and, in special regard for the business of such vessel may, with Coast Guard approval, be not less than 30 inches high, rails on decks accessible to passengers must have at least 3 courses and be at least 42 inches high.

Passenger decks of ferries, excursion vessels, and others of similar type must have the space below top of rail fitted with suitable wire mesh or its equivalent.

All other such rails shall be at least 36 inches high and have at least 3 courses, equally spaced; but vessels contracted for prior to Jan. 1, 1957, may continue with 2 courses.

Q. What are the requirements of the regulations with respect to storm rails on vessels?
A. Storm rails must be installed in all passageways and along deckhouse sides where passengers or crew have normal access. In passageways of 6 or more feet in width, the rails shall be fitted on both sides.

Q. Compare the advantages of closed type chocks to open type chocks. See illustration.

Closed Chock   Open Chock

A. Closed type chock possesses the safety feature of security against the line in use becoming disengaged from it, as where the quayside is higher than the deck, thus possibly resulting in damage to ship's rail or injury to personnel. In point of strength, it has a decided advantage over the open chock in the upward-sloping pull, for which reason, together with its closed feature, this type is required by Panama Canal authorities, in view of the varied levels of water in which vessels are moved through the Canal's locks.

Q. State why preparation of joints is essential to butt welds where the strength of the hull structure is involved.
A. Such preparation provides the required V or trough for the molten filler metal, as it is built up in the fusing process by a series of passes.

Q. How are joints prepared for butt welding?

A. On thin plating, no preparation is needed, but, in thicker metal, the butting edges are chamfered so that, when brought together, a V-shaped trough is formed to receive the filler metal. On very thick plating, the double-V joint is prepared by chamfering both corners of each plate.

Q. What provisions are made in the design and construction of pipe lines to allow for thermal expansion?

A. They are provided with expansion bends, loops, offsets, or slip-joints, the last being used in tank vessels only.

   All pipe supports must be designed and arranged so as not to interfere with expansion and contraction of piping, and to insure that no excessive forces or moments are imposed on connected equipment.

Q. Identify the welds illustrated.

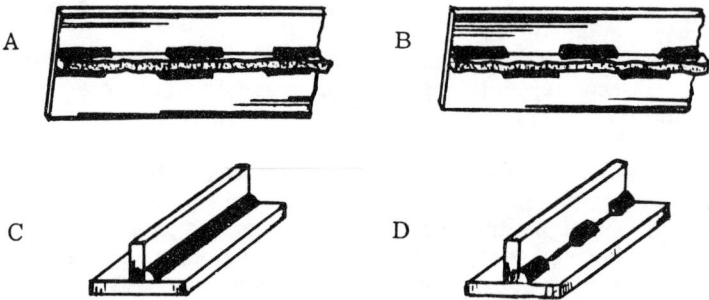

A. A: Intermittent chain fillet; B: Intermittent staggered fillet; C: Continuous fillet type of weld; D: Skip, or intermittent, welding.

Q. How are pipes terminating at the shell plating constructed in order to minimize danger of the pipes being cracked by blows or stress on the skin plating?

A. They shall be fitted with bends or elbows between the outboard openings and the first rigid connection inboard. Such pipes shall never be fitted in a direct line between shell opening and first inboard connection.

Q. Where should shut-off valves be located on piping to the shell?

A. As near the shell plating as practicable.

Q. What is the objection to cast iron for use in cocks and valves attached to a ship's side?

A. That such metal is not suitable to withstand shocks or stresses on the shell in the immediate vicinity.

Q. How is the stern bearing normally lubricated on an oceangoing vessel?

A. By the sea water which is allowed to enter tube along the shaft.

Q. What materials are used in fabricating stern tube bushings?

A. The liner, or liners, constituting the bearing surface of tail-end shaft, usually are made of bronze, while the shaft works in bearings usually of lignum vitae strips.

Q. How may it be determined if welding electrodes (welding rod) are suitable for use in construction or repair of vessels?

A. By consulting the Equipment Lists (CG-190) published by the U. S. Coast Guard. Also, approved electrodes listed by the U. S. Navy and the American Bureau of Shipping are equally suitable.

Q. Why may cracks spread rapidly once they have developed?

A. Unless some local pent-up stress is being thus relieved, rapid spreading of cracks may be attributed to the general stresses set up in ship's structure due to her motion among waves.

Q. On a tank vessel constructed with twin longitudinal bulkheads, what advantage is gained by using the wing tanks rather than the center tanks for ballast?

A. A much easier motion in a seaway will result, as compared with ballasting of center tanks only, because the moment of inertia about ship's midship fore-and-aft axis is greatly increased, with consequent increase in period of roll.

Q. Describe the advantages of welded ship construction with respect to repairs of shell damage.

A. Welding can be done under water. No beveling of frames to flange against side plating is required. Stud welding eliminates drilling a hole through plating and use of a nut on other side. Relatively inaccessible joints may be more conveniently made. Instead of punching out rivets to remove plating, and shaping, boring holes, etc., in replaced parts, in many cases repairs or renewals may be completed on the spot. Cutting may be done with a torch and new material fitted as, e.g., whole or part of a plate may be cut away, replaced, and welded without the time-consuming recourse to shore facilities as required in riveted construction.

Q. What precautions must be taken with respect to radiators and other heating apparatus to avoid injury to persons occupying the space?

A. The heating apparatus must be placed, and shielded if necessary, so as to avoid risk of fire or danger or discomfort to occupants. Where pipes leading to radiators or heating apparatus create a hazard to occupants, such pipes shall be satisfactorily lagged.

Q. On passenger vessels, what are the general requirements for rails?

A. Space between rail courses shall not exceed 18 inches, and on decks accessible to passengers rails shall be in at least 3 courses and at least 42 inches high; excepting that, on vessels of 65 feet in length or less, other than ferries, excursion boats, and those of similar type which carry large numbers of passengers, rails shall be at least 36 inches high, and in sport-fishing vessels and the like, as approved by the Coast Guard, rail above deck on which passengers stand may be not less than 30 inches in height.

On passenger decks of ferries, excursion vessels, and others of similar type, the space below top of rail shall be fitted with suitable wire mesh or the equivalent.

Q. What are the advantages of a tank in a vessel independent of the skin for potable water storage?

A. That no danger exists from outside contamination by leakage; also, where such tank is wholly or in part situated above ship's waterline, freezing of its contents may be obviated.

Q. How often must propeller tail shafts be withdrawn for examination?

A. Where tail shaft has two separate bronze bearing-liner, one at after end and the other in way of stuffing box, every 2 years; where bearing-liner is a continuous piece, every 3 years. However, at any time by request of classification society's inspector or of Officer in Charge, Marine Inspection (Coast Guard), the shaft must be drawn.

Q. At the stern post: (a) What is the purpose of the zinc plates usually fitted to a vessel? (b) When a ship is being painted, should such plates be painted?

A. (a) For protection of the steel against attack by galvanic action. Steel is electropositive to the near-by bronze, such as propeller blades, and accordingly will suffer corrosion if unprotected. Zinc, being electropositive to both steel and bronze, thus bears the attack, and corrosion in the steel is obviated.

(b) They should not be painted.

Q. How are hollow plated rudders usually treated to prevent internal corrosion?

A. They usually are filled with a bitumastic solution and then drained. Sometimes they are filled with molten pitch.

Q. When a vessel is drydocked, how may you detect small leaks, not readily apparent externally on a hollow plated rudder?

A. Connect an air hose and set up a pressure in the rudder. Leaks then will readily be seen or heard.

Q. Do Coast Guard regulations cover the maximum allowable clearance between propeller tail shaft and stern bushings?

A. Yes; in Marine Engineering Regulations.

Q. How is the clearance between tail shafts and bushings determined?
A. A wooden wedge may be inserted between shaft and bushing, and
the clearance measured thereon; or propeller may be jacked up
and its vertical motion measured by gauge. In the case of stern
tubes fitted with segmental rubber bushings, long feeler gauges
are used.

Q. How is the bossing about the tail shaft of a ship usually fitted
to prevent jamming of rope between the boss and the propeller?
A. A removable guard or hood is fitted to the boss to cover this
space.

Q. What inspection is mandatory by regulation when alterations, repairs, or operations involving riveting, welding, burning, etc.,
are to be made in or on the boundaries of oil tanks, oil lines,
or oil heating coils?
A. An inspection to determine that such operations may be under-
taken with safety. Such inspection shall be made by a gas chemist
who is either certificated by the American Bureau of Shipping or
supplied by the marine inspector, if vessel is within continental
United States; when not within such limits, the inspection shall be
made by the senior officer present, who shall make an appropriate
entry in ship's log.

Q. What is the maximum angle of efficiency for a rudder?
A. Approximately 35 degrees.

Q. What means must be provided to insure that the maximum angle
of efficiency for the rudder is not exceeded when the wheel is put
hard over?
A. Stop-cleats or buffers fitted in way of the quadrant, or other
efficient means, to prevent rudder from exceeding an angle of
38°. In smaller vessels, stops may be fitted on rudder itself or
on the rudder post.

Q. Describe how the upper stock of the rudder passes through the
hull of a vessel and the methods of lubrication employed at this
point.
A. Stock passes through the rudder casing, or trunk, which is
simply a watertight tubular housing. Usually located in the after
peak, just below the quadrant or steering attachments at the rudder head, is a stuffing box, and the stock is lubricated at this
point with grease. In larger vessels, connected with stuffing
box is a bearing arrangement which usually takes the form of a
thrust block in reverse, supporting entire weight of rudder and
working in a lubricant.

Q. How is a rudder removed for repair?
A. The inboard part of stock is disconnected, rudder is lifted
enough to clear pintles from gudgeons, then hoisted clear of ship.

Some types of balanced rudders, however, are not disconnected from stock, entire rudder being lowered to dock.

Q. How are the pintles and gudgeons constructed on a seagoing vessel?

A. Pintles are secured to rudder's leading edge and fit downward into the gudgeons, which are part of, and project aft from, ship's rudder post. The bearings contained in the gudgeons usually are made of lignum vitae or bonze.

Q. What is the nature of the force that pintles and gudgeons are built to withstand?

A. Heavy shearing stresses, maximum of which, in a heavy head or beam sea, with hard over rudder, is the combined force due to vessel's headway and the shock-like action of sea waves.

Q. How are pintles and gudgeons checked for wear?

A. Rudder is lifted, pintles and gudgeons sighted, and checking measurements taken.

Q. What is the name usually applied to the constructional features of a vessel indicated at A, B, and C?

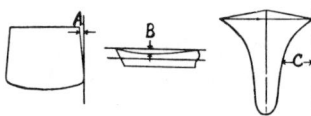

A. A = tumble home. B = sheer. C = flare.

Q. How are the pintle and gudgeon bearing surfaces on a seagoing vessel generally rebushed?

A. Rudder is removed; pintles reforged to required diameter, if worn; gudgeons cleared of old bushing and replaced with lignum vitae or bronze. Gudgeon bushings are lined up and reamed out to about one-sixteenth inch clearance from pintles by actual trial.

Q. How is the vertical weight of a rudder sustained?

A. In smaller vessels, by the bottom gudgeon, in which the bearing pintle sits on a rounded steel disk. Larger vessels have a bearing arrangement located either above or connected with the stuffing box. Such rudder bearing usually takes the form of a thrust block in reverse, its one or two "collars" working in a lubricant.

Q. When heavy concentrated loads must be carried on deck, how could you distribute the load or increase the bearing capacity of the deck?

A. Load might be distributed by spreading its bearing surface with heavy timbers. If this is impracticable, the additional strength of a 'tween deck may be brought to bear by shoring up the upper deck beams from a position immediately below such heavy load.

Q. What materials are employed in the manufacture of stern frames?
A. Usually cast steel of the nickel or the vanadium type, characterized by its toughness and ability to withstand shocks or local impact.

Q. When vessels are constructed with the stringer fastened to the sheer strake below the top of the sheer strake as shown at A, why are scuppers preferably constructed as at B rather than C?

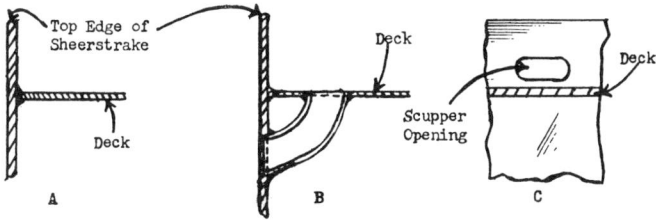

A. Because tensile strength of sheer strake is reduced in C, due to scupper opening being at a much greater distance from strake's neutral axis.

Q. How are the sections of a cast steel stern frame joined together?
A. They are scarfed together and the union made by riveting or welding, or by a combination of both. Heavy countersunk rivets are used and scarf seams may be "veed out" and welded to present a flush surface. Where an all-welded job is performed, "plug welding" takes the place of rivets and seams are V-welded as above. Welded scarf work is given stress-relieving treatment by slowly heating to about 1200° F. and as slowly cooling.

Q. Name the parts of the stern frame marked A, B, C, D, E, and F in the sketch.

A. A = gudgeons. B = rudder post. C = body post. D = shaft boss E = screw race. F = rudder-post heel.

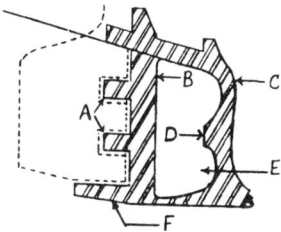

Q. Describe how a stern frame is secured to a vessel's structure and plating.
A. Rudder post extends upward to connect with the aftermost transom and may even reach to an upper deck beam. Body post connects with a transom or "deep floor." Each "post" usually terminates in a "palm," or a flattened-out section, by which a well-spread union is made with the transom, floor, or beam. Shell plating is tap-riveted to body post and archpiece of frame.

Q. What is meant by camber?
A. The convexity or rounding of a surface above the horizontal, as that of a deck.

Q. What is the strength deck of a vessel?
A. The uppermost continuous deck.

Q. State how decks are supported.
A. By the deck beams which are connected at each end with the transverse frames, beams in turn resting on pillars or stanchions rising from deck next below. In the longitudinal frame system, decks are supported by the longitudinals which span between deep, or web, frames, the latter having much wider spacing than in the usual transverse system.

Q. What are the functions of beams?
A. To support the decks and any weight carried thereon; to stiffen the side frames and hold them to their work; to withstand racking stresses; and to provide means of securing deck plating, which is a principal strength requisite in the structure.

Q. How is the upper stock joined to the rudder?
A. Its lower end is flanged to meet a corresponding flange in upper end of rudder. Both flanges are bolted strongly together.

Q. What is the skeg of a stern frame on a single screw vessel?
A. At its lower extremity, that part between rudder post and body post.

Q. How should freeing ports be fitted for protection of personnel and where shutters are installed, what precautions are necessary to prevent jamming?
A. Freeing ports shall be fitted with suitable guards across such openings. Where fitted with shutters or covers, these are to be the hanging type, i. e., suspended from their hinges, and so installed as to freely work without jamming or re-engaging their securing dogs or other devices.

Q. When riveting and welding are both used in fabricating a vessel's skin, which process is employed first? Why?
A. The welding; because the riveted joints might be strained or "sprung" by the extreme heat and stresses set up in the metal by the welding process.

Q. State the reason why freeing ports are important on a vessel fitted with bulwarks.
A. In that, when deeply laden, vessel may quickly rid herself of heavy water shipped in rough sea conditions. Besides lessening the probability of damage, as to deck fittings, hatches, deck cargo, etc., prompt freeing of water from deck obviates the undesirable effect of a free liquid surface on vessel's stability, plus the

loss of buoyancy due to superimposed weight of water.

Q. What is the purpose of the copper wire frequently fitted to stay turnbuckles?

A. To ground any stray currents, or static electricity, and thus prevent sparking across the gap between turn-buckle threads.

← COPPER WIRE

Q. What is the purpose of a thrust block?
A. To receive the push, driving force, or thrust of the propeller and trans-mit it to ship's hull.

Q. What type of bearings are usually employed for thrust blocks?
A. With reciprocating engines, usually the horseshoe thrust bear-ing, consisting of 3 or more thrust shoes fitted to engage corres-ponding collars on the shaft, the whole working in a bath of oil.
The Kingsbury patent thrust bearing is much used with turbines. In this system, a single shaft collar engages against a series of babbitt-faced shoes with an intervening pressure film of oil.

Q. How are the foundations for thrust blocks constructed?
A. Thrust block is firmly secured to a heavy plate supported by two longitudinal webs, which in turn are stiffened athwartships by two or more solid brackets, the whole based on the reinforced tank top. As maintaining the extra strength continuity required in this part of the hull, with its solid floors, extra intercostals, and heavier tank-top plating, the seating of a thrust block has for its aim an even distribution of the thrust forces in the structure.

Q. On the illustration shown, identify A, B, C, and D.

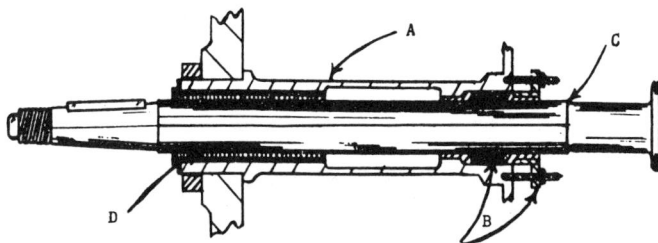

A. A = stern tube wall. B = stuffing box. C = bearing liner.
   D = tube bushing.

Q. Would you expect hogging or sagging stresses to be more severe on a vessel with machinery aft in the full load condition?
A. Sagging stresses.

Q. Where wooden doors are permitted in a superstructure, how must the doors be constructed to meet the strength requirements?
A. They shall be of hardwood and have a minimum thickness of 1-3/4 inches.

Q. Sketched is a pressure-vacuum valve such as is found on many tank vessels. Describe briefly the care and inspection such a valve requires.

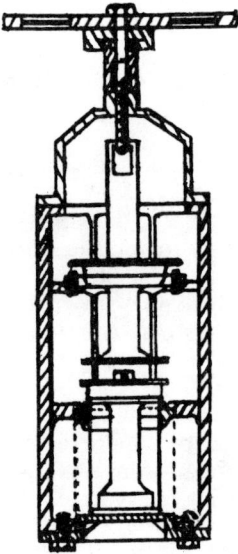

A. Such valves should be opened up for inspection at frequent intervals. The discs should correctly "seat," hand wheel should be set for proper operation, and guides kept clean and clear. Flame screens also should be kept clean and in good condition.

Q. If, in heavy weather, you notice buckling in the midship deck plating of your vessel, (a) What would it indicate? (b) What measures could you take?
A. (a) Strain in the structure due to the laboring to which vessel is subjected.
   (b) Reduce engine speed and alter course to a direction in which vessel will take the sea more kindly; or lie to before the sea until bad weather subsides. Any possible action, including bettering the weight distribution in the hull, might then be considered.

Q. What type of stress do the deck beam brackets of a transversely framed vessel resist?
A. Racking stress.

Q. Why might the stress for which the deck beam brackets provide part of the resistance be strongest at the vessel's midlength than at bow and stern?
A. Because of the massive expanse of the midship body compared with the more concentrated material toward the vessel's ends. Such stress would vary approximately as the moment of inertia of a point about ship's longitudinal axis at different positions in the fore-and-aft line.

Q. When scupper and sanitary discharge pipes lead through the ship's side below the freeboard deck, how must they be fitted to prevent water from passing aboard?
A. Where such discharge pipes lead through ship's side at more than 18 inches below the freeboard deck, each shall be provided with one automatic nonreturn valve fitted with a means of closing it from above the freeboard deck; or, with two such valves without

means of closing them, provided the upper valve lies above ship's deepest load line, so as to be always accessible for inspection, and is of a type which normally is closed.

Q. In the construction or the repair of gratings for use on the decks near a switchboard or resistor panel, would you use nails or wooden dowels? Why?
A. Wooden dowels; because it is most desirable that personnel at such location should stand upon nonconducting material, in case of an accidental "ground" through one's body.

Q. What basic considerations are followed in the design and maintenance of ships to ensure that they are ratproof?
A. Elimination of all nooks and possible nesting places.
   Stoppage of all means of communication through air ducts, pipe coverings, lockers, and partitions.
   Special attention to ratproofing of refrigerated spaces, storerooms, pantries, etc., where foodstuffs or provisions are carried.

Q. In machinery spaces where sources of vapor ignition are normally present, why should at least one vent duct go as low as possible?
A. So as to remove the petroleum vapors which tend to accumulate in the lowest parts of such spaces.

Q. Describe briefly how heavy steel castings, forgings, etc., are examined by magnetic particle testing (magnifluxing) for cracks or flaws invisible to the eye.
A. Fine steel dust is sifted over the weld. Then the weld with its adjacent metal is electromagnetized, which will result in dust being drawn into any crack that is present. Dust is then blown off by a very slight pressure of air, and a crack will be revealed by the line of dust remaining.

Q. In the construction of a vessel, how must fire hydrants be spaced and arranged?
A. They shall be of such number and so located that any part of the vessel (other than main machinery spaces), which is accessible to crew and passengers, and all cargo spaces may be reached with at least 2 streams of water from separate outlets, at least 1 of which being from a single length of hose. In main machinery spaces, at least 2 streams shall be from single lengths of hose in reaching all portions of such spaces.

Q. What are: (a) Soft patches? (b) Hard patches?
A. (a) Pieces of plate, sheet lead, or the like, temporarily secured to cover a damaged part, as a hole or fracture in plating, a pipe, etc.
   (b) Pieces of plate more permanently secured to cover a damaged part of a surface.

Q. How are they fastened on and made watertight?

A. Soft patches are tap-bolted to the surface concerned and set up with a gasket or waterproofing filler laid between faying surfaces; or, in the case of damaged pipe, they take the form of pieces of canvas or sheet lead secured by serving the whole with spun yarn.

Hard patches are secured by bolting, riveting, or welding. Where securing means is bolting, a gasket and/or red or white lead is used between faying surfaces.

Q. How is a B-15 bulkhead constructed to prevent the spread of fire?

A. It is so constructed that, if subjected to the standard fire test, it would be capable of preventing passage of flame for 1/2 hour; and also, its insulation value shall be such that the temperature of its unexposed side would rise not more than 250° F. above its original temperature within 15 minutes.

Q. Why is insulating material necessary on steel or aluminum bulkheads which are constructed to prevent an excessive rise of temperature on the unexposed side as well as to prevent smoke and flame passing?

A. So that progress of the fire may be delayed, and thus an opportunity afforded persons to escape from the compartment concerned or its vicinity in safety.

Q. In freeing up a reach rod, would procedure A or B be preferable? Why?

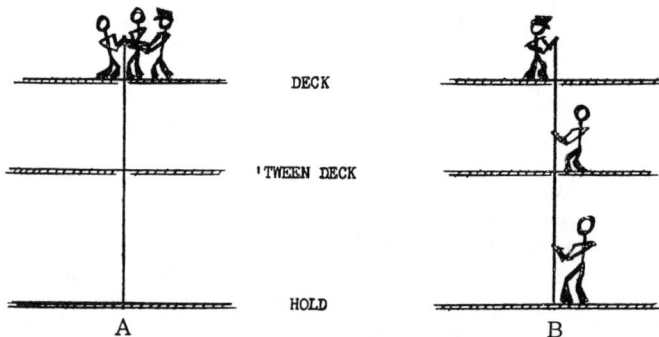

DECK

'TWEEN DECK

HOLD

A   B

A. Procedure B; because the accumulated torque in A would be damaging to the rod, as compared with the distribution of torsion effected in B.

Q. How must vessels of over 1600 gross tons be fitted in order that failure of the side, masthead, range, or stern lights is indicated at once to the officer on watch?

A. With a light-indicator panel located in wheelhouse to control electric side, masthead, range, and stern lights. Such panel shall provide visible and audible indications of failure of any of these lights.

Q. Is a mushroom vent as at <u>B</u> or a porthole as at <u>A</u> satisfactory for ventilation of a battery room? Why?

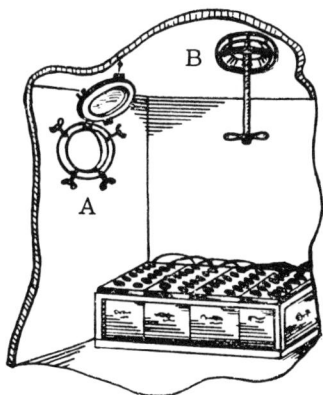

A. The mushroom vent <u>B.</u> Hydrogen gas emitted from batteries being lighter than air, an explosive mixture might accumulate at the deckhead, which condition a porthole could not prevent.

Q. Why do chain falls usually hold a load in position without the necessity of securing the hauling part? Why do turnbuckles hold a weight without securing against turning or walking back?

A. Chain falls hold a load because the friction due to multiplicity of power obtained is sufficient to bind or brake the hoist to a stop.

Turnbuckles hold because the screw parts have opposite threads, i.e., a right-hand turning force at one end occurs with a left-hand force at the other.

Q. What effects does vibration have upon such devices as chain falls or turnbuckles?
A. Vibration will tend to loosen or "walk back" such devices, because of a gradual shaking loose from the binding effect of friction in the working parts.

Q. With regard to fire protection, why is special care necessary in the construction and maintenance of stairways and elevator enclosures?
A. Because such construction is the principal requisite for escape of passengers and others from fire below decks.

Q. Can current flow to actuate the winch motor when the limit switch is in good condition and in the open contact position?
A. Winch might still run if failure should occur in motor control contactor, since limit switch usually is in the control circuit rather than on main power. Such failure might be caused by an accidental ground, by contacts becoming welded together, by frozen working parts, etc.

In view of the above, it is imperative that the emergency disconnecting switch be in reliable working order at all times. This switch is in the main power circuit.

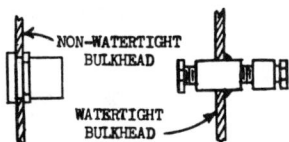

Q. Shown is a bushing for use where an electrical cable passes through a non-watertight bulkhead of less than 1/4 inch and a stuffing box for a watertight bulkhead. What is the purpose of the bushing for the non-watertight bulkhead?

A. To secure the cable against chafe on the plating edge and thus the possibility of a "short" occurring at this point.

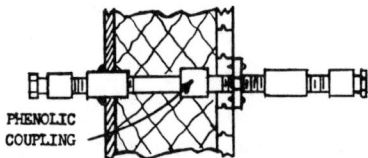

Q. Shown is a conduit where cable passes through an insulated bulkhead to a cold storage space. What is the purpose of the phenolic coupling?

A. As a heat insulator, for protection against fire.

Q. What points should be carefully checked in examining lifeboat limit switches (see illustration)?

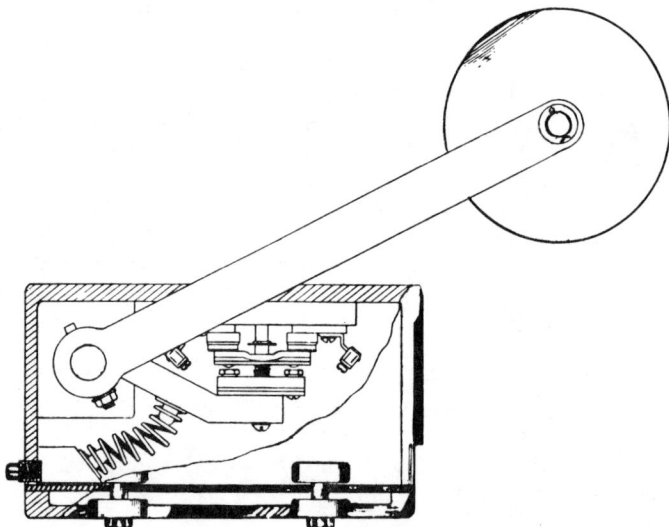

A. All internal mechanical and electrical parts should be dry and in good order; also see that all connections between roller arm, roller, and shaft are secure and in good condition, and check condition of gasket and tightness of drain plug.

Q. When damage to a ship's structure or fittings is occasioned by neglect, carelessness, or poor workmanship of a stevedore or his employees, what action on the part of the master is necessary to assure that the stevedore is held responsible for the cost of repairs?

A. The managing owner, agent, or master of such vessel shall notify the Coast Guard District Commander by letter within five days, or as soon thereafter as possible, stating name, port of registry, and official number of vessel; place, nature, occasion, and estimated amount of damage to ship; also shall furnish all other information as may be called for by the Coast Guard.

Q. What are the advantages and disadvantages of cork as an insulating material? Under what conditions is its use forbidden on passenger vessels?

A. Advantages of cork, which now usually is in "corkboard" or slab form of the granulated material, are its low thermal conductivity, extreme lightness, non-deteriorating qualities, and moderate cost of installation. Its disadvantages in passenger vessels chiefly lie in being unsuitable for insulation of bulkheads, partitions, or shell plating in way of accommodation spaces, because of its combustible nature and its noxious smoke-producing effect in case of fire; also it is likely to provide nesting places for rats.

Q. Illustrated is the type of receptacle outlet which is currently approved for outside use. What advantage is provided by the use of a three-pronged plug required to fit this type of outlet?

A. Third wire provides a ground in the event of a "short" in the instrument, light cluster, etc., plugged in, thus eliminating sparks from the connection.

Q. On a ship fitted with smoke-detecting apparatus and CO_2 fire-extinguishing systems for the cargo holds, how is the extinguishing system piping for the holds checked?

A. Smoke inlets in cargo holds must be examined at least once in each three months by ship's personnel, and smoke tests made in all holds. At annual inspection, "all piping, controls, valves, and alarms shall be checked to ascertain that the system is in working condition."

Q. What safety advantage is gained by the use of raked bows?

A. In the event of a vessel having such bow ramming another vessel, resulting damage very likely will be entirely above her waterline, and also likely to be above that of the other vessel.

Q. What two factors govern the rate at which water enters the hull of a damaged vessel?

A. Size of the opening and its distance below the surface, i.e., cross-section area of entrance flow and pressure of water.

Q. What name is given the three types of plans illustrated? Name _A_, _B_, and _C_.

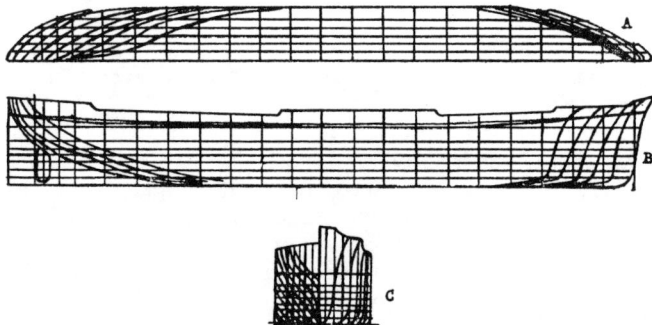

A. _A_ = half-breadth plan. _B_ = sheer or profile plan. _C_ = body plan.

Q. Would end _A_ or _B_ be most likely to continue to propagate? Why?

A. _A._ Continuity of cracking is stopped by hole at _B_.

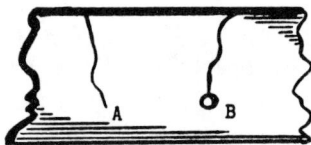

Q. In the carriage of refrigerated cargoes, such as fruit: (a) Why are vessels normally painted white? (b) Why are such vessels frequently fitted with a wooden deck?

A. (a) Because the white paint is best for reflecting the sun's rays, thus keeping ship's temperature at the most possible minimum in warm weather, and so assisting in the necessary cooling of fruit.

(b) Because a wood deck is an excellent nonconductor of heat, and thus maintains a comparatively cool temperature in the steel plating under such deck, and so assists in cooling of the fruit in compartments below.

Q. What is meant by slugging a weld?
A. The act of laying welding rods, wire, bolts, or other extraneous material in a welding groove and then welding over it, with the aim of quickly building up the weld.

Q. How may slugged welds be detected?
A. By radiographic examination.

Q. What is the block coefficient of a vessel?
A. Ratio of her underwater volume to that of a rectangular prism having same length, extreme breadth, and mean draft.

Q. What are molded dimensions on a vessel, as molded beam, molded draft, etc. ?
A. Measurements referred to outer edges of frames or of floors. (Thickness of shell plating is not considered in such terms.)

Q. Describe the function of a deck stringer plate.
A. Serves as a valuable connection between beams and ship's side: stiffens shell plating in its vicinity; forms a watertight boundary to deck; acts as a girder to the beams; and, especially in the upper or strength deck, contributes greatly to vessel's longitudinal strength in its "teamwork" with the sheer strake, to which it is strongly connected fore and aft.

Q. Why should heating coils in a tank be located as close to the bottom of the tank as possible?
A. Because the heated oil nearest the coils rises and the cooler oil sinks, thus setting up a vertical distributing motion in the liquid. Such convective heat distribution within a reasonable length of time is possible only with coils close to bottom of tank.

Q. Why are colliers built with wing tanks as illustrated; i.e., why does the inside bulkhead of the tank slope as shown? How is the strength of the vessel affected by the inclusion of these tanks in the construction?

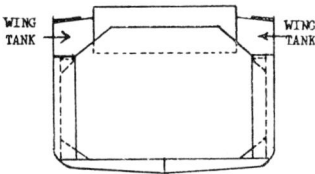

A. Sloped bulkhead of such tank, while structurally serving as a girder to the deep beam and frame system, also prevents the bulk cargo from shifting into the upper wings, in event of heavy weather, thus providing a safety measure akin to that supplied by shifting boards erected in the hold. While the vessel's transverse strength has been lessened by the removal of all pillars or stanchions and an intervening 'tween deck, that weakness is more than compensated for in the extra deep frames and beams, with web brackets and the plating of the tank slopes. The last-named also contributes greatly to ship's longitudinal strength, in lieu of a 'tween deck.

Q. Is the wind resistance encountered by a vessel greatest with the wind dead ahead or with wind ahead at an angle off the bow?
A. With wind off the bow, since vessel then presents a much greater area of resistance.

Q. Why does a ship require less fuel and why does her speed increase normally when she is in the light condition rather than in the loaded condition?
A. Because of the lesser resistance to her advance through the water accompanying a lighter draft. Less power is required to attain a given speed in the light condition, average weather only considered.

Q. What is the maximum amount of acetylene and oxygen a vessel is permitted to carry for the purpose of effecting her own repairs?

A. Acetylene: 600 cu. ft. on cargo and foreign or intercoastal passenger vessels; 300 cu. ft. on inland or coastwise passenger vessels.

Oxygen: 3000 cu. ft. on cargo and foreign or intercoastal passenger vessels; 1500 cu. ft. on inland or coastwise passenger vessels.

Q. If a vessel is in level trim but sagging, where would the location of her maximum draft be located?

A. Approximately amidships?

Q. If a vessel's bottom has a pronounced sag amidships when she is on a drydock, how is that considered in painting the forward and after draft marks?

A. The base line for marking in the forward and after draft figures is the fair extension of the curved line of bottom of keel.

Q. On the ship's length, where are the shearing forces on a ship's structure usually at their maximum?

A. At approximately 1/4 ship's length from each end.

Q. Why is it mandatory for safety in oil tanks that such fittings as ladder bolts, heating coil clamps, pipe clamps, etc., be of strong and substantial material in a good state of preservation?

A. In order that injury to men working in tanks may be prevented, as through a ladder bolt, pipe clamp, etc., carrying away.

Q. What is the function of the stern tube gland as illustrated?

A. As a stopwater to prevent leakage entering the hull through the tube.

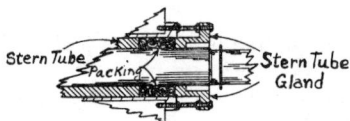

Q. What procedure is usually followed when a stern tube gland is leaking excessively and requires repacking?

A. At first opportunity when vessel is light, trim ship to raise the propeller out of water, open gland, remove old packing, repack, and set up gland.

Q. What type of power supply is required for the general alarm system?

A. A storage battery giving a nominal potential of not less than 6 volts and not more than 120 volts.

Q. How must fuses in the general alarm system be protected against unauthorized tampering?

A. Means shall be provided for locking the fuses.

Q. When compression members of a ship's structure, such as longitudinal girders or frames, have been badly buckled by collision or other cause, why is cropping out and renewal preferable to fairing in place?

A. Because, in the cropping out and renewal work, relief of pent-up structural stresses is effected, as compared with a forced retention of such stresses where fairing in place is the procedure.

Q. What ship's plan may be used to determine the dimensions, and location of plating?

A. The body plan, with necessary reference to the sheer plan. (Better to take plating dimensions from the plating model.)

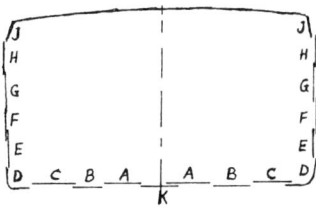

Q. Name the plates on the sketch shown here.

A. K = keel plate A = garboard strake D = bilge strake H = sheer strake.

Q. What is the difference between a solid floor and an open floor?

A. A solid floor is made of continuous plate throughout its depth and length, while an open, or bracket, floor is a skeleton arrangement consisting of a reverse frame as the tank top support and a continuation of a frame forming its bottom edge, connected to the vertical center keel and to the margin plate by brackets, and stiffened by intermediate struts set vertically between frame and reverse frame.

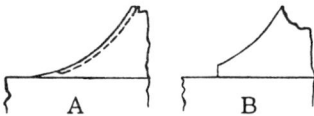

Q. In construction or repair of a ship or her fittings, would you regard the fashion plate at A or B most suitable? Why?

A. That at A. Such construction indicates a continuity of strength apparently not considered in B.

Q. Steel plating used for ship construction and repair is commonly referred to by its weight. (a) What thickness would 40.8 lb. plate be? (b) What thickness would 30.6 lb. plate be?

A. Steel being 490 lbs. per cubic foot in weight, and 40.8-lb. plate meaning the weight of 1 square foot of the material:
   (a) Thickness is $40.8 \div (490 \div 12) = 40.8 \div 40.8 = 1$ inch.
   (b) Thickness is $30.6 \div (490 \div 12) = 30.6 \div 40.8 = 3/4$ inch.

Q. What drainage and venting arrangement are made in solid floors?

A. By the limber holes, or small drains cut in floor near the vertical keel plate and near the bilge to allow drainage to the tank suction. Similar holes are cut near the keel plate and bilge for venting.

Q. What is meant by the pitch of rivets?
A. It indicates the spacing, or distance of each one from another
in a line of riveting, and usually is expressed in diameters of
the rivets used, as measured from center to center.

Q. Describe how the propeller of a vessel is removed for repair
or renewal.
A. Rig two good tackles over the quarter or use a suitable dock
crane. Place a good chain or wire sling around the boss. Hook
on and take the weight. Unscrew lock nut and remove key. Start
propeller by wedging from body post. Disconnect length of shafting forward of stern tube. Draw in tail shaft. Slack away tackles
or crane fall as required and land propeller clear of stern frame,
or lift it ashore by crane.

Q. Why are louvers or small screened openings desirable in bulkheads or doors between a passageway and a room for passengers
or crew members?
A. As a safety measure, to allow detection of presence of smoke
by the fire patrol or watchman.

Q. Why must a vessel's stern tube be of sturdy construction?
A. Because of the varying heavy shocks and stresses endured by
propeller in heavy weather, which forces are transferred to the
tube through the tail shaft. Structurally, the stern tube holds propeller to its work and distributes its shocks and stresses to the
hull.

Q. What report is necessary when repairs or alterations affecting
the safety of the vessel are to be made?
A. The Officer in Charge, Marine Inspection, shall be notified of
such alterations or repairs, and drawings of alterations shall be
submitted therewith.

Q. What is the difference between a built-up and a solid propeller?
A. A built-up propeller has removable blades, which are separately
bolted to the boss, or hub. A solid propeller is a single casting;
boss and blades are cast as a unit.

Q. What members of the ship's structure resist buckling of the
plating when the vessel's plating is in compression?
A. Principal members are sheer strake, deck stringer plate, vertical plate keel, intercostal keelsons, transverse framing; and
all longitudinals in the longitudinal frame system.

Q. In loading concentrated heavy weights, such as lead or pig iron
billets in a vessel's 'tween decks, where would the decks' load
bearing capacity be greatest, i.e., could more weight be carried
adjacent to shell and bulkheads or near hatch openings without
danger of setting down the decks?

A. Bearing capacity would be greatest close along the shell or adjacent to the bulkheads, and consequently less danger in such locations of setting down the deck.

Q. How are the tail shafts of vessels protected against corrosion where they pass through the stern tube?
A. If not entirely covered by a single bearing liner, shaft surface between liners may be freely coated with white or red lead and tallow, then covered with canvas and served with small tarred hemp line or ratline stuff; or a reliable bitumastic solution may be used.

Q. What tests are given to riveted work?
A. For watertightness of tanks, by filling tank and building up a pressure equal to not more than an 8-foot head, or about 3-1/2 pounds per inch^2. In dry cargo compartments, a strong stream of water from a hose is turned on the riveted work and its other side observed for leaks.

Cracked or loose rivets may be detected by tapping with a light hammer, while feeling the rivet for soundness. In dry dock, a loose rivet may often be detected by corrosion rings around its point; these should be tested by tapping as above.

Q. How is the length of rivets measured?
A. By length of the shank, i.e., from the neck, or beginning of the head, to the tail end, or point.

Q. When passenger vessels are fitted with hinged watertight doors in the cargo spaces, what precautions are required by the regulations?
A. These doors shall be closed before a voyage commences and shall be kept closed during navigation. Where any such doors are accessible at any time during the voyage, they shall be fitted with locks to prevent them from being opened.

Q. What advantage is gained by the use of a balanced rudder?
A. Less power is required to turn such rudder to large angles, thus providing more rapid helm movements than is possible with an ordinary rudder and similar steering-gear effort, with also a reduction of torsional stress on the rudder head. The balanced rudder eliminates the pintle and gudgeon arrangement required for the single-plate type.

Q. What is a stealer strake? State why it is necessary.
A. Where, in the shell plating, because of the reduced breadth of plating toward vessel's ends, two strakes may be merged into one, this single strake is termed a stealer. It is so called because each time it is fitted the number of strakes is reduced by one.

A. Bearing capacity would be greatest close along the shell or adjacent to the bulkheads, and consequently less danger in such locations of setting down the deck.

Q. What is the purpose of the expansion joint fitted on the superstructure of some vessels?

A. To relieve superstructure of compressive and tensile stresses set up during vessel's motion in a seaway. Due to the comparatively great distance of superstructure above the neutral axis, and also above the strength deck, such expansion joints are a most important protection against serious structural injury.

Q. Why must the deck plating above tanks be capable of withstanding forces acting upward as well as down?

A. Because of its required capacity, in the case of double-bottom tanks, to withstand the hydrostatic pressure due to vessel's bottom being injured and open to the sea. In all other cases, decks over tanks must be capable to withstand normal gas or overflow pressures, as in a tank vessel, and pressure set up by a greater head than is necessary, as in filling a lower deck or a double-bottom tank.

Q. How do you determine the thickness of plating, sizes of beams, girders, etc., that may be used in constructing or repairing a vessel?

A. By consulting the classification society's rules for scantlings of such. Considerations of vessel's length, breadth, and depth, as expressed in certain numerals, determining scantlings of structural members, are embodied in tables prepared by the society. For example, the First Numeral, which is vessel's length times her depth, gives required sizes of all component parts of double bottoms, flat plate keel, shell plating, propeller boss plating, etc.

Q. Where is zinc or magnesium anode protection most useful on the outer hull of vessels? Why?

A. In way of a propeller of different metal than the vessel's steel, as on the body post where propeller blades are of bronze.

Due to galvanic action set up through the medium of sea water, zinc or magnesium being electropositive to the bronze and also to the steel, such anode receives the resulting corrosive attack, thus protecting the steel.

Q. In addition to the compartmentation and the watertight division which bulkheads afford, what strength elements do they give the vessel?

A. They greatly stiffen the hull transversely against any tendency to distortion, in which respect they may be regarded as important members of the transverse framing.

Q. Are vessels designed to withstand abnormally severe stresses which may be set up by poor distribution of weight?

A. The naval architect designs a vessel of sufficient strength to prevent any material alteration of the hull form when engaged in a particular trade. Thus, while sufficient strength reserve is supplied to withstand all practical variations in distribution of weight, the unreasonable requirement of coping with "abnormally severe" stresses in this category is not considered. A vessel designed to withstand such stresses would prove far too weighty and costly to operate successfully.

Q. When passenger vessels are fitted with portholes below the bulkhead deck, what method is prescribed by the regulations to prevent their being opened by unauthorized persons?

A. They shall have fitted to one or more of the bolts a special round slotted or recessed nut requiring a special wrench. Such special nuts are to be protected by sleeves or guards which render the nuts not capable of being released by use of ordinary tools, such as pipe wrenches, etc.

Q. How are drain wells for holds constructed in order that damage to the outer bottom on a vessel fitted with a double bottom will not cause water to be admitted into the cargo spaces?

A. They are not to extend downward more than necessary and, in passenger vessels, must not be less than 18 inches from the outer shell, except at after end of a shaft alley, where they may extend to the shell.

Q. When sounding pipes terminate below the freeboard or bulkhead deck, what provisions are required to prevent flooding of the compartment in which the sounding pipe terminates, should there be a head on the double bottom tank?

A. They shall be fitted with gate valves, which, in passenger vessels, shall be the self-closing type.

Q. What provision is usually made to prevent damage to a vessel's shell plating where the sounding rods strike?

A. A small piece of plate is fitted flat to the shell, in way of the sounding pipe, for the purpose.

Q. Where breaks in the continuity of a vessel's shell structure are created by sideports, gangway apertures, etc., what structural compensations are made?

A. In order to maintain vessel's continuity of longitudinal structural strength, extra thickness of plating is fitted in way of such openings.

Q. Why is it, in general, the procedure in electric welding to weld butts before seams in repair or construction of vessels?

A. Because contraction upon cooling takes place under conditions of least restraint when butts are first welded.

Q. What protection must be afforded double bottom tanks against pressures in excess of that for which they are designed?
A. They must be fitted with at least 2 vents, so located as to provide venting under any service conditions. Aggregate area of such vents in each tank shall be at least equal to the area of the filling line, unless the tank is protected by an overflow, in which case area of overflow shall be not less than that of filling line.

Q. What is the dead rise of a vessel?
A. Height to which the thwartship line of vessel's bottom rises above the horizontal at molded breadth distance. Most modern vessels have no midship dead rise.

Q. What are garboard strakes?
A. Strakes of bottom plating next to the keel.

Q. What protection must be afforded manholes to double bottoms?
A. They must have efficient covers capable of being made thoroughly watertight and effectively protected from damage by cargo or bunker coal.

Q. What is the function of lightening holes in solid floors?
A. For lessening weight of material, while providing a means of access to any part of the half double-bottom tank concerned.

Q. What are intercostals?
A. Longitudinal girders fitted between the floors as stiffeners to the latter and as further support to the double-bottom tank top. Any piece similarly fitted, as between frames, may also be termed an intercostal, since the word itself means between ribs.

Q. What are margin plates?
A. The sloping longitudinal plate forming a side of a double-bottom tank. Extending from the shell at turn of the bilge, it lies along the line of outer ends of the floors.

Q. Why are hinge pins usually made with a loose fit or an elongated hole made for the hinge bolt or pin on hinged watertight doors and portholes?
A. So that hinge may not prevent complete contact against gasket when door is set tight by the dogs.

Q. Describe how you would check a hinged watertight door for tightness, and state the adjustments that may be made if necessary under operating conditions at sea.
A. Chalk the knife edge and then check its mark on gasket for high spots. Correction may be effected by an adjustable wedge liner, use of dog washers, repair or renewal of gasket, or fairing of knife edge or coaming.

Q. Why are the bulkhead stiffeners of freight vessels normally vertical while those of tank vessels are horizontal?

A. Because in both cases the span, or effective length, of stiffener is shorter than otherwise, and hence, with a given scantling, more efficiently stiffens the bulkhead.

Q. How are bulkheads in cargo holds tested for watertightness?

A. A strong stream of water from a hose is directed against the seams and butts while an inspector from the other side of bulkhead looks for leaks.

Q. How are galleys, living quarters, navigation spaces, general cargo, boiler rooms, and enclosed spaces containing machinery, where sources of vapor ignition are normally present, segregated from cargo spaces carrying grades A, B, C, or D liquids?

A. By cofferdams or tanks, either empty or carrying a liquid which has a flash point of 150° F. or above; by pump rooms; or by deck spaces either enclosed or open.

Q. Why does the plating of a bulkhead as well as its stiffeners decrease in size and strength from the lower to the upper part?

A. Because in the event of a hold being flooded, required strength to withstand the hydrostatic pressure involved must be greater at the lower part. (With a full hold, center of gravity of pressure is located at approximately one-third height of bulkhead.)

Q. Why must shaft alleys be of watertight construction?

A. To prevent entrance of water to machinery or cargo spaces in the event of damage to vessel in or about the stern tube.

Q. Where double bottom tanks are filled with fuel or water, how could you check suspected bottom damage that may have opened the outer bottom to the sea?

A. By noting the results obtained in tank soundings. If, after a few strokes of the pump, the oil or water remains in the sounding pipes at sea-level height, such damage is present.

Q. In the event of damage to a vessel's bow and flooding of the forepeak, what factors would influence the amount of water pressure on the collision bulkhead?

A. Vessel's speed and forward draft.

Q. When a passenger vessel is fitted with watertight doors of sliding type, against what list must the power of manually actuated closing mechanism be effective?

A. They must be capable of being closed against an adverse list of 15 degrees, whether mechanically or manually operated.

Q. Why must watertight doors which may be opened at sea below the subdivision load line of a passenger vessel be of the sliding type rather than of the hinged type?

A. So that such door may be closed regardless of a flow of water through the doorway. Such flow might render closing of a hinged door impossible.

Q. What provisions to maintain watertightness must be taken when electric cables penetrate a watertight bulkhead?
A. A watertight stuffing-tube must be fitted for this requirement.

Q. What provisions to maintain watertightness are necessary on passenger vessels bilge piping when the piping is located in a duct keel or within 1/5 of the beam from the side of the vessel?
A. A non-return valve shall be fitted to the end of the pipe in the compartment which it serves.

Q. In case of damage resulting in flooding: (a) What may be the effect of watertight longitudinal divisions? (b) What provisions may be made in longitudinal bulkheads to partly overcome this factor?
A. (a) Vessel may take a serious list due to flooding on one side of a midship longitudinal bulkhead.
   (b) Sluice valves at their lower extremity may be provided for allowing water to flow through the bulkhead to more or less equalize the flooding.

Q. What is a stepped bulkhead and what precautions are necessary where one is installed?
A. A bulkhead which is interrupted vertically by an intervening deck, at which it rises farther forward of, or abaft, its lower plane. Where such bulkhead occurs, additional subdivision must be provided in way of the step to maintain the same measure of safety as that secured by a plane bulkhead.

Q. State the usual minimum bulkhead requirements for a seagoing freight vessel of the United States.
A. A collision bulkhead at 5% of vessel's length abaft forward perpendicular; one at forward end and one at after end of boiler and engine space; and after peak bulkhead.

Q. How could you check inner or outer bottom plating for deflection due to grounding, severe buckling or compressive strains, pounding, etc. ?
A. Over a small area, by use of a batten laid along the plating over the apparently affected parts and measuring deflection by departure of batten from the fair lines. Over larger areas and where considerable "set" of the plating has occurred, by checking amount of departure from a wire tightly stretched over the area as required.

Q. What precaution is usual to prevent contamination of fresh water double bottom tanks by fuel oil and vice versa?

A. Separate pumps are used for fuel oil and fresh water.

Q. What is the name of the first bulkhead aft of the stem and what is its purpose?
A. Collision bulkhead. As its name implies, its purpose is to prevent entry of water into the forward hold in the event of severe damage to the stem or its immediate vicinity, as by a collision.

Q. What vessels are required by law to have effective double bottoms?
A. All passenger vessels 330 feet and upwards in length shall be fitted therewith in the entire extent from collision bulkhead to after peak bulkhead.

Q. For deep tank bulkheads and tank tops: (a) What tests are required? (b) What other test is sometimes employed to check tightness?
A. (a) Tank is filled and subjected to a pressure of usually an 8-foot head.
    (b) A strong stream from a hose is played upon the seams while an inspector observes the other side for leaks.

Q. Where are panting beams or stringers fitted and what is meant by panting?
A. Those structural parts which stiffen and strengthen a vessel's bows against panting, or the working in and out of the shell which otherwise would occur as ship runs into a heavy sea head-on or on either bow.

Q. What are the functions of partial bulkheads fitted in the cargo spaces of a vessel?
A. They are built as partitions or screens for separating different kinds of cargo, or cargo from fuel.

Q. What are the functions of pillars or stanchions in a vessel's hold?
A. To support and stiffen the deck beams against any tendency to sag, as from weight of cargo.

Q. In what part of the vessel may you expect to find deep floors, and floors increased in size or thickness to increase their strength?
A. In way of the engine and boiler spaces.

Q. When vessels have tanks for the carriage of bulk liquids, what measures are taken to minimize the dynamic effect of the liquid as the vessel rolls?
A. By the midship fore-and-aft bulkhead and swash plates in double-bottom tanks. In deep tanks, by the midship fore-and-aft swash bulkhead, which also is usually fitted in deep fore peak and after peak tanks.

Q. What are the functions of a hold-stringer?
A. It bridges or unites, and so stiffens and strengthens, the transverse framing, as well as reducing the span of the latter.

Q. Why are many modern vessels built without such stringers?
A. Because of longitudinal instead of transverse framing. Here the
longitudinals are bridged and kept to their work by web frames
spaced at much greater distances than the ordinary transverse
frames. The "web" or extra deep frames require no stiffening in
the form of a hold stringer.

Q. State why the stringer plate is normally a very important structural part of a vessel's deck which must resist the greatest stresses to the deck structure.
A. The stringer plate of any deck forms an important unifying and
stiffening unit in that it ties beams, frames, and shell plating, so
contributing much to longitudinal strength continuity. But its principal strength value is seen in the upper, or strength, deck, where,
secured to the upper edge of the sheer strake, it combines with
the latter in resisting stresses of compression and tension which
here reach a maximum as the hull is subjected to bending forces,
as in a seaway.

Q. Why are deep tank bulkheads normally built with the stiffeners
inside the tank?
A. To avoid possibility of damage to such stiffeners by heavy cargo.

Q. What are the three primary functions of bulkheads?
A. 1. To subdivide ship into convenient sections for cargo, living
accommodation, stores, etc. 2. To stiffen, consolidate, and
strengthen the hull against deformation by the various stresses
sustained. 3. To confine flooding to a single hold or compartment,
as resulting from collision damage; or to confine a fire, as in the
cargo, to a single location.

Q. What advantage is gained through the use of watertight longitudinal divisions in the double bottom tanks?
A. For reduction of the free liquid surface in a partly filled tank;
also for facilitating trimming ship by increasing or reducing weight
of liquid, as water or oil, on either side of the division.

Q. How may fire-alarm thermostats be tested?
A. By application of heat such as might be obtained from an electric
hand torch. By replacing the guard and globe with an open end
sheet-metal shield, such as a No. 3 fruit can, the heat therefrom
would usually serve to operate a thermostat without damage to
paint work or thermostat itself. Any thermostat showing material
delay in functioning when thus tested should be suspected of being
faulty and sent to Coast Guard Headquarters for further testing.

Q. How often should such fire-alarm thermostats be tested?

A. At least 25% of those installed should be tested annually.

Q. What are the primary functions of the deck or decks of a vessel?

A. To protect the holds and other enclosed spaces from the sea and weather; to support cargo and certain machinery; to provide floor space for the various units in passenger accommodation; to supply longitudinal strength to the hull, as well as binding and stiffening the structure in the required unification of beams, frames, shell, etc.

Q. What protection against damage by cargo or cargo gear should be provided to hatch coamings?

A. Lower edge of hatch coamings should be rounded off, so that no tearing effect of falls or engaging of the cargo fall hook is possible.

Q. State what is meant by propeller cavitation. What are the effects of cavitation?

A. Cavitation occurs where the "follow up" or "wake" current fails to replace the water driven astern by propeller action, thus creating a partial vacuum or cavity immediately abaft the screw. Its effects are seen in ship's failure to increase speed through the water corresponding to an increase of revolutions. Maximum slip thus produced, of course, results in wasteful use of engine power.

Q. Where vessels have little or no sheer, what compensation is made to provide extra buoyancy?

A. Vessel is allotted a greater freeboard, the measure of which depends upon her departure in this respect from the sheer of the standard hull of a vessel of her class.

Q. Define boss plate, intercostal floor, margin strake, gusset, and cant frame.

A. A boss plate is fitted around the boss of a propeller post and/or the curved frames in way of stern tube.

Intercostal floor, in the continuous side vertical plate keelson system, a section of a floor fitted between the vertical center keel and a longitudinal or vertical plate keelson, or between two of the last-named.

Margin strake is the sloping plate forming, along the outer ends of the floors, the wing boundary of a double-bottom tank.

Gusset is either a piece of plate roughly triangular in shape or a narrow continuous plate, fitted as a uniting and stiffening member where discontinuity occurs, as at the junction of frame-brackets and margin plate.

Cant frame is any frame lying obliquely to the fore-and-aft line, as those leading from the transom to form an overhanging counter.

Q. Why are bilge drain wells located as far outboard as practicable?
A. So that the best possible drainage may be obtained, especially in the event of vessel having a list.

Q. What is the purpose of peening the successive beads of weld deposited after each pass when making a weld in heavy plating?
A. To assist in relieving stress in the cooling metal due to contraction.

Q. What is the purpose of preheating heavy sections of steel prior to welding?
A. In order to hold down or control, as far as possible, the resulting extent of stress and distortion in the metal during the welding process.

Q. Describe in detail the construction of a portable magazine chest for the carriage of rockets, flares, Lyle gun black powder, and other ship's stores of an explosive nature.
A. Chest must be of 1/8" thick metal and lined with 3/4" wood sheathing. Its capacity must be from 6 to 40 cu. ft. All metal screws, etc., must be set in so as not to touch contents. Chest must also be fitted with 4 lashing rings and with 2 bottom runners at least 2" high.
   It should be smoothly surfaced and well painted; also marked with 3" letters: "PORTABLE MAGAZINE CHEST: INFLAMMABLE—KEEP LIGHTS AND FIRE AWAY.

Q. When vessels are provided with forced-air ventilation for quarters, what provisions are usually made to prevent air-ducts, diffusers, etc., from becoming filled with dust?
A. Filters usually are fitted in outboard bulkheads of fan-rooms for reducing the dust blown through such ducts, diffusers, etc.

Q. If a clinometer in the wheelhouse is used to determine the number of degrees a vessel is rolling, why might it show a greater than actual figure?
A. If, as with a "stiff" vessel, a comparatively sharp recovery takes place at termination of each roll, the clinometer indicator (as a pendulum, liquid in a curved tube, etc.) may be "thrown" farther to the low side and so register a deeper roll.

24. SEAMANSHIP

Q. Describe the various methods employed to absorb rudder shocks and prevent their being transmitted to the steering machinery.
A. By tension coil springs set in the steering chains before reaching the quadrant; by buffer or tension springs fitted between quadrant and tiller; by a friction brake set up to engage the quadrant arc; by a relieving tackle set to maintain a constant tension as an auxiliary to the usual steering chains or direct engine power.

Q. The sketch shows the method employed for fastening a grab rail
  to the shell plating of a lifeboat. Why are more rivets employed
  for attaching the small plate to the shell than for attaching the
  bracket to the small plate?

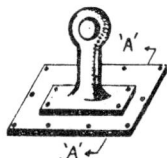

A. Because of the required spread of
  contact which provides appropriate distribution of stress to the shell.

Q. Discuss briefly the effect of list, speed,
  and rough weather on the draft of vessels operating in shallow water.

A. Considering the following: Increase of draft due to heel being in
  still water equal to ship's 1/2-breadth times sine of angle of heel.
  the "squat" produced by vessel's speed; and rough weather in
  which vessel sinks more due to the disturbed mean sea level; the
  combined effect in shallow water is a considerable increase of
  draft. Such increase will reach a maximum when vessel is proceeding at full speed and turning under a large rudder angle. It
  is not unusual in such conditions for a vessel of 50 feet beam
  with a 5° list to increase her draft at the bilge abaft amidships
  as much as 4 feet, as compared with the upright position and
  easy speed.

Q. A weight of 12 tons is being lifted with a three-fold purchase.
  Find the tension on the hauling part, considering loss of efficiency
  due to friction as 10 percent at each sheave.
A. Total friction = 12 × .10 × 6 = 7.2 tons;
  total weight = 12 + 7.2 = 19.2 tons;
  number of parts of rope at moving block = 6;
  tension on hauling part = 19.2 ÷ 6 = 3.2 tons.

Q. Describe briefly the possible effects of hugging the bank in a
  vessel proceeding in a narrow channel.
A. Vessel will tend to cant away from the bank. Thus, while proceeding close to the concave side of a bend, little or no helm is
  required to head parallel with bank; and, if on the convex side,
  usually a large amount of helm is necessary for that purpose.

Q. You are proceeding upstream in a loaded vessel, with an easy
  flood tide, and you have orders to dock starboard side to at a
  dock lying on your own port-hand. The face of the dock lies parallel with the stream. How would you maneuver your vessel to
  make the landing, assuming that no towboat is available?
A. Turn ship short around to head downstream off the dock. Ease
  her alongside with helm and engines to land against end of dock.
  Then heave ship around the corner, using engines as necessary,
  into berth.

Q. In construing the load line regulations, within what zone should a port be regarded as lying when load line regulations indicate that it lies on a boundary between two zones?
A. Within that zone where vessel's permissible load line presents the greater freeboard, i. e. , the lesser draft.

Q. In determining whether a ship is loaded below her load line: (a) What allowance for fuel consumption may be made? (b) Is an allowance for fuel consumption permitted for passenger vessels?
A. (a) Vessel's reduction in draft due to fuel consumed during passage from berth to sea.
    (b) Passenger vessels on foreign or on coastwise voyages (Great Lakes excepted) are not permitted such allowance.

Q. Taking a right-handed propeller steamer from wharves, buoys, docks, etc. , how would you get your ship away when lying head to tide, either side to the wharf, and heading the right direction?
A. Haul taut an after spring leading ahead and let go all other after lines. Take in all forward lines but a single breast. Come easy astern on engines. Slack away forward as ship cants away from berth; stop engines, take in both spring and breast, and proceed, using helm and engines as required.

Q. What is meant by the pivoting point of a vessel?
A. The point about which a vessel's hull appears to pivot while turning by action of the rudder and making headway.

Q. Where will the pivoting point usually be found in a vessel?
A. Depending upon speed and hull form, from one-sixth to one-fourth vessel's length from her stem.

Q. Knowing the location of a vessel's pivoting point, state why experienced ship handlers will observe the stern while turning in constricted waters.
A. Because vessel's after end sweeps through a much greater area than her forward end. Consequently, the degree or rate of vessel's swing is more readily noted.

Q. Explain the effect of bank cushion and bank suction on a vessel steaming in a narrow channel. State how a steamer should be handled when proceeding through a narrow channel in order to avoid these effects.
A. Bank cushion is the wedging effect of displaced water between vessel's bow and the nearer bank. Particularly when ship's draft closely approaches the depth of water and her speed is not substantially reduced, she will rapidly sheer away toward the opposite bank, unless timely preventive action is taken.
    Bank suction is the indraft of vessel's stern toward the nearer bank caused by return flow of displaced water predominating on the off quarter. Aided by the rotary action of a right-handed screw,

this <u>suction</u> becomes a serious factor in forcing vessel to sheer toward the farther bank when nearer bank is on her starboard hand.

With the foregoing in mind, especially in shallow depths vessel should proceed at slow speed, keeping as far as possible in mid-channel. When meeting another vessel, speed should be reduced to bare steerage way. Anchors should be always ready to let go at a moment's notice, in case of vessel taking a sheer. Particular care is required at a <u>bend</u> in such channel, the convex side, especially in heading into a current, having often proven a trap for the unwary.

Q. Where machinery such as gears or piston cranks is exposed, what safety measures are required by the regulations?

A. Suitable guards, covers, rails, etc., shall be placed for protection of persons approaching all such dangers or dangerous areas.

Q. If your vessel's engine became disabled in heavy weather, what steps might you take to avoid rolling in the trough of the sea?

A. If in soundings, unshackle a bower anchor and pay out a good length of cable to drag on the bottom. This will bring sea on the bow.

If in deep water, unship a cargo boom, weight it with chains or wire so that the whole will be just awash when in use. Rig a good bridle and make a hawser fast to it, so that boom will "drag" sideways. If vessel is substantially by the stern in trim, rig such "sea anchor" from the weather quarter; if about even keel, from the forecastle.

Q. How would you turn a right-hand screw vessel alongside a dock under her own power? Vessel is lying starboard side to dock and is to be turned port side to dock, no wind or tide.

A. Run a hauling line along the dock from starboard bow to about abreast of the quarter. Take in all other lines forward and aft, except a short back spring. Come ahead on the spring with dead slow engines and hard right rudder to cant ship's stern out from dock. When canted well out heave on the hauling line, go easy astern on engines, and take in the back spring. As ship's head is hove around, maneuver with the engines dead slow ahead and hard right rudder, or engines slow astern, until stern is within heaving-ling distance of dock. Then send the necessary lines ashore and make ship fast.

Q. Why is a vessel fitted with twin screws turning outboard easier to maneuver than a vessel with twin screws turning inboard?

A. Because the side thrust effect may be used to full advantage with out-turning screws, while that of in-turning screws hinders rather than assists in maneuvering.

Q. In maneuvering ahead at low speed is the rudder of a single
screw vessel or a single rudder on a vessel fitted with twin screws
more effective for turning the vessel? Why?

A. Rudder of a single screw vessel is more effective. This is because, with a given rudder angle, in addition to rudder effect due
to ship's headway, the screw race also gives the steering effect
of headway. No such advantage is obtained by rudder in the twin-
screw vessel.

Q. With a right-hand single screw ship, is it more advantageous
to dock port or starboard side to, no tide? Why?

A. Port side to, if ship is canted toward dock, as usually is the case;
because, in taking way off by engines, thrust of backing propeller
will straighten vessel parallel to her berth.

Q. What entries are required in the official logbook with respect
to the load line and draft?

A. Vessel's drafts forward and aft when leaving port; her freeboard,
as measured on both sides at the load line markings; and, when
any allowance for draft is made for density of water at the berth,
this density must be noted also.

Q. A wire rope rove through 2 single blocks with 2 parts at
the moving block is used for a lifeboat fall. The weight of the
boat and its equipment is 5 tons, and the boat has a capacity of
100 persons. Compute the required breaking strength for the wire
rope falls using the following factors. Show all work.
   A safety factor of 6 is required for boat falls by regulations.
   The weight of each person is considered 165 lbs. by regulations.
   Friction loss of 10 percent at each of the 2 sheaves.

A. Weight of persons = $(100 \times 165) \div 2240 = 7.37$ tons.
Total weight = $5 + 7.37 = 12.37$ tons.(Supported by 2 davits)
Friction loss = $.10 \times 2 = .20$ of total weight = $12.37 \times .20 = 2.47$ tons.
Total weight allowing for friction = $12.37 + 2.47 = 14.84$ tons.
Total weight allowing for safety factor $6 = 14.84 \times 6 = 89.04$ tons.
Breaking strength of rope required = $89.04 \div 4 = 22.26$ long tons,
or $22.26 \times 1.12 = 24.93$ short tons.

Q. State the formula used to obtain the tons per inch immersion
(T.P.I.) of a vessel in sea water.

A. $$\text{T.P.I.} = \frac{\text{area of waterplane}}{35 \times 12}$$

Q. Where is the information concerning the tons per inch immersion of a vessel usually found?

A. On vessel's deadweight scale.

Q. What consideration may make the tons per inch immersion value
in error unless a correction is applied?

A. That of vessel's draft; such value is least at light draft and attains a maximum at load draft.

Q. A vessel docking in an onshore wind decides to use her bower anchor to check the bow momentum towards the dock. (a) Noting the sketch, would you regard the inshore or offshore anchor as most effective? (b) What disadvantages might have to be considered in using an inshore anchor?

A. (a) Inshore anchor.

(b) Considerable area of paint on ship's bottom would suffer; localized pressure stress by cable on shell plating might rupture one or more seams or butts; it might be found impossible to heave anchor aboard after ship is berthed; and it is possible that, in weighing anchor upon departure, tidal or weather conditions may present a hazardous situation in getting away from dock.

Q. What duty does the regulations place on the master of vessels equipped with emergency lighting systems and emergency generators?

A. He must see that they are operated and inspected at least once in each week; motor-driven emergency generators shall be operated under load for at least 2 hours at least once in each month; storage batteries shall be tested at least once in each 6-month period that vessel is navigated; date of tests, with condition and performance of the systems shall be noted in the official log.

Q. What duty does the regulations place upon a master with respect to electric power operated lifeboat winches and their control apparatus?

A. That all winch control apparatus shall be examined at least once in each 3 months. This shall include removal of drain plugs and/or opening of drain valves in such appliances concerned to assure that enclosures are free of water. Date of examinations and condition of such equipment shall be noted in ship's official log.

Q. If your ship goes aground in an onshore gale, what should be the first measure to save the vessel, if the crew, etc., are in no immediate danger?

A. Try to hold ship from drifting farther inshore by filling all available ballast tanks or, if necessary, by flooding the lower holds.

Q. State what is meant by the term fleet angle in placing a lead block with relation to the axis of a drum or niggerhead for heaving on wire rope, or illustrate the meaning of the term by a rough sketch.

A. Departure from the perpendicular which a cargo fall or a hawser makes with the axis of the winch drum or the niggerhead, as such rope is wound around the latter in heaving. Thus, when the rope leads at right angles to the drum axis, <u>fleet angle</u> is <u>zero</u>; upon being wound on the drum, as in hoisting, the fall's fleet angle attains <u>maximum</u> value when the outermost turn is reached.

Q. A vessel is docked as shown, with her stern projecting from the pier into the current. What lines in addition to those shown would you consider necessary? (Illustrate, if you wish, by rough sketch).

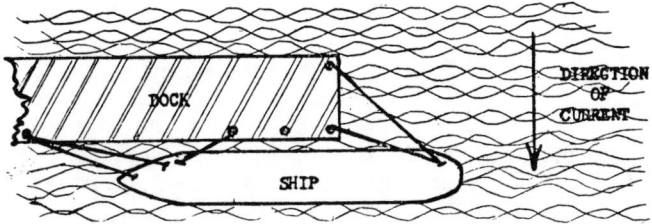

A. A breast line to off corner of dock leading from the after deck. Double up the back spring (line leading aft from fore deck).

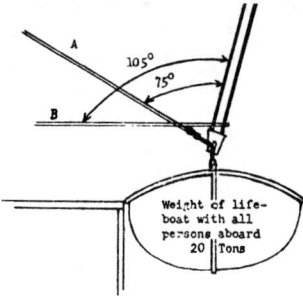

Q. Referring to the sketch: (a) Determine the stress on the tricing line <u>A</u> when a lifeboat is lowered to the embarkation deck. (b) Determine the stress on the frapping line <u>B</u> when the tricing line pelican hook is released.

A.

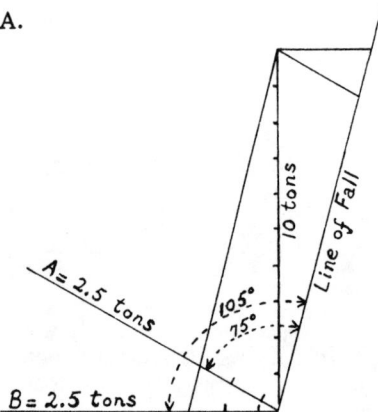

Solution by parallelogram of forces: Weight on each davit = 20 ÷ 2 = 10 tons

(a) Total stress on each tricing line is 2.5 tons; on each part, 1.25 tons.

(b) Total stress on each frapping line is 2.5 tons; on each part, 1.25 tons.

Q. How do you place a block for the most effective lead to a drum
or niggerhead when using wire rope?
A. In such position that fall or hawser will lead at right angles to
the axis, and at mid-length of, drum or niggerhead; also at such
distance from the winch that the rope will not "ride" over an adjacent turn at any time, upon being wound in during hoisting or
heaving.

Q. What precautions are necessary to insure that lifeboat winches and
hand propelling gear in lifeboats operate properly in cold weather?
A. The working parts and bearings should be kept well lubricated
with a nonviscous or light, penetrating oil. Lifeboat winches shall
be provided with suitable fabric covers for protection of exposed
mechanism, where ice conditions are likely to be encountered.

Q. Taking a right-handed propeller steamer from wharves, buoys,
docks, etc., how would you get your ship away under the following conditions: lying port side to, heading in the right direction,
no tide?
A. Take in all lines excepting a spring leading aft from fore deck.
Go dead slow ahead on engine with left rudder. When stern is
canted far enough away from dock, come slow astern with rudder
amidships, and take in spring. As ship cants to parallel with dock,
go ahead on engine and proceed.

Q. How would you dock a ship in a slip, coming in on the flood
with the tide running across the slip entrance?
A. I would turn ship so as to head into the current and land her
alongside the lee pier head, with stem as close as possible to
other pier. Then, depending upon which side of slip vessel is to
berth, run lines accordingly while turning into slip by engine power
and rudder as required. When approximately in berth, stop engines and haul ship by lines as necessary.

Q. In docking a vessel against a pier with a solid pier facing (that
is, one not built on pilings), what is the advantage in going astern
on the engine prior to landing the vessel broadside to?
A. To wash away any floating debris between ship and pier; also,
to provide a cushioning effect by the moving water between ship
and pier, on impact of hull with the solid pier wall.

28. LIFESAVING APPARATUS AND FIRE-FIGHTING EQUIPMENT
Q. What factor of safety is required for blocks, falls, fairleads,
padeyes, shackles, links, fastenings, etc., used in connection
with lifeboat gear?
A. A safety factor of 6 times the maximum working load.

Q. A lifeboat davit block with a maximum working load of 3000 lbs.
requires renewal. What breaking load would you specify for the
new block?

A. The breaking load should be 3,000 × 6 = 18,000 lbs.

Q. On vessels equipped with winches for lowering lifeboats, what speed of lowering the loaded boat should be regarded as satisfactory when the winch is fitted with a governor brake?
A. About 100 feet per minute.

Q. A vessel has a beam of 70 feet. The distance from the davit head to the light load line is 50 feet. The boat falls have 6 parts at the moving block; 25 feet are required to lead to the cruciform bitt and for turns on the bitt. What length of fall is required?
A. Length of fall must be sufficient to lower boat to water with ship listing 15°; so that

$$\text{Length} = (70 \div 2)\,(\tan 15° \times 6) + (50 \times 6) + 25$$
$$= (35 \times .268 \times 6) \quad + \quad 300 \quad + 25$$
$$= \quad 56.3 + \quad 300 + \quad 25 = 381.3 \text{ feet,}$$
$$\text{or 64 fathoms required.}$$

Q. What equipment is required on motor lifeboats using gasoline for fuel to prevent fires from carburetor backfire, and to prevent the accumulation of gasoline in the bilges of the boat?
A. Carburetor shall be fitted with an efficient backfire flame-arrester of an approved type; also, with a drip-collector to prevent fuel leakage from reaching bilges, so arranged as to permit ready removal of such leakage. Drip-collector shall be covered with a flame screen.

Q. What precautions must be taken on vessels fitted with lifeboat winches where possible icing conditions may occur?
A. Suitable fabric covers shall be provided for all lifeboat winches, so fitted over exposed mechanism that any ice formation may be readily broken adrift when use of winch is required.

Q. You suspect a fire watchman has taken all his keys to the mess-room and is "punching his clock" while sitting there. How would you determine if he was guilty of this practice?
A. Check for removal of keys from station boxes; also, arrange for an officer to pay a surprise visit to messroom after failing to see watchman cover his route.

Q. On passenger vessels fitted with magnetic controls on doors, is it permissible to install holdback hooks or other devices to keep the door permanently open?
A. Such devices will not be permitted.

Q. On firescreen doors and other doors which are not normally locked on passenger vessels, what is the maximum list that the door is required to close against? If you were obliged to adjust the spring tension on such a door, what other considerations should be borne in mind?

A. A 3-1/2-degree list. Considering the likelihood of vessel acquir-
   ing a greater list than that, as in a strong beam wind of considerable duration, the spring tension should be adjusted to make door
   close against at least a 5-degree list.

Q. How would you embark passengers in lifeboats suspended from
   gravity davits? Describe precautions in the use of tricing lines in
   particular.
A. Have tricing lines secured by slip hook to shackles at lower
   blocks of falls. As boat is lowered, tricing lines serve to draw
   her against ship's structure until frapping lines are passed around
   falls. When these are secured in place, see that men are seated
   in boat, and then let go tricing line slip hooks. Embark passengers with boat thus held in position by frapping lines. Then, depending upon vessel's motion, frapping lines may be slacked off,
   or boat may be lowered with them kept taut.

29. SHIP SANITATION

Q. What is the average maximum consumption of fresh wate per
   day per person required in the interest of adequate personnal hy-
   giene?
A. 30 gallons.

Q. What chemical is used to treat water in order to insure its
   safety for drinking?
A. Hypochlorite of lime (chlorinated lime).

Q. How should taps be marked when wash water of doubtful purity
   is used?
A. UNFIT FOR DRINKING.

Q. Describe the responsibility of the master with respect to nar-
   cotic drugs placed on a vessel for medicinal purposes?
A. He is charged with safeguarding the requisition, purchase, receipt, storage, issue, use, and record-keeping of such narcotics.

Q. What particular care should be exerted when procuring the following for shipboard consumption: (a) Milk; (b) Shellfish?
A. (a) Should be the pasteurized product and kept under refrigeration until required for use.
      (b) See that it is fresh and has been kept in cold storage up to
   time of delivery to ship.

Q. For what period is a deratization certificate or deratization exemption certificate issued?
A. 6 months.

Q. What conditions must exist for a deratization exemption certificate to be issued?
A. When the medical officer concerned is satisfied that vessel is
   free of rodents or their number is negligible.

Q. What is the duty of the master of a vessel with respect to sanitation?
A. To see that his vessel and, in particular, the passenger and crew quarters are in a clean and sanitary condition.

Q. What penalties is the master of a vessel liable to for failure to maintain his vessel in a sanitary condition?
A. A penalty of not more than 500 dollars.

Q. What is the purpose of a quarantine inspection?
A. To ascertain whether or not "the vessel, cargo, and passengers are each and all free from infectious disease, or danger of conveying the same."

Q. What persons are allowed aboard a vessel subject to quarantine inspection?
A. Except with permission of the quarantine officer, no person other than the pilot.

Q. What sanitary measures must be taken to bring cats, dogs, or monkeys into the United States on a ship?
A. Owner of such submits a sworn statement that animal was given a physical examination within 10 days prior to departure for the United States and found free of disease; or, animal is examined by a quarantine officer upon arrival in a United States port. If found not free of disease, animal is either destroyed or deported, according to the judgment of examining officer.

Q. Describe briefly the facilities available for obtaining medical and quarantine advice by radio.
A. Medical advice may be obtained from officers of U.S. Public Health Service or from physicians aboard nearby ships. U.S. Coast Guard radio stations are available for medical service to ships, each station having prearranged direct communication to a U.S Public Health Service Hospital or other medical relief station.
    Quarantine advice may be obtained from Medical Officer in Charge, Quarantine Station, at any principal U.S. seaport.

Q. What precautions must be observed in obtaining drinking water in port?
A. Drinking water should be obtained from a source of known purity If any doubt exists on this point, the supply should be chlorinated before being used. Also all necessary precautions as to cleanliness of hose and its connections must be observed.

Q. What provisions are required by regulation on new vessels for the crew to wash and dry their clothing?
A. Sufficient facilities, depending upon number of crew, shall be provided where crew may wash and also dry their own clothes. There shall be at least one tub or sink fitted with means of a supply of hot and cold running water.

Q. What recreational facilities for the crew are required on late construction vessels by regulation?
A. Adequate open deck space shall be available to the crew when off duty. Recreation accommodation shall be provided, and, where messrooms are used for such purpose, they shall be suitably planned.

Q. Why is screening desirable on the vents for potable water tanks?
A. So that foreign matter may be excluded from the tanks.

Q. What chemical is recommended for disinfection after contagious disease has been present in quarters?
A. Compound cresol—usually a 3% solution.

Q. What measures should be taken after washing dishes to insure that they are in a sanitary condition?
A. Dishes should be totally immersed in clean, scalding water (of at least 170° F.) for two minutes, or in boiling water (212° F.) for one-half minute. They then should be racked on edge to dry without use of dish towels.

Q. If a drinking fountain is not available, what facilities should be provided to furnish drinking water?
A. Individual disposable cups should be provided at the faucet in use.

Q. What is a certificate of provisional pratique?
A. A certificate issued by the medical officer in charge, signifying that vessel has passed quarantine and may enter port, but that certain measures, as specified in the certificate, must be taken in connection with discharge of cargo, landing of passengers, or the vessel's sanitary condition.

Q. What is radio pratique?
A. Permission by radio, granted to a vessel by the medical officer in charge at quarantine, to enter port without quarantine formalities. It is given on the basis of information regarding the vessel, her cargo, and persons aboard received prior to arrival.

Q. What precautions would you take in a port infected or suspected of being infected with plague?
A. Take particular care against access of rats to the ship, as via mooring lines or gangways, and adopt every practicable measure to exterminate all rats that may be on board. If possible, have every member of crew immunized against the disease. Maintain good sanitary conditions by keeping a clean ship, especially in removal of food scraps, grain, etc., which might provide sustenance for rats. If practicable, before leaving the port fumigate ship fore-and-aft.

30. RULES AND REGULATIONS FOR INSPECTION
OF MERCHANT VESSELS

Q. List the duties that must be shown in the station bill.

A. The following in general shall be included, with such other duties
as may be necessary in a particular vessel for proper handling of
a particular emergency:

1. Closing of airports, watertight doors, fire doors, scuppers,
sanitary and other discharges leading through vessel's hull below
margin line; stopping of fans and ventilating systems; and operation
of all safety equipment.

2. Preparing and launching lifeboats, life rafts, and buoyancy
apparatus.

3. Extinction of fire.

4. Muster of passengers, which shall in general be assigned to
the steward's department, and shall include the following:

(a) Warning the passengers. (b) Seeing that they are dressed
and have put on their life jackets in a proper manner. (c) Assembling passengers and directing them to their appointed stations.
(d) Keeping order in passageways and stairways, and generally
controlling movement of passengers. (e) Seeing that a supply of
blankets is taken to the boats. (f) Custody of the portable radio
apparatus which will be placed in lifeboats designated by master
or officer in charge.

Q. Describe in detail the manner of making an entry in the official
logbook for an offense by a crew member. State the steps which
must be taken to insure that the offender has been informed of
the charge against him, and the possible result of failure to follow the procedure detailed by law.

A. An entry describing the offense shall be made on the day in
which offense was committed, and it shall be signed by the master and the mate or other member of the crew; offender shall be
furnished with a copy of such entry before vessel arrives in next
port, or if in port at time of offense, before departure therefrom;
and such copy having been read over distinctly and audibly to
offender, who may thereupon make such reply as he thinks fit, a
statement in the log shall indicate that a copy of said entry has
been furnished, or it has been read over, together with offender's
reply, if any, and shall be signed in the same manner.

Failure to follow the above procedure may be considered by
the court hearing the case as in default of proof and, at its discretion, refuse to receive evidence of the offense.

Q. Under what conditions may a shipping commissioner act as an
arbitrator of a dispute between master and seaman and what is
the effect of his decision?

A. He shall hear and decide any question whatsoever between master
and seaman, which both parties agree in writing to submit to him,
and every award so made by him shall be binding on both parties

and, in any legal proceedings that may be taken in the matter before any court of justice, shall be deemed conclusive as to rights
of both parties.

Q. In docking, a seaman is caught in the bight of a hawser and his
leg is broken. What reports must be made by the owner, agent,
or master of the vessel to the Coast Guard?
A. Within 5 days after the accident, or as soon thereafter as possible, a report shall be sent by letter to the Officer in Charge,
Marine Inspection, at, or nearest, the port where accident occurred,
stating name and official number of vessel, her port of registry,
and nature and occasion of the accident; also shall be furnished,
upon request of Coast Guard, such other information as may be
called for.

Q. After his ship has been involved in a casualty, under what circumstances is the master permitted to omit reporting in person
to the Officer in Charge, Marine Inspection, at the port in which
the casualty occurred or nearest the port of first arrival?
A. When, because of distance, it may be inconvenient to report in
person.

Q. What quantity of gasoline may be carried when necessary for an
emergency generator aboard a passenger vessel and how must it
be carried?
A. Not more than 40 gallons, carried in a cylindrical tank or tanks
of approved strength and type.

Q. What type emergency generator engines are required for all new
construction and replacements?
A. Internal combustion engines of the Diesel type.

Q. On passenger vessels, is it permissible to use the emergency
loud-speaker system for the distribution of music?
A. No; the emergency loud-speaker system shall not be used for
entertainment purposes.

Q. How often must the emergency loud-speaker system be tested and
who must make the test?
A. At least once every week by an officer of the vessel.

Q. Describe the equipment required by the regulations to prevent
ship's personnel from being locked in the refrigeration compartment.
A. Such refrigerated space shall be fitted with an alarm system
operated within the space at the exit therefrom. The alarm may
be either a jingle bell sounded by a pull cord or a vibrating bell
or other audible device operated by an electrical push button; and
the audible signal shall be located where a person is regularly
employed. Where more than one lockable compartment have an

audible signal, an annunciator shall be provided to indicate the
compartment from which signal emanates.

Q. What is the minimum flash point of paints and enamels permitted
to be used aboard U.S. Merchant Vessels by regulations?
A. The minimum flash point is 80° F. for mixed paints, varnish,
or enamel as ship's stores. Also, compounds or nitrocellulose
known as "lacquer" are subject to same limiting flash point.

31. LAWS GOVERNING MARINE INSPECTION

Q. Prior to paying off or discharging a seaman, what does the law
require that the master furnish a seaman in order that he may
examine his accounts?
A. Master must furnish seaman with an account of wages at least
48 hours before paying him off; or, if discharged before a Shipping Commissioner, then to such Commissioner, a full and true
account of wages and deductions.

Q. What vessels are required to be provided with a slop chest?
A. Every vessel belonging to a citizen of the United States which
is bound from a port in the United States to any foreign port; or
being of 75 tons' burden or more and bound from a port on the
Atlantic to a port on the Pacific, or vice versa. Also every sailing vessel bound across the Atlantic or the Pacific Ocean, or
around Cape Horn, or Cape of Good Hope, or engaged in whaling,
sealing, or other fisheries. But slop chest is not required by vessels plying between the United States and Canada, the Bermudas,
Bahamas, the West Indies, Mexico, and Central America.

Q. Shortly after signing articles on a seagoing merchant vessel,
the boatswain requests that you discharge a seaman because he
has heard a rumor the man has a reputation for failing to work
diligently. What obligation might be placed upon the vessel if the
boatswain's request was carried out?
A. Vessel would be obligated to pay the man one month's wages.

Q. What are the stores which the slop chest is required by law to
provide?
A. A complement of clothing for the intended voyage for each seaman, including boots, caps, underclothing, outer clothing, oil-
skins, and everything necessary for a seaman's wear; also, a full
supply of tobacco and blankets.

Q. What is the duty of the master of a vessel in the event of the
death of a seaman during the voyage?
A. He shall take charge of all money, clothing, and effects left on
board by such deceased seaman and, if he thinks fit, cause all or
any of such effects to be sold by auction, and shall sign an entry
in the official log, duly attested by the mate and one of the crew,

indicating the following:
  1. Amount of money left by deceased.
  2. If sold, a description of each article and sum received for each.
  3. Statement of wages due deceased and total amount of deductions therefrom, if any.

Q. How often are the seamen on a American vessel entitled to receive an advance on their wages and what is the penalty for failing to comply with the provisions of this law?
A. They are entitled to half of balance of wages due in each port at which cargo is loaded or delivered, provided this occurs no more than once in five days, or no more than once in same harbor on same entry. Penalty is release of seaman from his contract and so his title to full payment of wages earned.

Q. How must sea stores, ship's stores, and bunker fuel be shown on a vessel's arriving in a U.S. port from a foreign port or place?
A. These must be separately specified in ship's manifest.

Q. In order to land any item of ship's stores from a vessel arriving from a foreign port or place, what steps must be taken?
A. Application by the master, owner, or agent must be made to the Collector of Customs for permission to land such item, specifying the intended purpose of such request. Upon Collector's approval of such landing, he will determine whether goods will be held in bond or the amount of duty payable, if any.

Q. When the master of a registered vessel is changed, what action of the new master or of the owner is required by law?
A. He shall report the change to Collector of Customs of the district where same has happened, and shall produce to him the vessel's certificate of registry. Under oath he shall show such new master to be a citizen of the United States and the manner in which he attained such status.

Q. What notice and reports are required and to whom are they made in the event that your vessel is involved in a marine casualty which results in one of the following: (a) Material damage to property in excess of $1500; (b) Material damage affecting the seaworthiness or efficiency of a vessel; (c) Stranding or grounding; (d) Loss of life; (e) Injury causing any person to remain incapacitated for a period in excess of 72 hours?
A. The managing owner, agent, or master, within 5 days after the casualty, or as soon thereafter as possible, shall send by letter to the Officer in Charge, Marine Inspection, at or nearest the port casualty occurred a report thereof stating vessel's name and official number, her port of registry, place where casualty occurred, nature and probable occasion of casualty, number and

names of those lost, and estimated amount of loss or damage to
vessel or cargo; also, he shall furnish, as required by Coast
Guard, such other pertinent information as may be called for.

Q. What is the duty imposed by law upon the master when repairs
are made in foreign port?
A. Upon first arrival in the United States he shall report, upon entering at Customs, the particulars as to materials and costs of
such repairs, and owner or master shall pay such duties as are
required therefor by Collector of customs.

Q. What responsibility does the vessel, and, therefore, the master
have toward the clothing and personal effects of crew members?
A. That of taking into custody all money, clothing, and effects of
deceased seamen and rendering account therefor to Coast Guard
at termination of voyage in the United States. Such accounting shall
be shown by entry in ship's official log, duly attested by the mate
and one of the crew, as follows: 1. Statement of money left by the
deceased. 2. Description of any effects sold and money received
for such. 3. Statement of wages due, with total amount of deductions therefrom.

Q. When a preferred mortgage is outstanding against a ship, what
means must be taken to inform people who might have business
with the vessel of the existence of the mortgages?
A. Upon the recording of a preferred mortgage by Collector of
Customs, mortgagor is directed to retain a certified copy of such
mortgage on board vessel concerned. Such copy and any pertinent
documents must be exhibited by vessel's master to any person
having business with the vessel which may give rise to a lien
upon, or to a sale, conveyance, or mortgage of, the vessel. Upon
request of any such person, master shall show him the vessel's
documents and the copy of any preferred mortgage placed on board.

Q. When a master of a vessel has been obliged to use his own
funds in order to secure the conviction and punishment of an offend-
ing seaman, can a court reimburse him at the offender's expense
when holding proceedings relating to the wages?
A. Yes; in an amount not exceeding 15 dollars out of the man's
wages.

Q. In order to prove a seaman a deserter in the eyes of the law,
what must be shown?
A. That seaman left without intending to return on board; that he
did not leave because of cruel treatment or threats; that he did
not leave because vessel makes a deviation or change of voyage
not provided for in the articles of agreement.

Q. What disposition must be made of the clothes, effects, and
wages of a deserting seaman?

A. These being forfeited for desertion shall be applied in payment of expenses occasioned to the vessel by such desertion, balance, if any, to be paid by master or owner to Shipping Commissioner at the port voyage in question terminates.

Q. To whom may a seaman make a lawful allotment?
A. To his grandparents, parents, wife, sister, or children; to a duly authorized agency for purchase of U.S. savings bonds for himself; or to a savings account at a bank, a U.S. postal savings depository, or other savings institution in which accounts are insured by the U.S. government.

Q. What entry is required in the official log in the event of illness or injury aboard?
A. Date of occurrence, nature of illness or description and cause of injury, and details of medical treatment and care administered.

Q. What entry is required in the official logbook in the event a crew member is paid off by mutual consent in a foreign port?
A. Entry shall indicate the place, time, manner, and cause thereof; also a statement of wages earned, deductions therefrom, and balance paid seaman.

Q. What is the penalty for omitting required entries in the official logbook?
A. For each offense, a penalty of not more than $25 for each entry.

Q. A case of assault occurs aboard a merchant vessel of the United States on the high seas. The identity of the offender and facts and evidence concerning the offense became known to the master. What steps must the master take to bring the offender to justice?
A. Master shall enter place, time, and nature of assault, together with names of witnesses, in the official log, and the entry shall be signed by the mate or one of the crew. Before arriving at next port, or if in port then before departure, offender shall be given a copy of said entry and have same read over to him distinctly and audibly. A statement that this has been done, together with the offender's reply, if any, also shall be entered in log in same manner.
  Upon arrival in a United States port, master will institute the necessary steps for prosecution in Federal Court, producing ship's official log in initial proceedings.

32. SHIP'S BUSINESS
Q. What is particular average?
A. The financial loss caused by damage or partial loss to ship, cargo, or freight money, and which is borne by owners of the property lost or damaged, or their insurers.

Q. What is meant by the term dispatch money?

A. A sum paid by the shipowner to charterer for completing loading or discharging a cargo in less time than that stipulated in
charter party as lay days.

Q. State whether a shipowner is liable to a passenger injured in
each of the following ways: (a) By an assault committed in the
cabin class accommodations by a third-class steward. (b) By a
large wave shipped on deck during heavy weather, the officers
having failed to warn the passenger of the danger of appearing
on deck at such a time. (c) By a collision due to the joint fault
of the vessel on which he is traveling and the other vessel.

A. Shipowner is liable in all 3 cases. The law provides for
absolute protection of a passenger against negligent or malicious
acts of members of the crew.

Q. Suppose a master abandons a vessel with crew and afterwards
some of the crew return and rescue the vessel. Can the crew
claim salvage?

A. Where the master's intent and act of abandonment is established,
the voluntary act of certain members of the crew in reboarding
and rescuing vessel gives such crew members the status of sal-
vors. Salvage, therefore, may be claimed.

Q. Suppose a ship finds another ship 1,000 miles at sea and tows
her within a mile from shore and then, by reason of an accident,
loses her. Is the salving ship entitled to salvage?

A. Since a major element in a valid salvage claim is that services
rendered must be successful wholly or in part, in this case the
towing ship is not entitled to salvage.

Q. If you are master of a vessel belonging to the same company as
another vessel and render aid in salvaging her, does the fact that
the owner is common to both vessels bar you or members of your
crew from a salvage claim?

A. No. The Salvage Act of 1912 states that the right to a salvage
award shall not be affected by common ownership of vessels rendering and receiving salvage services.

Q. State what action taken by a seaman, in case of wreck or loss
of the vessel on which he was employed, would bar his claim to
wages earned.

A. If he fails to do his utmost in the work of attempting to save
the vessel.

Q. When does a person appointed to command a vessel become
legally responsible as master?

A. When the Collector of Customs endorses on the vessel's certificate of registry a memorandum of appointment of master, or
change of masters, specifying such master's name, with date of
such endorsement.

Q. Suppose you have been appointed as master of an oceangoing vessel, what are the important details that must receive your immediate attention regarding your vessel, your equipment, business matters and the crew? What are your further duties?

A. As responsible both to the shipowner and the navigation laws of the United States, my care, management, and navigation of vessel will include such details as follows, in order of required attention:

1. That vessel is in seaworthy, shipshape, and sanitary condition fore and aft, and in a safe berth.

2. That immediate business of the ship, as loading or discharging, is properly supervised, and the officers have the situation well in hand.

3. That all lifesaving and fire-fighting equipment is in good order and condition, and ready for immediate use.

4. That all necessary charts, sailing directions, notices to mariners, and other navigational publications are on board, and condition of all navigational instruments is satisfactory.

5. That vessel's certificate of inspection, radio certificate, fumigation certificate, load-line certificate, and such important papers are currently valid; also that station bills, officers' licenses, and all notices required to be posted are in place.

6. If new crew has been engaged, check stores and crew list, and see that vessel is properly supplied and manned for the voyage.

7. Check all vouchers and accounts with former master, and, if in a foreign port, make entry in official log to that effect, with signatures of both men.

8. Consult chief engineer regarding fuel requirements, engine speed, safety arrangements in engine department, etc.

9. Note all information at hand regarding cargo, mails, insurance, charter, next dry-docking, any change in route next voyage, etc.

10. Become familiar with vessel's plans and stability information.

Further duties include care and supervision of official logbook procedure; presentation of monthly reports to Coast Guard, as fire and boat drills; number of passengers carried; general condition of vessel and equipment. As responsible for virtually all that occurs under his charge, master's duties toward his crew, his vessel's owner, the cargo and passengers, as well as to U.S. navigation laws, may be considered as practically unlimited.

Q. Before sailing for a foreign port, what document must you get?
A. The clearance or official permission to depart on voyage.

Q. If the crew refuse to go to sea through the alleged unseaworthiness of the ship, what should be done?
A. Master must submit the complaint to a local judge or a justice of the peace, if in a domestic port, or to the U.S. consul if in a foreign port, taking with him two or more of those making complaint. Such judge, justice, or consul will then direct 3 of the most skillful and experienced persons in maritime affairs that

may be procured, one of whom shall be a physician if complaint
includes or concerns ship's provisions, to board vessel and examine the alleged defects or deficiencies indicated in crew's complaint of unseaworthiness.

Such surveyors shall then make reports to the judge, justice, or
consul, in writing, of their findings and recommendations, if any,
to remedy the alleged defects or deficiencies. Master and crew
shall conform to conclusions reached by such board of inquiry. If
complaint is justified, master pays costs of survey; if otherwise,
costs and any reasonable detention charges are deducted from wages of the men making complaint.

Q. Suppose you had incurred losses during the voyage which are
proper subject for a general average: (a) What would you do on
your arrival at your port of destination? (b) Have you any lien
on the cargo for the shipper's share of the loss?
A. (a) Note a protest. Have ship's agent notify insurance interests,
arrange for a survey of cargo to determine losses suffered, and
ob'ain services of an average adjuster. Keep shipowner informed
and be guided by his advice in the circumstances.
(b) Yes. Consignees are required to sign an average bond before cargo is delivered, and master may require a deposit in
advance and in addition to the average bond.

Q. Suppose a merchant had stipulated to supply a full cargo, but
finds he cannot, what would you do?
A. Give merchant notice in writing of your legal claim for payment
of "dead freight," or that for unoccupied space or dead weight
shortage, as the case may be. Then advertise such space or dead-
weight as available to other shippers. If this brings results, set-
tlement of any remaining loss must be made good by merchant.
It would be to merchant's advantage, with a possible gain to shipowner, to aid in procuring the cargo necessary to complete a full
load.

Q. Although in most trades it is the practice to place the loading,
stowage, and discharge of cargo under direct charge of the first
officer, does this relieve the master of responsibility? If not,
what responsibility is he charged with?
A. No. It is the master's responsibility to safely and properly load,
stow, carry, and deliver the cargo; and such responsibility in-
volves supervision of his officers' activities in performing the
duties required of them by law toward the cargo.

Q. What would you do before signing a bill of lading?
A. Make certain that the count, description, and apparent condition
of the goods check with mate's receipts.

Q. Should a bill of lading list more cargo than is aboard, what
would you do?

A. If shipper may not be contacted for correction of bill before ship sails, sign bill with a note inserted stating the facts concerning the tally, with the proviso that the apparently missing goods "if on board will be delivered."

Q. If any cargo is carried on deck without the consent of the shipper or without being shown by the bill of lading as being "on deck," will the vessel be rendered liable for loss or damage sustained thereby from an excepted peril?
A. Yes; unless it is recognized as customary to carry the cargo in question on deck.

Q. What vessels are required to take a pilot under state laws?
A. Registered vessels, or those engaged in the foreign trade.

Q. What vessels are not subject to compulsory pilotage?
A. Enrolled and licensed vessels.

Q. In the event that a pilot offers his services to a vessel subject to compulsory pilotage and is refused, is the vessel liable for any pilotage charge and if so, how much?
A. Vessel is liable for pilotage charges, either wholly or in part, according to the particular state's laws governing pilots and pilotage.

Q. What report is required to be made by the master within 24 hours after the arrival of his vessel from a foreign port? To whom is it made? When is this report dispensed with?
A. Report of arrival. To nearest Custom House. In the case of a U.S. vessel from a domestic port not carrying bonded goods, or carrying foreign goods already entered.

Q. A crew has demanded their discharge from a vessel, claiming that the master has refused them a draw of one half their wages at a port, when the vessel loaded bunkers only. Admitting that a refusal of a draw in port when and where due is basis for the crew to demand their discharge from the vessel, in this case should the master accede to the demand or not? State your reason.
A. Master should not accede to such demand. The law states that seamen are entitled to one-half the balance of wages earned at the expiration of 5 days in a harbor where vessel shall load or discharge cargo.

Q. Where do you go to enter a ship upon arrival in the United States from a foreign port and what papers are you required to deposit?
A. The Custom House. Papers required are Certificate of Registry; Official Crew List; Bill of health and clearance from last port; Pratique Certificate; two copies of Official Manifest.

Q. What business would you transact at the United States Consulate in a foreign port?

A. Enter ship by depositing the articles of agreement, crew list, and certificate of registry, also giving particulars of cargo discharged or loaded at port in question, where from and where bound on voyage. Business of discharge or engagement of any crew members, sending men to the hospital, or noting a protest is also done at Consulate.

Q. You arrive in a foreign port and have reason to believe that your cargo has been damaged. What action would you take?

A. I would "note a protest" through the U.S. consul at a foreign port, or through a notary public if in a U.S. port, presenting, as is usually required, an officer and a seaman, with vessel's deck log, to substantiate the grounds for making such "protest." If suspicion of damage arises from heavy weather experienced, I would have the hatches surveyed and certified as being in good order. Noting the protest, with such survey, has for its objective the rebuttal of any damage claims by cargo interests which might arise against shipowner in allegedly providing a faulty or unseaworthy vessel.

Q. In regard to merchant vessels and all other private vessels of the United States, under what jurisdiction are crimes committed aboard while on the territorial coastal waters of a state?

A. That of the nation within whose boundaries the vessel is navigated or lies.

Q. You have bound yourself in the Charter contract to take the shortest route to your port of discharge; may you deviate from your course?

A. Yes; for the purpose of saving, or attempting to save, life or property at sea, or for any reasonable cause other than for the purpose of loading or unloading cargo or passengers.

Q. Explain briefly the distinction between jurisdiction in rem and jurisdiction in personam.

A. Jurisdiction in rem obtains when, in admiralty law, a vessel is treated as responsible for its own faulty actions; jurisdiction in personam is that in which proceedings are against a particular person or persons, as the shipowner or owners.

Q. State what rights, if any, an American seaman employed in an American ship will have against the owner if, while on the high seas, he contracts pneumonia.

A. Shipowner shall supply medicine, medical treatment, board, and lodging until seaman is cured, unless so limited by law that such care need not exceed 16 weeks, or if covered by other compensation laws. Shipowner pays full wages while seaman is on board and, if there are dependents, pays wages after man is landed and until cured, unless limited to not less than 16 weeks. If landed during voyage, he must be returned to home port or other port mutually agreed upon. If death results, shipowner must defray burial expenses and safeguard deceased seaman's property. (In cases in which there is in force at vessel's port of registry a scheme of compulsory insurance by which seaman becomes entitled to medical care and cash benefits, shipowner's liability ceases at such time as such care and cash payments begin.)

Q. What is a ship's register?

A. Ship's register, or certificate of registry, is a document serving as title deed of ownership and evidence of nationality of a vessel. It is issued by Collector of customs, in the case of a U.S. vessel, at ship's hailing port to her owners, and contains official particulars, including ship's name, port of registry, origin, date built, owner's name, type or rig, tonnage, power, principal dimensions, number of decks, etc., and must indicate name of master currently in command. The register is held on board while vessel is in the foreign trade.

Q. What is general average?

A. Financial loss made good by equitable contribution of ship, cargo, and freight money, to restore the value of any sacrifice or extraordinary expense incurred for the common safety in a maritime venture.

Q. What is a ship's enrollment?

A. Ship's enrollment is a document issued by Collector of Customs to a U.S. vessel engaged in the U.S. coastwise or domestic trade. Of the same import and purpose as the certificate of registry, and in lieu thereof if vessel changes from foreign to U.S. domestic trade, the enrollment contains particulars as to ownership, master, date and place built, principal dimensions, number of decks, tonnage, etc.

RULES OF THE ROAD

21. INTERNATIONAL

Q. When is a vessel to be considered under way by these rules?

A. When she is not at anchor, or made fast to the shore, or aground.

Q. At what moment are you "under way" from an anchorage; when your anchor is aweigh, or when it ceases to hold?

A. When your anchor is aweigh.

Q. Does the fact of your having or not having way upon your ship have any bearing on whether you are "under way" according to the Rules?

A. No; since vessel is neither anchored, nor made fast to the shore, nor aground to be "under way".

Q. At what intervals is a sailing pilot vessel required to show a flareup light or lights?

A. At intervals which shall never exceed 10 minutes.

Q. What is the range of visibility for the white light required to be carried by a sailing pilot vessel?

A. All round the horizon for a distance of at least 3 miles.

Q. At what point does a vessel cease to be privileged in a crossing or overtaking situation?

A. When, from any cause, she finds herself so close that collision can not be avoided by the action of the giving-way vessel alone. She then shall take such action as will best aid to avert collision.

Q. In a crossing situation, assuming that your vessel and the other steamer both hold course and speed, state how you could make use of the range of his masthead and after range light to determine:
(a) Whether he will cross ahead of you.
(b) Whether you will cross ahead of him.
(c) Whether risk of collision exists.

A. (a) If his lights continue to open out. (b) If his lights slowly come into line and begin opening out in the other direction.
(c) If his lights maintain their relative positions.

Q. Under the International Rules, are vessels showing "not under command" lights in distress? Explain.

A. No. They are to be taken that the vessel showing them is unable to maneuver and therefore cannot get out of the way. (Distress signals are given in Rule 31 only.)

Q. When are side lights exhibited on:
   (a) Ocean steamers;
   (b) Sailing vessels;
   (c) Cable vessels;
   (d) Fishing vessels?

A. (a) When under way from sunset to sunrise. (b) When under way from sunset to sunrise. (c) When making way through the water, from sunset to sunrise. (d) When fishing with trolling (towing) lines only; all others when not fishing; from sunset to sunrise.

Q. What is meant by the term "burdened vessel"?

A. The "giving-way" vessel, or the one of two vessels which is directed by the Rules to keep clear of the other.

Q. Give the definition of the word "visible" when applied to lights, according to the International Rules.

A. It means "that may be seen on a dark night with a clear atmosphere. "

Q. How can risk of collision be determined?

A. By carefully watching the compass bearing of an approaching vessel. Such risk is indicated if the bearing does not appreciably change.

Q. What are the day and night signals for a vessel aground?

A. She shall show by night the light or lights for a vessel at anchor, viz., if under 150 feet in length, one all _ round white light forward where it can best be seen and to be visible at least 2 miles; and, if 150 feet or more in length, one all _ round white light in fore part of vessel, and, at or near the stern, another such light not less than 15 feet lower than the forward light; both lights to be visible not less than 3 miles. Also, the lights for a vessel not under command, viz., two red lights not less than 6 feet apart in a vertical line one over the other, visible all round the horizon at a distance of at least 2 miles.
   By day, where they can best be seen, 3 black balls each not less than 2 feet in diameter, in a vertical line one over the other, not less than 6 feet apart.

The applicant for license should know Rules 22, 23, 27 and 29 verbatim.

Q. What shall be deemed to be the length of a vessel?

A. The length over all.

Q. The International Rules prescribe that a foremast light shall be at a height above the hull of not less than 20 feet, etc. If you were checking the height of a light, where would you take your measurements from?

A. From the weather or uppermost continuous deck immediately below the light.

Q. What signal should a vessel give to attract attention, if necessary?

A. At least 5 short and rapid blasts on the whistle.

Q. What lights are required for vessels being pushed ahead?

A. They shall carry at the fore end a green light on the starboard side and a red light on the port side, each to show an unbroken light over 10 points of the compass, viz., from right ahead to 2 points abaft the beam on their respective sides, and to be visible at least 2 miles. Any number of vessels pushed ahead in a group shall be lighted as one vessel.

Q. In addition to the lights and flares required for sailing pilot vessels, what light does a power-driven pilot vessel carry when on station and not at anchor?

A. She shall carry, 8 feet below her white masthead light, a red light visible all round the horizon at a distance of at least 3 miles.

Q. What may a power-driven pilot vessel use in place of a flare?

A. A bright, intermittent, all-round white light.

Q. Is there any provision made in the Rules for the use of additional whistle signals between ships of war or vessels sailing under convoy? Explain.

A. Rule 13 (a) prescribes that nothing in the Rules shall interfere with the operation of any special rules made by the Government of any nation with respect to additional station and signal lights for ships of war, for vessels sailing in convoy, or for seaplanes on the water.

Q. The Rules require that a power-driven vessel be provided with an efficient whistle. Does the siren meet this requirement? State your reason.

A. Yes. Rule l(xiii) states the word "whistle" means whistle or siren.

Q. What lights are vessels forbidden to exhibit by the Rules?

A. No other lights which may be mistaken for the prescribed lights, or impair their visibility or distinctive character, or interfere with the keeping of a proper lookout.

Q. What are the lights required on sail pilot vessels when on station?

A. When on station and not at anchor, shall carry a white light at the masthead visible all round the horizon for at least 3 miles; and shall show a flare-up light or lights at intervals which shall never exceed 10 minutes. On the near approach of or to other vessels, they shall flash or show their side lights at short intervals to indicate the direction in which they are heading. If at anchor on station, they shall carry the light and show the flares required, and the anchor light or lights prescribed in Rule 11, but shall not show the side lights.

Q. Describe the lights and day signals displayed by Coast and Geodetic Survey vessels under way and actually engaged in hydrographic surveying.

A. They shall carry 3 lights, where they can best be seen, in a vertical line one over the other not less than 6 feet apart. The highest and lowest of these shall be red, and the middle light shall be white, and they shall be visible all round the horizon at a distance of at least 2 miles. By day, in a vertical line one over the other, not less than 6 feet apart, where they can best be seen, 3 shapes each not less than 2 feet in diameter. The highest and lowest of these shall be globular in shape and red in color; the middle one diamond in shape and white. Such vessels, when not making way through the water, shall not carry the colored side lights or the stern light, but when making way, shall carry them.

Q. At sea, on what occasion would you display two red lights at night or two black balls during the day?

A. When my vessel is "not under command" and cannot get out of the way of another.

Q. A fishing vessel is under way with all sails set and a gasoline engine running. Under the Rules, is she a power-driven or sailing vessel?

A. She is a power-driven vessel.

Q. What is meant by "privileged vessel"?

A. That one of two vessels approaching each other so as to involve risk of collision which is directed by the Rules to "keep her course and speed".

Q. What are the characteristics, range of visibility, and location for the anchor light of a vessel less than 150 feet in length?

A. She shall carry in the fore part of the vessel, where it can best be seen, a white light in a lantern so constructed as to show a clear, unbroken light all round the horizon at a distance of at least 2 miles.

Q. Which of two crossing power-driven vessels has the right of way in a fog?

A. Neither vessel.

Q. What is meant by the term "engaged in fishing?"

A. It means fishing with nets, lines, or trawls, but does not include fishing with trolling lines.

Q. What is the fog signal for vessels engaged in fishing?

A. They shall sound, at intervals of not more than 1 minute, 3 blasts in succession, namely, 1 prolonged blast followed by 2 short blasts.

Q. Under what conditions are whistle signals given for alteration of ship's heading, as required by the Rules?

A. When vessels are within sight of each other and action is taken as authorized or required by the Rules. (See Rule 28)

Q. What are the fog signals for towing vessels?

A. They shall sound, at intervals of not more than 1 minute, 3 blasts in succession, namely, 1 prolonged blast followed by 2 short blasts.

Q. What are the fog signals for a vessel engaged in laying or in picking up a navigation mark?

A. Same as previous answer.

Q. What lights should a vessel carry when in tow of another vessel?

A. The colored side lights and a stern light.

Q. Describe the stern light which is carried by a vessel under way.

A. A white light constructed to show an unbroken light over an arc of the horizon of 12 points of the compass, so fixed as to show 6 points from right aft on each side of the vessel, and to be visible at a distance of at least 2 miles.

Q. What is the day signal for vessels at anchor?

A. Between sunrise and sunset, in the fore part of the vessel where it can best be seen, 1 black ball not less than 2 feet in diameter.

Q. When is a power-driven vessel engaged in towing in International waters required to carry three masthead lights?

A. When the length of the tow, measuring from the stern of the towing vessel to the stern of last vessel towed, exceeds 600 feet.

Q. What are the requirements of the Rules with respect to anchor lights for a vessel 150 feet or upward in length?

A. Vessels of 150 feet or upwards in length shall carry in the fore part of the vessel, not less than 20 feet above the hull, a white light, and at or near the stern, at a height not less than 15 feet lower than the forward light, another white light. Both lights shall be visible all round the horizon at a distance of at least 3 miles.

Q. What lights and signals are required for vessels fishing with lines or nets extending horizontally into the seaway more than 500 feet?

A. Two lights in a vertical line, one above the other, not less than 4 or more than 12 feet apart. The higher light shall be red in color and the lower one white, both visible all round the horizon.
   In addition, and in the direction of the outlying gear, at a horizontal distance of not less than 6 or more than 20 feet from the vertical lights, an all-round white light.
   By day they shall show where it can best be seen a black shape consisting of 2 cones with their apexes together, one above the other; and, in the direction of the outlying gear, an additional black conical shape, point upward.

Q. May signals other than fog signals be given when vessels are unable to see each other because of fog, mist, snow or rain? If so, state them.

A. No.

Q. What action shall a power-driven vessel take on hearing, apparently forward of her beam, the fog signal of a vessel whose position is not ascertained?

A. She shall, as far as the circumstances of the case admit, stop her engines, and then navigate with caution until danger of collision is over.

Q. Describe the lights and shapes required to be exhibited by a vessel engaged in laying or picking up a submarine cable by night and by day.

A. By night, in lieu of the white masthead lights specified in Rule 2 she shall carry 3 lights in a vertical line one over the other, not less than 6 feet apart. The highest and lowest of these shall be red and the middle light shall be white, and both shall be visible all round the horizon at a distance of at least 2 miles.

By day, in a vertical line one over the other not less than 6 feet apart, where they can best be seen, 3 shapes each not less than 2 feet in diameter. The highest and lowest of these shall be globular in shape and red in color; the middle one diamond in shape and white.

Q. Describe the arcs of visibility of the masthead light and stern light of an ocean steamer.

A. The masthead light shall show an unbroken light over an arc of the horizon of 20 points (225°) of the compass, so fixed as to show the light from right ahead to 2 points (22 1/2°) abaft the beam on either side, and to be visible at a distance of at least 5 miles.

The stern light shall show an unbroken light over an arc of the horizon of 12 points (135°) of the compass, so fixed as to show the light from right astern to 6 points (67 1/2°) on either side, and to be visible at a distance of at least 2 miles.

Q. When a small vessel is being overtaken by another, what lights is she required to show if unable to carry the fixed stern light because of bad weather?

A. She shall have an electric torch or a lighted lantern at hand ready for use and shall, on the approach of an overtaking vessel, show such signal in sufficient time to prevent collision.

Q. What power-driven seagoing vessels are not required to carry a range light?

A. Those having a length of less than 150 feet.

Q. What are the requirements of the Rules with respect to the lights for a power-driven vessel towing or pushing another vessel?

A. In addition to the colored side lights, 2 white lights in a vertical line one over the other, not less than 6 feet apart, and shall carry an additional bright white light 6 feet above or below such lights, if the length of the tow, measuring from the towing vessel's stern to that of the last vessel towed, exceeds 600 feet. Each of these lights shall be carried in the same position as the masthead light in Rule 2, except the additional light which shall be carried at not less than 14 feet above the hull.

Q. What vessels display a red all-round light vertically below the masthead light?

A. Power-driven pilot vessels on pilotage duty.

Q. You are proceeding toward a wide channel and sight a vessel showing an all-round white light on the bow and on the stern, together with two red all-round lights in a vertical line amid-ships. What do her lights indicate?

A. A vessel aground.

Q. What is the rule regarding two power-driven vessels meeting end on or nearly end on so as to involve risk of collision?

A. Each shall alter her course to starboard, so that each may pass on the port side of the other. Each shall indicate such action by one short blast on the whistle.

Q. How are orders to wheelsmen to be given?

A. They are to be given in the sense that "Right rudder" or "Starboard" means "put the vessel's rudder to starboard"; "Left rudder" or "Port", "put vessel's rudder to port".

Q. When should whistle signals be sounded for course alteration?

A. When such course alteration is being executed.

Q. Name the distress signals.

A. A gun or other explosive fired at intervals of about a minute.
A continuous sounding with any fog-signal apparatus.
Rockets or shells, throwing red stars, fired one at a time at short intervals.
The Morse Code signal SOS made by radio-telegraphy or by any other signalling method.
The spoken word "Mayday" sent by radio-telephony.
International Code Signal indicated by N C.
A square flag having above or below it a ball or anything resembling a ball.
Flames on the vessel, as from a burning tar barrel, oil barrel, etc.
A rocket parachute flare showing a red light.
An orange-colored smoke signal.
Repeatedly slowly raising and lowering the arms outstretched on either side.

Q. Do vessels not under command and vessels laying or picking up a telegraph cable carry side lights on the high seas?

A. Yes; but only when making way through the water.

Q. Quote Rule 27, the General Prudential Rule.

A. "In obeying and construing these Rules, due regard shall be had to all dangers of navigation and collision, and to any special circumstances, including the limitations of the craft involved, which may render a departure from the Rules necessary in order to avoid immediate danger."

Q. What is the meaning of two short blasts when sounded by one of two power-driven vessels which are meeting so as to involve risk of collision?

A. "I am altering my course to port."

Q. What do three short blasts denote when sounded by one of two power-driven vessels which are meeting or crossing so as to involve risk of collision?

A. "My engines are going astern."

Q. State the duties of the "privileged" vessel as outlined in the Rules. In other words, where by these Rules, one of two vessels is to keep out of the way, what shall the other vessel do? Answer in full.

A. The other vessel shall keep her course and speed. "When, from any cause the 'privileged' vessel finds herself so close that collision cannot be avoided by the action of the giving-way vessel alone, she also shall take such action as will best aid to avert collision."

Q. Are naval vessels required to carry lights as prescribed in Rules of the Road in peacetime?

A. Yes; but with the provision that their nation's Government shall determine what is to be their closest compliance with the Rules.

Q. Are squadrons and convoys prevented from carrying special lights?

A. No; by Rule 13(a).

Q. May vessels exhibit any lights in order to attract attention?

A. Yes; they may show a flare-up to attract attention.

Q. May a power-driven vessel use the five or more short-blast signal in fog when she is not visible to other vessels?

A. No; the signal is to be used only when vessels are within sight of each other.

Q. What vessels may use a bell to sound fog signals while under way?

A. A vessel less than 40 feet in length, a rowing boat, or a seaplane on the water.

Q. Has a vessel towing another vessel any right of way not usually allowed to other vessels?

A. No.

Q. Which has the right of way, a sailing vessel or a vessel fishing? State your reasons.

A. By Rule 26, a vessel fishing has the right of way. However, this Rule gives a vessel engaged in fishing no right to obstruct a fairway. This Rule is based upon the fact that the vessel fishing lacks the maneuverability of a vessel under way and unhampered with "nets, lines, or trawls."

Q. What is the meaning of one short blast when sounded by one of two power-driven vessels which are meeting so as to involve risk of collision?

A. "I am altering my course to starboard."

Q. What is the rule governing two power-driven vessels crossing so as to involve risk of collision?

A. The vessel which has the other on her own starboard side shall keep out of the way of the other.

Q. What is the rule for a power-driven vessel and a sailing vessel proceeding so as to involve risk of collision?

A. The power-driven vessel shall keep out of the way of the sailing vessel, except when by Rule 24, the latter is the overtaking vessel, or by Rule 26, the power-driven vessel is engaged in fishing.

Q. A towing vessel is required to make a fog signal. State that signal and the intervals at which it is made.

A. She shall sound, at intervals of not more than 1 minute, 3 blasts in succession, namely, 1 prolonged blast followed by 2 short blasts.

Q. A vessel being towed is required to make a signal. State the signal for a vessel being towed, the interval at which it is sounded, and how it is to be sounded with respect to the signal of the towing vessel.

A. She shall sound, at intervals of not more than 1 minute, 4 blasts in succession, namely, 1 prolonged blast followed by 3 short blasts. When practicable, this signal shall be made immediately after the signal made by the towing vessel.

Q. You are watch officer at anchor on an 8000 ton vessel, 400 feet long. The weather becomes foggy. State in detail the precautions you would take.

A. I would station a man forward with orders to ring ship's bell rapidly for about 5 seconds every minute, and another man aft to sound the gong likewise. Ship's whistle or siren would be ready to use in case of necessity to give warning of my position to a vessel approaching, the signal for this being 3 blasts in succession, namely, 1 short, 1 prolonged, and 1 short blast.

Q. Under what conditions other than fog are fog signals used?

A. In mist, falling snow, heavy rainstorms, or any other condition similarly restricting visibility.

Q. In foggy weather, what signals may be used when vessels can see one another?

A. The steering signals: 1 short blast = "I am altering my course to starboard"; 2 short blasts = "I am altering my course to port". The engine signal = "My engines are going astern". The "danger" signal = At least 5 short and rapid blasts on the whistle. An attention signal = A flare-up light or a detonating or other efficient sound signal that cannot be mistaken for any other signal authorized in the Rules.

Q. Of what duration are the following when used as fog signals:
   (a) Prolonged blast;
   (b) Short blast;
   (c) Ship's bell?

A. (a) A blast of from 4 to 6 seconds' duration.
   (b) A blast of about 1 second's duration.
   (c) A rapid ringing for about 5 seconds.

Q. Would a vessel be required to sound signals during the fog if she was moored at the end of a pier in such a manner that she projected beyond the pier into the channel? Explain.

A. Yes. Since the purpose of a fog signal primarily is to warn or advise vessels and all water craft of the presence of each other in navigable waters, and the vessel in question occupies part of a fairway in such navigable waters, such vessel virtually becomes a vessel at anchor and accordingly should sound the required signals during fog.

Q. On hearing the fog signal of another vessel close ahead, what signal should be sounded by a power-driven vessel which has reversed her engines and actually has sternway?

A. 1 prolonged blast at intervals of not more than 2 minutes. (Rule 15(c)(i) states that such vessel sounds this signal when "making way through the water. ")

Q. In fog, would you sound signals indicating an alteration of course?

A. No. Such signals are sounded only when vessels are in sight of one another.

Q. What are the fog signals for a vessel being towed and on what are they to be sounded?

A. At intervals of not more than 1 minute, 4 blasts in succession, namely, 1 prolonged blast followed by 3 short blasts on the whistle or the foghorn.

Q. Two vessels are meeting in the crossing situation. The vessel which has the other on her starboard bow blows two short blasts of her whistle and this signal is answered by a similar signal from the other vessel. Which is the burdened vessel and which the privileged vessel?

A. This situation has no place under International Rules. The vessels in question, according to Rule 28, have indicated their respective actions, viz. , "I am altering my course to port." There are no "answers" to passing signals under the Rules.

Q. What signal should be made by an overtaken vessel in answer to a one- or two-blast signal from a vessel which is overtaking her?

A. None.

Q. May a power-driven vessel in sight of another alter course without blowing the whistle?

A. Yes; if she is not taking any course authorized or required by the Rules.

Q. Are both the burdened vessel and the privileged vessel obliged to sound whistle signals? Explain your answer in detail.

A. The burdened vessel only is obliged to sound the appropriate whistle signal, since the Rules require such signal to be given "in taking any course authorized or required by these Rules. "

Q. If a whistle signal is sounded by a vessel indicating a change of course, is she obliged to change course in accordance with her signal?

A. No. Such whistle signal is obligatory only when vessel is in the act of changing her course.

Q. Assume that you are the officer in charge of the watch and you observe on your port hand a crossing vessel whose course appears to be 090° to the right of your own. Her bearing does not appreciably change and she has apparently made no change in course or speed since you first observed her. Is there any signal which you can make which will indicate to the vessel the presence of your ship?

A. Yes; by Rule 28, I may give at least 5 short and rapid blasts of the whistle, as signifying my doubt the other vessel is taking action to avoid collision.

Q. What is the fog signal for a power-driven vessel under way, but stopped, and having no way upon her?

A. At intervals of not more than 2 minutes, 2 prolonged blasts, with an interval of about 1 second between them.

Q. What is the duty of the Officer in Charge of a power-driven vessel upon hearing a fog signal apparently forward of the vessel's beam?

A. He shall, as far as the circumstances of the case admit, stop the engines, and then navigate with caution until danger of collision is over.

Q. When a vessel is skirting a fog bank but is not herself in the fog, should she sound fog signals? Why?

A. Yes; so that any approaching vessel or vessels actually in the fog may be warned of the presence of such vessel.

Q. What lights and signals are shown by a vessel fishing with nets or lines extending horizontally not more than 500 feet into the seaway?

A. They shall carry 2 all-round lights in a vertical line, one above the other, not less than 4 or more than 12 feet apart. The upper of these lights shall be red in color; the other white.
   By day, shall display where best can be seen a black shape made of 2 cones apex to apex, one over the other. If under 65 feet in length, may substitute a basket for such shape.

Q. What lights, in addition to the required lights, may fishing vessels and fishing boats use at any time when engaged in their occupation?

A. They may, if necessary to attract attention of approaching vessels, show a flare-up light. They also may use working lights.

Q. What are the lights to be displayed by a sailing vessel engaged in trawling?

A. Two all-round white lights in a vertical line one above the other, not less than 4 or more than 12 feet apart, the higher green and the lower white in color.

Q. What is the signal of a vessel of 400 feet length which is aground in fog?

A. In the fore part of the vessel the bell shall be rung rapidly, at intervals of not more than 1 minute, for about 5 seconds; and in the after part of the vessel, at intervals of not more than 1 minute for about 5 seconds, a gong or other instrument, the tone of which cannot be confused with that of the bell. In addition, if aground, she shall give 3 separate and distinct strokes on the bell immediately before and after each such signal.

Q. What is the rule regarding day signals to be displayed by a fishing vessel at anchor with her gear out?

A. She shall show, from sunrise to sunset, forward where it best can be seen, a black shape consisting of 2 cones one above the other, apex to apex; and, in the direction of the outlying gear, an additional black conical shape, point upward, if such gear extends more than 500 feet horizontally.

Q. How does a fishing vessel indicate to an approaching vessel that she has nets, lines, or trawls out in the daytime?

A. By the black shape indicated in previous question. Also, if her length is less than 65 feet, a basket may be substituted for the shape.

Q. What fog signal is required to be sounded by a power-driven vessel having way upon her?

A. At intervals of not more than 2 minutes, 1 prolonged blast.

Q. What fog signal must be sounded by a vessel picking up a submarine cable?

A. At intervals of not more than 1 minute, 3 blasts in succession, namely, 1 prolonged blast followed by 2 short blasts.

21. INTERNATIONAL AND INLAND RULES

Q. What do towed vessels use to make fog signals in International waters?

A. The whistle or the foghorn.

Q. What do towed vessels use to make fog signals in Inland waters?

A. The foghorn.

Q. What is positive evidence that risk of collision is present in a crossing situation?

A. When the compass bearing of the approaching vessel does not appreciably change.

Q. When shall the Rules concerning lights be complied with?

A. In all weathers, from sunset to sunrise.

Q. When navigating in a large vessel, have you any special privileges over yachts and other small craft?

A. No.

Q. Where specific lines of demarcation are not prescribed, how would you determine whether International or Inland Rules would govern at entrances from seaward to bays, sounds, or other estuaries?

A. By noting that the waters inshore of a line approximately parallel with the general trend of the shore, drawn through the outermost buoy or other aid to navigation of any system of aids, are inland waters. Within this limit, the Inland Rules govern; without, or to seaward, the International Rules.

Q. Name the lights required for sailing vessels.

A. A green light on starboard side; a red light on port side; and a stern light.

Q. What is the rule regarding speed in fog?

A. Every vessel shall, in fog, mist, falling snow, heavy rainstorms, or any other condition similarly restricting visibility, go at a moderate speed, having careful regard to the existing circumstances and conditions.

Q. What is the difference in the location requirements of the masthead light of a power-driven vessel on the high seas and on Inland waters of the United States?

A. On the high seas, the light shall be carried at a specified height above the hull, viz., not less than 20 feet, and if the breadth of the vessel exceeds 20 feet, then at a height above the hull not less than such breadth, so, however, that the light need not be placed at a greater height than 40 feet above the hull. On Inland waters of the United States, it shall be carried at no specified height, but "on or in front of the foremast, or if a vessel without a foremast, then in the fore part of the vessel".

Q. Under what circumstances is the privileged vessel required to hold her course and speed?

A. Where, by any of the Rules, one of two vessels is to keep out of the way, the other, or "privileged" vessel, shall keep her course and speed.

Q. At what point in a crossing situation is the privileged vessel bound to alter course or speed?

A. When, from any cause, she finds herself so close that collision cannot be avoided by the action of the giving-way vessel alone.

Q. What is the only case in which a starboard-to-starboard passing would be proper for two steam vessels meeting end on or nearly end on?

A. When it is clear that their respective courses will take them a safe distance to starboard of each other, as when a green light without a red light is seen ahead, or the masts are a little "open" to starboard.

Q. In what two situations at sea may a privileged vessel use 5 or more short and rapid blasts provided by the Rules to call the attention of the burdened vessel to its obligation to keep clear?

A. In the crossing and the overtaking situations.

Q. What precautions are required by the Rules for vessels nearing a bend in a channel where approaching vessels may not be visible?

A. When they shall arrive within 1/2 mile of the bend, shall sound 1 long blast, which signal shall be answered with a like blast by any approaching power-driven or steam vessel that may be within hearing around the bend. Whether or not an approaching vessel on the farther side of the bend is heard, such bend shall be rounded with alertness and caution.

Q. Do the Rules give any specific or special privilege to naval vessels to take the right of way over a commercial vessel at any time during the crossing situation?

A. No.

Q. What are the lights required for rowing boats whether under oar or sail?

A. They shall have ready at hand an electric torch or a lighted lantern which shall be exhibited temporarily in sufficient time to prevent collision.

Q. What is the rule governing narrow channels?

A. Every power-driven vessel shall, when safe and practicable, keep to that side of the fairway or mid-channel which lies on the starboard side of such vessel.

Q. What is the meaning of the one blast signal:
 (a) In International waters;
 (b) In Inland waters?

A. (a) "I am altering my course to starboard."
 (b) "I intend, propose, or desire to pass you on my port side; accordingly, if my signal is answered in assent thereto, I shall, if necessary, alter my course to starboard."

Q. If two sailing vessels, each having the wind on the port side, are approaching each other so as to involve risk of collision, which must keep out of the way?

A. The vessel which is to windward shall keep out of the way of the vessel which is to leeward.

Q. What shall a power-driven vessel, which is directed by the Rules to keep out of the way of another vessel, do, if necessary, on approaching the other vessel?

A. She shall, if necessary, slacken her speed, or stop, or reverse.

Q. When sail vessels are close hauled on different tacks, which must keep clear?

A. The vessel which is on the port tack.

Q. How can risk of collision be determined?

A. By carefully watching the compass bearing of an approaching vessel. If such bearing does not appreciably change, such risk should be deemed to exist.

Q. State the steering and sailing rules for two sailing vessels approaching one another so as to involve risk of collision.

A. (a) When each has the wind on a different side, vessel having wind on port side shall keep out of the way. (b) Each having wind on same side, vessel which is to windward shall keep clear. (c) For this Rule's purpose, the windward side is that opposite the side on which the mainsail is set, or, in a square-rigged vessel, the side opposite that spreading the largest fore-and-aft sail.

Q. When one sail vessel is running free and the other is close hauled, which must keep clear?

A. The vessel having the wind on her port side.

Q. When two sailing vessels have the wind on different sides, and they are approaching one another so as to involve risk of collision, which must keep out of the way?

A. The vessel having the wind on her port side.

Q. Under what conditions does the General Prudential Rule, or Rule of Special Circumstances, Article 27, apply? State several situations where it must be applied.

A. When circumstances arise which may render a departure from the Rules necessary in order to avoid immediate danger.
    1. In misty weather, when vessels find themselves dangerously close.   2. When more than 2 vessels are involved in the risk-of-collision situation.   3. When the privileged vessel suddenly alters course to avoid a danger.   4. When a whistle signal contrary to the Rules is assented to by the other vessel.   5. When one vessel is making sternway toward another.

Q. Does the rule for an overtaking vessel apply to a sailing vessel overtaking a power-driven vessel?

A. Yes.

Q. Quote Rule (or Article) 29, the "Precaution Rule".

A. "Nothing in these Rules shall exonerate any vessel, or the owner, master, or crew thereof, from the consequences of any neglect to carry lights or signals, or of any neglect to keep a proper lookout, or of the neglect of any precaution which may be required by the ordinary practice of seamen, or by the special circumstances of the case."

Q. Name 5 situations which could be classed as special circumstances.

A. 1. Where, from any cause, two vessels get so close to each other that collision cannot be avoided by the giving-way vessel alone.

2. Where compliance with the Rules is prevented by apparent physical conditions, such as a tug with a tow heading down a swift river current and meeting a free vessel crossing her course.

3. Where more than two vessels are approaching each other.

4. Where the situation is not specifically covered by the Rules, as when one vessel is backing toward another.

5. Where one powered vessel proposes action contrary to the Rules and the other assents.

Q. In what respects do the International and Inland Rules regarding fog signals differ?

A. Inland Rules require a vessel towed to sound signals on the fog-horn; International, on the whistle or the foghorn. Under Inland Rules, there is no signal specified for a power-driven vessel under way but stopped, for a vessel not under command, or for a vessel laying or picking up a submarine cable or a navigation mark; also, the Rule for a vessel at anchor, unlike the International, makes no provision for a vessel's length, for a warning whistle signal when at anchor, or for a vessel aground. A vessel towed, under Inland Rules, gives same signal as the towing vessel — not the prolonged blast and 3 short blasts of the International. Again, under Inland Rules, all water craft, including vessels fishing, "not herein provided for", sound the same signal as in International Rules for a less than 40-foot vessel, a rowing boat or a seaplane on the water. All fog signals are required to be sounded at intervals of not more than 1 minute under Inland Rules; the interval is "not more than 2 minutes" in the case of a power-driven vessel making way through the water, according to International Rules.

Q. In thick weather, the wind is S by W and you hear a schooner blowing one blast of her foghorn; about how would she be heading?

A. Between E by S and SE. (Allowing vessel to sail 5 points from wind).

Q. If you observe a vessel's green light bearing NNE, how may that vessel be heading?

A. Between East and SSW.

21. INLAND RULES

Q. What are the lights required to be carried by double-end ferry-boats in inland waters?

A. They shall carry the range lights and the colored side lights required by law on Inland waters, except that the range shall be a central one of clear, bright, white lights, showing all round the horizon, placed at equal altitudes forward and aft.

Q. State Article No. 3 of the Inland Rules relating to the special requirements with respect to lights for steam vessels towing or pushing another vessel.

A. They shall carry the side lights and 2 all-round white lights in a vertical line one above the other not less than 3 feet apart; and, when towing one or more vessels astern, shall carry an additional white light 3 feet above or below such lights. Each of these lights shall be the same as that prescribed in Article 2(a) or the after range light in Article 2(f).

Such vessels, when pushing another vessel or vessels ahead, shall also carry at or near the stern two bright amber lights, one above the other in a vertical line, not less than 3 feet apart, each to show an unbroken light from right astern to 6 points on each side of the vessel.

When towing one or more vessels astern may carry a small white light abaft the funnel or after mast for the tow to steer by, but such light shall not be visible forward of the beam.

Q. What signal is required by the Pilot Rules when steam vessels are moved from their docks or berths and other boats are liable to pass from any direction toward them?

A. The required signal is the same as that given when approaching a short bend, viz., a long blast, but immediately after clearing the berths so as to be fully in sight, the vessel shall be governed by the steering and sailing rules.

Q. Describe the lights for rowing boats, under oars and sail.

A. They shall have ready at hand a lantern showing a white light which shall be temporarily exhibited in sufficient time to prevent collision.

Q. What are the fog signals for steam vessels under way and also steam vessels under way but stopped and having no way upon them?

A. A steam vessel under way shall sound, at intervals of not more than 1 minute, a prolonged blast. Such vessel under way, but stopped and having no way upon her, shall sound the same signal.

Q. During what period of each day shall the Rules concerning lights be complied with?

A. From sunset to sunrise, in all weathers.

Q. Your steamer is being overtaken by another steamer which blows one short blast. You regard it dangerous to comply with the overtaking steamer's request but are willing to allow him to pass you on your port side. What signals would you sound to indicate this?

A. I would sound several short and rapid blasts of the whistle, not less than 4; then, being sure that all is clear for his passing on my port side, I would sound 2 short blasts. If the overtaking steamer then wished to pass on that side, he would announce his intention to do so by answering my signal with 2 blasts and proceed accordingly.

Q. Describe the day and night signals for self-propelling dredges under way with suctions on the bottom.

A. By day, they shall display 2 black balls not less than 2 feet in diameter in a vertical line not less than 15 feet above the deck house, and where they can best be seen from all directions.
By night, in addition to the regular running lights, 2 red lights of the same character as the white masthead light, and in the same vertical line beneath that light; the red lights to be not less than 3 feet nor more than 6 feet apart, and the upper red light to be not less than 4 feet nor more than 6 feet below the masthead light; also, on or near the stern, 2 red lights in a vertical line not less than 4 feet nor more than 6 feet apart, to show through 4 points of the compass, that is, from right astern to 2 points on each quarter.

Q. What lights are required to be shown by all fishing vessels and fishing boats, of 10 gross tons or upwards, when under way and when not having their nets, trawls, dredges or lines in the water?

A. They shall carry and show the same lights as other vessels under way.

Q. If, when nearing a short bend or curve in the channel, you blew the signal of one long blast on the whistle and it was answered by a similar whistle signal from another steamer on the other side of the bend, what action would you take?

A. I would proceed with caution and, immediately upon sighting the other vessel, would announce my intention by whistle signal (usually the 1 short blast for a port-to-port passing) as to which side I would pass.

Q. State Article No. 18, Rule 8, of the Inland Rules which governs the overtaking situation.

A. "When steam vessels are running in the same direction, and the vessel which is astern shall desire to pass on the right or starboard hand of the vessel ahead, she shall give 1 short blast of the steam whistle, as a signal of such desire, and if the vessel ahead answers with 1 blast, she shall direct her course to starboard; or, if she shall desire to pass on the left or port side of the vessel ahead, she shall give 2 short blasts of the steam whistle as a signal of such desire, and if the vessel ahead answers with 2 blasts, shall direct her course to port; or, if the vessel ahead does not think it safe for the vessel astern to attempt to pass at that point, she shall immediately signify the same by giving several short and rapid blasts of the steam whistle, not less than 4, and, under no circumstances, shall the vessel astern attempt to pass the vessel ahead until such time as they have reached a point where it can be safely done, when said vessel ahead shall signify her willingness by blowing the proper signals. The vessel ahead shall, in no case, attempt to cross the bow or crowd upon the course of the passing vessel. "

Q. What warning signals for day and night are displayed by Coast Guard vessels while handling or servicing aids to navigations?

A. By day, they display from the yard 2 orange and white vertically striped balls in a vertical line not less than 3 feet nor more than 6 feet apart; and by night, where they best may be seen, 2 red lights in a vertical line not less than 3 feet nor more than 6 feet apart.

Q. State the day signal required for vessels at anchor with fishing gear out.

A. No day signal is required by such vessel.

Q. When a vessel is backing (that is, proceeding stern first), what rule governs its meeting with another vessel?

A. The "Special Circumstances" or "General Prudential" Rule, Article 27.

Q. What precautions are required by the Rules for vessels nearing a bend in a channel where approaching vessels may not be visible?

A. Whenever a steam vessel arrives within half a mile of such bend, she shall give a signal by one long blast of the whistle, as a warning to any approaching steam vessel that may be within hearing on the farther side of the bend. If this signal is answered with a similar blast, both vessels shall proceed with caution and, when within sight of each other, the usual signals for meeting and passing shall be immediately given and answered.

Q. What would you do if cross signals had been sounded in answer to your passing signal?

A. I would sound the danger signal, stop, and, if necessary, reverse the engines until such apparent misunderstanding is cleared up.

Q. How are dredge or floating plant moorings marked and, at night, how is their location shown to an approaching vessel?

A. Breast, stern, and bow anchors of floating plant working in navigable channels are marked by barrel or other suitable buoys. By night, approaching vessels shall be shown the location of adjacent buoys by throwing a suitable beam of light on the buoys from the plant, until the approaching vessel has passed, or the buoys may be lighted by red lights, visible in all directions at a distance of at least 2 miles.

Q. What is the rule regarding the speed of vessels passing floating plants working in a channel?

A. Vessels passing such plants shall reduce their speed sufficiently to insure safety of both plant and themselves, and, when passing within 200 feet of the plant, their speed shall not exceed 5 miles per hour. While passing over lines of the plant, propelling machinery shall be stopped.

Q. What lights and day signals are required to be displayed by inland steam vessels, derrick boats, lighters, or other types of vessels made fast alongside a wreck, or moored over a wreck which is on the bottom, or partly submerged, or which may be drifting?

A. By day, they shall display, where best can be seen, 2 shapes, one above the other not less than 6 feet apart, lower shape to be not less than 10 feet above the deck house. The shapes shall be in the form of a double frustum of a cone, base to base, not less than 2 feet in diameter at the center nor less than 8 inches at ends of the cones, and to be not less than 4 feet lengthwise from end to end. Where more than one vessel is working under these conditions, the shapes need be shown only from one vessel on each side of the wreck from which they can best be seen from all directions. The shapes shall be painted a solid bright red.

By night, a white light from the bow and stern of each outside vessel or lighter shall be displayed not less than 6 feet above the deck, and in addition, in a position where they can best be seen from all directions, 2 red lights in a vertical line not less than 3 nor more than 6 feet apart, and not less than 15 feet above the deck.

Q. What is the Inland Rule danger signal?

A. Several short and rapid blasts, not less than 4, of the steam whistle.

Q. When should the Inland Rule danger signal be used?

A. When steam vessels are approaching each other and either one fails to understand the course or intention of the other from any cause, the vessel so in doubt shall immediately sound the danger signal.

Q. Do the Rules give any specific or special privileges to naval vessels to take the right of way over a commercial vessel at any time during the crossing situation?

A. No.

Q. How would you know on which side it would be clear to pass a dredge working in a channel, by day and by night?

A. When within a reasonable distance from such dredge, not in any case over a mile, I would indicate my intention to pass by 1 long blast of the whistle. The dredge would then direct me to the proper side for passage by sounding the signal prescribed in the local pilot rules for vessels under way and approaching each other from opposite directions, which I would answer in the usual manner. If the channel is not clear, the dredge would sound the danger signal, upon which my vessel would slow down, or stop, and await further signal from the dredge.

Q. Describe the lights to be displayed on pipelines attached to dredges and either floating or supported on trestles.

A. By night, one row of amber lights not less than 8 feet nor more than 12 feet above the water, about equally spaced and in such manner as to mark distinctly the entire length and course of the line, intervals between lights where the line crosses navigable channels to be not more than 30 feet. Also, on the shore or discharge end of the line, 2 red lights, 3 feet apart, in a vertical line, with the lower light at least 8 feet above water, and if the line is opened for passage of vessels, a similar arrangement of lights is displayed at each side of the opening.

Q. In the crossing situation, should either vessel fail to understand the course or intention of the other, what shall she immediately do and what action must then be taken by both vessels?

A. The misunderstanding or objection shall at once be made apparent by blowing the danger signal, and both vessels shall be stopped and backed, if necessary, until signals for passing with safety are made and understood.

Q. How should all orders to helmsmen be given?

A. "Right Rudder" to mean "Direct the vessel's head to starboard."
"Left Rudder" to mean "Direct the vessel's head to port."

Q. What are the rules for sound signals in a fog for:
(a) A steam vessel;
(b) A sailing vessel;
(c) A vessel at anchor;
(d) A steam vessel when towing, or a vessel being towed;
(e) Rafts or other water craft?

A. (a) A steam vessel under way shall sound, at intervals of not
more than 1 minute, a prolonged blast.
(b) A sailing vessel under way shall sound, at intervals of not
more than 1 minute, when on the starboard tack, 1 blast; when
on the port tack, 2 blasts in succession; and, with the wind abaft
the beam, 3 blasts in succession.
(c) A vessel, when at anchor, shall, at intervals of not more
than 1 minute, ring the bell rapidly for about 5 seconds.
(d) A steam vessel when towing shall, at intervals of not more
than 1 minute, sound 3 blasts in succession, namely, 1 prolonged
blast followed by 2 short blasts. A vessel towed may give this
signal and she shall not give any other.
(e) All rafts or other water craft not herein provided for, navigating by hand power, horsepower, or by the current of the river,
shall sound a blast of the foghorn, or equivalent signal, at intervals of not more than 1 minute.

Q. What is indicated by a vessel which displays a day signal consisting of 2 red balls, 2 feet in diameter and 3 to 6 feet apart
vertically, 15 feet above the deckhouse?

A. A dredge held in stationary position by moorings or spuds.

Q. What is indicated by a vessel which displays a day signal consisting of 2 balls, 2 feet in diameter, 3 to 6 feet apart vertically,
about 20 feet above the deckhouse, if the upper ball is painted in
alternate black and white vertical stripes and the lower ball is a
solid bright red?

A. "A vessel moored or anchored and engaged in laying cables or
pipe, submarine construction, excavation, mat sinking, bank grading, dike construction, revetment, or other bank protection operations."

Q. State the Pilot Rule governing the action required when vessels
are approaching each other at right angles or obliquely, so as to
involve risk of collision, other than when one vessel is overtaking
another.

A. The steam vessel which has the other on her own port side shall hold her course and speed; and the steam vessel which has the other on her own starboard side shall keep out of the way of the other by directing her course to starboard so as to cross the stern of the other vessel, or, if necessary, slacken her speed, or stop, or reverse.

If, from any cause, the conditions covered by this situation are such as to prevent immediate compliance with each other's signals, the misunderstanding or objection shall be made apparent at once by blowing the danger signal, and both vessels shall be stopped and backed, if necessary, until signals for passing with safety are made and understood.

Q. How do the whistle signals under Inland Rules for the overtaking situation differ from the whistle signals under International Rules?

A. Under Inland Rules, an overtaking steam vessel announces her desire to pass by blowing either the 1 or 2 short-blast signal, and makes no alteration of course until the overtaken steam vessel answers by repeating such signal. Under International Rules, the overtaking powered vessel directs her course to starboard or to port as she sees proper and, at the same time, announces such action by the appropriate steering signal, no answer to which signal is required by the overtaken vessel. For an overtaking sailing-vessel under either Rules, no signals are provided.

Q. You are overtaking another steamer and, without altering your course, will pass him a quarter mile off to port when abeam. Would it be necessary to sound a passing signal? Why?

A. Yes; so that, in the interests of safety, the overtaken vessel may be advised of your vessel's presence and procedure.

Q. When two vessels are meeting in a crossing situation, which vessel should blow a passing signal first?

A. The Rules make no requirement as to which shall blow a passing signal first. It is considered good practice, however, for the privileged vessel to initiate the signal (1 short blast) in ample time to be answered and complied with by the burdened vessel, i. e., the vessel having the other on her own starboard side.

Q. Describe the lights required in United States Harbors (except the Hudson River, etc.) for barges and canal boats towed astern of steam vessels, when towed singly, or what is known as tandem towing.

A. Each shall carry a green light on the starboard side, a red light on the port side, and a white light on the stern, except that the last vessel shall carry 2 lights on her stern, athwartship, horizontal to each other, not less than 5 feet apart, and not less than 4 feet above the deckhouse, so placed as to show all round the horizon. A tow of one such vessel shall be lighted as the last vessel of a tow.

Q. Describe the lights required in United States Harbors (except the Hudson River, etc.) for barges and canal boats towed astern of steam vessels, when two or more boats are abreast.

A. When two or more of such craft are abreast, the colored side-lights shall be carried at the outer sides of the bows of the out-side boats. Each of the outside boats in last tier of a hawser tow shall carry a white light on her stern.

Q. Describe the lights required in United States Harbors (except the Hudson River, etc.) for barges, canal boats or scows, when being pushed ahead of a steam vessel.

A. They shall display a red light on the port bow and a green light on the starboard bow of the head barge, canal boat, or scow, carried at a height sufficiently above the superstructure of the craft as to permit said side lights to be visible; and, if there is more than one barge, canal boat, or scow abreast, the colored lights shall be shown from the outer side of the outside barges, canal boats, or scows.

Q. When two vessels are approaching each other at right angles or obliquely, what signal signifies the intention of the steam vessel, which is to starboard of the other, to hold course and speed?

A. One short blast.

Q. What is the rule regarding obstruction of a channel by a float-ing plant?

A. Channels shall not be obstructed unnecessarily by any dredge or other floating plant. While vessels are passing such plant, all lines running therefrom across the channel on the passing side, which may interfere with or obstruct navigation, shall be slacked to the bottom of the channel.

Q. What is the rule for the protection of marks placed for the guidance of dredges or floating plants?

A. Vessels shall not run over anchor buoys, or buoys, stakes, or other marks placed for guidance of floating plant working in channels; and shall not anchor on the ranges of buoys, stakes, or other marks placed for guidance of such plant.

Q. What is the rule regarding clearing of channel by dredges or floating plants, where regulations have not been prescribed?

A. They shall, upon notice, move out of the way of vessels a sufficient distance to allow them a clear passage. Vessels desir-ing passage shall, however, give the master of the floating plant ample notice in advance of the time they expect to pass.

Q. What is signified by a steamer displaying a day signal consisting of two shapes in the form of a double frustrum of a cone, base to base, both shapes painted a solid bright red?

A. Such signal is displayed by steam vessels, derrick boats, lighters, or other types of vessels made fast alongside a wreck, or moored over a wreck which is on the bottom or partly submerged, or which may be drifting.

Q. State the rule governing the bunching of tows.

A. In all cases, where tows can be bunched, it should be done.

Q. Under what circumstances must passing signals be given and answered?

A. Passing signals must be given and answered, not only when meeting end on, or nearly so, but at all times when steam vessels are within sight of each other, when passing or meeting at a distance within half a mile of each other, and whether passing to starboard or to port.

Q. State what action you would take if a vessel, on your port bow and crossing your course so as to involve risk of collision, fails to answer your passing signal of one short blast.

A. I would immediately blow the danger signal. If no answer were then forthcoming, I would at once take such action as would be necessary to avoid collision.

Q. Do the special signals prescribed for surveying vessels give such vessels the right of way or obviate the necessity for strict observance of the rules for preventing collision of vessels?

A. No. The special signals serve only to indicate the nature of the work upon which the vessels are engaged.

Q. Are Coast Guard cutters or war ships of the United States permitted to operate without running lights?

A. Yes; where the special character of the service may require it, according to Article 30.

Q. State the rules relating to the carrying of unauthorized lights on vessels.

A. Article 1 states that between sunset and sunrise "no other lights which may be mistaken for the prescribed lights shall be exhibited"; and under the Pilot Rules, "any master or pilot of any vessel who shall authorize or permit the carrying of any light, electric or otherwise, not required by law, that in any way will interfere with distinguishing the signal lights, may be proceeded against looking to a suspension or revocation of his license."

Q. What lights shall be carried by any raft being propelled by hand power, or by the current of the river, or when being towed, or which are anchored, or moored in or near a channel, or fairway?

A. (1) A raft of 1 crib in width shall carry 1 white light at each end.

(2) One of more than 1 crib in width shall carry 4 white lights, 1 at each outside corner.

(3) An unstable log raft of 1 bag or boom in width shall carry at least 2 but not more than 4 white lights in a fore-and-aft line, 1 of which shall be at each end. The lights may be closely grouped clusters of not more than 3 white lights, rather than single lights.

(4) An unstable log raft of more than 1 bag or boom in width shall carry 4 white lights, 1 at each corner. The lights may be closely grouped clusters of not more than 3 white lights, rather than single lights.

These lights shall be visible all round the horizon at a distance of at least 1 mile. Lights for rafts shall be suspended from poles at a height not less than 8 feet above the water, except that those for unstable log rafts shall not be less than 4 feet above water.

Q. Describe the lights required where a string-out of moored vessels or barges is engaged in the operation of vessels moored or anchored and engaged in laying cables, pipes, or submarine construction, etc.

A. By day, they shall display, not less than 15 feet above the deck, where they can best be seen from all directions, 2 balls not less than 2 feet in diameter, in a vertical line not less than 3 feet nor more than 6 feet apart, the upper ball to be painted in alternate black and white vertical stripes 6 inches wide, and the lower ball a solid bright red. By night, at the channelward end of the string-out, 3 red lights carried in a vertical line not less than 3 nor more than 6 feet apart, in a position where they can best be seen from all directions, with the lowermost light not less than 15 feet above deck.

Where the string-out crosses the navigable channel and is to be opened for the passage of vessels, the 3 red lights shall be displayed at each side of the opening instead of at the outer end of the string-out. Also, upon such string-out, 1 horizontal row of amber lights not less than 6 feet above the deck, or above the deckhouse (where the craft carries a deckhouse), in a position where they can best be seen from all directions, spaced not more than 50 feet apart so as to mark distinctly the entire length and course of the string-out.

Q. Your steamer is being overtaken by another steamer which blows one short blast. You regard it as dangerous to comply with the overtaking steamer's request but are willing to allow him to pass you on your port side. What signals would you sound to indicate this?

A. I would answer with the danger signal, a series of short rapid blasts, not less than 4; thereafter, I would blow 2 short blasts as indicating the overtaking vessel has a clear passage on my port hand. Then, if that vessel decides to pass on my port side, she will answer with 2 short blasts and proceed to do so.

Q. What navigation light (or lights) is/are required for a vessel propelled by hand power, horsepower, or by the current of the river; except rafts and rowboats?

A. One white light forward not less than 8 feet above the surface of the water.

Q. What information can be determined about the heading of a vessel by observing her colored side lights?

A. A vessel's heading within 10 points of the compass is thereby indicated. Thus, a red light bearing South from an observer may be steering between ESE and North; or a green light, WSW to North. The vessel will be heading, according to the old rule, "Between 6 points to the left and the opposite bearing, for a red light; and between 6 points to the right and the opposite bearing, for a green light".

Q. Describe the lights required in United States Harbors (except the Hudson River, etc.) for barges, canal boats, or scows towing alongside a steam vessel if the deck, deckhouses, cargo of the barge or canal boat be so high above water as to obscure the side lights of the towing steamer.

A. If towed on the starboard side of the steamer, shall carry a green light upon the starboard side; and, when towed on the port side of the steamer, a red light on the port side of the barge, canal boat, or scow; and, if there is more than 1 barge, canal boat, or scow abreast, the colored lights shall be displayed from the outer side of the outside barges, canal boats, or scows.

Q. In thick weather, the wind is northeast and you hear a schooner blowing one blast of her fog horn; about how would she be heading?

A. Between N by W and NW.

Q. What is the rule for light draft vessels passing floating plants?

A. Vessels whose draft permits shall keep outside of the buoys marking the ends of mooring lines of floating plant working in channels.

Q. What is the permissible length of a tow of seagoing barges within inland waters?

A. Such length is limited to 5 vessels, including the towing vessel or vessels.

Q. What is the maximum length of hawser permitted between vessels in a tow on inland waters?

A. 75 fathoms, as measured from the stern of one vessel to the bow of the following vessel; and, in all cases, should be as much shorter as weather or sea will permit.

Q. What is the length of a "long blast" as this term is used in the Inland and Pilot Rules?

A. It is customarily considered as a blast of from 8 to 10 seconds' duration.

Q. What does the term "floating plant" as used in the Rules include?

A. It includes dredges, derrick boats, snag boats, drill boats, maneuver boats, hydraulic graders, survey boats, working barges, and mat-sinking plant.

Q. State the distress signals for vessels in inland waters.

A. When in distress and requiring assistance, the following shall be the signal to be used or displayed by her, either together or separately, namely: In the daytime: A continuous sounding with any fog-signal apparatus, or firing a gun. At night: 1. Flames on the vessel as from a burning tar barrel, oil barrel, etc. 2. A continuous sounding with any fog-signal apparatus, or firing a gun.

Q. When is the sound signal of one long blast used by vessels in inland waters of the United States?

A. Whenever a steam vessel is nearing a short bend or curve, where, from the height of the bank or other cause, a steam vessel approaching from the opposite direction can not be seen for a distance of half a mile, when she shall have arrived within half a mile of such curve or bend. When a steam vessel is moved from her dock or berth and other craft are liable to pass from any direction toward her. Also, by a vessel intending to pass a dredge or other type of floating plant working in a channel, when within a reasonable distance therefrom.

Q. What signal is given by a steamer nearing a bend or curve in a channel if, because of height of the banks or other cause, a steam vessel approaching from the opposite direction cannot be seen for a distance of a half mile?

A. A long blast.

Q. Describe the day and night signals for vessels moored or anchored and engaged in laying cables or pipe, submarine construction, excavation, mat sinking, bank grading, dike construction, revetment, or other bank protection operations.

A. They shall display, by day, not less than 15 feet above the deck, where best may be seen from all directions, 2 balls not less than 2 feet in diameter, in a vertical line not less than 3 nor more than 6 feet apart, the upper ball to be painted in alternate black and white vertical stripes 6 inches wide, and the lower ball to be a solid bright red. By night, they shall display 3 red lights, carried in a vertical line not less than 3 nor more than 6 feet apart, in a position where best seen from all directions, with the lowermost light not less than 15 feet above the deck. Where a string-out of moored craft is engaged, the 3 red lights shall be displayed at the channelward end of the string-out. Where the string-out crosses the navigable channel and is to be opened for passage of vessels, the 3 red lights shall be displayed at each side of the opening, instead of at outer end of the string-out. Upon such string-out there shall be displayed 1 horizontal row of amber lights not less than 6 feet above the deck, or above the deckhouse (where the craft carries a deckhouse), in a position where best seen from all directions, spaced not more than 50 feet apart, so as to mark distinctly the entire length and course of the string-out.

Q. What are the day and night signals for dredges held in stationary positions by moorings or spuds?

A. By day, they shall display 2 red balls not less than 2 feet in diameter, in a vertical line not less than 3 nor more than 6 feet apart, at least 15 feet above the deckhouse and in such a position where best seen from all directions. By night, a white light at each corner, not less than 6 feet above the deck, and also in a position where best seen from all directions, 2 red lights carried in a vertical line not less than 3 nor more than 6 feet apart, and not less than 15 feet above the deck. Scows moored alongside such dredges shall display a white light on each outboard corner, not less than 6 feet above the deck.

Q. What is the penalty for any licensed officer not observing the provisions of the Inland Rules?

A. He shall be liable to a penalty of five hundred dollars, and for all damages sustained by any passenger in his person or baggage by such neglect or refusal.

Q. What is the penalty for any vessel navigated without complying with the provisions of the Inland Rules?

A. The vessel shall be liable to a penalty of five hundred dollars, one-half to go to the informer, for which sum the vessel so navigated shall be liable and may be seized and proceeded against by action in any district court of the United States having jurisdiction of the offense.

Q. Describe the anchor lights required by steamers.

A. If under 150 feet in length, shall carry forward where it can best be seen, but at a height not exceeding 20 feet above the hull, a white light in a lantern so constructed as to show a clear, uniform, and unbroken light visible all round the horizon at a distance of at least 1 mile. However, vessels not more than 65 feet in length, when at anchor in a special anchorage area designated by the Secretary of the Army, shall not be required to carry such light.

If 150 feet or upward in length, shall carry in the forward part of the vessel, at a height of not less than 20 feet and not more than 40 feet above the hull, one such light, and at or near the stern and at such a height that it shall not be less than 15 feet lower than the forward light, another such light.

Q. (a) What is meant by the term "steam vessel" in the Rules?
(b) What is the meaning of "visible" when applied to lights?
(c) When is a vessel "under way" within the meaning of the Rules?

A. (a) The term "steam vessel" shall include any vessel propelled by machinery.
(b) Visible on a dark night with a clear atmosphere.
(c) When she is not at anchor, or made fast to the shore, or aground.

Q. Describe the running lights of a steam vessel under the Inland Rules — other than seagoing vessels and ferryboats.

A. (a) On or in front of the foremast, or, if a vessel without a foremast, then in the fore part of the vessel, a bright white light so constructed as to show an unbroken light over an arc of the horizon of 20 points of the compass, so fixed as to throw the light 10 points on each side of the vessel; namely, from right ahead to 2 points abaft the beam on either side, and of such a character as to be visible at a distance of at least 5 miles. A central range of 2 white lights in line with the keel, the after light being carried at a height of at least 15 feet above the above-mentioned forward light and to show all round the horizon.
(b) On the starboard side, a green light and on the port side, a

red light, each of which shall be so constructed as to show an unbroken light over an arc of the horizon of 10 points of the compass, so fixed as to throw the light from right ahead to 2 points
abaft the beam on their respective sides, and to be of such a
character as to be visible at a distance of at least 2 miles.

Q. Describe the signals to be made by a vessel intending to pass
dredges or other types of floating plant working in navigable channels.

A. When within a reasonable distance therefrom and not, in any
case, over a mile, they shall indicate such intention by 1 long
blast of the whistle, which shall be answered by the plant by the
signal prescribed in the local pilot rules for vessels under way
and approaching each other from opposite directions, and this signal shall be answered by the approaching vessel. If channel is not
clear, the plant shall sound the danger signal and the vessel shall
slow down or stop and await further signal from the plant.

Q. An ocean steamer 550 feet long is being shifted at night from
one dock to another in New York harbor by three tugs. One tug
is on a hawser 100 feet ahead of the steamer and one tug is a-
longside on each quarter. What lights are required to be shown
by each of the four vessels?

A. The tug ahead, in addition to her side lights, will show 3 white
lights in a vertical line not less than 3 feet apart, which shall be
of the same construction and character, and carried either in the
same position as the 20-point masthead light or the all-round
range light required by Article 2. The tugs alongside also will
show side lights, but, instead of the 3 white lights carried by the
tug ahead, will show 2 white lights in a vertical line and of same
character, construction, and visibility. The steamer towed will
show her side lights only.

Q. What lights and day signals are carried by a vessel of the Coast
and Geodetic Survey when at anchor in a fairway on surveying
operations?

A. She shall display from the mast, by day, 2 black balls in a
vertical line and 6 feet apart. By night, 2 red lights shall be
shown in the same manner. On a small vessel, the distance between both the balls and lights may be reduced to 3 feet, if necessary. In addition, such surveying vessels shall have at hand
and show, if necessary, a flare-up light in order to attract
attention.

Q. Describe the lights carried by a Pilot vessel engaged in pilotage
duty in United States waters and at anchor.

A. Sailing pilot vessels carry the all - round white masthead light
required of all pilot vessels; and steam pilot vessels carry, in
addition, an all - round red light 8 feet below the masthead light,
visible at a distance of at least 2 miles. Both vessels are required also to show a flare-up light, or lights, at short intervals
which shall never exceed 15 minutes. While at anchor, neither
shall show their colored side lights.

Q. A sailing pilot vessel 150 feet in length anchors at night on the
way out to her station, but not on it. What light or lights must
she display?

A. She shall carry in the fore part of the vessel, not less than 20
nor more than 40 feet above the hull, a white light visible all
round the horizon at a distance of at least 1 mile; and at or
near the stern, not less than 15 feet lower than the forward light,
another such light.

Q. Where must the two anchor lights be shown in vessels of 150
feet and upwards?

A. The forward light must be shown in the fore part of the vessel
at a height of not less than 20 and not more than 40 feet above
the hull; the light at or near the stern must be carried at least
15 feet lower than the forward light.

Q. What day signal must be displayed in the forward part of the
vessel where it can best be seen from other vessels when a vessel more than 65 feet in length is moored or anchored in a fairway or channel between sunrise and sunset?

A. One black ball, not less than 2 feet in diameter.

Q. Why is an inland steam vessel not required to show a stern
light, when her lights are fitted in accordance with the inland
rules?

A. Because her all - round range light gives ample warning of her
presence to an overtaking vessel.

Q. What lights are shown by vessels not under command in inland
waters?

A. No lights are prescribed for such. They must show ordinary
underway lights or those for a vessel at anchor, as appropriate.

Q. What lights are shown by vessels aground in inland waters?

A. No lights are specially prescribed. It is customary to display
the light or lights for a vessel at anchor.

Q. What are the lights for seagoing steam vessels in inland waters?

A. On the foremast or in the fore part of the vessel, a bright white light, to show an unbroken light over an arc of the horizon of 20 points of the compass, fixed to throw the light 10 points on each side of the vessel; namely, from right ahead to 2 points abaft the beam on either side, and to be visible for at least 5 miles. She may carry another such light of similar construction, in which case the 2 lights shall be placed in a line with the keel so that one shall be at least 15 feet higher than the other, the lower light to be forward of the upper one. The vertical distance between these lights shall be less than the horizontal distance.

On the starboard side, a green light and on the port side, a red light, each to show through 10 points of the compass; namely, from right ahead to 2 points abaft the beam on their respective sides, and to be visible at a distance of at least 2 miles.

Q. Where do the Pilot Rules apply?

A. They apply to vessels navigating the harbors, rivers, and inland waters of the United States, except the Great Lakes and their connecting and tributary waters as far east as Montreal; the Red River of the North; the Mississippi River and its tributaries above Huey P. Long Bridge; and that part of the Atchafalaya River above its junction with the Plaquemine-Morgan City alternate waterway.

Q. What is meant by the "danger" signal?

A. It is a signal given when steam vessels are approaching each other and either vessel fails to understand the course or intention of the other, from any cause. The vessel so in doubt immediately signifies the same by giving several short and rapid blasts, not less than 4, of the steam whistle. This is called the "danger" signal.

Q. What is the Rule relating to use of searchlights or other blinding lights?

A. Flashing the rays of a searchlight or other blinding light onto the bridge or into the pilothouse of any vessel under way is prohibited. Any person who shall flash or cause to be flashed the rays of blinding light in violation of the above may be proceeded against in accordance with law, looking to revocation or suspension of his license or certificate.

Q. What is the fog signal for a steam vessel under way?

A. She shall sound, at intervals of not more than 1 minute, a prolonged blast.

Q. Of what duration are the blasts of the whistle which are used as passing signals?

A. Of about 1 second's duration, called the "short" blast.

Q. What signal shall be given by steam vessels when moving from their docks or berths and other vessels are liable to pass from any direction toward them?

A. They shall give one long blast on the whistle; but immediately after clearing the berths, so as to be fully in sight, they shall be governed by the steering and sailing rules.

Q. What is the rule in regard to sailing in a narrow channel?

A. When it is safe and practicable, every vessel shall keep to that side of the fairway or mid-channel which lies on the starboard side of such vessel.

Q. Describe the lights and day signals required to be shown by a fishing vessel under way with her nets or lines in the water.

A. By day, they shall indicate their occupation to an approaching vessel by displaying a basket where it can best be seen. By night, they shall exhibit, from some part of the vessel where they can best be seen, 2 lights. One of these shall be red and the other white. The red light shall be above the white light, and shall be at a vertical distance from it of not less than 6 and not more than 12 feet; and the horizontal distance between them, if any, shall not be more than 10 feet. These lights shall be visible all round the horizon, the white light at a distance of not less than 3 miles and the red light at not less than 2 miles.

Q. What are the day and night signals to be carried by a steamer when towing a submerged, or partly submerged, object when no signals are displayed upon the object towed?

A. By day, such vessel shall display, where can best be seen, 2 shapes, one above the other, not less than 6 feet apart, lower shape to be carried not less than 10 feet above the deckhouse. The shapes shall be in the form of a double frustum of a cone, base to base, not less than 2 feet in diameter at the center nor less than 8 inches at the ends of the cones, and to be not less than 4 feet lengthwise from end to end, the upper shape to be painted in alternate stripes of black and white, 8 inches in width; the lower shape to be painted a solid bright red. By night, she shall display the regular side lights, but, in lieu of the regular white towing lights, shall display 4 lights in a vertical position not less than 3 nor more than 6 feet apart, the upper and lower lights to be white, and the 2 middle lights to be red; all of such lights to be of the same character as the regular towing lights.

Q. What signal must a steamer give in addition to the one long blast when backing out of her berth with other vessels in sight?

A. Immediately upon clearing the berth, 3 short blasts to indicate she is going astern.

Q. What is the rule governing lights for barges, canal boats, scows, and other nondescript vessels temporarily operating on waters requiring different lights from those of their customary route?

A. Such vessels shall not be required to change their lights from those required on the waters on which their trip begins or terminates; but, should they engage in local employment on waters requiring different lights from those where they are customarily employed, they shall comply with the local rules where employed.

Q. What navigation lights are required by motorboats when propelled by sail and machinery or by sail alone?

A. Classes 2 and 3 motorboats, or those 26 or over and less than 40 feet, and those 40 or over and not more than 65 feet in length, respectively, when propelled by sail and machinery, or by sail alone, shall carry the colored side lights, suitably screened, but not the white lights prescribed by this section. But motorboats of all classes, when so propelled, shall carry ready at hand a lantern or flashlight showing a white light which shall be exhibited in sufficient time to prevent collision. Motorboats of classes A and 1, or those less than 16, and those 16 or over and less than 26 feet in length, respectively, when so propelled shall not be required to carry the combined lantern prescribed in this section.

Q. What lights are required by fishing vessels of less than ten gross tons when under way and when not having their nets, trawls, dredges or lines in the water?

A. They shall not be obliged to carry the colored side lights; but shall, in lieu thereof, have ready at hand a lantern with a green glass on one side and a red glass on the other, and on approaching, or being approached by, another vessel, such lantern shall be exhibited in sufficient time to prevent collision, so that the green light shall not be seen on the port side nor the red light on the starboard side.

Q. Under what circumstances should the inland danger signal be used in fog?

A. Whenever the approaching signals of another vessel seem to indicate impending collision. Articles 27 and 29 would authorize such use of the danger signal in fog.

Q. Describe the day and night signals for self-propelled dredges under way with suctions on the bottom.

A. By day, they shall display 2 black balls not less than 2 feet in diameter in a vertical line not less than 15 feet above the deckhouse, where they can best be seen from all directions. By night, they shall carry, in addition to the regular running lights, 2 red lights of the same character as the white masthead light, and in the same vertical line beneath that light, the red lights to be not less than 3 feet nor more than 6 feet apart and the upper red light to be not less than 4 nor more than 6 feet below the masthead light; and, on or near the stern, 2 red lights in a vertical line not less than 4 nor more than 6 feet apart, to show through 4 points of the compass, that is, from right astern to 2 points on each quarter.

Q. What are the whistle signals for a vessel moving from her dock or berth when other vessels are liable to pass toward her?

A. If using her own power, she shall blow a long blast and, immediately after clearing the berth and fully in sight, she shall be governed by the steering and sailing rules.

Q. What navigating lights would be required on self-propelled dredges which are proceeding to or from a dredging site?

A. The regular running lights required for a steam vessel under way.

RADAR OBSERVER

Q. Define and state the cause of: a) Super-refraction; b) Sub-refraction.

A. (a) A bending downward from the normal of the radar ray caused by its passing from a denser medium to a lighter one.
(b) A bending upward from the normal of the radar ray, caused by its passing from a lighter to a denser medium.

Q. How may radar be used for short range weather predictions?

A. Rain or heavy squall clouds, depending upon their height and size, may be seen from a distance of 15 to 25 miles. Thus, from successive observations, it is possible to predict the weather changes in the path of such disturbances. Heavy dark clouds distinctly appear as woolly masses of brightness on the screen.

Q. What weather phenomena are detectable by radar?

A. Precipitation areas and weather activity, such as heavy rain squalls, in the neighborhood of hurricanes and typhoons.

Q. State the precautions necessary when using the sea-return suppressor or anticlutter device.

A. On the smaller range scales, a slight maladjustment of the controls may cause a "poor response target" to disappear from the screen altogether, especially if sea is rough.

Q. How can heavy rolling influence detection of targets by radar?

A. If the period of roll coincides with the time required for one complete revolution of the scanner, the radar ray may repeatedly miss the target by being thrown either too high or too low at each revolution.

Q. Is the relative bearing or the true bearing presentation best for clarity of presentation on the PPI scope? State reasons for your answer.

A. Relative bearing presentation is preferable in the case of entering or leaving port, where piloting the vessel through a channel or fairway is required. True bearing presentation, on the other hand, as when approaching the land, where laying off bearings and distances from the PPI information is required, is much simpler than using relative bearings which must be converted to true bearings (unless the gyro repeater arrangement is included in the set) before being laid off on the chart.

Q. How can radar blind spots be located?

A. By changing the pulse repetition frequency and noting results.

Q. What measures may be taken to minimize dangers from blind spots?

A. Frequent change of pulse repetition frequency from low to high and vice versa, with close observation of any resulting change on the screen.

Q. How was the name "radar" derived?

A. From a suggestive abbreviation of the term indicating its use, viz., "Radio Direction and Ranging"; or it may have been formed from the like terms, "Radio Aid, Direction, and Range".

Q. Explain briefly, in non-technical terms, the principle upon which radar is based.

A. As a means of determining a vessel's position relative to floating objects, coast outlines, or prominent landmarks, radar is based upon the time elapsed for return of the echo, or reflected wave, of a radio oscillation or pulse directed outward in a continuously revolving beam over the surrounding area. As shown in the picture presented in the "screen" from such information, the reflected or return wave from each obstacle in the radio beam's path, both the distance and bearing of every spotted feature, and so the vessel's position with relation to other ships in the vicinity, coastal marks, etc., is determined.

Q. What are the elements of a radar installation that affect its range?

A. Minimum range is governed by "pulse width", height at which "scanner" is mounted, vertical beam width, and receiver sensitivity. Maximum range is obtained by a low pulse repetition frequency.

Q. Name the principal components of a marine radar installation and briefly in non-technical terms, describe their functions.

A. 1. The Timing Unit, also known as synchronizer or modulation generator, which supplies the synchronizing signals timing the pulses and the indicator, and coordinates other associated units.
2. The Transmitter, which generates radio-frequency energy in the form of short, powerful pulses.
3. The Antenna system, which radiates the transmitted pulses in a highly directional beam and receives the returning echoes, passing them on to the receiver.
4. The Receiver, which amplifies the weak return echoes and passes them on as pulses to the indicator.
5. The Indicator on which the echo pulses from the target produces a visual outline of the latter.

6. The Power Supply, furnishing all AC and DC voltages required for operation of the system.

Q. In basic terms, what is radar?

A. A system of determining distance and bearing of an object by measuring the elapsed time between transmission of a radio pulse signal and its reception as an echo, or the reflected wave, from the object, and noting the orientation of the directional antenna.

Q. What is meant by the term "bearing resolution" when applied to radar? On what does bearing resolution depend?

A. The discrimination between two objects at the same range but on different bearings. It depends upon the range at which targets are situated and the horizontal beam width.

Q. What is resolution in range? On what does it depend?

A. The showing up of two targets as separate objects when they lie in the same bearing but at different ranges. It depends upon the reflecting qualities of the farther object's surface, and the "pulse width" which governs minimum range at which targets can be seen separately in the scope.

Q. What are relative bearings as seen on a radar PPI scope?

A. Those indicating an arc of the horizon measured from the vessel's heading, or relative to the fore-and-aft line, as in the "heading upward" presentation on the scope.

Q. What are true bearings as seen on a PPI scope? How is the course of the vessel usually indicated when using true bearings?

A. Those indicated on the "north upward" presentation, or bearings relative to the true meridian. A radial line is provided to show the true heading of the vessel.

Q. What range scale would you use in the open sea? What scale would you use to make a landfall? What scale would you use in a crowded channel?

A. 15 to 20 miles range. 10 miles range. 1 to 5 miles range.

Q. What precautions should be observed during poor visibility if the radar scope shows heavy sea return?

A. On the smaller range scales (1, 3, and 5 miles), "clutter control", in conjunction with the "differentiator", should be used with caution, for the reason that a slight maladjustment of this control may result in a "poor response" target disappearing from the screen altogether.

Q. What effect does the material composing an object have on its being detected by radar?

A. Different materials have greater or lesser reflecting qualities, so that detection of echoes from the transmitted radar ray presents no problem in the case of metals or sea water, but may severely tax the system's ability to receive a clear response from foliage, wood, and other non-metallic substances. In general, conductors of electricity are good reflectors; non-conductors, poor.

Q. How could you identify low flying aircraft appearing on the radar scope?

A. By the unusual rapidity with which the target blips move in the scope, either in range or bearing, or both.

Q. What limits the effective range of radar?

A. The pulse repetition frequency, pulse width, and peak power of the set.

Q. Describe briefly the essential parts of a radar set.

A. 1. The Timing Unit, which starts the sequence of operation of the set, and may be called the master control, as synchronization of the different parts is required for accuracy, especially in determining the range of targets. The pulse repetition frequency is also controlled by this unit. 2. The Transmitter, which generates and sends out radio-frequency energy in the form of short, powerful pulses. 3. The Antenna system, featuring the Scanner, takes radio-frequency energy from the transmitter, radiates it in a highly directional beam, receives the returning echoes, and passes the echoes to the receiver. 4. The Receiver amplifies the weak pulse-echoes from the target and applies them to the indicator. 5. The Indicator produces a visual indication of pulse-echoes on the scope, both as to bearing and distance from the observer. 6. The Power Supply furnishes all DC and AC voltages required for operation of the set.

Q. What is the effect of a radar reflector on a buoy?

A. It strengthens the reflectivity of the target, thus increasing the detecting ability of the set.

Q. Is a bearing obtained through use of radar or visually preferable? Why?

A. A visually observed bearing is preferable. Apart from any error caused by interference of a part of ship's structure with the pulse-ray or its echo, and which increases directly as the range, the 2 to 3 degrees horizontal beam width of the radar sweep itself gives an uncertainty by just that amount in the scope.

Q. In using radar to obtain navigational positions, which should be more accurate:
(a) A fix obtained by cross-bearing of two objects.
(b) The intersection of the arcs obtained using the ranges from the objects as radii.
Explain your answer.

A. (b) should be more accurate, for the reason that range readings are found to be more accurate than bearing readings.

Q. Do atmospheric conditions affect the range at which objects may be discerned by radar? State the reasons for your answer.

A. Yes, because the transmitted ray is subjected to a bending from the horizontal as it passes through different atmospheric media. Thus, under what is termed "sub-refractive" conditions, in which the cooling of rising air masses produces increase of humidity, the radar ray is bent upward with consequent decrease in detecting range; conversely, with the sea relatively cooler than the air masses above it, condensation results in excess humidity conditions near the surface, and "super-refractive" conditions obtain, or those in which the radar ray bends downward, giving increased detecting range.

Q. What safety precautions must be taken when examining or working on the interior of a radar set?

A. Since many of the voltages occurring in the set are dangerous to life, whenever the particular test or adjustment permits, power supply should be switched off and safeguarded against possible switching on while the person is working on the equipment. Great care should be exercised where it is necessary to have the power on for adjusting or testing purposes.

Q. Navigating in ice, how may areas of clear water be distinguished on the PPI scope? What are the limitations on the effectiveness of radar in detecting icebergs and growlers?

A. Outline of ice appears about same as responses from a low-lying rocky shoreline, so that a baylike appearance of a clear-water lead is shown by its reeflike limits in the scope. Regardless of size, it is possible to miss an iceberg or a growler altogether because these targets have sloping sides and smooth regular surfaces. Sometimes a berg, once having been detected, may disappear suddenly from the screen. Altogether, the iceberg is a dangerous target at any time.

Q. Define: (a) Relative movement; (b) Relative speed; (c) Relative distance.

A. (a) If 2 sides of a triangle are drawn to represent the direction and magnitude of the respective velocities of 2 bodies, the third side will represent the bodies' relative movement to each other; or, relative movement may be defined as the motion of one body or object relative to another.
(b) The rate at which two moving objects approach or separate from each other.
(c) Distance travelled in the direction of relative movement at relative speed.

Q. In each of the following cases, give the approximate direction and rate at which the pip would move on your PPI scope:
(a) If your vessel, while proceeding North at 15 knots, observed by radar a stationary object.
(b) If your vessel, while proceeding East at 10 knots, observed by radar a vessel proceeding West at 10 knots.
(c) If your vessel, while proceeding South at 10 knots, observed by radar a vessel proceeding South at 10 knots.

A. (a) South at 15 knots. (b) West at 20 knots. (c) Stationary.

Q. What does a sudden increase or decrease of the signal strength of another vessel's pip on the PPI scope usually denote when the vessel observed on the PPI scope is close to your vessel?

A. Increase of signal strength usually occurs upon change of "aspect", in the sense of the target presenting a greater reflecting area, as when vessel observed presents a broadside view following an end-on or quarterly one. Decrease of signal strength would occur upon vessel observed presenting a more end-on aspect following a more broadside-on one.

Q. What factors aboard ship would cause blind sectors on the PPI scope?

A. Where the beam of radar energy is obstructed by some part or parts of ship's structure.

Q. Explain how the course and speed of another vessel is determined by ranges and bearing taken by an observer on a moving vessel.

A. A succession of bearings and ranges of the other vessel is taken. These are plotted and a faired line is drawn to connect all. Such line, extended if necessary, will represent the magnitude and direction of the vessel's approach or divergence from your own vessel's course, or her relative movement. Then, with the line representing course and speed of my own vessel plotted as forming the two sides of a triangle, the third side will indicate course and speed of the vessel observed.

Q. What precautions should be observed when operating a radar set with a high degree of sea return suppression?
A. Radar is then operating at reduced sensitivity, and will miss small targets which may be a source of danger to the ship. Under such conditions a close visual lookout continues to be the most reliable method of discovering potential danger.

Q. For what purpose is a Performeter or Echo Box?
A. It is used to check and tune the set.

Q. A point of land lying between your ship and a small boat, why may the boat not be seen on the radar scope?
A. Because of shadow effect.

Q. Ability of a radar to show objects observed close together on same bearing as separate pips depends upon what condition?
A. Pulse length.

Q. Your vessel is on course 230° True at a speed of 8 knots.
At 0800, a vessel is observed on the PPI scope bearing 290° True at a distance of 7.6 miles.
At 0815, the vessel is observed bearing 283° at a distance of 6.0 miles.
At 0830, the vessel is observed bearing 273° at a distance of 4.6 miles.
(a) Assuming that both your vessel and the vessel observed maintain course and speed, determine the distance between your vessel and the vessel observed at their closest point of approach.
(b) Determine the course and speed of the vessel observed.
(c) Determine the time of the closest point of approach.

A. (a) 3 miles. (b) 185° at 10 knots. (c) 0858.

Q. Your vessel is on course 135° True at a speed of 9 knots.
At 0028, a vessel is observed on the PPI scope bearing 110° True at a distance of 10 miles.
At 0032, the vessel is observed bearing 109° at a distance of 9 miles.
At 0036, the vessel is observed bearing 107°.5 at a distance of 8 miles.
(a) Assuming that both your vessel and the vessel observed maintain course and speed, determine the distance between your vessel and the vessel observed at their closest point of approach.
(b) Determine the course and speed of the vessel observed.
(c) Determine the time of closest point of approach.

A. (a) 1.8 miles. (b) 280° at 6.7 knots. (c) 0107.

Your vessel is on course 060° True at a speed of 8 knots.

At 1500, a vessel is observed on the PPI scope bearing 080°
True at a distance of 7 miles.

At 1508, the vessel is observed bearing 080° True at a distance
of 6 miles.

(a) Determine the course and speed of the vessel observed.

(b) Determine that course to which to alter at 1512 which will
enable you to pass the observed vessel at a distance of 3 miles on
your port side.

A. (a) 350° at 2.7 knots. (b) 95°.

Q. Your vessel is on course 140° True at a speed of 6 knots.

At 1200, a vessel is observed on the PPI scope bearing 200°
True at a distance of 5 miles.

At 1206, the vessel is observed bearing 200° True at a distance
of 4 miles.

At 1212, the vessel is observed bearing 200° True at a distance
of 3 miles.

(a) What would be the effect of altering your course to 080°?
Explain in full.

A. Altering course to 080° would not eliminate danger of collision,
because direction of relative motion remains unchanged. However,
the rate at which other vessel approaches, or relative speed,
would be considerably lessened.

Note: Since 1 January 1959, the Coast Guard has required an applicant for an original, raise of grade, or increase in scope of license for
service as a deck officer on ocean, coastwise, or Great Lakes vessels
of 300 gross tons and over to qualify as a radar observer. This requirement is met by successfully passing an examination given at a Marine
Inspection Office or by presenting a certificate of successful completion
of a course of instruction at a Maritime Administration Radar Observer
School or other Government operated school approved by the Commandant.

An officer who has qualified as a radar observer in order to obtain
an original, raise of grade, or increase in scope of license is not required to qualify again as a radar observer for the issuance of any subsequent raise of grade or increase in scope of his license. However, the
examination for such a subsequent raise of grade or increase of scope
of license embraces the proper operation and utilization of marine radar
equipment and includes at least one practical plotting problem. A certificate of successful completion of a course of instruction is not acceptable in lieu of this examination in radar by the Coast Guard.

Every master who obtained a license prior to 1 January 1959 is not
presently required by Coast Guard licensing regulations to become a
qualified radar observer. Similarly, every deck officer who obtained a
license prior to 1 January 1959 is not required to qualify if he simply
renews his license without ever obtaining a raise of grade or increase

in scope. Nevertheless, all officers who serve aboard radar equipped vessels are expected to be able to properly interpret and utilize the information presented to them by the radar equipment. Consonant with this expectation the Coast Guard has proposed a regulation which is a step towards insuring that end for the manning of inspected vessels. This regulation, on the Merchant Marine Council Public Hearing Agenda scheduled to be held beginning on 21 March 1960, required that every radar equipped vessel of 300 gross tons and over which, on or after 1 January 1961, is issued a Certificate of Inspection for the navigation on ocean, coastwise, or Great Lakes waters shall have in its complement of deck officers (including the master) only officers who have qualified as radar observers.

The masters and other deck officers who would be affected by the adoption of the above proposed regulation are encouraged to qualify as radar observers as soon as practicable, either by passing the Coast Guard examination or by successfully completing a course of instruction at an approved school. Those persons who desire to qualify by Coast Guard examination may appear at their convenience at a Marine Inspection Office to take the examination. Many have already taken the examination and have been furnished documentary evidence of their professional qualifications as radar observers.

COAST GUARD DISTRICT COMMANDERS AND MERCHANT MARINE ACTIVITIES

District	Title	City	State	Address
1st	Commander, 1st Coast Guard District	Boston	Mass	1400 Customhouse.
	Marine Inspection Officer	do	do	Do.
	Officer in Charge, Marine Inspection	do	do	447 Commercial St.
	do	Portland	Maine	P. O. Box 108, Pearl St. Sta.
	do	Providence	R. I	409 Federal Bldg.
2d	Commander, 2d Coast Guard District	St. Louis	Mo	224 Old Customhouse, 8th and Olive Sts.
	Marine Inspection Officer	do	do	222 Old Customhouse, 8th and Olive Sts.
	Officer in Charge, Marine Inspection	do	do	216 Old Customhouse, 8th and Olive Sts.
	do	Cairo	Ill	425–427 New Post Office Bldg.
	do	Dubuque	Iowa	301 Post Office and Courthouse Bldg.
	do	Cincinnati	Ohio	748 Federal Bldg., 5th and Main Sts.
	do	Louisville	Ky	254 Francis Bldg., 4th and Chestnut Sts.
	do	Memphis	Tenn	426 Falls Bldg.
	do	Nashville	do	670 U. S. Courthouse, 801 Broadway.
	do	Pittsburgh	Pa	1215 Park Bldg.
	do	Huntington	W. Va	328 Federal Bldg., 5th Ave. and 9th St.
3d	Commander, 3d Coast Guard District	New York	N. Y	6?0 Customhouse.
	Marine Inspection Officer	do	do	626 Customhouse.
	Officer in Charge, Marine Inspection	do	do	720 Customhouse.
	do	New London	Conn	302 Post Office Bldg.
	do	Albany	N. Y	313 Federal Bldg.
	do	Philadelphia	Pa	801 Customhouse, 2d and Chestnut Sts.

COAST GUARD DISTRICT COMMANDERS AND MERCHANT MARINE
ACTIVITIES—Continued

District	Title	City	State	Address
5th	Commander, 5th Coast Guard District	Norfolk	Va	Box 540, U. S. Post Office and Courthouse.
	Marine Inspection Officer	do	do	Do.
	Officer in Charge, Marine Inspection	do	do	204 Customhouse.
	do	Baltimore	Md	209 Chamber of Commerce Bldg.
7th	Commander, 7th Coast Guard District	Miami	Fla	Pan American Bank Bldg., 150 S.,E. 3d Ave.
	Marine Inspection Officer	do	do	Do.
	Officer in Charge, Marine Inspection	do	do	Do.
	do	Tampa	do	406 Federal Bldg.
	do	Charleston	S. C	32 U. S. Customhouse.
	do	Savannah	Ga	205 Customhouse.
	do	Jacksonville	Fla	210 Federal Bldg.
	do	San Juan	P. R	P. O. Box 3666, 302 Federal Bldg.
8th	Commander, 8th Coast Guard District	New Orleans	La	328 Customhouse.
	Marine Inspection Officer	do	do	309 Customhouse.
	Officer in Charge, Marine Inspection	do	do	310 Customhouse.
	do	Mobile	Ala	563 Federal Bldg.
	do	Port Arthur	Tex	General Delivery.
	do	Galveston	do	232 Customhouse.
	do	Corpus Christi	do	101 Federal Bldg.
	do	Houston	do	7300 Wingate Ave.
9th	Commander, 9th Coast Guard District	Cleveland	Ohio	Main Post Office Bldg.
	Marine Inspection Officer	do	do	Do.
	Officer in Charge, Marine Inspection	do	do	1055 E. Ninth St.
	do	Buffalo	N. Y	440 Federal Bldg.
	do	Oswego	do	205 Federal Bldg.
	do	Detroit	Mich	430 Federal Bldg.
	do	Duluth	Minn	311 Federal Bldg.
	do	Toledo	Ohio	Veterans Bldg., 501 Huron St.
	do	Saint Ignace	Mich	Municipal Bldg.
	do	Chicago	Ill	10101 So. Ewing Ave.
	do	Ludington	Mich	National Bank Bldg.
	do	Milwaukee	Wis	551a Federal Bldg.
11th	Commander, 11th Coast Guard District	Long Beach	Calif	706 Times Bldg.
	Marine Inspection Officer	do	do	1105 Times Bldg.
	Officer in Charge, Marine Inspection	do	do	Do.
12th	Commander, 12th Coast Guard District	San Francisco	Calif	903 U. S. Appraisers Bldg., 630 Sansome St.
	Marine Inspection Officer	do	do	Station B, Box 2129.
	Officer in Charge, Marine Inspection	do	do	Do.
13th	Commander, 13th Coast Guard District	Seattle	Wash	618 2d Ave.
	Marine Inspection Officer	do	do	Do.
	Officer in Charge, Marine Inspection	do	do	Do.
	do	Portland	Oreg	202 Lincoln Bldg., 208 S. W. 5th Ave.
14th	Commander, 14th Coast Guard District	Honolulu	T. H	P. O. Box 4010.
	Marine Inspection Officer	do	do	P. O. Box 2997.
	Officer in Charge, Marine Inspection	do	do	Do.
17th	Commander, 17th Coast Guard District	Juneau	Alaska	P. O. Box 2631.
	Marine Inspection Officer	do	do	Do.
	Officer in Charge, Marine Inspection	do	do	Do.